Japan: Economic Success and Legal System

Japan: Economic Success and Legal System

Edited by

Harald Baum
Max-Planck-Institute for Foreign and Private International Law, Hamburg

1997
Walter de Gruyter · Berlin · New York

Printed with the support of the
Förderverein japanisch-deutscher Kulturbeziehungen e. V., Köln (JaDe)
[Organization for the Promotion of Japanese-German Cultural Relations, Cologne].

∞ Printed on acid-free paper which falls within the guidelines of the ANSI
to ensure permanence and durability.

Library of Congress Cataloging-in-Publication Data

Japan : economic success and legal system / edited by Harald Baum.
p. cm.
Includes bibliographical references.
ISBN 3-11-015160-X (cloth : alk. paper)
1. Commercial law – Japan – Congresses. 2. Justice. Administration of – Japan – Congresses. 3. Contracts – Japan – Congresses. 4. Business enterprises – Law and legislation – Japan – Congresses. 5. Trade regulation – Japan – Congresses. I. Baum, Harald.
KNX919 1995
346.52′07–dc20
[345.2067] 96-45041
CIP

Die Deutsche Bibliothek – CIP-Einheitsaufnahme

Japan: economic success and legal system / ed. by Harald Baum.
– Berlin ; New York : de Gruyter, 1997
ISBN 3-11-015160-X
NE: Baum, Harald [Hrsg.]

Printing: WB-Druck, Rieden am Forggensee – Binding: Mikolai GmbH, Berlin. – Printed in Germany.

Acknowledgements

The conference on "Japan: Economic Success and Legal System" at the Japanese-German Center Berlin, Germany, from November 22-24, 1995, would not have been possible without the generous support of the following institutions and donors: *Fritz Thyssen Foundation, Deutsche Forschungsgemeinschaft, Society of Friends of the Japanese-German Center Berlin*, *Daimler-Benz AG, Robert Bosch GmbH,* and *E. Merck KGaA*. The publication of this volume was generously supported by the *Förderverein japanisch-deutscher Kuturbeziehungen e.V.*, Cologne, and the law firm *Sonderhoff & Einsel*, Tokyo.

Many people have provided their advice and time in organizing the conference and editing this volume. In Berlin, four persons have been particularly helpful: the secretary general of the Center, Dr. *Thilo Graf Brockdorff*, readily agreed to host the meeting, and Dr. *Wolfgang Brenn* and his colleagues *Tatjana Wonneberg* and *Jörg Reinowski* undertook every possible effort to secure an absolutely perfect order of events. From Tokyo, *Peter Rodatz* has been a source of inspiration, encouragement, advice, and indispensable help throughout the whole project. In Hamburg at the Max-Planck-Institute, *Dörte Liebrecht*, *Olaf Kliesow,* and *Ingeborg Stahl* have participated with the greatest dedication in the editing process of this volume. And *Kristen Zetzsche* never tired of smoothing manuscripts written by scholars from different countries into coherent English.

I am very much indebted to all of the above for their manifold assistance.

Hamburg, August 1996 *Harald Baum*

Foreword

One of the highlights of the *Japanese-German Center Berlin*'s (JGCB) 1995 programs was a joint conference with the *Max Planck Institute for Foreign and Private International Law* (MPI), Hamburg. Japan legal system experts from legal traditions as disparate as the Japanese, the Anglo-American, and the German met in Berlin for three days at the end of November to discuss their responses to the hidden question in the title: "Japan: Economic Success and Legal System".

The economic success of Japan and the globalization of industry, trade, and finance in conjunction with the growth and strength of the Japanese economy encouraged scholars of law as well as lawyers to intensify their study of the Japanese legal system. This endeavor to become familiar with another country's legal system was the very effort Japan itself was forced to undertake in the fields of European and American law over a century ago, and again after the Second World War when Japan had to modernize its state and administration and compete with Western countries.

The study of Japanese law and Japan's legal system is also of significance in doing business with other economies of the region. Various Asian countries have asked Japan, an Asian power, to support the restructuring of their legal system. The Japanese Ministry of Justice has responded to this request, for instance, by establishing an *International Center of Civil and Trade Law* in Osaka.

In addition to the previously mentioned adoption of Western and American law by Japan, a conference aiming at a broad and intense discussion on the given issue could not be conducted without participants from the U.S., Australia, and New Zealand for at least two other reasons: a) expertise on the Japanese legal system is higher in these countries than in Germany, and b) litigation in the different countries varies considerably. While litigation in America is extremely high, it is remarkably low in Japan. Litigation in Germany, on the other hand, seems to fall somewhere between the two extremes. It speaks in favor of the conference that these differences and different concepts of rights (e.g., individual rights vs. administrative guidance) were spoken of freely, while investigating the reasons behind the Japanese approach.

It was a wise decision by Dr. *Harald Baum* (MPI), who drafted the concept for the conference in cooperation with *Peter Rodatz* (Tokyo), not to discuss the questions of the Japanese legal system on an abstract level, but rather to choose Japanese business, enterprise, and bureaucracy as specific phenomena for the conference. This approach and the final panel discussion on "The Japanese

Legal System: A Non-Tariff Trade Barrier?" also made the conference interesting for corporations doing business with Japan.

The conference fulfilled the aim of the JGCB - namely, to promote and deepen German-Japanese and international cooperation in the fields of science and culture in the context of economic life, including the American and Asian-Pacific dimension - in an exemplary way.

I wish to thank first of all Dr. *Baum* for all his effort in arranging the conference and bringing the right people together. We owe thanks to Mr. *Rodatz* for his never-waning advice and comments and his great and valuable support in contacting sponsors. Furthermore, I want to thank all speakers and active participants for their presentations and especially those from places as far away as New Zealand, Japan, Australia, and California for coming to Berlin. The contribution of one scholar we would have liked to have with us should not go unmentioned: Professor *John Owen Haley* (University of Washington) was unfortunately unable to attend because of other duties. Nonetheless, he wrote a paper for the conference which was read out on the second day and which is included in this book.

The conference would not have been possible without the generous support of the *Fritz Thyssen Foundation, Deutsche Forschungsgemeinschaft (DFG), Daimler-Benz AG, Robert Bosch GmbH, E. Merck KGaA,* and the *Society of Friends of the JGCB*. In the name of the President of the JGCB, Ambassador *Hiromichi Miyazaki*, and the other members of our Board, I would like to express our most cordial thanks for this substantial support.

Thilo Graf Brockdorff

Table of Contents

List of Contributors

BAUM, Harald	Senior Research Associate, Max-Planck-Institute for Foreign and Private International Law, Hamburg
BENNETT, Frank	Lecturer, Law Department, School of Oriental and African Studies, London
BROCKDORFF, Thilo Graf	Secretary General, Japanese-German Center Berlin, Berlin
FOOTE, Daniel H.	Dan Fenno Henderson Professor of East Asian Legal Studies, School of Law, University of Washington, Seattle
GÖTZE, Bernd	Attorney at Law, Reeg & Born, Singapore
HALEY, John O.	Director, Asian Law Program, Garvey Schubert & Barer Professor of Law, Professor of International Studies, School of Law, University of Washington, Seattle
HAYAKAYA, Masaru	Professor, Faculty of Law, Doshisha University, Kyoto
HEATH, Christopher	Head of Department (Japan/East Asia), Max-Planck-Institute for Foreign and Int'l Patent, Copyright and Competition Law, München
HENDERSON, Dan Fenno	Professor, Hastings College of Law, University of California, San Francisco
KANDA, Hideki	Professor, Faculty of Law, University of Tokyo, Tokyo
KEEHN, E.B.	President, Japan America Society; Visiting Scholar at the Center for International Business Education and Research at the University of Southern California, Los Angeles

KITAGAWA, Zentaro	Professor, Faculty of Law, Meijo University, Prof. em. Kyoto University; Chief Director, Kyoto Comparative Law Center, Kyoto
KÖDDERITZSCH, Lorenz	Attorney at Law, Düsseldorf
KONO, Toshiyuki	Associate Professor, Faculty of Law, Kyushu University, Fukuoka
LIEBRECHT, Dörte	Research Assistant, Max-Planck-Institute for Foreign and Private International Law, Hamburg
MARFORDING, Annette	Senior Lecturer, Faculty of Law, University of New South Wales, Sydney
NOTTAGE, Luke R.	Lecturer in Law, Victoria University of Wellington; Barrister and Solicitor, JHJ Crawford Law Office, Wellington. (From April 1997: Associate Professor, Faculty of Law, Kyushu University, Fukuoka)
RAHN, Guntram	Attorney at Law, Hoffmann, Eitle & Partner, München
RODATZ, Peter	Attorney at Law, Sonderhoff & Einsel, Tokyo
SAKURADA, Yoshiyaki	Professor, Faculty of Law, Kyoto University, Kyoto
SCHAEDE, Ulrike	Assistant Professor, Graduate School of International Relations and Pacific Studies, University of California, San Diego
SCHEER, Matthias K.	Secretary General of German-Japanese Lawyers' Association [DJJV]; Attorney at Law, Lawyer's Office Dr. Scheer, Hamburg
TAKAHASHI, Eiji	Associate Professor, Faculty of Law, Osaka City University, Osaka
WOLLSCHLÄGER, Christian	Professor, Faculty of Law, University of Bielefeld, Bielefeld

List of Abbreviations

List of Abbreviations of Laws, Periodicals, and Other Legal Materials

All E.R.	All England Reports
Am. Ec. Rev.	American Economic Review
Am.J.Comp.L.	American Journal of Comparative Law
Am. Pol. Sci. Rev.	American Political Science Review
Am. Soc. Rev.	American Sociological Review
APL	Administrative Procedure Law [*Gyôsei tetsuzuki-hô*]
Asia Pac. L. Rev.	Asia Pacific Law Review
Bell J. Econ. & Man. Science	Bell Journal of Economical and Managment Science
BGBl.	Bundesgesetzblatt [Federal Law Gazette]
B.Y.U. L. Rev.	Brigham Young University Law Review
Cal. L. Rev.	Californian Law Review
Case W. Res. J. Int'l L.	Case Western Reserve Journal of International Law
Colum. L. Rev.	Columbia Law Review
Comp. Lab. L.	Comparative Labor Law
Comp. L. Rev. Chuo University	Comparative Law Review of the Chuo University
Daiten-hô	*Dai-kibo kouri tenpo ni okeru kouri-gyô no jigyô katsudô no chôsei ni kansuru hôritsu* [Law to Adjust Business Activities of Retailers in Large-Scale Retailing Stores]
EEOL	Equal Employment Opportunity Law [*Koyô no bunya ni okeru danjo no kintô na kikai oyobi taigû no kakuho to joshi rôdô-sha no fukushi no zôshin ni kansuru hôritsu*]
EHS	*Eibun-Horei-Sha*, EHS Law Bulletin Series [Legal publisher, Translation Series, Tokyo]
Emory L.J.	Emory Law Journal
E.R.N.Z.	Employment Reports of New Zealand
European Econ. Rev.	European Economical Review
Georgetown Immig. L.J.	Georgetown Immigration Law Journal
Geo. Wash. J. Int'l & Econ.	The George Washington Journal of International Law and Economics
GRUG Int.	Gewerblicher Rechtsschutz und Urheberrecht/Internationaler Teil
Harv. Int'l L.J.	Harvard International Law Journal

Harv. L. Rev.	Harvard Law Review
Harv. Women's L.J.	Harvard Women's Law Journal
Houston J. Int'l L.	Houston Journal of International Law
IIC	International Review of Industrial Property and Copyright Law
Int'l Org.	International Organization
Japan Lab. Bull.	Japanese Labor Bulletin
Jap. An. Int'l L.	Japanese Annual of International Law
J.C.L.	Journal of Contract Law
J. Int'l L. Bus	Journal of International Law and Business
J. Jap. Stud.	Journal of Japanese Studies
J. L. & Econ	Journal of Law and Economics
J. Leg. Stud.	Journal of Legal Studies
J. of Asian Studies	Journal of Asian Studies
Kentucky L. Rev.	Kentucky Law Review
Kobe U. L. Rev.	Kobe University Law Review
Lloyd's Rep.	Lloyd's Report
Loy. L. A.Int'l & Comp. L.J.	Loyola of Los Angeles International and Comparative Law Journal
L. & Soc. Rev.	Law and Society Review
L.Q.R.	Law Quarterly Review
LSL	Labor Standard Law [*Rôdô kijun-hô*]
Mich. Y.B. Int'l L. Studies	Michigan Year Book of International Law Studies
Minso	*Minji soshô-hô* [Civil Procedure Law]
M.L.R.	Modern Law Review
M.U.L.R.	Melbourne University Law Review
NBL	New Business Law (in Japanese)
N.W.U.L. Rev.	North Western University Law Review
N.Z.C.L.C.	New Zealand Company Law Cases
N.Z.L.J.	New Zealand Law Journal
N.Z.L.R.	New Zealand Law Review
N.Z.U.L.R.	New Zealand Universities Law Review
ORDO	Jahrbuch für die Ordnung von Wirtschaft und Gesellschaft

Pacific Basin L. & Policy J.	Pasific Basin Law and Policy Journal
Pacific Rim L. & Policy J.	Pacific Rim Law and Policy Journal
Q.B.	Queen's Bench
RabelsZ	Rabels Zeitschrift für ausländisches und internationales Privatrecht
RGBl.	Reichsgesetzblatt [Reich Law Gazette]
S. Cal. L. Rev.	Southern California Law Review
SEL	Securities and Exchange Law [*Shôken torihiki-hô*]
U.B.C. L. Rev.	University of British Columbia Law Review
UCLA L. Rev.	University of California Los Angeles Law Review
U. Det. Mercy. L. Rev	University of Detroit Mercy Law Review
U. Pa. L. Rev.	University of Pennsylvania Law Review
U. Pa. J. Int'l Bus. L.	University of Pennsylvania Journal of International Business Law
U.S.C	United States Code
V.U.W.L.R.	Victoria University of Wellington Law Review
Wash. L. Rev.	Washington Law Review
West. Aust. L.R.	The University of Western Australia Law Review
Yale L.J.	Yale Law Journal
ZfbF	Schmalenbachs Zeitschrift für betriebswirtschaftliche Forschung
ZJapanR	Zeitschrift für japanisches Recht

General Abbreviations

ADR	alternative dispute resolution
AG	Aktiengesellschaft [stock company]
App. Cas.	Appeal Case
AZ	Arizona
bil.	billion
BOJ	Bank of Japan
CALPERS	California Public Employees Retirement System

CEO	Chief Executive Officer
cf.	compare
ch.	chapter
CLCS	Central Labor Standards Council [*Chûô Rôdô Kijun Shingi-kai*]
Cong.	Congress
CPA	Certified Public Accountant
Ct.	Court
DM	Deutsche Mark [German Mark]
doc.	document
EC	European Community
EDI	Economic Development Institute of the World Bank
ed./s.	Editor/s
e.g.	for example
et al.	and elsewhere, and others
etc.	and so forth
et. seq.	and the following
EU	European Union
fig.	figure
FTC	Fair Trade Commission [*Kôsei Torihiki I'inkai*]
FY	fiscal year
GHJB	*Gaikoku-hô jimu bengoshi* [Lawyers for Foreign Legal Services]
GM	General Motors
GmbH	Gesellschaft mit beschränkter Haftung [limited liability company]
GNP	gross national product
H. Ct.	High Court
ibid.	in the same place
id.	the same
i.e.	that is to say
ILO	International Labor Organization
Inc.	incorporated
Int'l	international
J.D.	Jurist Doctor
JFBA	Japan Federation of Bar Associations [*Nihon Bengoshi Rengô-kai*]
JGCB	Japanese-German Center Berlin

JIL	Japan Institute of Labour
KGaA	Kommanditgesellschaft auf Aktien [partnership limited by shares]
K.K.	*kabushiki kaisha* [stock company]
LDP	Liberal Democratic Party
LL. B.	Bachelor of Law
LL. M.	Master of Law
Ltd.	limited
LTRI	Legal Training and Research Institute [*Shihô Kenshû-jo*]
m.	million
MDR	main dispute resolution
MITI	Ministry of International Trade and Industry [*Tsûshô Sangyô-shô*]
MOF	Ministry of Finance [*ôkura-shô*]
MOL	Ministry of Labor [*Rôdô-shô*]
Nikkeiren	*Nihon Kei'ei-sha Dantai Renmei* [Japan Federation of Employers Association]
no.	number
N.Z.	New Zealand
OB	Old Boy
OECD	Organization for Economic Cooperation and Development
p.	page
p.a.	per anno
Ph.D.	Doctor of Philosophy
P.L.	product liability
RCSL	Research Committee on Sociology and Law
SCAP	Supreme Commander for the Allied Powers
SEC	Securities and Exchange Commission (US)
SESC	Securities and Exchange Surveillance Commission [*Shôken Torihiki Tô Kanshi I'inkai*]
sess.	session
SII	Structural Impediments Initiative
Sup. Ct.	Supreme Court
Sup. Ct. G.B.	Supreme Court Great Britain

trans.	translator
U.S.	United States
v.	versus
VER	Voluntary Export Restraints
vol.	volume
WIPO	World Intellectual Property Organization

Notes

1) The transcription of Japanese terms and names follows a modification of the *Hepburn* system. In the case of well-known geographical terms, the internationally used form was given preference over a strictly correct romanization. The names of persons have been romanized according to their own personal preferences.

2) Japanese names are written according to Western fashion with the family name following the personal name.

3) The exchange rate of the yen to the dollar is calculated at a rate of 100:1.

Introduction

Emulating Japan?

Harald Baum

Contents

A. The Perennial Question

In recent years there has been much discussion about the so-called "Japanese model" and its possible emulation by other countries. But in spite of much spilled ink and endless heated discussions, the challenge of analyzing and understanding the roots and origins of the Japanese success in economic, social, and legal terms still looks considerable. The number of Western publications on Japan, its society, and its industrial system is growing by the day; books on the Japanese firm and its management methods are to be counted by the dozen. Even the Japanese legal system can finally count on a growing comparative interest. But still the central issue seems to be highly controversial and unresolved: the question of whether Japan is running on a fundamentally different but obviously very efficient track. If one sees a system with a fundamentally different balance of incentives and constraints at work, a second question inevitably follows: What is the cause? A cultural setting or some kind of clever institutional arrangement? This of course is the (in)famous and wonderfully persistent "Japanese question" which looms large in the background of almost every conference focused on Japan.

From the *economic* perspective, the issue boils down to the question of whether we see a third way between plan and market, between a socialist and a capitalist society in Japan. Is a wise and benevolent state guiding the economy successfully in the interest of the common good? Can we observe a truly corporatist system at work where people compete less against each other and cooperate more in some kind of "culturally determined altruism"?[1] From the *social* perspective, we may ask whether we see a society whose citizens have recognized that they form a community and whose "communitarian orientation" is the basis for economic success and a stable democracy.[2] From the *legal* perspective, we may wonder how Japan - the second largest world economic power and a modern industrial nation - manages to function with a significantly lower number of judges and lawyers and correspondingly fewer civil and administrative proceedings than (for example) Germany or the United States. Is a non-litigious people cleverly *not* wasting scarce resources on lawyers and lawsuits and still providing for an adequate measure of intrasocietal justice? If so, what alternative conflict-avoiding or conflict-solving mechanisms take the place of contentious disputes?

It may be appropriate to begin with a few general observations which will embrace Japan, the U.S., and Germany. These three countries are not only the main powers of the so-called economic "Triad" which has lately become en vogue in comparative studies, but their legal systems are also indirectly interconnected: in modern times, Japanese law was influenced at first to a significant degree by German law and doctrine; later, after the end of World War II, the American legal system played an important role, especially with respect to economic law. This relationship was of course one of the reasons for inviting contributors from the civil as well as from the common law world to participate together with our Japanese colleagues in the conference, in hopes that this triangular perspective might enable us to discuss our subjects in a particularly productive way.

---

1 *Cf.* R. DORE & H. WHITACKER in their very readable albeit disputable - introduction to the English version of "Business Enterprise in Japan: Views of Leading Japanese Economists" (K. Imai & R. Komiya, eds. 1994) at 4; *see* in general R. DORE, Taking Japan Seriously: A Confucian Perspective on Leading Economic Issues (1987).

2 *Cf.* J.O. HALEY, Lessons from a Changing Japan, 2 PACIFIC RIM L. & POLICY J. 1, 3 (1993).

B. Some Introductory Considerations

1. Mutual Perceptions

On the occasion of the 50th anniversary of the end of World War II, three leading newspapers from the U.S., Japan, and Germany - the *Wallstreet Journal,* the *Nihon Keizai Shinbun*, and the *Handelsblatt* - commissioned a comprehensive survey.[3] In each of the three countries, some 1,500 persons were questioned on the same topics in March 1995. The aim of the survey was to supply a comparative picture of public opinion in these countries. Some of the results offer an illuninating background picture for our further discussion.

In all three countries, three issues were perceived as the biggest problems of the mid-1990s: *unemployment*, *high taxes,* and *the national debt*. However, there were significant differences in the evaluation.[4] The Germans considered unemployment in general to be *the* predominant economic problem by a wide margin (2/3). For both the U.S. and Japan this was obviously not regarded as a pressing social issue (the figures are 19% and 9% respectively). The Americans perceived the national debt as their number one problem (1/3), whereas in Japan the polled persons were most concerned about high taxes. Interestingly in our context, for the Japanese the third biggest problem was *bureaucracy* and *state intervention* (16%) - far more serious than unemployment.[5]

When the question concerning the employment situation was changed to an evaluation of the *individual* job security of the polled person, the picture was quite different: only one quarter of the Germans and Americans thought that their job was *not* sufficiently secure - or that there were no appropriate *chances* to find another one - whereas the same figure for Japan was over 70%.[6] This seems somehow to run counter to the usual conception of the U.S. as a "hire and fire" society in opposition to Japanese society with its famous alleged "lifelong" employment system.

Significant differences can also be seen in the degree of satisfaction with the living conditions in the three countries. The polled parameters included the personal financial situation, cost of living, health care, provisions for old age,

---

3 HANDELSBLATT & INFAS (eds.), USA, Japan, Deutschland 1995. Wirtschaftsmächte im Spiegel der Nationen [The U.S. Japan, Germany 1995: Economic Powers in the Mirror of the Nations (1995).

4 *Id.*, at 5.

5 Although our focus is on Japan and not on Germany, the following observation may be added: in Germany, where the state's share in the gross national product is nearly twice as high as in the U.S. or Japan (roughly 57% : 34%) and where it takes on average four times as long to get the necessary permission for establishing a production facility as in Japan, "big government" is obviously *not even realized* by the public as a problem and a direct threat to the employment situation.

6 HANDELSBLATT & INFAS, *supra* note 3, at 6-8.

and job security, among others. On average, half of the Germans were content with their present situation, and the figure for the Americans was marginally but not significantly lower. The big surprise was the Japanese. Despite Japan's tremendous economic success in the decades after World War II and once more during the so-called "*heisei*-boom" between 1986 and 1992, only 15% of the Japanese were content with their situation.[7] That means that three quarters of those polled were dissatisfied with the conditions of life in Japan in early 1995.

The survey further delivered some revelations with respect to moral concepts: quite contrary to popular beliefs in the West, according to the poll, only 39% of the working populace in Japan saw their life fulfillment in their work, though this figure is still higher than in the U.S. or Germany (30% and 27% respectively). Asked whether they would rather live for their obligations towards other people or try to develop their own personality, the Japanese were split evenly between choosing obligations and their own personality. In the U.S. and Germany, 58% voiced a preference for fulfilling their duties. These figures, too, seem to contrast with commonly held beliefs about Japanese values.[8]

Finally, the subjects of the poll were asked which economy they regarded as the leading economic power today and which would be the strongest ten years from now. Not surprisingly, the Japanese and the Americans still saw the U.S. as the leading economy - albeit by a very small margin - followed by Japan. The Germans saw the Japanese economy in first place by a very wide margin and - quite puzzling - Germany in their view came as number two, before the U.S.[9] Expectations for the future differed: the Americans thought - realistically - that they would not only hold their leading economic position but enlarge it significantly again, leaving Japan behind and Germany coming as a distant third. The Germans, on the contrary, saw only a relative decline of Japan's economic power that ultimately would not affect its leading position. The *Japanese* voiced a strongly diverging opinion: they predicted Mainland China as the clear winner in only ten years time and, correspondingly, as the future leading political power in Asia as well.[10] The significance given to Japan in all three countries as one of the leading economic powers in the second half of our century is of course supported by well-known facts, such as the following.

7 *Id*. at 6-8.
8 *Id*. at 14-16.
9 *Id*. at 17-20.
10 *Id*. at 20, 37.

2. *Success*

As of today, Japanese have attained the highest life expectancy in the world and achieved the highest per capita income of the world - at least in dollar terms. In the late eighties, the country had become the leading creditor nation and the biggest foreign investor worldwide. Its persistent trade surpluses are infamous. In the five-year period between 1986 and 1990, the accumulated increase of the Japanese GNP equaled the average GNP of France in one of those years, France being the fourth-largest economy in the world at that time. A considerable part of those riches has been spent on acquisitions of foreign corporations and other assets. In 1992, the cumulated foreign direct investments of Japanese companies amounted to nearly U.S.$ 400 billion, whereas the entire direct investments of foreign companies in Japan summed up to a meager U.S.$ 30 billion. In other words, all foreign direct investments in Japan to date are less than what Japanese corporations have invested in Great Britain alone.[11]

These few examples of Japan's admirable success speak for themselves. These are also the facts which caused a mild panic in the 1980s when we saw a seemingly endless flood of articles concerned with the perceived threat of Japan turning the Western societies into technological colonies and attaining its allegedly imminent world supremacy.

3. *A Miracle Lost?*

But that was before the *baberu keizai*, the so-called "bubble economy", burst and the *heisei* recession started to drag on - repeated official declarations proclaiming its end notwithstanding - at least until 1996, making it the worst recession in Japan in more than four decades. Meanwhile, *Matsushita* has been forced to sell its famous acquisition, the *MCA Studios*, and *Mitsubishi* has had to seek protection under Chapter 11 for the *Rockefeller Center*, the New York landmark it had acquired some years before, both of them losing hundreds of millions of dollars. This has changed the tune: a leading German newspaper wrote about Japan as the country of the "miracle economy" which had lost its miracle.[12] Increasingly the talk is about Japan's unstoppable decline, about the "setting of the sun", and the like. The Western media have obviously decided all of a sudden that the challenge from Japan has ended for good. Although this might suggest that we have chosen the wrong subject for our conference, the reality is different.

11 For further details and references, *see* H. BAUM, Marktzugang und Unternehmenserwerb in Japan [Market Access and Acquisition of Companies in Japan] 29-52 (1995).

12 SÜDDEUTSCHE ZEITUNG, October 23, 1995, p. 4.

Each of the preceding views seems to be as exaggerated as the other. There has never been a serious danger of Japan taking over the world economy, but Japan has become one of the great economic powers of the world and will stay that way - notwithstanding the fact that the country finds itself in the mid-nineties in a severe structural recession and in a time of transition. Actually, this is an especially interesting period for studying Japan, as it allows us to observe and analyze the sources of Japan's economic competitiveness more precisely because we can now also see some of its limitations more clearly. This in turn might prevent us from drawing the wrong conclusions and adopting strategies which may appear superior but in fact would be detrimental to our future growth and may cause great harm if implemented. Suddenly it has become clear that the Japanese system has not only given rise to companies like *Toyota*, *Sony*, or *Kyocera* - as was commonly thought in the heydays of the 1980s - but has also created a financial industry with banks like *Daiwa* and others which were collectively responsible for the possibly biggest peacetime economic loss in history amounting to many hundreds of billions of U.S. dollars in bad loans. In spite of the overall success, therefore, parts of the system seem to work in a rather problematic way. In fact, it looks as if it were exactly those parts which were accredited by Japan watchers in the past with the most praise for their instrumental role in Japan's economic success: the guiding hand of the state as at least a partial substitute for the market forces. This brings us back to our initial question: Is there a third way between market and plan, a new, socially refined form of Japanese capitalism?

C. Posing the Wrong Questions

1. A New Capitalism?

Many highly influential Japanese scholars and writers insist on just that. A prominent example is *Eisuke Sakakibara,* at the time these lines were written one of the top bureaucrats in the Japanese Ministry of Finance, who published a book called *Beyond Capitalism* in the early 1990s.[13] According to *Sakakibara,* the Japanese economy is best described as a "non-capitalistic market economy". In his view, the real choice facing the world nowadays is not between capitalism and socialism, but between the capitalistic market economy and the Japanese model which he describes as an "extremely humanitarian economic regime" in comparison to capitalistic societies.[14] And, in his opinion, this owes much to the guiding and supervising role of the state or the administrative

---

13 E. SAKAKIBARA, Beyond Capitalism: The Japanese Model of Market Economics (1993).

14 *Id.* at 1 *et seq.*

sector. Nonetheless, at least the Japanese citizens polled in 1995 seemed to have different views of their living conditions under that regime, and they perceived this influence and power of bureaucracy as one of their major problems, as mentioned at the beginning. The perspective seems to change depending on one's immediate standpoint.

However, this idea of the state - meaning the bureaucracy - not only supplementing but at least partially *replacing* the market is supported not only by other high-ranking bureaucrats (which of course is no surprise) but by Japanese scholars as well. A thoughtful study from 1993 called *Governing the Japanese Economy* argues vehemently against "any permanent surrender of economic direction to market forces" which are described as "some of the least admirable elements of Western ideology and values".[15] Government is perceived as an integral element in the economic system, and government-led concerted action must be defended against "free marketeers" and conserved as a "valuable national capacity".[16]

What are the views of Western observers? They differ, naturally. The label "capitalism" is widely used to describe Japan's economy, but the term is usually modified. Thus we find a "strategic capitalism",[17] a "human",[18] a "consultative",[19] a "corporate",[20] an "alliance",[21] a "developmental-state" capitalism,[22] or something, as in the titles of well-known studies, "between MITI and the market"[23] or like " strategic pragmatism".[24] These are but a few of the attempts to describe a phenomenon which obviously eludes clear categorization. Although most foreign experts stick to a broad description of a market-driven economy as a model, it is not a free market in the neo-classical sense they have in mind. It seems more to be what one analyst called a "planned market"[25] - regardless of the fact that this term is a contradiction in

15 K. SHERIDAN, Governing the Japanese Economy 7 (1993).

16 *Id.* at 2.

17 *See* K.E. CALDER, Strategic Capitalism: Private Business and Public Purpose in Japanese Industrial Finance (1993).

18 *See* R.S. OZAKI, Human Capitalism: The Japanese Enterprise System as World Model (1991).

19 *See* U. SCHAEDE, Change and Continuity in Japanese Regulation, 1 ZJAPANR 21, 26 (1996).

20 *See* S. TSURU, Japan's Capitalism: Creative Defeat and Beyond 181 (1993).

21 *See* M.L. GERLACH, Alliance Capitalism: The Social Organization of Japanese Business (1992).

22 *See* C. JOHNSON, Japan: Who Governs? The Rise of the Developmental State (1995).

23 *See* D.L. OKIMOTO, Between MITI and the Market: Japanese Industrial Policy for High Technology (1989).

24 *See* M. SCHMIEGELOW & H. SCHMIEGELOW, Strategic Pragmatism: Japanese Lessons in the Use of Economic Theory (1989).

25 W.K. TABB, The Postwar Japanese System: Cultural Economy and Economic Transformation 297 (1995).

itself. What is meant is not "big government" in the sense of the ubiquitous welfare state à la Europe, but a policy of constant interference in or meddling with the markets by a dominant bureaucracy to achieve previously stipulated goals. *Chalmers Johnson* put it clearly: "The institutions of capitalism inherited from the occupation . . . were modified by the government's industrial policy. Lying behind industrial policy is the strong Japanese state itself. It is the *sine qua non* of Japan's economic achievements"[26].

2. *Industrial Policy as a Road to Success?*

The fact that the Japanese bureaucracy has been and still is heavily interfering in the market process obviously doesn't need to be discussed, but it needs to be perceived precisely to understand the Japanese system. However, the question remains dubious as to whether this interference, or "industrial policy" as it is usually called, has been predominantly instrumental in Japan's economic success. I am of course in no way qualified to give a definite judgment, but, in my view, it has *not* been the main reason for that success. Even if it should prove to have been partially useful - and this is a decisive limitation - it must be seen in a historical context which will not repeat itself and - even more important - which is not transferable to Europe or the U.S.

In the past, the main goals of Japanese industrial policy were primarily to strengthen Japanese exports and to earn much-needed foreign currency in return.[27] It has helped to shape a producer- instead of a consumer-oriented society, which may explain some of the discontent shown in the 1995 poll mentioned above. In the first two or maybe even three decades after World War II, the Japanese economy was a late-comer in a catch-up situation where foreign technology could be easily bought, where it was possible to at least partly shelter the home market against foreign competition while at the same time having a ready market for exports in the United States. All of this is well known - though often officially denied - and has recently been described with rare clarity by a former government adviser: ". . . paternalistic administrative guidance enabled [the leading industries] to strike a happy balance between competition at home and government support for sales abroad".[28] With respect to intellectual property and competition law, the protection of national interests by the bureaucracy is analyzed in this volume by *Christopher Heath* (ch. 13).

---

26 JOHNSON, *supra* note 22, at 66.

27 *See* J.R. BROWN, Industrial Policy and the Dangers of Emulating Japan, 27 GEO. WASH. J. INT'L L. & ECON. 1, 56 (1993).

28 TSURU, *supra* note 20, at 82. With respect to basic materials industries in Japan, the ongoing formal and informal governmental protection of cartels is described by M. TILTON, Restrained Trade: Cartels in Japan's Basic Materials Industries (1996).

Besides this kind of state-led "affirmative action" for the national champions,[29] the success of industrial policy seems questionable.[30] Even during the catch-up phase, it is highly disputable whether the industries promoted by the state were what laid the basis for Japan's economic miracle. There is ample evidence that the state has *not* been picking winners. Rather, it seems to be the market-oriented entrepreneurs who have secured the lasting success. Another less state-oriented new American study recently summarized Japanese capitalism as "corporate-led strategic capitalism" which is described as "neither state dominated nor laissez-faire".[31] This description seems more accurate, but one must be aware that it has been the "laissez-faire" aspect which has led to success. The striking pluralism and vigor of the Japanese private sector, and especially the new sectors like automobiles and consumer electronics, have led the dynamic growth. Fortunately, they have not been inhibited by the Ministry of Trade and Industry's (*Tsûsan-shô*, hereinafter MITI) infamous concept of "excessive competition" or stifled by a convergence of views on broad policy objectives.[32]

In any case, the catch-up position has long since ended. New technology must be developed rather than simply acquired, and comparative advantages like low labor costs have disappeared.[33] Consequently, MITI has tried to foster technological development and innovations by encouraging and financing research cartels and the like.[34] But obviously with little success: the so-called "Fifth Generation Computer Project" has failed to deliver the expected results, and the collective effort to develop high-definition television has turned out to be a flop in the face of independent American producers' advanced technology.[35] U.S. companies have successfully seized back various markets long thought lost, like the ones for semiconductors or computer technology.[36]

---

29 A new study suggests that even this kind of industrial policy was not overly successful, *see* G. SCHNABEL, Handelsbilanz und staatliche Intervention - Japan als Vorbild? [Balance of Trade and and State Intervention: Japan as a Model?], on file with the author.

30 The critical stance towards the idea that active industrial policy was decisive for Japan's success does not, of course, mean that it does not help a lot if the public sector has a positive attitude towards business and is not disinterested or even outright hostile towards business as I fear the situation in Germany could sometimes be described. Less antagonistic government-business relations certainly allow a greater flow of information, to name but one example.

31 CALDER, *supra* note 17, at 251.

32 *See* CALDER, *supra* note 17, at 249, 251; BROWN, *supra* note 27, at 56.

33 BROWN, *supra* note 27, at 57.

34 For a general critical comparative analysis on state-induced research activities, *see, e.g.*, H. HOLZKÄMPER, Forschungs- und Technologiepolitik Europas, Japans und der USA [Research and Technology Policies in Europe, Japan, and the U.S.] (1995).

35 BROWN, *supra* note 27, at 58.

36 *See* C. WOOD, The End of Japan Inc. and How the New Japan Will Look 157 et seq. (1994); BROWN, *supra* note 27, at 58 *et seq.*

In telecommunications or multimedia, the hesitant bureaucratic attitude has been described by Japanese industry itself as a kind of "negative industrial policy".[37] Japan still lacks a flourishing domestic industry in these areas thanks to overregulation and interference in the market by the responsible Ministry of Posts and Telecommunications.[38] It looks as if - not surprisingly - it is competition based on a risk-taking ethic combined with an active venture capital industry rather than state-induced cooperation which creates the optimal environment for innovation.[39]

3. *Successful Paternal Supervision?*

Another - and even worse - case in point seems to be the financial sector, a pet industry of the Japanese bureaucracy. The Ministry of Finance (*Ôkura-shô,* hereinafter MOF) with its far-reaching powers can easily be described as the most powerful public institution in Japan, regulating, guiding, and protecting almost every aspect of the financial industry over the last fifty years. But was it a success? The aforementioned Japanese scholar in her criticism of market forces expressively quotes Japan's banking and financial system as an example of successful management of the markets and the positive outcome of bureaucratic paternalism.[40] In her view, it is "more strictly and prudently governed than most others".[41] No observer would again dispute the fact that especially Japan's financial markets have indeed been and - ten years of discussion about deregulation notwithstanding - still are intensely regulated,[42] but the idea that this has been a great success seems rather outlandish if one

37 WOOD, *supra* note 36, at 177.

38 *Id.* at 178 *et seq.*

39 For a general criticism of the misguided - though in no small part because of Japan's example increasingly fashionable - concept of industrial policy, *see* M. H. DUNN, Neue Industriepolitik oder Stärkung der Marktkräfte? [New Industrial Policy or Strengthening of Market Forces?], 46 ORDO 165 *et seq.* (1995); J. STARBATTY, Die ordnungspolitische Dimension der EG-Technologiepolitik [Market Oriented Policy and EC Policy on Technology], 38 ORDO 155 *et seq.* (1987). The dangerous international implications raised by the increasing tendency of governments to intervene in international trade with the aim of helping their respective national enterprises are described by E.-J. MESTMÄCKER, Wirtschaftsordnung und Geschichtsgesetz [Economic Order and the Law of History], 46 ORDO 9, 19 *et seq.* (1995).

40 SHERIDAN, *supra* note 15.

41 *Id.* at 5.

42 A comprehensive overview of the present regulation and its developement can be found with H. BAUM & M. HAYAKAWA, Die rechtliche Gestaltung der japanischen Finanzmärkte [The Regulation of Japan's Financial Markets], *in* Japanisches Handels- und Wirtschaftsrecht 495-639 [Japanese Economic and Business Law] (H. Baum & U. Drobnig, eds. 1994).

looks at the gigantic losses mentioned above which have been accumulated by that industry. The result of that specific paternalistic treatment is what Western observers have called the "antediluvian" or "archaic" nature of Japanese finance.[43] Due to the permanent guidance of MOF and its refusal to let clear winners and losers emerge - as has been the case in the Japanese electronic industry, for example, which is significantly less guided - Japanese banks and securities companies are far behind their American or even European competitors.[44] Although it is seldom realized, the Japanese financial institutions have so far not been able to catch up to the impressive international success of the Japanese manufacturing industry; *Sony* and *Toyota* have no counterparts in the financial world.

The tight control together with the feeling of being ultimately protected by the authorities bred complacency and gave little incentive to prepare for the deregulation of the 1980s and the growing international competition. While during the postwar period the banks mainly served as instruments for collecting and allocating scarce resources to the manufacturing industries based on fixed and low interest rates, by the 1980s when industry started to make use of liberalization and to look for cheaper direct financing at home and abroad, the banks had increasingly turned to other business. The banks' lack of preparation for new business has been attested to by the mountain of bad loans, huge losses in derivative trading, and the forced exit of *Daiwa* Bank from the U.S. market in 1995, to name but a few examples. The collapse or virtual bankruptcy of banks, various credit cooperatives and nearly all housing loan companies (*jûsen*) - something unheard of during the first five decades after World War II - only followed a wave of scandals in the securities industry just a few years earlier. In other words, in more or less all sectors of the financial system, severe regulatory problems surfaced in the first half of the 1990s to expose systemic defects. *E.B. Keehn* vividly describes how the financial bureaucracy manages to keep its power and stick to its way of regulating the markets in spite of obvious set-backs, strong public criticism, and calls for an overhaul of the whole system towards a more market-orientated regulatory structure[45] (ch. 12).

Besides the hugh losses for investors and taxpayers in general, a further effect of the financial crisis and a typical result for the ministry's interference in the market was a severe shortage of capital in the first half of the 1990s, although Japan has the highest saving rate in the industrial world. Banks had

---

43 WOOD, *supra* note 36, at 132; E.R. DATTEL, The Sun that Never Rose: The Inside Story of Japan's Failed Attempt at Global Financial Dominance 5 (1994).

44 A good description of this problem can be found with DATTEL, *supra* note 43.

45 *See*, e.g., Y. ENDO, Looking Towards the Twenty-First Century, *in* Japanese Financial Markets 258 *et seq*. (S. Hayakawa, ed. 1996).

restricted their lending to their safest customers only because of their bad debt problems. In addition, there was and still is no efficient corporate bond market thanks to a regulatory overkill, and the stock market had been closed to new equity issues by administrative guidance of the ministry as part of the so-called "price keeping operation".[46] As a result, capital was inefficiently allocated and a recovery of the Japanese economy was further delayed.

One conclusion seems to be obvious: the clash between market forces in the form of liberalized access to foreign markets for investing or raising capital, increasing international competition at home, and new financial products, to name but a few examples, and the paternalistic guidance by the (very) visible hand of the finance bureaucracy was clearly lost by the latter, causing a considerable welfare loss for the Japanese public. It may not be a great exaggeration to say that the Japanese financial industries in the 1990s are to a significant degree subsidized by the Japanese manufacturers and consumers. The reason why the financial crisis occurred at all, and then was not handled efficiently, is closely connected with what one observer has called "collusive regulation".[47] One aspect of this is the close relationship between the regulators and the regulated. Many former finance bureaucrats held responsible positions in failed financial institutions, and some of the *jûsen* were even headed by them.[48] This refers to the phenomen of *amakudari*, the "descent from heaven" (which, financially, might be more appropriately called "ascent into heaven"), a common practice of retired bureaucrats in their mid-fifties taking well-paid positions in the industries they had formerly been supervising. Sometimes this occurs directly, sometimes indirectly via a stop-over in a semi-public institution. The resulting "Old Boy" network and its effect on the government-business relations are analyzed in depth in this volume by *Ulrike Schaede* (ch. 14).

Another aspect of this particular regulatory structure is informality or situational regulation by administrative guidance (*gyôsei shidô*). The laws and ordinances grant the authorities wide discretionary powers which are used to persuade and guide the party concerned to act in a certain way, in order to realize an administrative goal through the party's cooperation. As compliance with the ministerial suggestions is considered legally "voluntary", there is little

46 WOOD, *supra* note 36, at 111.

47 U. SCHAEDE, The Bad Loan Debacle: MOF and the Japanese Banking Crisis, paper 1996, on file with the author.

48 Between 1990 and 1995, nine out of sixteen presidential or vice-presidential positions with the seven *jûsen* companies were held by former officials of the Ministry of Finance; *see* O. KLIESOW, *Jûsen*: Absurdes Theater in Japans Finanzwelt [*Jûsen*: Theater of the Absurd in Japan's Financial World], 2 ZJAPANR 1996 (in preparation for autumn 1996); a detailed report can be found with SCHAEDE, *supra* note 47.

ground for a judicial review by the courts and the whole process has a rather non-transparent character.[49] This leads to the question of which concept of administrative law allows an administrator to apply a vaguely worded law or ordinance while exercising a great deal of discretion in the process; in other words, how formal or informal are administrative processes in Japan? *Hideki Kanda* answers these questions by developing a theory of monitoring to analyze the role of bureaucrats. He expressively rejects the view that MOF exercises market control (on top of its usual functions of law enforcement and rulemaking), but rather sees a process of *ex ante* monitoring at work where parties with multiple interests participate in the administrative rulemaking process via the *shingi-kai* (advisory councils). As a result, there are no judicial challenges to financial legislation or administrative rules in Japan; in this view the *ex post* monitoring by the courts is replaced by compromise reached informally with the parties concerned during the rulemaking procedure (ch. 11).

4. *Two Dangers*

Why did we elaborate on the (questionable) role of the state? For two reasons: first, as already mentioned, one cannot understand the functioning of the Japanese economy without giving sufficient attention to bureaucratic interference in the markets. But, second, at least in the view presented here, the past discussion has put far too much emphasis on the alleged role of industrial policy and paternal governmental guidance and supervison as *the* cause of Japan's success. This inadequate perspective engenders two negative consequences: first, in its distraction with an illusionary concept, it fosters the danger of overlooking the *real* sources of Japan's strength, which in this opinion are its distinctive social, organizational, and legal features. Based on competition, these facilitate the functioning of a perfectly capitalistic, non-planned market economy by formulating the rules of the game in a different but still efficient way within the specific constraints of an institutional setting molded, of course, by Japan's tradition and culture. Second, and more important, we face the danger of adopting strategies from Japan which are at best neutral, but most probably are detrimental to growth and non-causal to Japan's success. In other words, as important as it is to know what to learn, sometimes it appears to be equally important to know what *not* to adopt. Important examples for this misguided approach are the constantly repeated calls for an industrial policy à la MITI in Europe, for so-called "good cartels", or for concerted actions à la japonaise.[50] It is quite alarming to observe a new

49 For a detailed analysis, *see*, e.g., BAUM & HAYAKAWA, *supra* note 42, at 516 *et seq.*

50 One hair-raising example was reported in the press: with obvious reference to a perceived Japanese model, the European Commission is apparently contemplating

growth of interventionist tendencies among those - critics of the capitalist system and others - who, for whatever reasons, believe in a strong interventionist state. These critics tend to blindly cite Japan as a justification for their beliefs. The faulty argument that Japan has succeeded by avoiding free market methods serves their purpose well.[51] The regulatory failure of that approach should be demonstrated beyond any sensible doubt by looking at the mess in Japan's financial markets; the failed attempts of pushing innovation by state-led action mentioned above should at least give rise to serious doubts and disqualify the Japanese experience from any continued perception of suitability as a positive example.

If one understands the market with *Hayek* and *Kirzner* as a process of discovery and spontaneous learning driven by dynamic competition, it becomes clear that innovation cannot be achieved by concerted action and pre-described goals. Only the discovery function of the market allows the use of information that was initially at nobody's command. The market process, made up of acts of "entrepreneurial discovery", spontaneously offers the incentives and opportunities that inspire market participants continually to "push back the deep fog of mutual ignorance" that surrounds every decision.[52] There exists no centralized access to the dispersed information - not even in Japan.

D. Defining the Relevant Aspects

After this exploration of the concept of state intervention as a historically informative aspect that is indispensable to an understanding of the Japanese system, though not overly promising for the future, let us shift the focus to other more rewarding aspects of Japan's remarkable economic achievements and try to set the background for the chapters of this volume not yet touched upon. Three aspects may be of special interest: first, there seems to be a high degree of social trust in Japan that works as a basis for long-term strategies and interpersonal dealings. Second, flexibility, informality, and pragmatism rather

---

plans for spending huge amounts of public money to help the European car industry develop the "car of the future". One would think that the industry might be able to manage *this* by itself, wouldn't one? *Cf.* FRANKFURTER ALLGEMEINE ZEITUNG, November 11, 1995, p. 13.

51 WOOD, *supra* note 36, at 158, 186.

52 *See* F.A. v. HAYEK, Die Verwertung des Wissens in der Gesellschaft [The Use of Knowledge in Society], *in* F.A. v. HAYEK, Individualismus und wirtschaftliche Ordnung [Individualism and Economic Order] 104 et seq. (1976); I.M. KIRZNER, Discovery, Capitalism, and Distributive Justice 11, 85, 92 (1989); *id.*, The Limits of the Market: The Real and the Imagined, *in* Marktwirtschaft und Rechtsordnung. Festschrift zum 70. Geburtstag von Erich Hoppmann [Market Economy and Legal Order: Festschrift for the 70th Birthday of Erich Hoppmann] 103 (W. Möschel, M.E. Streit & U. Witt, eds. 1994).

than strict law enforcement are obviously dominating the business practice, as can be observed, for example, in contract practice. From the organizational perspective, there seems to be a remarkable ability to create and widely use something between market and organization, or what might be termed a combination of both aspects: networks, which faciliate the flow of information at various levels of society.

1. Trust and Communitarian Values

Francis Fukuyama, the American analyst well-known for controversial theses, has argued that trust and other social virtues are the decisive basis for the creation of prosperity[53]. He sees a strong positive influence of communitarian values on the long-term economic development in the three big industrial nations that he predicts as the future winners: it is no surprise that Japan is among them. What may appear surprising is that the U.S. and Germany score equally high for the levels of trust within their societies. China, for all its Confucian heritage - and the Japanese concerns about its future dominance mentioned above - is *not* among them, nor are France or Italy, to name but a few. The theory maintains that there is not a pan-Asian challenge, but rather that the similarities among the above-named three countries scoring high on social trust are much larger and more important than a shared Confucian heritage between Japan and China or other Asian countries.

These views obviously run counter to quite a number of entrenched opinions: first, insofar as the emphasis is put on culture-based social trust as a prerequisite for network organizations, which in turn can reduce transaction costs significantly, a conflict with economic theory emphasizing the importance of strictly enforceable property rights appears likely. Second, when *Fukuyama* puts Japan in the same camp as the U.S. and Germany, he challenges the popular idea of a pan-Asian success story modeled along Confucian lines,[54] as neither of the latter are heavily indebted to the legendary Chinese sage. Third, there is obviously no room for the notion of the uniqueness of the Japanese economic system voiced by many of the Japanese analysts mentioned above.[55]

The communitarian aspect is strongly emphasized by *John O. Haley*, too, who expressively links Japan's economic achievements to a substantial degree to the recognition by the Japanese that they form a community.[56] But he differentiates this sharply from the U.S. society, which he sees in need of a

53 Trust. The Social Virtues and the Creation Prosperity (1995).
54 *Cf.*, e.g., DORE, *supra* note 1; J. FALLOWS, Looking at the Sun. The Rise of the New East Asian Economic and Political System (1994).
55 *Cf.*, e.g., SAKAKIBARA, *supra* note 13.
56 HALEY, *supra* note 2, at 3 *et seq.*

stronger communitarian orientation although "[m]any of the communitarian aspects of Japanese life run counter to deeply held American beliefs and preconceptions".[57] In his contribution to this volume, *Haley* asks whether community counts with respect to relational contracting and its implications for law. He argues that differences between Japan and the United States exist and can be understood best by the communitarian orientation of Japanese society and law enforcement as Japanese relational contracting, unlike American, occurs in a communitarian context that both encourages relational contracting and provides a system of ordering that effectively substitutes for the formal legal system. Although such substitution may not reduce contract rules to irrelevance, it does restrict their application and thus their role in regulating transactions and determining outcomes (ch. 5).

2. *Flexibility and Informality*

Zentaro Kitagawa, too, differentiates the Japanese way of contracting to some degree from the American way of doing business and questions the common assumption that contracts are better the more detailed they are. In his view, a good contract is not necessarily one in which the interests of the contracting parties are balanced equally. Instead, within the limits set by the principle of private autonomy, we should expect a certain amount of imbalance under our market system of competition. A functioning contract in his opinion is one in which the parties disclose information in good faith and without terms that are unjustly advantageous to one party. He emphasizes one often overlooked aspect of special importance in Japanese practice: the unique interrelationship between the role of administrative standards in resolving contract disputes and the laxity of legal control over unfair contract terms in Japanese contract law (ch. 4). *Luke Nottage* continues along the same lines with his focus on the development of criteria necessary for a meaningful comparison of contract law and usage (ch. 7).

From the practitioner's perspective, *Guntram Rahn* emphasizes flexibility. Studies of the late 1980s indicate that more than two thirds of commercial contracts made by Japanese companies were concluded only orally. *Rahn* observes that, in his view, Japanese companies are sometimes hesitant to conclude detailed written contracts as they prefer to retain their flexibility. Accordingly, contracts quite often are not formally concluded in Japan, but evolve. In these cases, the party interested in entering into a business relationship will not formally negotiate, presenting instead what it has to offer and then trying to involve the other party by frequent contacts and personal

57 *Id.* at 5.

communication, impressive hospitality, free ancillary services, and a flow of constant information. In this manner, a personal relationship is gradually built up until sooner or later a point of no return is reached and business orders just have to follow (ch. 6).

This informal approach a type of relational contracting seems to point to the functioning contract as a means ot building up trust and of avoiding conflict rather than predominantly as a legal instrument for safeguarding one's interests in the case of a dispute. Shifting the perspective from contract law and practice to the broader question of the use or non-use of litigation and the role of trained lawyers in Japanese business life, we find not surprisingly that the percentage of people involved in the legal profession and, correspondingly, the rate of litigation, is much lower in Japan than, for example, the U.S. This is, of course, standard knowledge about Japan, but it has seldom been examined in depth, and the point that differences exist in different areas of law with varying causes is rarely noted.[58]

3. A "Non-Litigious Society" and a "Dearth of Lawyers"?

Two voluminous contributions in this volume, both based on extensive empirical as well as comparative research, tackle these questions. It is probably the first time ever that these issues have been analyzed - at least in a Western language - in such a profound way. *Christian Wollschläger* utilizes the historical information offered by Japanese judicial statistics. He shows the historical origins of the avoidance of litigation as well as the continuity of effective private means of dispute resolution and norm enforcement. The low demand for civil justice is traced back to the 18th century for metropolitan courts. His findings confirm the traditionalist explanation of the avoidance of litigation as it was laid down in *Takeyoshi Kawashima's* historical studies. Social attitudes towards law which continue from an agrarian feudal state are judged as the only basis to explain the stable secular development of litigation in Japan as well as the wide distance to Western nations. *Wollschläger* regards competing theories as hardly compatible with the conclusions which were drawn from judicial statistics in his contribution. The low demand for civil justice is seen as a genuine element of legal culture insofar as it distinguishes the practical operation of Japanese law from that of Western nations. This is the Japanese aspect of Japanese law which otherwise comprises many foreign imports. On the other hand, *Wollschläger* shows that the criticisms of *Kawashima's* emphasis on mentality is probably justified. Its underlying

58 See this has been rightly criticized by D.H. FOOTE, Resolution of Traffic Accident Disputes and Judicial Activism in Japan, 25 LAW IN JAPAN 19 *et seq.* (1995).

evolutionary notion of a progressive parallel rise of litigation rates and rights consciousness finds no support from historical judicial statistics. Instead, time series of four nations show individual national patterns on the way to modernity. In the foreseeable future, the avoidance of litigation will continue as a distinctive element of the Japanese legal culture and *Wollschläger* sees the historical origins of the avoidance of litigation as safe grounds for ongoing research (ch. 3).

The historical roots of present-day dispute settlement in Japan are also emphasized by *Dan Fenno Henderson* in his contribution about the role of lawyers, quasi-lawyers, and the Japanese legal profession in general. He emphasizes the continuation of a strong tradition of Japanese bureaucratic governance as indispensable for understanding social constraints on law and lawyering in Japan and the prominent role of quasi-lawyers in helping the bureaucrats. These are more concerned with facilitating compliance with bureaucracy than enforcing rights of citizen vs. citizen or government. The administrative system - as differentiated from the legal one - can be seen to work quite well: it is flexible; it adjusts by consensus and cooperation; and it deals with recalcitrance by give-and-take or potential withholding of favors rather than rigid orders, universalistic rules, lawyerly posturing, ultimatums, adjudications, and sanctions of law. Instead there is a vast network of mediators to adjust the citizenry's complaints against officialdom. These other perhaps better ways of settling disputes are likely the main reason why the Japanese litigate comparatively little. In context, these may be better ways to settle disputes because they are quicker, cheaper, and leave less rancor among the disputants. At this level of otherwise private transactions, too, social administration, bereft of lawyers' law, may work tolerably well. *Henderson* sees the social density of Japan - with its lack of American-style mobility to move from job to job, place to place, or spouse to spouse - as enhancing this ordered but lawless way of managing society, an option which mobile individualistic Americans in his view neither have nor probably want (ch. 1).

A third contribution by *Toshiyuki Kono*, again based on extensive empirical research, completes the picture by examining the role of the aministration as a mediator. First, he finds that large Japanese companies have tended in the past to resolve most disputes through negotiations within the framework of "business". With smaller companies and outside enterprise groups, the Japanese administration comes in as a mediator. It tends to establish "forums" for dispute resolution, especially when the gap between the relative power of the parties is wide. However, within these forums the administration remains quite "motionless" and often urges the parties to find a "voluntary" solution. The question is how these methods of dispute settlements will develop in the face of the growing frequency of derivative suits. *Kono* sees a growing reluctance among executive directors to resolve disputes within the framework of business judgments. In this context, calls for reform and improvement of the Japanese court system from the industry are not surprising. Despite the remaining difficulties with regard to access to courts, the demand for court intervention and legal service will probably increase. Nonetheless, the administration will likely still try to act as mediator. Depending upon how the administration approaches the situation, it may change from *de facto* to *de jure* mediator (ch. 2).

4. *Relational Environment, Cooperation, and Networks*

We have already described the relational aspect with respect to contracting and to some degree in the above-mentioned buraucratic rulemaking where the parties concerned are involved in a consensual process. If we look at the Japanese firm we see again a highly relational environment. Many of these companies operate within one of the various enterprise groups or *keiretsu* that function as networks. From the organizational perspective these can be labelled somewhere between market and organization, where cross-shareholding, interpersonal exchange, a common main bank, preferential trading relations, and technical cooperation among each other prevail. These phenomena and possible future changes are analyzed in this volume by *Eiji Takahashi* (ch. 8).

In general, Japanese enterprises appear to operate in less rigid legal surroundings and to enjoy greater flexibility. Shareholder rights may be less developed and less frequently enforced in Japan than in the United States. The formal legal protection of workers in Japan seems less stringent than in Germany with its absurdly protective labor laws and its system of mandatory co-determination, yet Japanese workers seem more closely involved in the actual decision-making process. In general, labor relations appear to be more cooperative, with the employee treated more - to use the famous catch phrase - like a stakeholder in the firm and enjoying greater power in relation to the owner. As retroactive look back clearly shows that this was not always so and has come about not by chance or some kind of cultural destination but rather as a result of a clever institutional setting.[59]

Daniel H. Foote picks up here and analyzes the *governmental* - not union - efforts to reduce working hours in Japan. His extensive study gives one of the very few insights in a Western language of how the administration is trying to influence business and labor practices and the difficulties of doing so by legislation.[60] The *shingi-kai* process already mentioned above is described in

59 *See*, e.g., the very infomative study by W.D. KINZLEY, Industrial Harmony in Modern Japan: The Invention of a Tradition (1991).

60 Another aspect, the relevance of the judiciary in creating an extensive body of law in the employment area is treated by the same author elsewhere: *see* D.H. FOOTE,

great detail, allowing a glimpse at the balance of power between administration, enterprises, and labor. *Foote's* analysis supplements the other studies in this volume about the roles of the bureaucracy as mediator, supervisor, and administrative rulemaker in the financial sector. The fact that it was the government that started to press for change seems in itself remarkable; from the German perspective one would expect the unions to be the initiators. As *Foote* points out, reducing working hours had not been a major issue for most unions; labor was not heavily involved in the initial push for lower hours in spite of heavy overtime work. He cites several interrelated factors to help explain labor's reluctance to press the hours issue. First, job security has long been a critical issue for unions in Japan. Presumably, reducing working hours and limiting use of part-time employees would have resulted in more jobs for full-time employees. De facto, the retrenchment served the interests of union members by enhancing their job security. In the event of a future turndown in economic activity, cutting back overtime and reducing the part-time work force would serve as buffers to protect them from layoffs. Second, overtime work also represented a bread-and-butter issue for workers. Even with an overtime premium of only 25%, overtime wages constituted an important part of the family budget for many workers. Furthermore, as *Foote* emphasizes, Japanese unions have faced a fundamental structural weakness that limits their ability to press effectively for shorter working hours. This lies in the well-known phenomenon of "enterprise unions" - unions organized at individual enterprises and typically embracing the full range of non-managerial full-time regular employees at that firm, as opposed to trade unions linking workers in similar fields across companies. The prevalence of enterprise unions in Japan has left unions weak when it comes to bargaining for benefits that might affect a company's competitive position. *Foote*'s contribution may raise some doubts about the perceived charming side of the cooperative, communitarian stakeholder magic normally attributed to labor relations in Japan (ch. 10).

Shifting the position to the other side of the stakeholder panorama, the shareholder comes into sight. What kind of role has the shareholder played so far vis-à-vis labor in the corporate networks? *Masaru Hayakawa* presents us with a rare picture of shareholder behavior in Japan. This topic seems to be absolutely basic to an understanding of the ongoing discussion of corporate governance in Japanese firms - an intensely discussed subject of interest in more or less all major industrial countries[61] - but it has been only marginally

---

Judicial Creation of Norms in Japanese Labor Law: Activism in the Service of - Stability? 43 UCLA L. REV. 636 *et seq.* (1996).

61 It is quite intriguing to watch a kind of rotary traffic: American scholars study the Japanese and German corporate and financial structures with their main bank and universal banking systems respectively as a possibly better way of monitoring managers. Their Japanese colleagues, on the other hand, are looking for ways to

covered so far in Western literature on Japan.[62] *Hayakawa* gives an overview of various types of shareholders, most of them committed shareholders as opposed to payout-oriented ones with a preference for exit. Since the latter half of the 1960s the number of individual shareholders has decreased, and a cross-shareholding system has taken hold. In such a system, if a company in its role as a corporate shareholder were to demand a high rate of dividends, it would be counterproductive to its own economic interests. As *Hayakawa* points out, under the cross-shareholding system, such a demand would result in the other party - the company conversely holding shares in the corporate shareholder - claiming dividends in a similar way. Cross-shareholding thus eventually works as a device to usurp the rights of shareholders. Low dividends have been criticized as disregarding the interests of the average shareholder. However, for the committed majority shareholder (which here includes companies with interlocking share ownership relationships such that their interests sufficiently converge to make them act as a majority shareholder), low dividends do not conflict with their own economic interests. Consequently, they have little incentive to actively exercise their rights and sue. But this restrained practice does not necessarily answer the question of consciousness of their rights. How the growing activities of foreign institutional investors in Japan will affect these practices remains to be seen. Legal reforms easing the filing of derivative actions have already resulted in a significant increase in those actions and consequently a somewhat strengthened exercise of supervisory authority over management. Whether this is the beginning of a "shareholder revolt" in Japan is at the moment still an open question (ch. 9).

---

loosen up the restraints of just that system, while the Germans - having second thoughts about the influence of their universal banks - are trying to curb that influence by revamping their capital markets along the lines of the U.S. model.

62 A list of some recent works on corporate governance in Japan or on a comparison with Japan might include J.M. ROE, Some Difference in Corporate Structures in Germany, Japan, and the United States, 102 YALE L. J. 1927 (1993); U. SCHAEDE & H. BAUM, Institutional Investors and Corporate Governance in Japanese Perspective, *in* Institutional Investors and Corporate Governance 609 *et seq.* (T. Baums, R. Buxbaum & K.J. Hopt, eds. 1994); U. SCHAEDE, Understanding Corporate Governance in Japan: Do Classical Concepts Apply? Industrial and Corporate Change 3 (1994) 285 *et seq.*; S PROWSE, Corporate governance in an international perspective: A survey of corporate control mechanisms among large firms in the United States, the United Kingdom, Japan and Germany, BIS Economic Papers, No. 41 (Basle 1994); M. FUKAO, Financial Integration, Corporate Governance, and the Performance of Multinational Companies (1995); C.J. MILHAUPT, A Relational Theory of Japanese Corporate Governance: Contract, Culture, and the Rule of Law, 37 HARV. INT'L L.J. 3 *et seq.* (1996).

E. Communitarian Romanticism?

Relational rulemaking, relational contracting, cooperative labor relations, and firms operating within networks - do we see a communitarian paradise in Japan? Maybe. Despite a one hundred-year history of adoption and formal validity of codified (Western) law, modern Japanese society is still controlled to a great degree by consensus. In this context, the often-cited "struggle for law" is of less decisive significance than a skilled, institutionalized social administration, consciously supported by a manipulated shortage of the resource of law. However - and the contributors to this volume agree on this point without exception - this does of course not mean that law does not count in Japan. As in other industrial nations, Japanese parties also bargain in the "shadow of the law", but the resort to law, as a means of regulating business and solving disputes may not be the most prominent cause of action. The advantages of this approach - greater flexibility and the necessity of cooperation - are obvious. A less positive aspect, however, may be the corresponding loss of individual rights, a topic which surfaced time and again during our discussions (see the report of *Dörte Liebrecht*, ch. 15).

With this problem in mind, some Japanese commentators are rather critical of the currently dominant legal culture in Japan as they perceive it. *Tatsuo Inoue*, for example, sees a strong parallel between the Western communitarian visions and Japanese society, but warns that the Japanese experience shows that a closed community may well impoverish life if individual rights are neglected for the sake of shared goals and the "pervasive pressure of social tyranny" is applied to individuals who try to seek an alternative life of their own.[63] *Setsuo Miyazawa*, following the criticism of *Inoue*, expressively calls for a "liberal transformation of Japanese legal culture and legal system" in a society which he regards as too tightly organized and controlled.[64] In his view, Japan has to find a middle way between "[t]he danger of becoming like the United States or the danger of remaining a right-blind society".[65] I very much doubt whether the German model with its soft tyranny of the all-embracing welfare state slowly throttling life - at least as it has developed during the last decades - could offer the necessary middle way. In a society where it is legally much easier to get rid of a spouse than of a tenant in a flat, things seem to be a bit out of balance. In

63 The Poverty of Rights-Blind Communality: Looking through the Window of Japan, B.Y.U. L. REV. 517, 540, 550 (1993).

64 Taking Merry Seriously: A Neo-Culuralist Review of the Recent Scholarship and Practice in Japan, *in* The Proceedings of the 1995 Annual Meeting. Legal Culture: Encounters and Transformations 133, 168 (Japan Committe for the Research Committee on Sociology of Law, Japanese Association of Sociology of Law, ed. 1995).

65 *Id.* at 164.

any case, those who take seriously the "communitarian values" should first take a look at Japan - for better or for worse.

Relational contracting and rulemaking, cooperative labor relations and interlocking corporate networks, described above as to some degree typical for the Japanese system seem to be inseparable from a rather informal approach to the law. This last element has also been identified for various areas of law in Japan. In light of Japan's outstanding economic success, does this mean that a strict judicial enforcement of property and contract rights is not a prerequisite for growth? Does the Japanese experience indeed show that legal informality rather than legal formalism, enhances economic growth, as one American scholar speculated from analyses of Asia and particularly Japan?[66] Possibly, yet not necessarily. In any case, it does seem to show that there are different ways to success within the capitalistic spectrum, which furthermore may change along a single path of development. Whether these ways are actually contradictory, as is sometimes suggested, appears questionable. Instead, each society's set of institutions, formed by its unique cultural and historical conditions, shapes its economic life and legal process in a peculiar way by creating a distinctive balance of constraints. As mentioned above, within these constraints, rational behavior and the competition at the core of a market-oriented society are the main factors for the Japanese success. Whether those systems like Japan's characterized by legal informality are converging with those emphasizing a formal approach to law in the course of the much-cited globalization is yet another question.[67] The Japanese experience does not suggest that this will happen any time soon.

This brings us back to our initial question: emulating Japan? The answer should have become clear by now: emulating, no - learning, yes. There can no (longer) be any question about the rewards of remaining involved in the most fascinating undertaking of analyzing the Japanese legal and economic system, its sources of success, and its elements which might be helpful for improving one's own system. This does not necessarily always mean the adoption of such features; the mere sharpening of one's own focus and the accompanying more critical evaluation of what is to be seen in one's own "backyard" can be a significant achievment in itself.[68] This of course is the basic aim of every

---

66 *See* F.K. UPHAM, Speculations on Legal Informality, 28 L. & SOC. REV. 233, 236 et seq. (1994).

67 *Cf. id.* at 238, 240.

68 From this perspective, the growing comparative interest in Japanese law to be seen internationally appears to be of great importance. A helpful overview of recent Western publications on Japanese law can be found with H. HOHMANN, Modern Japanese Law: Legal History and Concept of Law, Public and Economic Law of Japan, 44 AM.J.COMP.L. 151-173 (1996). For a review of three major publications on Japanese law of the 1990s and some general oberservations on comparison of law with Japan, *see* H. BAUM, Rechtsdenken, Rechtssystem und Rechtswirklichkeit

comparative endeavor, and here Japan is an excellent model: if there is something in particular to learn from Japan, it is (1) the willingness to look across its borders for usable solutions to import, and (2) the inherent flexibility of the system, the pluralistic structure of the country with its diverse interplay of inherited and modern values, and the resulting spectrum of alternative modes of action which have been significant elements in its economic success. Herein lies one of Japan's strengths, one which seems to have been largely overlooked in the current discussion regarding the competitive advantages of nations.

in Japan - Rechtsvergleichung mit Japan [Legal Thought, Legal System, and Legal Reality in Japan: Comparison of Law with Japan], 59 RABELSZ 258-292 (1995).

Part One:
Lawyers, Mediators, and Legal Culture

Chapter One

The Role of Lawyers in Japan

Dan Fenno Henderson

Contents

> They've got about as many lawyers as we've got *sumo* wrestlers.
>
> Chrysler chairman, *Lee Iacocca*

If we think of the English common law as built by judges, the German system as made and refined by professors, then, of course, in the American legal system the key role is the lawyer.[1] In like sense, for Japan, it is clearly the bureaucrat.[2]

This is not by recent contrivance. Partly, the Japanese bureaucrat finds his roots in age-old Chinese state examinations thought to legitimate government-by-meritocracy;[3] in part official prestige derives from the ruling *samurai's* role in the Tokugawa hereditary caste system, still vaunted in *kabuki*, the movies, literature, and daily business and political jargon. Surely, too, the Meiji Constitution enhanced the role of imperial bureaucrats (both civil and military) right up to 1945. And finally, McArthur's choice[4] in 1945 to democratize, required by the Potsdam Declaration, by using rather than replacing the Japanese administrators, tended to entrench further a talented officialdom of great coherence, autonomy and political power. Only against this backdrop of Japanese bureaucratic governance can we understand social constraints on law and lawyering in Japan and the prominent role of quasi-lawyers[5] to help the bureaucrats.

---

1 It has become conventional to cite *Alexis de Tocqueville*, Democracy in America (1837), for the peculiar influence of lawyers in our society from the beginning, and of course it persists.

2 *See* J.O. HALEY, Authority Without Power: Law and the Japanese Paradox 140 (Oxford, 1991); D.F. HENDERSON, Foreign Enterprise in Japan 196-216 (1975).

3 The Tokugawa hereditary *samurai* intervened between Japan's sinic experience and importation of Western models. The Meiji government decided to rely on a meritocracy based on exams, and it has intensified since World War II. *See* a recent account, I. AMANO, Education and Examination in Modern Japan, ch. 1 (1990).

4 C. JOHNSON, Japan, "Who Governs?": An Essay on Official Bureaucracy, 2 J. JAP. STUD. (No. 1) 16 (1975); HALEY, *supra* note 2, at 147.

5 The Japanese literature on the role of law and lawyers is voluminous, because Japanese scholars are generally more aware that Western justiciable law was a misfit in their traditional Japanese society and culture, and therefore Japanese comparativists better understand the enormity and slow pace of change required to accommodate the Meiji Code reception. Also they realize that law, lawsuits, and lawyers came to Japan in a package; therefore, the lawyer's role has been treated along with the novelty of law and lawsuits, and against a background of much social autonomy and bureaucratic oversight. *See,* e.g., the early post-war work of T. KAWASHIMA, *Nihonjin no hô-ishiki* [Legal Consciousness of the Japanese] 125 (1967); also T. TANASE, *Gendai shakai to bengoshi* [Present-Day Society and Lawyers] (1987); S. KATÔ, *Bengoshi yakuwari-ron* [Discourse on the Role of Lawyers]; M. ÔKI, *Nihonjin no hô-kannen: seiyô-teki hô-kannen to no hikaku* [The Idea-of-Law of the Japanese: A Comparison with the Western Idea-of-Law] (1983); and G. NAKAGAWA, *Nihonjin no hô-kankaku*, [The Legal Sense of the Japanese] 71

The conventional wisdom has Japan short of lawyers. Whether that is true or not depends on the definition of "lawyer" or quasi-lawyers and how we count them.[6] These are comparative law problems of much subtlety, but in sum, however many of them we may choose to count, the quasi-lawyers are more concerned with facilitating compliance with bureaucracy than enforcing rights of citizen vs. citizen, or against government. Lawyers in Japan monopolize the rights-enforcing function important in democracies to a rule-of-law. Still the quasi-lawyers' assistance with compliance overlaps considerably the work of American lawyers, whose practices are uniquely broad, recently embracing even alternative dispute resolution which is more sociological than legal.

In Part I, I will discuss the problem of definition and lawyers' relationships to other law-related professions, because comparability, especially with the

---

(1989); T. KOJIMA, *Bengoshi no shakai-teki yakuwari* [The Social Role of Lawyers] *in*: *Gendai no bengoshi* (HÔGAKU SEMINARU, special issue, p. 44 (1982)).

This is not a neglected subject in English either. F.K. UPHAM, Law and Social Change in Postwar Japan (1987); H. TANAKA, The Role of Law in Japanese Society, 19 U.B.C.L.REV. 375-388 (1985); J.O. HALEY, The Role of Law in Japan, 18 KOBE U.L.REV. 1-20 (1984); I. SHAPIRO & M. YOUNG, The Role of Law and Lawyers in Japan and the United States, 7 MICH. Y.B. INT'L L. STUDIES 25 (1985); M. KATÔ, The Role of Law and Lawyers in Japan and the United States, 1987 B.Y.U.L.REV. 627-698 (1987); D.F. HENDERSON, Conciliation and Japanese Law 2 Vol. (1965); *id.*, 38 WASH. L.REV. 1 (1963); G. DAL PONT, The Social Status of the Legal Profession in Japan and the United States: A Structural and Cultural Analysis, 72 U. DET. MERCY L.REV. 291-325 (1995); T. HATTORI & D.F. HENDERSON, Civil Procedure in Japan, ch. 2 (Professional Legal Assistance), p. 2-1 to 2-52 (1985); J.M. RAMSEYER, Lawyers, Foreign Lawyers, and Lawyer-Substitutes: The Market for Regulation in Japan, 27 HARV. INT'L L.J. 499-539 (1986); and many others.

6 The question of how to count and compare "lawyers" as well as "cases" across national boundaries has its share of literature too: COURT STATISTICS PROJECT STAFF, State Court Caseload Statistics: Annual Report 1992, 272 (1994), treats the problem of what is a case, kinds of cases, and reporting diversities as encountered in gradually giving us a better national view of the State Court workload in the fifty American states.

My own initial attempt at counting "lawyers" was *in* Conciliation and Japanese Law, Vol. 2, 195-197 (1965); thereafter twice again I have given the problem a closer look: *id.*, *supra* note 2, at 176-85; and HATTORI & HENDERSON, *supra* note 5, at 2-43 § 2.09 (1985).

Recently, *see* a careful study by S. ÔTA & K. ROKUMOTO, Issues of the Lawyer Population: Japan, 25 CASE W. RES. J. INT'L L. 315-332 (1993); also one of the better ones is M. KATÔ, *supra* note 5; also *see* R.S. MILLER, Apples vs. Persimmons: Let's Stop Drawing Inappropriate Comparisons Between the Legal Professions in Japan and the United States, 17 V.U.W. L.REV. 201, 202-204 (1987); R.L. BROWN, A Lawyer by Any Other Name: Legal Advisors in Japan, *in*: PRACTICING LAW INSTITUTE, (ed.), Legal Aspects of Doing Business in Japan 1983, 201 and 479 (1983). Y. KAGO (ed.), *Shimin no tame no hôritsu-ka* [Law Specialists for the Citizenry] 213-47 (1983), includes detailed valuable descriptions of other special professions doing law-related work, but excluded from my list based on my own judgment as to comparability with lawyers.

American bar, is awkward unless we cast the net very widely. Even then precise comparability is illusive. Part II focuses on lawyers (*bengoshi*) only and their history as it affects their current role in society. Part III is a synopsis of the current institutional setting of the legal profession and its geographic distribution, internal organization, scope of services, ethics and fees. In Part IV special issues of transnational law practice and the status of foreign lawyers will be reviewed.

PART I: DEFINING LAWYERS AND LAW-RELATED PROFESSIONS

A. Counting Lawyers (*bengoshi*)

Though "barrister"[7] would be a better English term for *bengoshi*, the standard translation has long been "lawyer," though I notice the *Japan Federation of Bar Associations* (hereafter, JFBA) is currently calling its *bengoshi* members, "attorneys" in English.[8] There is some sense in using "attorney" too, just to avoid "lawyer."

There are 15,541 lawyers (1,070 women, 7%) registered with the JFBA in 1995,[9] or roughly one for every 8,043 people. These lawyers alone comprise a small bar compared to some 850,000 lawyers in the U.S. or one for about 306 Americans.

7 *See* R.W. RABINOWITZ, The Historical Development of the Japanese Bar, 70 HARV. L.REV. 61, 64 note 5 (1956).

8 JFBA, *Japan Federation of Bar Associations* (1995), gives the current information on the profession; also *see* a handsome brochure, *Bengoshi kaikan* [Bar Association Building] (1995); it celebrates the move into the brand new 17-story building at Kasumigaseki 1-1-33 in Tokyo, August 1, 1995. On the site previously occupied by separate bar buildings, the *Japanese Federation of Bar Associations* and the three Tokyo Bars (*Tokyo Bar Association, First Tokyo Bar Association, and Second Tokyo Bar Association*) have built a single building to be shared (Floors 14-17 by JFBA, *Japan Legal Aid Association* and other groups; Floors 11-13, *First Tokyo Bar Association*; Floors 8-10, *Second Tokyo Bar Association*; Floor 7, Joint Library; Floors 4-7, *Tokyo Bar Association*; Floors 1-3, reception, and consulting centers).

9 JFBA, *supra* note 8, at 1.

Table 1: 1990: Lawyers in Several Nations (per 100,000 people)

Japan	12.4
Vietnam	1.2
Korea	4.7
France	99.2
United Kingdom	121.4
Australia	157.2
Germany	199.4
United States	327

Source: S. ÔTA & K. ROKUMOTO, Issues of the Lawyer Population: Japan, 25 Case W. Res. J. Int'l L. 315, 320 (1993), with updating to 1995 for Japan and the U.S.

As Table 1 shows, Japan is on the low end of lawyer density, counting *bengoshi* only, except in Asia, where it is on the high end. It follows that east Asia simply does not have much experience with justiciable law.

The trouble with taking Japanese lawyers alone for comparison with legal professions abroad is that *bengoshi* have been essentially right-enforcing litigation lawyers, though their other work is increasing.[10] There are other separately licensed professions, as well as other law-trained company and government employees, who assist with compliance with the bureaucracy and who do much work that is ordinarily done by American lawyers. If these "quasi-lawyers"[11] are added to the *bengoshi*, the U.S. would still have over twice as many lawyers per capita as Japan, but not twenty-six times as suggested by Table 1 above.

In global comparison, then, we must emphasize that the American lawyer, ubiquitous, numerous, and playing multiple roles in business, government, and society, is atypical and not necessarily a model for comparison, especially given the growing American criticism of the bar's performance nowadays.[12] In this Part I we will briefly canvass other Japanese legal workers, who, added

10 Survey Report: NIHON BENGOSHI-KAI BENGOKAI (ed.), *Nihon no hôritsu jimu-shô, '90 - bengoshi gyômu no keizai-teki kiban ni kansuru jittai chôsa hôkoku-sho* [Japanese Law Offices, 1990: A Report on a Fact-Finding Survey Concerning the Economic Base for Law Practices], 42 JIYÛ TO SEIGI (NO. 13) (*rinji zôkan* [special edition] 1991).

Compared to the earlier survey of 1980, this report states that lawyers' *gross* revenues had increased 1.87 times in the decade (1980 to 1990), and that lawyers' *income* was up 2.2 times, also that work handled by lawyers not related to disputes had increased in the 1980-1990 period from 7.3% to 16.2% of their total work. Court cases were correspondingly reduced from 78% to 63% of their work.

11 KAGO, *supra* note 6, at 212-236.

12 For fun, *see* T.W. OVERTON, Lawyers, Light Bulbs, and Dead Snakes: The Lawyer Joke as Societal Text, 42 U.C.L.A. L.REV. 1069-1114 (1995).

together with the lawyers, will give a total of legal workers perhaps more, if not precisely, comparable to the total American lawyers (850,000). We hasten to add, though, that comparability only holds for the kind of work they do. Qualifications, training, role in society, and the like are not comparable at all, hence the term, quasi-lawyers. Some of them are trained, examined, licensed and regulated by the government, and have their own associations and some autonomy. Others are petty bureaucrats or corporate staff, who do mostly registry paperwork.

Before canvassing the full panoply of legal workers, it is essential to note the historically important distinction in Western legal development between (1) justiciable law (with adjudication of rights as its model), and (2) administration without rights based on authority, orders, hierarchy, and duties. Of course in governance, administration historically predates justiciable law just as society predates a power structure or government which sets about preempting management of some prior purely societal concerns. Then the overlap of laws and authority in governance (limited government; constitutionalism) may eventuate to bring justiciable law (and adjudication with lawyers) into the public law arena. This did not happen in Japan, even on paper, until the Showa Constitution (1947), so lawyers have been only recently admitted to that sphere. But the welfare state also brought much pure administration into the sphere of "law" in the West, and with it the lawyer's role has expanded to include advising on compliance and avoidance in this whole sphere of administration often with little or no effective adjudicatory remedies. In Japan as well, quasi-lawyers gradually appeared in the compliance business, hence the comparison of the expanded U.S. bar, which has all sorts of compliance as well as adjudicating lawyer roles, with lawyers and quasi-lawyers in Japan.

B. Quasi-Lawyers

1. Tax Agents (zeiri-shi)

Tax agents are the most numerous (over 62,000 in 1995) and they have their own examination.[13] They choose five accounting or tax subjects from the following: bookkeeping, financial statements, income tax, corporation tax, succession tax, liquor tax, consumption tax, national tax collection, and real estate tax. They can choose to be examined on the subjects, one at a time. On passing all five subjects chosen, and after two years of practical experience,

---

13 KAGO, *supra* note 6, at 212 has descriptions of the various quasi-lawyers; I have relied also on ÔTA & ROKUMOTO, *supra* note 6, at 315, for important recent information on quasi-lawyers; also HATTORI & HENDERSON, *supra* note 5, ch. 2 (Professional Legal Services). I am indebted also to *Toshio Miyatake* for obtaining up-to-date statistics from the several associations in Tokyo.

they are qualified as tax agents. They then do tax returns, tax consulting (mostly small business), and represent clients in tax audits and administrative proceedings. In 1988, 61,589 took the exam; the pass rate is said to be about 10%. Lawyers and CPAs are also qualified for tax practice, but the tax agents' specific skills are high enough to discourage, so far, much overlap of the two professions.

2. *Patent Agents (benri-shi)*

Patent agents are not so numerous (1995: 3,500), and are highly specialized in intellectual property. They too have their own organization and some autonomy under the regulation of the Ministry of International Trade and Industry, which examines and licenses them. They draft and file patent, trademark, and utility model applications and represent clients at hearings concerning industrial property in the Patent Agency, and in court with clients and lawyers present.[14]

Certain patent office personnel with seven years of experience can become patent agents without examination, and all lawyers can serve as patent agents. Special, narrow competence of patent agents generally discourages lawyers from entering their domain, though lawyers and patent agents sometimes office together.

3. *Judicial Scriveners (shihô shoshi)*

Judicial scriveners are slightly more numerous (1995: 17,000) than lawyers, and in some of their work seem to be substitutes for lawyers, in rural areas particularly, where lawyers are scarce.[15] Judicial scriveners' main work is to handle property registrations (see below 8.), and paperwork for small businesses at the corporate registry. They also help with attachments and drafting papers to use at court for *pro se* litigation. Though forbidden to give legal advice for fees, judicial scriveners, in drawing up litigation and other papers, would seem to be involved in legal decisions of sorts, and are occasionally subject to complaints for unauthorized practice of law by the bar. Estimates suggest litigation and counseling is less than 10% of the legal scriveners' work. They are examined on civil, commercial, and criminal law in a preliminary multiple-choice test; and on the laws of the real property and corporate registries as well as civil procedure.

---

14 HATTORI & HENDERSON, *supra* note 5, § 2.09. KAGO, *supra* note 6, at 220.

15 KAGO, *supra* note 6, at 90-177, gives a full description of Judicial Scriveners' work in several areas: personal status (p. 120), immovable property (p. 129), commercial registry (p. 145), procedure in civil suits (p. 156-177).

The legal scrivener is supervised by the Ministry of Justice, under which the registries also are regulated.[16] In 1988, only 404 (2%) of 18,014 applicants passed the exam. Ministry of Justice officials and procurators with ten years of experience as well as court clerks and court secretaries can also be authorized by the Ministry of Justice to be judicial scriveners. Lawyers may function as judicial scriveners. A 1987-1988 sample survey showed only about a third of the judicial scriveners had degrees from law faculties, so overall they are definitely a lower caliber than the bar.

4. *Certified Public Accountants (kônin kaikei-shi)*

The Japanese CPA is a post-World War II creature of securities law reform (1948) under the Allied Occupation, which required audits for corporations issuing or registering shares for sale to the public. Since there was no adequate auditing profession then,[17] the CPA profession was created for the purpose, and since CPAs can do tax agent work, as well as corporate accounting required by the Commercial Code,[18] and the Securities Exchange Law,[19] there is some overlap with what we call legal work in the United States, where we have some conflict between CPAs and lawyers as well. They also give financial advice (CPA Law,[20] Article 2). The growing tendency of Japanese lawyers to enter the business planning area, including tax, suggests increasing potential overlap with CPAs' services in the future, as we have in the U.S.

Training and examinations are in three stages. After passing the first general exam and the second exam on accounting, business, economics, and commercial law, the candidate becomes an assistant CPA. After two years of apprenticeship, he may take a third exam (tax, audits, etc.) and become a CPA. The pass rate in 1990 for the first exam was 27%; for the second, 7.2%; and for the third, 52%. In 1990 there were about 8,800 CPAs including 18 foreign CPAs, and 109 institutional CPAs.

For comparison, CPAs should not be counted as quasi-lawyers in Japan, unless they are counted also in the U.S. They are very similar in function in both countries, but perhaps the American CPAs have expanded more rapidly into business consulting and planning.

---

16 *Cf.* Article 4 of the *Shihô shoshi-hô* [Judical Scrivener Law], Law No. 197 of 1950 as amended by Law No. 7 of 1971. For an English translation *see* EHS Vol. II, EA, No. 2060.

17 *Ibid* at 224.

18 *Shôhô*, Law No. 48 of 1899 as amended by Law No. 66 of 1994. For an English translation *see* EHS Vol. II, JA, No. 2200.

19 *Shôken torihiki-hô*, Law No. 25 of 1948 as amended by Law No. 106 of 1995. For an English translation *see* CAPITAL MARKETS RESEARCH INSTITUTE (ed.), Securities and Exchange Law (1994, suppl. 1995).

20 *Kônin kaikei-shi-hô*, Law No. 103 of 1948 as amended by Law No. 40 of 1992.

5. *Administrative Scriveners (gyôsei shoshi)*

Administrative scriveners assist the citizenry to interface with the administrative agencies both central and local. The Ministry of Home Affairs (*Jichi-shô*) supervises them, but the prefectures give the exam for administrative scriveners, covering the Administrative Scriveners Law,[21] constitution, civil code, administrative law, local autonomy law and general knowledge. In 1989, out of 21,167 examined, 1,672 (about 8%) passed.[22] They are quite numerous, about 35,000 in 1995. But lawyers, patent agents, tax agents, and CPAs are also qualified as administrative scriveners, as well as national and local bureaucrats of twenty years' service. Each prefecture has a local Administrative Scriveners' Association to which local administrative scriveners must belong.

6. *Notaries (kôshô-nin)*

The Japanese notary follows more the European model than the petty "notary public" of American practice, who does little more than simply authenticate signatures. The Japanese notaries are real professionals and are also public officials appointed by the Ministry of Justice, but they subsist on clients' fees, rather than salaries.[23] They authenticate and keep their own registry of private documents: corporate, contractual, or commercial. Overlap with lawyers work is generally slight because there are so few of them, but they do review some documents for content or compliance, and also counsel parties on required content. Judges, procurators, and lawyers may be notaries without exams. Of the 534 notaries, judges are 30%, procurators 45%, and other high officials 25%, so that selection from the general public is insignificant. These law officers are highly qualified, and it has been suggested that they might better be regarded as a part of the legal profession along with the judges, procurators, and lawyers.[24]

7. *"House Councel" (kigyô hômu-in)*

They are part of the permanent staff of an increasing number of Japanese corporations, which have established legal sections. These employees are not licensed professionals, nor are they private advisors either. They are listed here only because they are generally graduates of a university law faculty, and

---

21 *Gyôsei shoshi-hô*, Law No. 4 of 1951 as amended by Law No. 25 of 1991.

22 ÔTA & ROKUMOTO, *supra* note 6, at 326.

23 KAGO, *supra* note 6, at 22-89.

24 ÔTA & ROKUMOTO, *supra* note 6, at 32; HATTORI & HENDERSON, *supra* note 5, at 2-41 to 2-42.

because, being law trained, they are designated to do law-related corporate work for their companies. They are assigned to a specialized legal section (*hoki-ka* or *homu-ka*) within the corporate organization to review contracts, handle corporate paperwork for directors' and shareholders' meetings, and other regulatory work as well. In some cases these specialists include registered *bengoshi*, but this is very exceptional and requires approval from the lawyer's bar. Though the legal section's staff has no official status or title, they can be described by the term "enterprise legal staff" (*kigyô hômu-in*).[25] This term distinguishes them from the majority of law graduates who also join business corporations as line officers and who do general managerial work. This larger group in corporate management, who are also trained in law, presumably also reduce the legal advice needed in corporate Japan from outside lawyers. But here we are focusing on only the staff of the legal sections whose work correlates more closely with that of corporate "house counsel" in the U.S.

If and when the Japanese bar continues to expand its business counseling role, the corporate legal sections will interface with outside counsel more, and indeed probably deprive lawyers of more work. As it is now, corporations normally hire outside lawyers only to handle disputes and suits. It was estimated that there are 2,500 to 3,000[26] of such staff members in legal sections, but by 1995 it is probably higher. Undoubtedly they do much legal work that would be done by licensed lawyers as "house counsel" in the U.S. About 10% of the U.S. bar of licensed lawyers are salaried house counsel for corporations (i.e., with only one "client").

8. *Public Registry Clerks*

Before leaving the matter of quasi-lawyer, whose services overlap what American lawyers do, we must note the extensive Japanese use of public registries in three broad areas served instead by private documents prepared by lawyers in America: Land Registry (*fudôsan tôki*); Family Registry (*koseki*), including succession; and Commercial Registry (*shôgyô tôki*).[27] The public registries, though now operating in efficient modern format and staffed by

---

25 *See* ÔTA & ROKUMOTO, *supra* note 6, at 327; C. STEVENS, Multinational Corporations and the Legal Profession, the Role of the Corporate Legal Department in Japan, *in*: Current Legal Aspects of Doing Business in Japan and East Asia 34 (J.O. Haley, ed. 1978).

26 ÔTA & ROKUMOTO, *supra* note 6, at 328. Probably including only the 3,000 *kigyô hômu-in* (and not the larger core of other law-trained management) seriously understates these Japanese functional counterparts of U.S. "corporate house counsel."

27 *See* J.O. HALEY & D.F. HENDERSON, Law and Legal Process in Japan, 171-186 (1988).

skilled public clerks, can be traced through many changes to a long tradition perfected in Tokugawa times of harnessing all of the Shogun's subjects to the land, to their househeads (*koshu*), to the temples (to stamp out Christians),[28] and to the rice tax.[29]

The significance of the registries to today's lawyers is, however, the removal of vast areas of private transactions from law offices to the public clerks, judicial scriveners, and registries in Japan; whereas in the U.S. these are handled by private deeds and other documents produced by law offices. Merely to suggest removing the following list of matters from American law offices would cause panic in the bar: divorce, probate, other domestic relations; conveyancing, loans and mortgages, liens, leases; corporation formation, corporate meetings, and agency.

Exceptionally some registry matters involve Japanese lawsuits and lawyers,[30] but no doubt the meticulous maintenance of the registries by public officials and quasi-lawyers (legal scriveners) greatly increases pure administration and reduces the need for justiciable law and practicing lawyers to enforce rights engendered by use of alternative private deeds fraught inevitably with variety and ambiguity. Not to be overlooked also is the relative ease of fact-finding in a society regimented by comprehensive registrations for centuries. When a considerable amount of information about all sorts of private transactions must be registered in order to confirm personal relations and property interests, the resulting shrinkage of privacy, as well as the resulting efficacy of police surveillance, may forebode certain problems in the area of civil liberties as well.

These registry practices have their roots in tradition, despite similarities with some other civil law countries. Clearly they do reduce reliance on law and lawyers, for good or for bad, in broad areas of daily intercourse. Perhaps the registry officials should be added to our list of lawyer substitutes?

---

28 *Shûmon aratame-chô* and *ninbetsu aratame-cho* are described in N. SEKIYAMA, *Kinsei Nihon jinkô* [Population Structure in Japan in the Recent Era] 34 (1958).

29 R. ISHII, *Nihon hôsei-shi gaisetsu* [General Survey of Japanese Institutional History] 444 (1960) describes details of the Three Rural Registries (*jikata sanchô*). *See* also T.C. SMITH, The Land Tax in the Tokugawa Period, 18 J. OF ASIAN STUDIES 8 (1958); *id.*, The Agrarian Origins of Modern Japan (1959).

30 *See Nagano* v. *Takahashi*, 15 MINSHû 901 (Sup. Ct., April 27, 1961) and *Suzuki* v. *Orita*, 14 MINSHû 8933 (Sup. Ct. 1st P.B., April 14, 1960), both translated into English in HALEY & HENDERSON, *supra* note 27, at 178 and 182 respectively. These exceptional cases allowed the plaintiffs to avoid registry "facts" contrary to actual facts.

9. *Another Try at Counting Quasi-Lawyers*[31]

The several law-related professions reviewed above, plus the amorphous group of law-trained staff in the corporate legal sections now found in more and more large Japanese corporations, all have their differences that make comparison difficult. Surely none of the quasi-lawyers are comparable to either the Japanese *bengoshi* or American lawyer. But most of them deserve to be lumped together with *bengoshi* in comparing Japanese legal services with legal services in the U.S., a major portion of which is *compliance* practice too.

CPAs have some overlap with lawyers in both Japan and the U.S., but not enough to be counted in either country. American notaries are essentially clerical and should not be counted, though Japanese notaries have important legal responsibilities and should be counted with the Japanese legal professionals. All Japanese procurators and judges (2,740) should be added to the total in Japan, because in the U.S., with an integrated bar, judges (29,000) and prosecuting attorneys are also counted as lawyers first. While recognizing these difficulties, it is surely more accurate to include some of these quasi-lawyers with the lawyers of Japan in trying to measure the comparative quantity of "legal services" available to the people of the two countries.

*Table 2: Providers of Legal Services in Japan**

Judges	2,740 **
Procurators	2,000
Lawyers (*bengoshi*)	15,541
Tax Agents (*zeiri-shi*)	62,000
Administrative Scriveners (*gyôsei shoshi*)	35,000
Legal Scriveners (*shihô shoshi*)	17,360
Patent Agents (*benri-shi*)	3,500
Notaries (*kôshô-nin*)	534
Enterprise Legal Staff	3,000
Total Providers of Legal Service	141,675

* CPAs are not counted in either Japan or the U.S.
** Most of these statistics are rounded.

Most of the types of quasi-lawyers have increased (especially the *zeiri-shi*) since the last time I looked at them. With a population of about 125 million,

31 This essentially frustrating exercise of counting and comparing "lawyers" in the U.S. and Japan has a history at least as far back as my *Foreign Enterprise in Japan* 176-185 (1973). See citations in footnote 6 above.

this means that Japan has one "provider of legal service" for about every 882 people. Adjusting Table 1 (*supra*) to reflect the above recalculation of providers of legal services would raise the Japanese to 113 per 100,000 people, or about to the French and United Kingdom's level, half the German level and over a third of the U.S. level at 327.

As a postscript, my guess is that we may not have included enough Japanese law-trained business managers and bureaucrats to make the whole Japanese array fully comparable to U.S. statistics because so many (27%) American lawyers are salaried business house-counsel (12%) and government officials (10%), or inactive (5%). The figures[32] are shown below in Table 3.

*Table 3: Lawyers in the U.S.**

Total lawyers, 1991				805,000
In private practice				586,000
Salaried business, etc.			94,000	
Total government:	Administrative	66,000		
	Judicial	22,000		
			88,000	
Inactive or retired			37,000	
U.S. lawyers not practicing				219,000

* Figures rounded.

It is accurate to say that Japan does not have as many lawyers as the U.S., even if we include the quasi-lawyers, but Japanese lawyers really are not scarce compared to European lawyer populations. Surely, however, Japan is, by either European or American standards, indeed quite short of litigating lawyers (15,541) to enforce the rights of its citizens, conferred presumably upon them by justiciable law, imported on paper at least in the private law since about 1900, and in the public law since 1947. By democratic Western standards a bar of 15,541 litigating lawyers is small to enforce the rights of 125,000,000 people.

Increases are planned to bring the apprentices admitted to the *Legal Training and Research Institute* up to a class of 1,000 annually by 1998, and also a reduction of the training period to one year instead of the present two years has been suggested by the Ministry of Justice and the Supreme Court, and it seems that much of the bar is opposed to both initiatives,[33] but since 1991 the admittees have been raised from 500 to over 700 (740 in 1994). But still the

32 From 1991 survey, Statistical Abstract of the United States, 210 (1994).

33 *Tokushû: Shihô shiken kaikaku mondai shiryô-shû* [Special Edition: Compilation of Materials on the Problem of Judicial Exam Reform], 45 JIYU TO SEIGI (No. 12) 231 (1994).

reasons for the continuing inefficacy of justiciable law must be found in Japanese society - in the governance by social entities interfacing with bureaucracy through nontransparent administrative guidance outside the law.

PART II: THE ROLE OF LAW, LAWSUITS, AND LAWYERS

Here we are discussing only today's *bengoshi*, and justiciable law as imported from the West a century ago and as an override on a social and administrative system functioning well enough without law and lawyers. Justiciable law entails rules which create rights assertible by citizens in independent courts with trained judges, due process, and an autonomous bar to assist in right assertion. This is to be distinguished from pure administration (do-as-you-are-told law) of which Asia has had plenty from time immemorial. All modern governments are acquiring unreviewable administration, at an increasing rate with the steady growth of welfare bureaucracies everywhere. Unfortunately even in our professional discourse both administration (non-justiciable) and justiciable law are promiscuously called just plain "law." In Japan, the term "administrative guidance" (*gyôsei shidô*) has become fashionable to describe much Japanese administration (some say 85% of all) which is non-transparent and outside the law.

The whole apparatus of justiciability, a Western creation, has not been a part of the Asian tradition, until recently in varying degrees in certain places. We have seen that it is only about a century old in Japan, and still of rather shallow bite in Japanese society, especially in public law. The bureaucracy is largely exempt because it operates largely outside the law by administrative guidance. Proof of the dearth of justiciability in administration is the low case filings in administrative matters.[34] In private law, too, the dearth of case filings confirms the shallowness of justiciable law.[35] This is because of the efficacy of

34 Only 1,310 administrative law cases were filed at first instance in the entire Japanese court system in the latest year available, 1993, and this was on the high side. In the prior fifteen years (1979-1993), filing ranged between 1,000 and 1,200 per year. *See* SAIKÔ SAIBANSHO JIMU SOKYOKU MINJI-KYOKU, *Heisei gô-nendo gyôsei jiken no gaikayô* [General Situation of Administrative Cases in 1993], 46 HÔSÔ JIHÔ 1555, 1556 (1994). *Cf.* ECONOMIST 35 (Oct. 30, 1993) stating that in Germany there were "around 450,000 contests against governmental action." Query whether these Japanese court filings are comparable to the German "contest"?

35 In 1993, filings of ordinary civil cases in the District Courts were 152,000, and 228,000 in the summary courts. SAIKÔ SAIBANSHO JIMU SOKYOKU MINJI-KYOKU, *Heisei gô-nendo minji soshô jiken no gaikyô* [General Situation of Civil Cases in 1993], 46 HÔSÔ JIHÔ 1996 (1994). These include administrative cases, but they are only 1,300 and distort little. These initial filings are substantially up (in 1992: 138,000; 169,000). 1993 filings were up 10.2% in the district courts and 35% in the summary court. For the prior decade the district court filings were in the 125,000

mediation. Mediation and compromise have always been the "main dispute resolution" (MDR, not ADR)[36] methods in Japan, unlike our latter-day "alternative dispute resolution" (ADR) of the past couple of decades. Ironically our ADR may be viewed as a recognition of the shortcomings of law, lawsuits and lawyers, and our move toward Japanese ways of solving disputes.[37]

A. The Pre-World War II Legacy

Law, lawsuits, and lawyers were imported into Japan in a bundle just before 1900, and they can not be easily unbundled, to discuss the role of today's lawyers alone. Nor can the remarkable reception of Western law into Japan's refined Asian civilization be adequately presented in capsule form.[38] A few salient aspects of both the reception and the setting can, however, be set forth as the context into which lawyers were introduced just before 1900.

First, Japan was for more than a millennium within the Chinese sphere of influence (Confucius, Buddha, language, painting, literature, rice culture and T'ang Codes), yet insular and isolated for the last 250 years (1603-1868) by Tokugawa policy to avoid European interference and accompanying factional bickering of the Christian churches in the 17th century.[39] This means that not only did Japan have the unique experience of several centuries of peace in order to grow and get pretty socially sophisticated[40] and set in its ways, but Western

---

range and summary court filings declined from 224,000 to 97,000 in 1990. To compare with U.S. state filings alone: Japan: 304 per 100,000 pop.; state courts (U.S. median): 6,610 per 100,000 pop.

These "cases" (as filed in Japan and U.S. state courts) are generally comparable but certainly not precisely the same. Nevertheless the immense numerical difference simply reflects the fact that Japanese and Americans are at opposite poles of the spectrum of litigators. American source: State Court Caseload Statistics: Annual Report 1992, p. 11 (1994).

36 *See* D.F. HENDERSON, Conciliation and Japanese Law, Vol. 1, p. 6 (1965).

37 Y. TANIGUCHI, The Changing Attitude to International Commercial Dispute Settlement in Asia and the Far East, 29-35 (1994), notes that arbitration (with conciliation) might become another half-way technique to resolve disputes in Asia.

38 *See* T. TORU, *Meiji minpô hensan-shi kenkyû* [Study of the History of the Meiji Compilation of the Civil Code] 515 *et seq.* (1943), R. ISHII, Japanese Legislation in the Meiji Era (W. Chambliss, trans. 1958) 741 *et seq.*; N. HOZUMI, The New Japanese civil code as Materials for the Study of Comparative Jurisprudence (1912) 166 *et seq.*

39 *Tokugawa* Japan was a society of some scope; it grew to about 30 million people by the time *Commodore Perry* began to open the country to the outside world in 1853. Japan at that time had a population slightly larger than the U.S. Now the U.S. has twice Japan's population (260 million to 125 million). *See* HENDERSON, *supra* note 36, at 15.

40 *R. Mitsukuri & J. Kurimoto* were two pioneers who were sent to France by the Shogunate (1867) before it fell, and by their publications aroused some interest in what the foreigners call "law". *See* K. MUKAI & N. TOSHITANI, The Progress and

law (as an idea and set of institutions) was wholly unknown and alien to the cohesive Japanese cultural enclosure. Law was, thus, introduced into an entirely distinct and refined civilization, without even the *idea-of-law*, as we have known it since the Bible, Greeks, Romans, and onward to Montesquieu, Napoleon, Savigny-and-Thibaut, and new-world judicial review in *Marbury* v. *Madison*,[41] to name a few of the milestones of Western law; such law *with rights* was, of course, quite unfathomable to even Japanese educated elite before 1868. They had never been aware "law" existed abroad; nor did they need it.[42] This was because Japanese theory of governance was purely a rule-of-man: hierarchical, disciplinary, and administrative. It was based on authority (said to be legitimatized by the rulers' wisdom and virtue), hierarchy (no equality), and duties (no rights). For us realists, it was do-as-you-are-told "law," familiar to soldiers. Its rigors were to be mitigated by presumed beneficence of superiors in exchange for loyalty and filial piety underwritten by the orthodox Tokugawa confucianistic ideology (*shushi-gaku*).[43] Its genius was decentralization and a comprehensive power-structure reaching down to villages and households empowered to run their own affairs. Whatever its merits or shortcomings, it worked tolerably well for the time and place.

Disputes were dealt with by *ad hoc* settlements reached by negotiation, conciliation, compromise, and purely situational adjustments between the parties, generated from within rather than imposed by rules from outside.[44] In the last resort, didactic official instruction prevailed, but not by adjudication, as we know it. In the Sino-Japanese civilization, justice was situational and consensual between the parties, making their own interpersonal adjustments ("law") for their immediate problem only. There was no such "law" as transcendent, externally given, reified rules (Moses on the Mount), universally

---

Problems of Compiling the civil code in the Early Meiji Era, 1 LAW IN JAPAN 23, at 35 (D.F. Henderson, trans. 1967).

41 5 U.S. (1 Cranch) 137 (1803).

42 T.D. STEPHENS, Order and Discipline in China: The Shanghai Mixed Court, 1911-27 (1992) discusses this problem (p. 47).

43 This is the Japanized version of the Chinese, *Chu Hsi* (1139-1200). *See* HENDERSON, *supra* note 36, at 37.

44 Perhaps the earliest analysis of these adjustments-without-law was addressed to Chinese governance by U. GRANET, La pensée chinoise, 457 (1934). The early foreign missionaries and lawyers who wrote about Chinese and Japanese administrators were generally unsuccessful in discovering that law-external-to-the-parties was a Western ethnocentricity, and so they introduced their own Christian conceptual baggage into their descriptions and analysis of Chinese practices without being aware that it didn't fit. *See* also J. NEEDHAM, Science and Civilization in China, Vol. II, Ch. 18 (1956); T.B. STEPHENS, *supra* note 42, Foreword by *Henderson*; D.F. HENDERSON, Introduction to the *Kujikata Osadamegaki* (1742), *in*: COM. FOR MEMORIAL ESSAYS IN HONOR OF DR. HIRAMATSU YOSHIRO (ed.), *Hô to keibatsu no rekishi-teki kôsatsu* [Historical Consideration of Law and Punishment] 489-544 (1987).

applicable by a judge to all individuals, equal and similarly situated. That kind of law would have been quite dysfunctional in a Confucian world without equality and rights. Not only did such law not exist, even the *idea* of such given, external law (i.e., not worked out *at hoc* for and by the parties) was not a part of thought or discourse.

Second, though social functions such as maintenance of order and dispute resolution knew nothing of justiciable law in Tokugawa times, there was of course "justice" and *administration* of justice.[45] It operated in extended households and villages in large part. Disputes that did come to higher officialdom for *settlement* (and some did) were handled by the *administrative* officers (*bugyô*), as a matter of *grace*, not right. Petitions were settled by *ad hoc* compromise, discrete agreement or instructions of superiors.[46]

There was no role for lawyers, so anyone who sought to assist disputants was forbidden. Such few pettifoggers and shysters (*kuji-shi*) as did exist in the shadows of the Shogunal offices were despised and repressed. Suit inns (*kuji-yado*)[47] were legitimate and licensed custodians of itinerant disputants while in Edo, not legal professionals, though in fact they did some instructing in procedures and paperwork, and made sure petitioners appeared for appointments. Such was the heritage of the bar up to 1872.

Third, by Meiji times when the decision was made in the 1870s to begin transplanting European codes in Japan, a whole new set of invented Japanese terminology had to be assigned to represent European legal concepts from another conception of governance as well as from another continent.[48] Once the Meiji Constitution (1889) and codes were all enacted by 1900, Japanese professors and lawyers had then to devote several decades up to World War II studying the reception and domesticating primarily German theory and commentaries for use in Japan.[49] Of course, the reverse side of that insight is

---

45 Y. HIRAMATSU, Tokugawa Law, 14 LAW IN JAPAN 1, at 38 (D.F. Henderson, trans. 1981); *see* also D.F. HENDERSON & P. TARBERT, Contracts in the Far East: China and Japan, *in*: 7 Encyclopedia of Comparative Law, Vol. VII, ch. 6, p. 13 (1992).

46 *See* HENDERSON, *supra* note 36, at 131-169.

47 *See* M. TAKIGAWA, *Nihon bengoshi zenshi kuji-yado no kenkyô - kuji-yado henshû "hikae" no shokai* [A Pre-History of the Japanese Lawyer: A Study of the Suit Inns - An Introduction to the "*Hikae*" Compiled by a Suit Inn] WASEDA DAIGAKU HIKAKUHÔ KENKYÛSHO KIYÔ [Bulletin of Waseda U. Research Institute of Comparative Law] (1959); M. TAKIGAWA (ed.), *Nijô jinya no kenkyû - kuji-yado no kenkyû (zoku)* [Study of the Nijo Office: A Study of the Suit Inns (continuation)], 21 Waseda U. Research Institute of Comparative Law Series (1962).

48 MUKAI & TOSHITANI, *supra* note 40, at 38.

49 *See* Z. KITAGAWA, Theory Reception: One Aspect of the Development of Japanese Civil Law Science (R.E. Lee, trans.) 4 LAW IN JAPAN 1-16 (1970) for an introduction. For fuller treatment *see* Z. KITAGAWA, Rezeption und Fortbildung des europäischen Zivilrechts in Japan (1970); or *id.*, *Nihon hôgaku no rekishi to riron* [The History and Theory of Japanese Legal Science] (1968).

that, if even the professors and law students did not fully understand the applications of the imported codes, of course the folk (with few lawyers accessible to them) could not comprehend the codes, and of course the incomprehensible codes could not influence popular behavior, nor become the basis of lawsuits needing lawyers. In our realists' rhetoric the gap between "law-in-the-books" and "law-in-action" was enormous.

Fourth, in the Meiji period the pioneers of the Japanese bar suffered from the poor image of the prior forbidden shysters (*kuji-shi*), some of whom became the first registered attorneys (*daigen-nin*) in 1876.[50] Supported by foreign advisors such as Boissanade, rights-to-counsel were gradually recognized by the government in both civil and criminal trials by 1876. There was, however, no integrated bar; both judges and procurators were exalted public careers, but they were not selected from those who were already lawyers (*bengoshi*). This system perpetuated lawyers in an inferior private position. Lawyers long chafed at their private status compared to the public position of judges and procurators. It was accentuated by traditional respect for officials, shown in the slogan, "Respect official; but despise subject" (*kanson minpi*). This common phrase captures all the Japanese Confucianistic reverence for officialdom assiduously nurtured by centuries of official ideology. It cheapens the subjects (not citizens), and is difficult to capture in English of another culture. The sharp contrast in philosophy is seen in Lord Acton's "Power tends to corrupt and absolute power corrupts absolutely." From this outlook flows, of course, our rule-of-law to limit power by law and enforce the limitation with right assertion by lawyers.

The bar lacked adequate admissions criteria, lacked remedies against unauthorized practices, and was denied adequate autonomy by refusing it the right until 1933 to organize as a juristic person and by placing it and the courts under the supervision of the Ministry of Justice, until after World War II. Courts were seriously crippled in pursuing even a rule-by-law by elitist imperial bureaucrats who smothered the whole judiciary as well as the bar in bureaucratic and political controls rather than allowing them to follow their conscience limited only by law.

Fifth, in 1890 in the midst of the reception of Western law, a pivotal event occurred, called by later historians the "postponement Controversy".[51] During the course of enacting the civil code and transplanting European institutions

---

50 *See* Y. KAGO (ed.), *Gendai no bengoshi (shimin hen)* [Present-Day Lawyers (popular edition)] *Sogo Tokushu* Series, No. 20 (HÔGAKU SEMINARU, *zôkan*) p. 290-295 (1982) has a detailed chronology of the events in the development of the Japanese bar; *see* also RABINOWITZ, *supra* note 7, at 61.

51 *See* T. HOSHINO, *Minpôten ronsô-shi* [History of the Dispute Over the Civil Code] 262 *et seq.* (1944); R. EPP, The Challenge from Tradition: Attempts to Compile a civil code in Japan, 23 MONUMENTA NIPPONICA 15-48 (1967).

based on equality and justiciable law, the first Japanese Diet dramatically reversed course and rejected the draft civil code, being then debated on the floor, because it included French ideas of natural law, individualism and equality of family members. Then the Diet postponed (1890) enactment of a civil code until the family and succession provisions (Books IV and V) could be wholly redrafted. The so-called "postponement controversy" was a crucial accommodation of Asian family authority (of great importance to administration and theocratic imperial rule) at the expense of secular Western equality.

Regrettably little is known outside Japan about this Japanese highly significant switch because of language and cultural difficulties. The reception ended with a newly drafted civil code enacted in 1898 with a general German Pandectist framework in place of the French, and specifically preserving the authoritarian, collectivistic concepts of the traditional Confucian family and governance: primogenitive, inequality and hierarchy (male over female, all ranked by age), absolute loyalty (*chû*) to superiors. These monumental changes in the final stages of the code reception marked the triumph of traditionalists and neatly preserved for another half century and longer[52] the essence of the Asian societal discipline at the expense of individualism, equality, law, and rights to sustain them. It even strengthened the administrative command channels down to the depth of society in the family. The key to understanding its significance was that, by this adroit move, the new civil code was integrated with the absolutism of the Meiji Constitution based on theocratic imperial sovereignty, a cabinet with military ministers responsible directly to the throne not the Diet, and an elite and aloof civil service, beholden only to the Emperor, not his subjects.

Sixth, the shallow bite of the codes was, thus, partly attributable to an underprivileged and inadequate bar, right up to the end of World War II. But preservation of the prior discipline of the Confucianistic *administrative* order was the main cause for not only both shallowness of law and weak lawyers but

---

52 See the assorted views of Japanese Supreme Court justices mulling over the question whether a higher penalty for crimes against a father are inconsistent with the equality provision in the Showa Constitution (Article 14). *Yamato* v. *Japan*, 27 KEISHû 256 (Sup. Ct. G.B., Oct. 11, 1960) and *Aizawa* v. *Japan* 27(3) KEISHû 256 (Sup. Ct. G.B., April 14, 1973). These decisions will show that the Confucian thinking still had some strength in 1973, even among Supreme Court justices, and it was not until 1995 that the Criminal Code Article 200 was changed to repeal the unequal penalty for murder of fathers, even though the Supreme Court found the provision unconstitutional more than twenty years earlier (1973) in *Aizawa supra*. The interesting quirk in *Aizawa*, however, was in the reasoning that found Article 200 unconstitutional, not because it assessed a separate higher penalty when the victim was a father, but rather because the difference in penalty was too severe - a clear evasive tactic to avoid embracing equality of family individuals including fathers and to avoid rejecting Confucian family values valiantly preserved by *Hozumi* and supporters in the "postponement controversy".

also for the elitist military and bureaucracy. The resulting imperial bureaucracy bottled up both the bench and the bar under the controls of the Ministry of Justice and effectively minimized the importance of lawyers by thrusting them outside[53] the pale of official prestige and power, and by denying them even autonomy.

Another movement was important. Especially from the 1920s onward up to 1945, intensive efforts in the administration to conciliate civil disputes by implementing a series of conciliation (*chôtei*) statutes further reduced the functioning of law, lawsuits, and lawyers by shunting disputes away from courts until the end of World War II.[54]

The several features of pre-World War II Japanese governance, in relation to the reception of codes, bar, and bench highlighted above, portray a system which could function bureaucratically rather well (militarists aside) in the old Sinic, authoritarian ways, leaving only a shallow role for the new and alien law, striving ineffectually for autonomy but serving essentially as a facade (*tatemae*).

B. The Second "Postponement Controversy"

A second "postponement" of an operative rule-of-law occurred after World War II when the Supreme Commander for the Allied Powers (SCAP) preserved the administration and the bureaucracy invented "administrative guidance" (*gyôsei shidô*) to be used to side-step the application of law to administration, and again to reduce the role of law, lawsuits, and lawyers. I will review how this has worked briefly below.

Even for today, in reviewing Japan's experience - my six points above - two things stand out to reduce the role of present day lawyers: (1) despite now maintaining for a century an override of justiciable law from the West, Japan still permits the society to be largely *socially* managed by the decentralization

53 The Japanese division of the "legal profession" (*hôsô*) into three branches (*i.e.*, without a "legal profession from a single source" (*hôsô ichigen*)) had the effect of excluding and degrading lawyers even after their legitimacy was gradually recognized from 1872 to 1893, strengthened in 1933 and finally made largely autonomous in 1949. The pre-World War II bar was always referred to as "the opposition" or "in countryside" (*zaiya*). The slang expression "out in the boonies" may better capture the feeling of the term in relation to "judicial officials" (*shihô-kan*) used to refer to judges-procurators (*han-kenji*). Procurator sat on the same level as the judge in criminal trials. *See* T. USHIOMI, *Hôritsu-ka* [Legal Workers] 143 (1970). The term "*zaiya*" is still a part of the discourse. *See*: *Shihô no genjô o kangaeru* [Contemplating the Current Judiciary], *in*: *Bengoshi seido hyakunen kinen* [Commemoration of the 100th Anniversary of the Lawyer System], 27 JIYÛ TO SEIGI (No. 7) 2 (*rinji zôkan* [special edition] 1976).

54 *See* a summary *in* D.F. HENDERSON, Conciliation and Japanese Law, Vol. 2, at 210-214 (1965).

and personal status relationships familiar in the past, but adapted to modern needs (e.g., the company is now the "village," the business (*kyôkai*), or communal association); (2) governmental input is made by a bureaucratic nexus with the competent social functionaries on a personal basis by official use of so-called administrative guidance in large part bypassing the legal system. This dual governance system - social groups discoursing with bureaucrats - removes major areas of social activity and governance from the ambit and transparency of a rule-of-law, which becomes in large part a facade or ideal (*tatemae*). We might call this reality "bureaucratic social administration."

The resultant administrative system (not legal) can be seen to work quite well: it is flexible; it adjusts by consensus and cooperation; and it deals with recalcitrance by give and take or potential withholding of favors rather than rigid orders, universalistic rules, lawyerly posturing, ultimatums, adjudications, and sanctions of law. Instead there is a vast network of mediators to adjust the citizenry's complaints against officialdom.[55]

Similarly, within each of the social groups in the channels of "bureaucratic social administration," private law disputes may arise internally or across group lines, and they too can be dealt with by invoking the experience, prestige, and concern of the social superiors to bargain, make concessions, and settle. At this level of otherwise private transactions, too, social administration, bereft of lawyers' law, works tolerably well. Or so we are told, and persuaded to believe, by the modest volume of filings of civil suits. No doubt the social density of Japan - lack of American-style mobility to move from job-to-job, place-to-place, or spouse-to-spouse - enhances this ordered but lawless way of managing society, an option which mobile individualistic Americans do not have, or probably want.

Back to the role of lawyers in this sort of society, it becomes quite clear that the major reason that present-day Japan has few right-enforcing lawyers is because Japanese lawyers are indeed still primarily litigating lawyers, and because Japanese litigate comparatively little.[56] But perhaps more important is

---

55 I have summarized this network *in*: Dispute Resolution other than Litigation, *in*: Encyclopedia of Japan, 69-71 (KODANSHA, ed. 1985). In 1980 there were 190,000 complaints handled by the Administrative Inspection Bureau (*Gyôsei Kansatsu-kyoku*), Administrative Management Agency (*Gyôsei Kenri-chô*) compared to only about 1,000 cases in the entire court system. But this informal administrative dispute settlement system needs more attention in Western literature.

56 In 1965 I tried to compare Japanese and American (New York and California) per capita filings in the courts. HENDERSON, *supra* note 54, at 200. That exercise of mine at the time (1960-1961 statistics) showed 23 times as many suits-per-capita in California as in Japan and over twelve times as many in New York. Comparison problems and inadequacies of statistics of the 1960s have been, to considerable extent, overcome by 1995. *See* STATE JUSTICE INSTITUTE (ed.), State Court Case Load Statistics: Annual Report 1992 (1994), a joint project of the *Conference of State Court Administrators*, *State Justice Institute*, and *National Center for State Courts*.

the fact that Japanese litigate comparatively little *because they have other ways, perhaps better ways, to settle disputes*. In context, these others ways may be *better* ways to settle disputes because they are quicker, cheaper, and leave less rancor with the disputants. The recent sudden rise of ADR in America may indicate that we are beginning to suspect there are better ways, even for us, than hip-shooting in court.[57]

Western observers have speculated about other causes for the relatively low litigation rate in Japan. Still I find the main cause to be simply better *social* ways to resolve problems. The explanations most often mentioned by others include (listed in order of importance in my view): (1) better alternatives are available; (2) hostility of officialdom to suits, and accompanying orthodox ideology against suits; (3) the inefficacy and costs of suits; (4) indeed a lack of judges and lawyers may be a reason Japanese sue so little; and (5) Japanese preference for harmony or psychological aversions to suits (or confrontation).[58]

The federal court filings were reported for 1994 as 190,739 at first instance: 135, 853 (federal question cases) and 54,886 (diversity cases). *See* News Release, *Administrative Office of the U.S. Courts* entitled "Caseload of Federal Courts Remained High in FY 1994" (Mar. 28, 1995). A gross comparison shows that American state courts (federal cases not included) had just under 20,000,000 civil filings at first instance for a population of 260,000,000, and Japan had 381,000 filings of civil and administrative (1,300) filings in the district courts and the summary courts for 125,000,000 people. This means an American case for every 13 people and a Japanese case for every 329 people; that is, in 1995 Americans bring lawsuits to the courts about 25 times as much as Japanese. That is not so different from my less comprehensive comparisons thirty years ago. Japanese statistics used were from 46 Hôsô Jihô 1996 (1995).

57 One of the more interesting American debates in recent years is over the questions: Are Americans excessively litigious? Getting more litigious? And if so why? And what are its impacts on productivity? *See* M. Gallanter, Reading the Landscape of Disputes: What We Know and Don't Know (and Think We Know) About our Allegedly Contentious Society, 31 U.C.L.A. L.Rev. 4-71 (1983); Compare W.K. Olson, The Litigation Explosion 388 *et seq.* (1991). Whether there is an explosion of lawsuits seems to require a negative answer but certain kinds of highly publicized litigation has given lawyers a high profile and generally reflected negatively on the profession. There can be no doubt that there has been a veritable explosion of lawyers in the U.S. and gradual growth in the bar in Japan as well:

	1964	1995
U.S. Lawyers	200,586	850,000
Japan Lawyers	7,136	15,541
U.S. Population	190,000,000	260,000,000
Japan Population	95,000,000	125,000,000

58 This whole issue has been canvassed repeatedly and need not be rehashed here. *See* Kawashima, *supra* note 5; Henderson, *supra* note 54, at 244; N. Noda, Introduction to Japanese Law (1976); J.O. Haley, The Myth of the Reluctant Litigant, 4 J. Jap. Stud. (No. 2) 359-390 (1978); S. Miyazawa, Taking Kawashima Seriously, 21 L. & Soc. Rev. 219-241 (1987) for a sampling.

Except for the social and bureaucratic preemption of dispute resolution described above, there is probably no single simple answer to why the Japanese use their courts so little compared to us. But surely one is a difference in the *way* litigants use the American courts as opposed to the way Japanese use theirs. In Japan, once a suit is filed it is more likely to go to judgment; only about 50% are settled after filing but before judgment.[59] In the U.S. well over 90% of all suits filed are settled before judgment.[60] This difference suggests that individualistic Americans lack close social affiliations (available in Japan) to help them settle before filing suit as in Japan; so they sue, then rely on hired lawyers to bargain it out and settle between filing and judgment. As an aside, one might suppose the American settlement results worked out by litigating lawyers would better reflect the legal positions of the parties than would be the case in Japan where so many cases are settled before filing and without legal participation. The might-is-right principle could better function in the Japanese context. But this remains largely speculation because of the difficulty of measuring such matters. Comparison of settlements after filing suggests not only that Japanese filings are lessened by having readily available other mediating processes to reach a consensus, not available to Americans, but also that once a Japanese lawsuit is started it will be harder to settle before judgment because much settlement effort has already been expended, and the suit is a result of irreconcilable positions.

When we turn to the explanation variously offered by the literature, the idea that the Japanese people are congenitally harmony-minded and avoid courts for that reason has been rejected by most of us, although intuitively we can presume that the Japanese certainly share with mankind in general the dread of lawsuits. Indeed compared to us, Japanese in fact sue very little.

For myself I also think that, however sublimated it may be, official opposition to law, lawsuits, and lawyers is important;[61] and that it has persisted up to the present in most of Japanese administration: in appointments, budget making, remedies and implementation of alternatives. Though post-World War II constitutional imperatives have caused the administration to pay lip service to rights and their enforcement, still little is done by the ministries to enhance the facilities for right enforcement and to improve the procedure for administrative suit or introduce legislation for better remedies to improve the efficacy of law. Also we should not overlook the effect of the establishment's official ideology on the popular psychology and its possible enhancement of alleged disin-

59 *Cf.* 46 Hôsô Jihô (No. 10) 2006 (1994). 47% went to judgment, 53% settled, of which 32% were settled by compromise (*wakai*), 17% withdrawn (*torisage*).

60 State Court Caseload Statistics: Annual Report 1992, 16 (1994).

61 *See* M. Katô, *supra* note 5, at 643, footnote 24, for similar views (1987).

clination to sue. The bar too is little interested in enlarging the bench and bar, seeing it as only productive of competition.[62]

Finally the cost, efficacy, and convenience of suit, including access to reasonably priced, reliable lawyers and cheaper and better courts, certainly does affect their use in any system of justiciable law. Parties are not fools with their time and money. The old quip "The courts are open to everybody - like the Ritz Hotel!" tells an important part of the story. Below we will discuss the costs and efficacy of suits as an important aspect of the social role of lawyers in Japan.

C. Cost of Litigation as a Deterrence to Suit

No generalized, careful, and concrete comparison of litigation costs between the two countries has come to my attention,[63] and part of the costs it seems cannot be measured precisely - time, effort, and lost opportunity. But several aspects of the problem can be mentioned, which suggest that Japanese litigation may be relatively expensive when weighed against the rewards from a possible suit. Certainly the trade-off between costs and rewards are a prominent factor in a decision to go to court, or a defendant's decision to defend rather than pay up or settle, regardless of the strength of the case in substantive law. This analysis assumes as suggested above that relatively few Japanese disputes survive the efficient social dispute resolution process. But the cost of suit is also relevant to that social settlement process itself; in bargaining, even plaintiffs with good claims will settle for less, presumably in proportion to the cost of suit - what we vulgarly call the nuisance value of litigation.

This trade-off is of the highest significance: settlement is only legitimate if it is truly consensual, and consent is only voluntary when there is an alternative to settlement by way of a *practical* suit, especially if for any reason one party is weaker and forced to settle at a discount. As they say, when the lion and lamb lie down together the lamb is likely to be inside the lion.

---

62 *Id.* at 644 (1987).

63 The following studies look at certain facets of the problem: J.M. RAMSEYER, The Costs of the Consensual Myth: Antitrust Enforcement and Institutional Barriers to Litigation in Japan, 94 YALE L.J. 604 (1985); J.O. HALEY, Sheathing the Sword of Justice in Japan: An Essay on Law Without Sanctions, 8 J. JAP. STUD. (No. 2) 265-281 (1980); M.D. WEST, The Pricing of Shareholder Derivative Actions in Japan and the United States, 88 N.W.L.REV. 1436 (1994); N. YAMANOUCHI & S. COHEN, Understanding the Incidence of Litigation in Japan: A Structural Analysis, 25 INTERNATIONAL LAWYER 443 (1991).

1. Filing and Lawyer Fees

So what are the costs? Filing fees and lawyer fees are prominent on the list. Burdens of proof and standards thereof are another cost or risk, as are language, translation, and the availability of discovery or access to opponent's or third-party documents or testimony to assist in proving one's case. Finally, the remedies available are important to justify the plaintiff's expenditure of time, money, energy and adrenalin entailed in litigation. Punitive damages, triple damages, contingent fees, loser pays winner's fees, class actions, shareholders suits, private causes of action for regulatory offenses, as well as the ambiance of jury awards are all remedies encouraging plaintiffs to use the courts, all largely unavailable in Japan. Sorting through these factors is surely a step in a party's decision to become involved in the Japanese courts.

Taking filing fees first, Japanese filing fees in general are measured by the value of the claim asserted.[64]

Table 4: Filing Fees

The amount of claim in Yen	Court fee in Yen	Fee calculation in Yen on a 10 m. Yen claim
up to 300,000	500 for each 50,000 claimed	3,000
over 300,000 and up to 1 million	400 for each 50,000 claimed	5,600
over 1 million and up to 3 million	700 for each 100,000 claimed	14,000
more than 3 million	1,000 for each 200,000 claimed	35,000
10 million claimed ($100,000)		57,600 ($576)

For a claim of $100,000 (10 million yen at ¥100 to 1), in Japan the $576 filing fee is compared to $120 in the U.S. Federal District Court. Or, for a one million-dollar claim it would be $5,076, compared to $120 in the Federal District Court.[65]

---

64 *Minji soshô hiyô to ni kansuru hôritsu* [Law No. 40 of 1971] Article 3 (plus annexed list); HATTORI & HENDERSON, *supra* note 5, ch. 10 on Litigation Expenses (1985).

65 28 U.S.C. § 1914(a) (1988).

Lawyer fees are subject to a recommended fee schedule of the *Japan Federation of Bar Associations*.[66] For undertaking a lawsuit, the lawyer's fee is also based on the amount to be claimed. My sources tell me that despite an obligation to charge the minimum set by the bar, many lawyers vary their fees by agreement with clients depending on the circumstances. One source reports rumors that now only 20% of the lawyers follow the schedule consistently.[67] The retainer (*chakushu-kin*) schedule for the *First Tokyo Bar Association* effective to October 1, 1995, is as follows in litigation cases:[68]

Table 5: Lawyer Fees

Claim amount in Yen	Retainer fee	Success fee
up to 500,000	15%	15%
500,000 to 1,000,000	12%	12%
1,000,000 to 3,000,000	10%	10%
3,000,000 to 5,000,000	8%	8%
5,000,000 to 10,000,000	7%	7%
10,000,000 to 50,000,000	5%	5%
50,000,000 to 100,000,000	4%	4%
all above 100,000,000	3%	3%

Thus a ¥10,000,000 ($100,000) claim requires an advance retainer of $8,450, whereas many claims in the U.S., especially tort claims, would be taken on a contingent fee basis. Plaintiff would pay no fees unless or until the case is won or settled and payment would be made out of the recovery. Then the usual fee determined by contract would be about one third of the amount recovered. For a million dollar claim, the Japanese lawyer's retainer would be $48,450 to be paid up-front. Both the filing fees and lawyer fee paid in advance of filing suit are substantially higher than normal in the U.S. and presumably would discourage use of the courts by many poor clients.

66 Note that there is no legal barrier like *Goldfarb* v. *Virginia State Bar*, 421 U.S. 773 (1975). There is a very recent JFBA update of suggested fee schedules for lawyers effective October 1, 1995. As an example of local bar associations rules *see: Dai-ichi Tôkyô Bengoshi-kai* [First Tokyo Bar Association], *Dai-ichi Tôkyô Bengoshi-kai kaisoku, shô-kisoku* [The First Tokyo Bar Association-Rules and Various Regulations] 77-98 (1994). It has a detailed set of rules for recommended fees, not only for suits but also for conciliation, for negotiation, counseling, for drafting, either set by piece-work or by the hour or a percentage of the value involved. It will be soon updated to conform to the new JFBA rules mentioned above.

67 M. KATÔ, *supra* note 5, at 670, footnote 61.

68 New JFBA Rule 17; also *Dai-ichi Bengoshi-kai, Bengoshi hôshû kisoku* [Lawyers Compensation Rules] Rule 18.

The new rules effective October 1, 1995, are changed considerably to reduce the retainer (*chakushu-kin*) and increase the success fee (*hôshû-kin*), thus making fees more dependent on winning, akin to our contingency fees:

Table 6: New Fee Schedule

Claim amount in Yen	Retainer fee	Success fee
Under 3 million	8%	16%
3 to 30 million	5%	10%
30 to 300 million	3%	6%
Over 300 million	2%	4%

2. *Procedural Disincentives*[69]

The trial procedures and remedies can add to costs, or enhance or reduce rewards of litigation, thus influencing the decision to use lawyers and lawsuits. Major disincentives to suing in Japan include the lack of discovery procedures[70] to obtain evidence necessary to prove one's case, and the heavy burden of proof enforced by a generally conservative bench, which increases pressure on the settlement process and discourages litigation. In addition, damages and other remedies are relatively inadequate.

In discovery proceedings in the U.S., pre-trial discovery looms large as necessary preparations for a jury trial to avoid surprise. For the jury the trial must be concentrated and finished without recess. In Japan, without a jury, the "trial"[71] begins a few weeks after filing and continues by way of a series of sessions strung out a few weeks apart. In such an episodic trial, pre-trial discovery is not needed because surprise by an opponent is not a problem. There is always a chance to answer at another session. Viewed another way, discovery is always going on in the ongoing sessions, until the judge decides the case is ripe for judgment or until it is settled, often with the judge's active encouragement (*wakai*).[72] Needless to say, the American jury cannot be assembled several times for a series of such sessions. So the Japanese and American trials are fundamentally different because of the jury, and in the

69 See, for all of these remedies and procedural points, HATTORI & HENDERSON, *supra* note 5, ch. 7.

70 But *see* Japanese preservation of evidence (*shôko hozen*), Article 343 of the *Minji soshô-hô* [Code of Civil Procedure, hereafter *Minso*], Law No. 29 of 1890 as amended by Law No. 66 of 1994,; for an English translation *see* EHS Vol. II, FA, No. 2100. HATTORI & HENDERSON, *supra* note 5, at 6-5 to 6-7 (1985).

71 K. HARADA, Civil Discovery Under Japanese Law, 16 LAW IN JAPAN 21-53 (1983).

72 Article 136 of the *Minso*.

preparation for trial discovery becomes much more important in America. Even though many American trials do not actually have juries, the procedures of all trials are designed for them.

But if pre-trial discovery is unnecessary in Japan, there is still a major problem in obtaining evidence from the opponent or third parties, because of the narrowness of the code provisions[73] concerning parties' rights to demand documentary or testimonial evidence from the opponents or third-parties. For example, in a personal injury case, the injured's medical records have been held to be beyond the reach of the defendant;[74] whereas American procedures make them normally available. This lack of rights to obtain evidence can often force a party to discount his otherwise valid claim. Especially in product liability cases for damages caused by a defectively designed or manufactured product, lack of access to defendant's plant and records may be fatal on the issue of liability as well, especially in Japan where negligence was the only basis for a claim, until the Product Liability Law was changed (1995).

Also, the burden of proof is higher in Japan in civil cases, said to be akin to the "beyond-a-reasonable-doubt" formula in American criminal trials.[75] This high burden on plaintiffs, plus lack of a jury's evaluation, makes Japanese courts a tough forum for plaintiffs.

In proving one's case, judicially imposed strict requirements for factual allegations and proof can be onerous because of what one comparative scholar has called "precision justice" proceeding in accordance with shifting burdens of proof by judicially established rules difficult to divine from the codes.[76] The result can be dismissals for failure to comply with its strict standards.[77] It has even been suggested that these strictures imposed by the bench implement an administrative policy to discourage litigation and promote "non-justice"[78] through the social settlement processes (see above) to preserve "harmony."

As to remedies, the attempts to impose uniformity and standardization on damage awards, while commendable to assist in settling cases in general, have

---

73 Article 312 of the *Minso*.

74 In re *Ôoka et al.*, 31 *Kosai minshu* 187 (Osaka H. Ct. May 17, 1978). But *see Nîppon Chiba Takeda* v. *Ciba Geigi K.K.*, HANREI JIHÔ (No. 869) 35 (Fukuoka H. Ct., Sept. 17, 1977) for a decision upholding defendant's right to get plaintiff's medical records under Article 312 of the *Minso*. My firm represented defendants in this case. *See* HARADA, *supra* note 71, at 43 (1983).

75 HATTORI & HENDERSON, *supra* note 5, at § 7-77, or generally *see* § 7.05(13) and 7.05(14).

76 This important feature of the Japanese judiciary is described in English in I. KITAMURA, The Judiciary in Contemporary Society: Japan, 25 CASE W. RES. J. INTL. L. 263, 270-275 (1993). It states (p. 270) that this new method (*yôken jijitsu-ron*) has been developed not by scholars but by the LTRI during the past 30 years.

77 HATTORI & HENDERSON, *supra* note 5, at 7-78.

78 KITAMURA, *supra* note 76, at 275.

had the effect of setting levels of recovery comparatively low especially in injury and death cases, and the higher burden of proof also reduces the damages provable against such standards.

Neither Japan nor the U.S. have a general rule to award lawyer fees as damages to the winner, as in England. And despite the difficulties and unfairness of awarding winners lawyer fees as damages in close cases that have to be tried, still it is fatuous to say that a winner is "made whole" by the law of compensatory damages when in the bulk of cases lawyer fees take no small portion of those damages awarded. Besides there is no punitive damages in Japanese law, nor triple-damages found in some American statutory actions. All of these features surely reduce the awards and incentive to sue in Japan.

Whether U.S. practices such as jury trials which generally award higher damages, punitive damages, broad discovery and more flexibility of remedies (drawn from equity) or judicial activism are something to emulate is arguable, but surely such practice are incentives to use the courts.

PART III: CURRENT INSTITUTIONAL SETTING OF LAWYERS

The foregoing discussion measured the legal services available in Japan by relating the bar to the quasi-lawyers who facilitate compliance with regulation and guidance. In addition we have related the work of the bar to the social and bureaucratic practices which seem peculiarly effective to date to reduce the function of the Japanese judiciary. We suggested that the bureaucratic and social practices carried on outside of the justiciable legal system also greatly reduce the need for lawyers. So the tension that might be caused by side-stepping the legal system seems to have been checked by deliberately keeping the bar small and privileged with little competition, and hence well paid. These are the problems of alien law still only partially accepted in a lingering civilization headed by mandarins chary of law.

Finally, we have seen that these Japanese practices enable the society itself to provide ample *social* means of governance and dispute resolution which function well enough to substantially reduce the filing of lawsuits. In this Part III we will discuss major institutional features of the bar and try to assess their impact on the role of lawyers and lawsuits.

A. Legal Education

Japan's 15,541 lawyers are well trained and as a rule highly talented, and in the past forty years while I have been a member the social status of the bar has improved immensely. The normal access to the bar is, first, a four-year course in law at a University faculty of law.[79] Liberal arts takes up much of the first two years, and then the constitution, codes, and other legal subjects are studied mostly by the lecture method emphasizing code interpretation and legal theory. The application of law is little studied, this is in contrast to the American law schools by use of the case method. A wide array of courses in legal history, jurisprudence and foreign law enrich the curriculum, and are given more weight than in American law schools, where as non-bar-exam courses they get secondary attention. This kind of undergraduate law training has become the main avenue to power in both business and the bureaucracy and the curriculum reflects that goal, rather than a goal of training legal professionals.

On graduation, the Judicial Examination (*shihô shiken*) must be passed by those seeking to be lawyers. The pass rate is about 2%. Successful students enter the one and only *Legal Training and Research Institute* (LTRI; *Shihô Kenshû-jo*) for two years of study including classroom study (four months); then practical experience for sixteen months: eight months at a court, four months at a procurator's office, then four months at a law office; and back to the Institute for more classes (four months); and the final written and oral exams of the Institute. Most everyone passes these exams, and then each graduate chooses in which branch of the "legal profession" (*hôsô*)[80] he will pursue his career, usually for life: judge, procurator, or lawyer?

In this process just summarized, the Judicial Exam is an extremely difficult hurdle. Of roughly 24,000 examinees annually only about 2% pass; very few pass the first time, and most take the exam several times, and the time in between exams they spend at cram schools (*juku*) in special preparation for the next attempt to pass. Many spend more time in *juku* than they spend in the university or LTRI. The exam process is often criticized by academics because it seems to be used more to limit and to exclude than to ascertain qualifications. The reason is that there are now only 700 seats at the Institute for about 24,000 examinees, and until 1992 only 500. Still, this only points to the LTRI as the restrictive wicket, and in a country of Japan's wealth, presumably the LTRI could be doubled or tripled in capacity. The real reason for the small bar is that, once a member, lawyers also prefer a small bar and the bureaucracy has no incentive to implement a rule-of-law.

---

79 *Shihô shiken kaikaku mondai shiryôshû* [Collection of Materials on the Problem of Reforming the Judicial Exam] 45 JIYÛ TO SEIGI (No. 12) (*rinji zôkan* [special edition] 1994). M. KATÔ, *supra* note 5, at 629-643; M.J. KRASNOW, The Education and Development of Legal Professionals in Japan, 18 J. OF THE LEGAL PROFESSION 93-104 (1993).

80 *Hôsô* can be translated "legal profession" but specifically it is used to designate those trained at the LTRI and to refer to judges, procurators, and lawyers as a group.

In recent years the traditional preference among graduates of the LTRI to become officials (judges or procurators) is said to have changed to favor lawyers; annually only about 60 choose to become assistant judges, and about 50 elect to become procurators; the rest (about 590) will join the bar. The earning power of present-day Japanese lawyers may be a reason that more talented young men choose the bar, and no doubt the highly publicized difficulty of the judicial exam, plus their income and integrity, have combined to raise the social status[81] of today's lawyers to heights previously undreamed of even when I joined in 1954. Perhaps the biggest attraction of becoming a lawyer is the independence: lawyers are their own bosses in a society where most people are organizational cogs in large bureaus or companies.

B. Integration of the Bar (*hôsô ichigen*): The Relation Between Judges, Procurators and Lawyers

The relations between the three elements of the legal profession (*hôsô*) have always been somewhat strained. Pre-war lawyers long sought unsuccessfully to be treated equally with judges and procurators. This may seem ironical to American lawyers who do not think of essential prestige or success as coming from official status, but rather from independence and autonomy of the bar. Arguably the American bar takes too lightly the lawyer's role as an "officer of the court." One Japanese step in the direction of seeking prestige from association with officialdom was to support a single legal profession (*hôsô*) to which all belonged initially (*hôsô ichigen*),[82] and *from which* judges and procurators might later be chosen, as in England or the U.S.

The move after World War II to allow all would-be judges, procurators, and lawyers to become official apprentices, together with government stipends at the LTRI, was progress. Intermingling with each other as equal apprentices (before choosing careers) has improved relations between the three branches of the profession, divided for life into separate careers immediately after graduation. Once a lawyer, very few members of the bar make lateral moves to the bench or procuracy, though it is possible. Also an occasional judge or procurator will practice law after retirement from office. The strength of the ancient ideology of respect for officials (*kanson minpi*) is however still shown in the bar journals even today and even after these changes.

81 DAL PONT, *supra* note 5, at 299 has an interesting view of the Japanese lawyer's social status.

82 *See*: *Bengoshi seido hyakunen kinen* [Centennial Commemoration of the Lawyer System] 27 JIYÛ TO SEIGI (No. 7) 8 (*rinji zôkan* [special edition] 1976).

C. Organization of the Bar

The organized bar was placed under the Supreme Court when the judiciary was reconstituted by the Showa Constitution (1947). Courts were made independent from the Ministry of Justice for the first time, and the Supreme Court was given rule-making power and authority to administer the courts, judges, and lawyers.[83] In practice the Supreme Court has allowed the *Japan Federation of Bar Associations* (JFBA) complete autonomy to manage the local bars.

There are 52 local bar associations, one in each prefecture, except for Tokyo which has three for historical reasons having to do with early factionalism.[84] Each bar association is then a member of the Japan Federation of Bar Associations (*Nihon Bengoshi Rengôkai*; acronym: JFBA or *Nichibenren*) in Tokyo, of which each individual lawyer is also a member, upon first registering with his local bar. Each lawyer must be a local bar member and have a law office in the prefecture where he practices, and he may have only one office in Japan, but is licensed to appear in all courts throughout the country.

Lawyers have habitually been sole practitioners,[85] probably because their model was the English barrister whose conventions eschew partnerships. But soon after World War II, small partnerships for the practice of law began to appear in Tokyo and later in Osaka. I think this important innovation was embraced initially by lawyers in international work, to handle counseling in complex transnational business with patent, tax, corporate, contract, and conflict-of-law problems, among others. Such office practice, not centered around the courtroom, was more efficiently handled by a division-of-labor derived from several specialty lawyers working together. In the 1950s, many but not all of the pioneers in this new kind of practice were foreign quasi-members (*jun-kaiin*) of the Tokyo bars. Though growing in number and size, these firms are still small (a dozen lawyers or so, forty at the most) and still largely confined to Tokyo and Osaka.

D. Geographic Distribution

The bar's operation is heavily concentrated[86] in the three largest metropolitan areas - Tokyo, Osaka, and Nagoya - where fully two thirds of the lawyers may be found. Nearly half of the entire bar is in Tokyo. The rural areas such as the northern prefectures (Uwate, Aomori, and Akita) have only one lawyer for

---

83 Article 77 of the Japanese Constitution [*Kenpô*] from November 3, 1946.

84 RABINOWITZ, *supra* note 7, at 70.

85 *Nihon no hôritsu jimu-sho* '90 [Law offices of Japan, 1990], 42 JIYÛ TO SEIGI (No. 13) 14 (*rinji zôkan* [special edition] 1991).

86 M. KATÔ, *supra* note 79, at 672, gives the number of lawyers in each of Japan's prefectures and the ratio of people per lawyer in each.

every 40,000 or more people, compared to one for about every 2,000 in Tokyo, or one for every 5,400 in Osaka. Of the 201 places throughout the countryside where the District Courts have branches, fifty do not even have a single lawyer's office.[87] In other words, there is a judge and a courthouse, but no lawyer. In such rural areas, justiciable law is either obtained *pro se* or through quasi-lawyers, or not at all.

E. Scope of Services[88]

In 1995 most lawyers are still essentially litigators, or engaged in criminal defense. Their mission is stated much more broadly, though, as follows:

Article 1 of the *Bengoshi-hô*[89] (The mission of a practicing attorney)

> A practicing attorney is entrusted with a mission to protect fundamental human rights and to realize social justice.
>
> A practicing attorney shall, in keeping with the mission specified in the preceding paragraph, sincerely perform his duties and endeavor to maintain social order and to improve legal systems.

Increasingly legal opinions, consulting, drafting, negotiating, and such services together are becoming the focus of practices in Tokyo and Osaka, often in connection with transnational business. Still major portions of office paperwork done by American lawyers (corporate, real estate, estate planning, contracts) are done by quasi-lawyers without much involvement of the bar.

One significant trend is to have lawyers, patent agents, and even tax agents officing together to enhance the mix of specialties and the efficiency of delivering one-stop services to businesses. Needless to say, there is a rich mix of other skilled staff required in the big city transnational practice to investigate, translate to English, report, and work with the registries. In bilingual practice documentation is routinely bilingual, and the languages are difficult and require special staffing.

---

87 *See* K. YONEMOTO, The Shimane Bar Association: All Twenty-One Members Strong (D.H. Foote, trans.) 25 LAW IN JAPAN 115 (1995).

88 There is a detailed report of a comprehensive survey of law office services; *see*: *Nihon no hôritsu jimusho '90*, *supra* note 85, at 34-77.

89 Lawyer's Law, Law No. 205 of 1949 as amended by Law No. 89 of 1993. There is an English translation of it *in* R.H. WOHL, S.M. CHEMTOB & G.S. FUKUSHIMA, Practice by Foreign Lawyers in Japan 113-134 (ABA, 1989); another English translation can be found *in* EHS Vol. II, CA, No. 2040.

F. Ethics of the Profession

The Lawyer's Law assigns to lawyers the mission of defending fundamental human rights and promoting social justice.[90] They are also required to perform their work with integrity, and to strive to maintain social order and to improve the legal system.[91] With these lofty goals provided by law, the bar has encouraged individual lawyers to take their public role as officers of the court seriously, as well as pursue the private interests of clients.[92] Within these two roles the lawyer treads a difficult path.[93] In Japan, the officer-of-court role seems relatively strong compared to American practice, probably because of the lawyers' own striving for equal treatment.

Lawyer's Ethics (*Bengoshi rinri*) is a set of precepts and principles established by the JFBA and revised in 1990 and declared applicable to all members of the bar. In the case of the *First Tokyo Bar Association*, the revised ethics "code" is at the beginning of its effective rules.[94] Among other matters, lawyers are admonished to improve the judiciary and uphold its independence; to refrain from unseemly advertising; conciliate at the bar association any disputes between themselves and clients, or other lawyers; avoid delaying litigation; obey the law and the bar rules; avoid conflicts of interest; and avoid direct contact with opponent lawyer's clients among many others.

In 1989, only 28 lawyers were disciplined,[95] mostly for embezzling clients' funds, though *Nichibenren* has had a policy until 1991 to not reveal the nature of wayward lawyers' misconduct. This policy of non-disclosure has been reversed in order to nurture more trust from the public. *Nichibenren* has had 2,291 complaints of lawyers' misconduct between 1979-1990. Two hundred lawyers were punished, of which 12 were disbarred, 14 were ordered to withdraw, 98 suspended for up to two years, and 76 were merely reprimanded. But with about 200 complaints annually, only about one in 18 cases results in penalties. This too seems low.

Those statistics surely show a low level of disciplinary actions taken against lawyers, which is consistent with the integrity, talent, and general prosperity of the bar in recent years.

---

90 Article 1(1) of the *Bengoshi-hô*.

91 Article 1(2) of the *Bengoshi-hô*.

92 In the United States the pursuit of client's interest seems to be the overriding mission.

93 S. KATÔ, *Bengoshi yakuwari-ron* [Discussion About the Role of the Lawyer] 5 (1992).

94 *Dai-ichi Tôkyô Bengoshi-kai kaisoku, sho-kisoku* [First Tokyo Bar Association Rules and Various Regulation] 11-17 (1994) gives the *Lawyer's Ethics* in sixty-one articles; it is adopted and issued by JFBA to the local bars for adoption by them.

95 S.A. LEONARD, Attorney Ethics and the Size of the Japanese Bar, JAPAN QUARTERLY 86, 91 (Jan-Mar, 1992).

It is interesting that many lawyers do attribute the high moral and professional quality of the bar to the fact that membership has been kept, apparently deliberately, at a low level.[96] And lawyers today defend the smallness of the bar as a way to insure its high ethical standards and the members' continued integrity. Their reasoning has it that a large bar with low per capita earnings and high competitive efforts would spawn miscreants and multiply malpractice, leading to deterioration of the whole profession's reputation in the community.

It is easy to be skeptical of such a justification for the small bar, when the self-interest in limiting competition is so clear. Nevertheless, the skill and ethics of Japanese lawyers on the whole is high, and the bar is severely limited in size by restricted funding at the LTRI. And, it is quite plausible that these things are related; just as it is true that the remarkable growth of the American bar (200,000 in 1964 to 850,000 in 1996) coincides with a massive increase in lawyer-bashing, born presumably of lower performance and client dissatisfaction with fees and services.[97] Direct correlation between size and ethics of the bar have not been measured precisely in either country. But Japanese lawyers remember a time (1920s) when in their mind an over-population of lawyers seriously endangered the prosperity and ethics of the Japanese bar.[98] Those memories fortify them in their desire to avoid over-population, as we have it in the U.S. today according to some views.

Advertising is subject to rather strict bar rules established in 1987,[99] and there is no limit on the bar's advertising controls as in the U.S.[100]

G. Lawyer Fees

Costs of litigation, along with high burdens of proof, inflexible and ineffective remedies, no punitive damages or triple damages, lack of discovery, lack of a jury system, no contingency fee system or winner's fees have been mentioned as reasons for reluctance of Japanese to sue. Especially lawyer fees may be a disincentive. The posting of a recommended minimum fee schedule by the bar is not an anti-trust problem, as it can be in the U.S.[101] The First Tokyo Bar Association's fee schedule for lawsuits was discussed above (part II.C.1.).[102]

---

96 *Id.* at 90.
97 OVERTON, *supra* note 12, at 1081.
98 RABINOWITZ, *supra* note 7, at 73.
99 *Dai-ichi Bengoshi-kai kaisoku, sho-kisoku* p. 93-96 (1994).
100 *Cf. Bates* v. *State Bar of Arizona*, 433 U.S. 350 (1977).
101 *Goldfarb* v. *Virginia State Bar* 421 U.S. 773 (1975).
102 *Dai-ichi Tôkyô Bengoshi-kai bengoshi hôshû kisoku* [Lawyers' Compensation Rules of the First Tokyo Bar Association] Rule 18(1) (1995) *in* DAI-ICHI TÔKYÔ BENGOSHI-

The revised rules on fees reflect the trends in the law practice in recent years. More law offices earn a larger portion of their fees from office work, unrelated to suits, or settlement of disputes. Consequently the new fee schedule has suggested fees for drafting various documents, for negotiating contracts, wills, and estate administration. Methods of charging now include piece-work rates, hourly rates and rates, based on the value of the matter involved.

The JFBA fee schedule is, however, not always followed. In one study we are told that only about 20% of the lawyers consistently comply with it in charging their clients.[103] There is a long-standing bar practice of not relying on contingent fees, without the up-front retainer. However, several lawyers practicing in Tokyo told me that there are increasing numbers of lawyers trying to serve impecunious plaintiffs by not charging retainers or only small ones; they rely mainly on fees contingent on victory in court,[104] like much of the plaintiff's personal injury bar in the U.S.[105] Under new rules effective October 1, 1995, this practice is reflected in the revised schedule. Nearly 30% of the retainer plus success fee for handling a suit is shifted from the up-front retainer to success fees at the end, thus making the total fee one third retainer and the success fee becoming two thirds if the suit is won.[106]

The Tokyo transnational lawyers who do mostly office work, outside of the courts, tend to charge by an hourly rate,[107] as in the U.S. Charging by the hour has been quite uncommon in typical domestic law practice, except for

---

KAI, *Kaisoku, kisoku* [Rules and Regulations of the First Tokyo Bar Association] 82 (1995). A revised fee schedule was issued, effective October 1, 1995.

103 M. KATÔ, *supra* note 5, at 670 footnote 61.

104 This is authorized in Rule 4 (on variances). *Dai-ichi Tôkyô Bengoshi-kai kaisoku, sho-kisoku* 77 (1994) or new Rule 8.

105 See criticisms and suggestions for regulating contingency fee practice in the United States, mainly that they do not make sufficient allowance for quick settlements of strong cases with little actual contingency. This can amount to over-reaching as well as over-charging, because often the client lacks the skill to evaluate his legal claim, and only the lawyer can know it is likely to be a winner and likely to settle with little effort on his part. L. BRICKMAN, M. HOROWITZ & J. O'CONNELL, Rethinking Contingency Fees, 17 Manhattan Institute (1994).

106 JFBA, *Hôshû no kijun kitei* [Rules of fee standards] Rule 17:

Claim in Yen	*Retainer*	*Success Fee*
To 3,000,000	8%	16%
3 million to 30 million	5%	10%
30 million to 300 million	3%	6%
Over 300 million	2%	4%

Note that this new rule (October 1, 1995) assesses much less of the total fee for a case as an advance retainer and leaves much more contingent, to be paid later as a success fee, thus increasing the contingency aspect of Japanese litigation expense.

107 JFBA new rules, *supra* note 102, Rule 11 (1995): first consultation: ¥5,000 to ¥10,000 for 30 minutes; other: 30 minutes for ¥5,000 to ¥25,000.

occasional consultations. It is not difficult to imagine that many plaintiffs with a million-dollar claim might balk at a request to pay a $48,450 retainer, but if such a plaintiff should win the million dollars, the total Japanese fee of $96,900[108] would look good alongside an American lawyer's usual one fourth ($250,000) or one third ($333,333). The real deterrence of Japanese retainers is simply the inability to pay a large advance retainer, or unwillingness to risk losing the suit and the retainer.

Untrained in law, a client must rely on his lawyer to put a value on his lawsuit, whose strongest interest may be to bank the retainer. We may suppose intuitively that retainers might influence lawyers to be excessively optimistic. Another side effect of the retainer system is its obviously sobering effect on plaintiffs who might otherwise have a tendency to claim too much in damages in their complaints, or gamble on a weak case on the liability issue. Anyway just now (October 1995) we learn from the revised fee schedule that advance retainers henceforth are to be reduced.

PART IV: FOREIGN LAWYERS

The post-World War II period has had three phases in regulating foreign legal services. The first (1949-1955) commenced with the passage of the Lawyers' Law[109] (1949) and ended with the repeal of its provisions[110] permitting qualified foreign lawyers to join the bar as quasi-members (*jun-kaiin*). In the second phase (1955-1986), no additional foreign lawyers were allowed to join the bar, but those foreigners (about 70) who had already become quasi-members by 1955 when the bar was closed to new foreign members were permitted to remain as quasi-members and practice as before. Also during this phase,

---

108 JFBA Rule 18 (old rules). Under the new Rule 17, the up-front retainer would be reduced to ¥36,900. Under the revision, therefore, the retainer will be less of a disincentive to sue.

109 *Bengoshi-hô*, see *supra* note 89.

110 Article 7 of the *Bengoshi-hô*:

(1) A person who is qualified to become an attorney of a foreign country and who possesses an adequate knowledge of the *laws of Japan* may obtain the recognition of the Supreme Court and conduct the affairs prescribed in Article 3 *[the affairs of an attorney]*. Provided, however, that this does not apply to the persons listed in the prior article *[persons disqualified for various reasons such as disciplinary action by an attorneys' association, bankruptcy, and being sentenced to punishment by simple imprisonment or greater]*.

(2) A person who is qualified to become an attorney of a foreign country may obtain the recognition of the Supreme Court and conduct the affairs prescribed in Article 3 in regard to *aliens or foreign law*. Provided, however, that this does not apply to the persons listed in the prior article.

(3) The Supreme Court may impose an examination or screening in those cases where it grants the recognition of the prior two paragraphs. . . .

foreign lawyers were permitted to work as "trainees" in Japanese law offices for a limited term, usually two years. They were required to work under the supervision of a Japanese lawyer, and could neither join the bar nor practice law alone. The third phase (1986 onward) is the era of the Lawyer-for-Foreign-Legal-Services (*gaikoku-hô jimu bengoshi*; hereafter GHJB) authorized by a new law of 1986[111] enacted after a prolonged negotiation between the Japanese government and the U.S. government, which treated the restrictions on foreign legal services as a trade barrier.

A. Quasi-Members (*jun-kaiin*)

The Lawyer's Law was introduced in the Diet in 1949 as a private member bill, which is probably significant. Private bills are quite rare in Japan. The fact that it took a private bill to finally launch a bar with independence and autonomy after a fifty-year struggle with the procuracy and then the Ministry of Justice is not surprising. One might suppose that the quasi-members created by the new law were creatures of Allied occupation pressure, too, but we are told this was not the case.[112] Surely this was then nothing like the clamoring of aspirant foreign lawyers leading up to the 1986 authorization of the GHJB.

The status accorded foreign lawyers by Article 7 (repealed 1955) of the Lawyer's Law was of two types: (1) foreign lawyers with "an adequate knowledge of the laws of Japan"; and (2) foreign lawyers "recognized by the Supreme Court" with rights to advise specified nationalities on law of specified countries. The proof of adequate knowledge of Japanese law inhibited all but one American (the late Thomas L. Blakemore) from qualifying; but the other less rigorous status was attained by about seventy foreigners. By 1995, there are said to be only ten of us left, including two in Okinawa.[113]

The certification or license from the Supreme Court of Japan specified which foreign law the licensees could practice (in my case: American-English, *beiei-hô*), presumably to any clients including Japanese. Also it specified what nationalities could be advised (in my case: American and English *beiei-jin*). *Beiei* is not a term commonly used in law (as opposed to *eibei-hô*, the common term for Anglo-American law), and whether it includes Scotland or indeed maybe Australia, New Zealand, or Canada could be argued.

---

111 *Gaikoku bengoshi ni yoru hôritsu jimu no toriatsukai ni kansuru tokubetsu sochi-hô* [Special Measures Law Concerning the Handling of Legal Business by Foreign Lawyers] Law No. 66 of 1986 as amended by Law No. 65 of 1994. There is an English translation in WOHL, CHEMTOB & FUKUSHIMA, *supra* note 89, at 91-112.

112 T. FUKUHARA, The Status of Foreign Lawyers in Japan, 17 JAP. AN. INT'L L. 27 (1973).

113 These figures are found in the promotional brochure distributed in 1995 by the JFBA on moving into a new building entitled Japan Federation of Bar Associations.

In 1955 Article 7 was repealed,[114] but quasi-members already admitted were allowed to continue practice with the same privileges and restrictions. In retrospect, the quasi-member system seems to have served Japan well. Certainly a vast array of incorporations, technology licensing, financing, joint venturing, transportation and sales transactions between Japanese and foreign participants passed through the so-called "liaison law offices" with one or more *jun-kaiin* in partnership with Japanese lawyers working six or seven days a week for the first forty-odd years after 1949. Actually the quasi-members would be a better model for serving the public and the business community than the GHJB, but the public's interest in legal services seems to get lost in the political fray and lawyerly self-seeking.

B. The Lawyer-For-Foreign Legal Services[115]

Despite the clamoring for entry, so far the new regime for foreign lawyers has not been very useful; the elephant has whelped a mouse. The Japan Federation of Bar Associations reports that in 1995 there are 73 Lawyers-for-Foreign-Legal-Services (GHJB) registered in Japan, probably less than that actively practicing. A couple of years earlier there were 76. So several seem to have withdrawn. In fact, there have been media reports[116] to the effect that practice permitted for foreign lawyers is so limited that few of the new offices are profitable, especially because of the high expense of opening and operating an office in Tokyo.

The major restrictive features of the new GHJB status as enacted in 1986 are discussed below:

First, the application process requires dual scrutiny and approval by the Ministry of Justice and the Japan Federation of Bar Associations as well as the local bar.[117]

---

114 Again, the repeal of Article 7 was by private bill. Law Concerning Partial Amendment of the Lawyer's Law, Law No. 155 of 1955.

115 The voluminous recent literature on foreign lawyers in Japan fully reflects an intensity of the lawyers' interest in this subject, but the public interest is not necessarily the same and it gets little expressed attention. Most useful is WOHL, CHEMTOB & FUKUSHIMA, *supra* note 89. Among its 43 appendices are translations of the Special Measures Law Concerning the Handling of Legal Business by Foreign Lawyers (*supra* note 111) Appendix 1; and The "Practicing Attorney" Law (*supra* note 89) Appendix 2. *See* also an extensive discussion *in* Symposium Proceedings: Japan-American Society/ABA Seminar on American Lawyers in Japan, April 28, 1988, *in* 21 LAW IN JAPAN 1-218 (1988), containing (p. 193-218) another English translation of the Special Measures Law Concerning the Handling of Legal Business by Foreign Lawyers (*supra* note 111).

116 *See* Exodus of Foreign Lawyers Has Begun: Japanese Legal Market Not Lucrative, 8 THE JAPAN LAW JOURNAL (No. 1) p. 1-2 (Feb, 1995).

117 WOHL ET AL., *supra* note 89, at 25-41 and appended application forms 135-221.

Second, the applicant is only eligible to practice the law of his home state, which in a federal system like the U.S. includes the federal law. Thus, a California lawyer may advise on California and federal law, but not New York or any other state law, and of course he is not permitted to advise on Japanese law or appear in court.

Third, the GHJB is not permitted to hire Japanese lawyers to supply clients with advice on Japanese law, nor is he allowed to form partnerships or joint ventures with Japanese lawyers, though he might share offices. Changes have been made in 1994 (see below).

Fourth, only lawyers from states which offer reciprocity to Japanese lawyers are eligible. So far, in the United States only California, New York, Michigan, Hawaii and the District of Columbia qualify, although there are moves in progress in several other states to grant reciprocity.

Fifth, the applicant must have completed five years of practice at home before applying in Japan. Here too changes were made in 1994 (see below).

Sixth the GHJB must practice only in his own name as a GHJB. He was not allowed to use the name of his firm at home. There are changes here too (see below).

Finally, he must spend at least 180 days of each year resident in Japan.

The long and contentious U.S./Japan negotiation leading up to the law enabling GHJB to join the Japanese bar show that the American side remained dissatisfied in the end with the restrictions imposed, especially the prohibitions against hiring (or joining partnerships with) Japanese lawyers. So, soon after the new regime took effect in 1986, American requests of changes ensued and finally in 1995 the following changes have gone into effect.[118]

The new law allows joint ventures (but not partnerships) between GHJB and Japanese, and still foreigners may not hire Japanese lawyers. Also, a maximum of two years spent in a Japanese office (as a "trainee") may be applied to the five-year requirement, hence only three years of home practice is needed. Finally, the home firm's name may be used.[119]

---

118 *Gaikoku bengoshi ni yoru hôritsu jimu no toriatsukai ni kansuru tokubetsu sochi-hô no ichibu o kaisei suru hôritsu* [Law Amending a Part of the Special Measures Law Concerning the Handling of Legal Business by Foreign Lawyers] (Law No. 65 of 1994).

119 *See* a recent review of foreign lawyers: L. COULTER, Japan's Gaiben Law: Economic Protectionism or Cultural Perfectionism, 17 HOUSTON J. INT'L L. 431-461 (1995); K.B. DE VERE STEVENS, Liberalisation of Law Governing Foreign Lawyers in Japan: Commentary on the Developments Between 1984-1994, 4 ASIA PAC. L.REV. 49-68 (1995); L. COOPER, Is the Door Half Open or Half Shut? Japan's Special Measures Law Concerning the Handling of Legal Business by Foreign Lawyers, 18 KENTUCKY L.REV. 417-430 (1990); S. KIGAWA, *Gaikoku Hô,* Foreign Lawyers In Japan: Dynamics Behind Law No. 66, 62 S. CAL. L.REV. 1489-1521 (1989). There are many others.

Thus ended the second round of agitation for rights to practice for foreign lawyers. In retrospect the present regime is still quite unsatisfactory, it would seem, from the public's viewpoint. In fact, neither the public's need for services nor the best way to provide them, which one might hope would have been the focus, were given anywhere near the attention that was lavished on the lawyers' interest on both sides. It is therefore no surprise that the Japanese public interest and that of American business are not very well served by a crippled species of transnational lawyer, the GHJB.

What is the public's interest? Presumably it is to get competent inexpensive legal services in matters (1) governed by foreign law, or, just as important, (2) where there may be a choice-of-law, or (3) where elements of a transaction are concerned with both Japanese and foreign law. In case 1, say a Japanese or foreign resident in Japan has a legal matter in the U.S., a GHJB could adequately handle this case; but for efficiency, case 2 and 3 require (1) either a comparativist (bilingual and bilegal) or (2) a one-stop law office with both Japanese and foreign law experts practicing together. Certainly to require clients to get foreign law from the local lawyers who by definition are "local" simply puts them in a monopoly position to broker off the only people competent, the foreign lawyers.

Clearly, from the standpoint of the public need for services, the old concept of the quasi-member (*jun-kaiin*), abolished in 1955, would have been a better model to start with. But improvements might have been added too, such as a requirement of some Japanese language capability and a basic understanding of Japan and the Japanese legal system, as originally required in the old law for one category of quasi-member.[120] Nowadays there are a considerable number of young bilingual and bilegal lawyers, both foreign and Japanese,[121] who might serve the public better, if their considerable skills were distinguished by a bar status and distinguished from the hordes of hungry, garden-variety foreign lawyers excelling in marketing skills above all else.

120 Article 7(1) (repealed) of the *Bengoshi-hô*.

121 The Asian Law Program, University of Washington, alone has trained about 350 LL.M.s and 25 Ph.D.s in a curriculum designed to develop bilingual comparative law skills in U.S./Japanese transactions, and other programs have also introduced these skills at the J.D. level.

Chapter Two

Judges and Mediators in Japan: The Administration as Motionless Mediator?

Toshiyuki Kono

Contents

A. The Experience of *Daiten-hô*[1]

1. The United States Government and Daiten-hô

When the U.S. government, under President Bush, proposed the *Structural Impediments Initiative (SII)* Meeting to the Japanese government in 1989, one of its crucial objectives was to remedy the Japanese "closed" distribution system. The American government asserted that *Daiten-hô* was blocking the

---

1 The abbreviation of *Dai-kibo kouri tenpo ni okeru kouri-gyô no jigyô katsudô no chôsei ni kansuru hôritsu* [Law to Adjust Business Activities of Retailers in Large-Scale Retailing Store], Law No. 109 of 1973 as amended by Law No. 80 of 1991.

flow of American products into the Japanese market. From the American perspective, an appropriate access point for entry into the Japanese distribution system seemed to be large-scale stores, such as supermarkets, in the outskirts of big cities. This is so, it was reasoned, because such stores have the personnel and financial resources to import products. However, in light of restrictions found in *Daiten-hô*, it was difficult at that time to open a large-scale store. For example, *Itôyokadô*, the second largest supermarket chain in Japan, planned to open a branch in Shizuoka City in 1977, but the opening was not accomplished until nine and a half years later.

2. *Procedural Provisions of Daiten-hô*

Under the provisions of *Daiten-hô*, it is not easily understandable why *Itôyokadô* needed so much time to open its Shizuoka branch store. *Daiten-hô* requires only two reports to the governor before the commencement of business activities: a report concerning the construction of the store (Article 3 report) and a report concerning the retailer who is opening the store (Article 5 report).[2]

Pursuant to the *Daiten-hô* application practice at that time, however, some additional procedures were required. First, a retailer who planned to open a large-scale store was required to officially announce the opening of the new store (*shutten hyômei* announcement) and to provide an explanation of the project (*jizen setsumei*) before submitting the Article 3 report. The Article 3 report would then have to be made within six months after the official announcement. After the Article 3 report was accepted, the Article 5 report would have to be completed within eight months.[3] In the interim between the two reports, the Minister for International Trade and Industry would ask the local chamber of commerce if the opening of the store would affect the business of small- or medium-sized retailers in the area. If these retailers answered this inquiry in the affirmative, a so-called *Shôchô-kyô* (business coordinating meeting) would be held. The members of such a meeting typically consisted of consumers, scholars, and local retailers.

If local small- or medium-sized retailers objected to the opening of the large-scale store, they could interfere with the opening through passage of a resolution of objection in the local assembly before the official announcement. In yet another time-consuming procedure, local retailers might resort to the *Shôchô-kyô*. If such a meeting were called, the retailer who planned the new large-scale store would often undertake *nemawashi* (preparatory) negotiations with local retailers prior to the official announcement of the opening in order to

---

2 Articles 3 and 5 of the *Daiten-hô*.
3 These four- and eight-month terms were established by an administrative order.

expedite the proceedings of the *Shôchô-kyô*. Since this *nemawashi* negotiation begins before the official announcement of the opening, the above official regulations do not apply to this stage of negotiation. Thus, local retailers could resist as long as they desired. Due to these additional procedures[4] and the burden of the application procedures, the retailers of large-scale stores often had to reduce the size of the project and, therefore, the entire project took enormous time to complete. For example, in the above-mentioned case of *Itôyokadô* in Shizuoka, the current size of the new store is 5,500 m^2, while original plans called for it to be 28,000 m^2.

3. *Daiten-hô and Dispute Resolution*

In light of the above, it is fair to say that *Daiten-hô* was a symbol of the Japanese "closed" market. For our purposes, however, other aspects of this law are perhaps more pertinent. Suppose, for example, that the local retailers, as members of the *Shôchô-kyô*, would not approve of the opening of the new store, even following several years of negotiations. If the large-scale retailer were to submit the Article 5 report required by *Daiten-hô* without obtaining the admission, what would be the result? The Article 5 report is theoretically not different from other reports of facts such as birth, marriage, etc. In theory, then, the reports could be made, upon fulfillment of procedural prerequisites, and would have to be accepted by the administrative office. In practice, however, the administrative office often did not accept the Article 5 report when the members of a *Shôchô-kyô* had failed to reach a consensus. Due to this negative attitude on the part of the administration, those wishing to open large-scale stores were often forced to negotiate with local retailers until they reached a solution. When considering this process from the viewpoint of dispute resolution, one could say that the administration played the role of mediator at least to the extent that a solution might be realized pursuant to its (albeit negative) direction. What would this suggest to us?

In my opinion, to analyze the theme "Dispute Resolution in Japan" with respect to the nation's economic success, we should set aside the classical dichotomy of "litigation or settlement." It is truc that social costs for dispute resolutions are related to the economic performance of each country. Japan is famous for its relatively low litigation rate. Thus, as one author argues, Japan can direct more of its resources towards the enhancement of GNP rather than to lawsuits and legal fees.[5] Approaching this discussion from the perspective of

4 Most municipalities have rendered additional regulations with local ordinances. *See* NIHON KEIZAI SHINBUN, May 30, 1991.

5 *See* E.J. HAHN, Perspective: An Overview of the Japanese Legal System, 5 J.INT.L.BUS. 528 (1983).

the "litigation or settlement" dichotomy might, however, lead to a discourse on cultural differences which would stop further discussion.[6] It might also lead us to overlook that disputes can occur at various social levels, such as those between two individuals, between two big companies, or between a manufacturer and consumers of its products.

In the following section I will describe how Japanese enterprises have resolved disputes in the course of their activities and, based upon consideration of this, I will then formulate a hypothesis. I will then examine the relationship between Japanese economic success and national dispute resolution mechanisms. For this purpose I will focus on situations related to business activities.

B. Statistical Behavioral Patterns of Large Japanese Companies

1. Statistics of the Shôji Hômu Kenkyû-kai Association[7]

In the 1960s, when the current success of the Japanese economy emerged, the number of legal departments in Japanese companies started to increase.[8] It would not be wrong to assume that the development of business and demands for specialized legal sections were closely connected. It is possible, therefore, to detect some tendencies of Japanese companies from an examination of information on legal departments' activities.

By way of background, this report will refer to surveys done by the *Shôji Hômu Kenkyû-kai* Association. Since 1965, this association has investigated the activities of legal departments in Japanese companies every five years.[9] The association sends questionnaires to major Japanese companies and classifies collected data as statistics. Although the number of the companies and the method of data classification changes every time[10], these are probably the most comprehensive surveys on legal departments and their activities in Japan. In the latest survey in 1990, the association sent questionnaires to listed companies (*jôjô kigyô*) (2,032), the companies registered as over-the-counter companies (*tentô tôroku kigyô*) (276), and the unlisted, powerful companies (*hi-jôjô*

6 For example, *see* T. KAWASHIMA, *Nihônjin no hô ishiki* [The Legal Consciousness of the Japanese] 139 (1967).

7 This association was founded in 1955 to support legal departments of companies.

8 *See* T. KITAGAWA, *Kigyô hômu no rekishi-teki hatten (sengo)* [Historical Development of Legal Departments after World War II], 167 HÔGAKU KYÔSHITSU 41 (1994).

9 *See* 360 SHÔJI HÔMU 225 (1965), 537 ibid. 6 (1970), 722 ibid. 86 (1976), 109 NBL 25 (1976), 110 ibid. 26 (1976), 111 ibid. 24 (1976), 112 ibid. 32 (1976), 113 ibid. 32 (1976), 8 *Bessatsu* NBL 124 (1987), 16 ibid. 141 (1986), 464 NBL 47 (1991).

10 The first survey focused on organizational aspects of the departments responsible for legal matters. The second and third surveys included questionnaires to 100 leading companies. Beginning with the fourth survey, the association did not limit the number of respondents to 100.

yûryoku kigyô) (374).The association received replies from 440, 38, and 69 companies, respectively.[11]

Table 1

Capital of Companies in yen (1990)	Number of Respondents (1990)
Less than 10 bil.	299
More than 10 bil./less than 100 bil.	205
More than 100 bil.	41
Mutual insurance company	2

This table shows that the respondent companies are among the leading companies in Japan. The results from this recent survey, therefore, apply mainly to major Japanese companies.

2. *Questionnaires on Dispute Resolution in the Most Recent Surveys*

a. Some Results

The surveys discussed above considered a number of issues related to dispute resolution. Five such questions are analyzed below. These questions concerned only those disputes without international aspects. In order to clarify the information, I simplified the results of the survey and compared the results from the last two surveys.

aa. Causes of Disputes in Last Five Years (Respondents may make several choices).

Table 2

	1980 survey	1985 survey	1990 survey
Business Contracts	62.9%	73.9%	69.7%
Intellectual Property	(5.7%)[12]	34.9%	34.0%
Public Pollution/Consumer	35.1%	29.0%	30.0%
Labor/Workmen's Compensation	(6.0%)	24.2%	24.9%
Corporation Law	16.4%	16.5%	14.1%

11 *See* 464 NBL 66 (1991).

12 In the survey of 1980, there was no option for intellectual property. This number was for the categorie "other disputes causes".

bb. Methods of Dispute Resolution

Table 3

	1980 survey	1985 survey	1990 survey
Negotiation between Parties as First Choice	85.0%	89.0%	69.3%
Litigation as Third Choice	25.0%	33.1%	24.9%

The surveys also reveal that the more capital a company has, the more likely it is to prefer litigation or settlement in court.[13] Litigation is generally not the first choice of large companies. In the 1990 survey, for example, only 2.9% of respondent companies chose litigation as the primary resolution method.[14]

cc. Roles of Legal Departments in the Event of Dispute

The 1990 survey shows that legal departments of 42.8% of the respondents handled only important cases. Of these companies, 88.5% have no certain criteria to determine what is an "important" case. The percentages in the 1985 survey are not much different. In the 1985 survey, 45.1% of respondent legal departments handled only important cases and 87.5% had no criteria for determining which cases were "important."

dd. Who Decides the Method of Dispute Resolution?

According to the 1990 survey, directors of legal departments decided the method of dispute resolution in only 5.3% of the respondent companies. In 44.2% of the respondent companies, legal departments had meetings with the employees in charge of a given case. In 35.3% of the respondent companies, the method of dispute resolution was chosen during meetings of executive directors. Finally, in 23.6% of the respondent companies, methods of dispute resolution were selected by the board of directors following consultation with corporate legal departments. In the 1985 survey, dispute settlement methods were chosen according to the following statistics: (1) chosen by directors of legal departments, 5.4%; (2) chosen in meetings with employees in charge of the case, 39.9%; (3) chosen by executive directors, 44.9% and (4) chosen by the board of directors, 25.3%.

---

13 *See* 16 *Bessatsu* NBL 142 (1986).
14 *See* 464 NBL 56 (1991).

ee. Cooperation with Lawyers

In the 1990 survey, 75.3% of the respondents reported having no regular contact with lawyers. On the other hand, many respondents consider dispute resolution as the most important matter over which to consult with lawyers. The larger the company is, the more pronounced is this tendency. In fact, 87.8% of the respondent companies with more than ¥100 billion in capital chose the need for dispute resolution as an important incentive for contacting a law firm.

b. Analysis

The above results may lead to the following conclusions:

First of all, the majority of disputes derive from business contracts. We can assume that the other party in such disputes is also a business enterprise. Secondly, most of these disputes are resolved through negotiation between both parties. In fact, *Noboru Kashiwagi*, ex-director of the legal department of Mitsubishi Trading Company,[15] admits that he never conducted a business trip within Japan for the purpose of dispute resolution.[16]

According to the 1975 survey, if a given contract includes some provision for dispute resolution, 72% of respondents followed such provisions, while 18% did not follow the provisions. The main reasons given for avoiding the dispute resolution provisions in the contract were the future business relationship with the other party and the balance of power between the two parties.[17] Generally, however, Japanese companies tend to follow the provisions for dispute resolution found in the contract. It should be pointed out, however, that contracts between Japanese companies often include the following clause: "Both parties shall deliberate separately when important issues arise."[18] In addition, when one considers that legal departments generally handle only "important" disputes and that boards of directors often decide how to resolve disputes, one can assume that disputes are often resolved not as legal matters, but as purely business matters. *Toshimitsu Kitagawa*, ex-director of Toshiba's legal department,[19] points out, in fact, that most Japanese companies still fail to grasp the legal nature of matters among various business activities. In his opinion, legal matters are not handled properly as "legal" matters.[20] In

15 Now a professor at Tokyo University.

16 *See* N. KASHIWAGI, *Kigyô hômu heno sasoi* [Invitation to the Legal Department] *supra* note 8, at 20.

17 In the 1970 survey, 52% of respondents neglected the criteria in the contract. The recent surveys do not include this question.

18 *See* KASHIWAGI, *supra* note 16.

19 He is now a professor at Kyûshû University.

20 *See* KITAGAWA, *supra* note 8, at 42.

addition, before the amendment of the Commercial Code[21] in 1993, this tendency must have been furthered by the fact that derivative suits were rarely used. As a result, executive directors of companies would not take into consideration the risk of being sued as a result of their choice of dispute resolution method or compensation paid as a result of such activities.

From these facts, one could probably say that large Japanese companies tend to resolve most disputes through negotiations within the framework of "business". As long as the economy constantly expands, companies can expect larger profits in the future by accepting short-term loss. For this purpose, flexible decisions are indispensable and deliberation may be the best means for resolving disputes. Large companies, such as the respondents of the surveys, have the ability to absorb such losses. Even if the powers between both parties are very divergent, deliberation is effective as long as both companies belong to the same "family" of companies (*keiretsu*).

C. The Administration as Motionless Mediator?

If the difference in the balance of power between two parties is enormous and if the companies are not in the same *keiretsu*, how are disputes resolved? If both parties are very small enterprises or if one party is a consumer, how can disputes between them be resolved? The statistics cited above do not provide any answers to these questions. To find possible answers to these questions, the following examples will be considered.

1. Daiten-hô, Reconsidered

The first matter to be considered is the *Daiten-hô* itself. Based on the SII agreement between the U.S. and Japanese governments, the *Daiten-hô* was amended in 1991.[22] Pursuant to the 1991 amendments, the required store opening announcements and subsequent *Shôchô-kyô* were abolished. Today, when Article 3 and Article 5 reports are submitted, a special council, the so-called *Daiten Shin*,[23] hears opinions from representatives of consumers, scholars, and retailers, and summarizes opinions from local chambers of commerce and their members. Within eight months after submission of an Article 5 report, the council must complete its deliberations. Notwithstanding

---

21 *Shôhô*, Law No. 48 of 1899 as amended by Law No. 66 of 1994.

22 *See* J. TAKAHASHI, 983 JURISUTO 71 (1991).

23 The abbreviation stands for *Dai-kibo Kouri Tenpo Shingi-kai* [Large Scale Retailing Council]. Even before the amendment, each prefecture could establish this council (Article 15-4 of the *Daiten-hô*). When this was done, however, it was in name only.

these amendments, however, the reality is that some cases are no different from those before the amendments. In Shizuoka City, for example, where *Itôyokadô* took almost ten years to open a new store, the representatives of local retailers at the *Daiten Shin* are still able to thwart company efforts in much the same way as was done before the amendments.[24] The government administration failed to intervene or to propose anything at the council.

2. *Bunya-tô chôsei-hô*[25]

In order to alleviate the business pressures often inflicted upon medium- and small-sized enterprises, this law adjusts the commencement or the expansion of businesses of large enterprises.[26] In the case of the commencement or the expansion of large businesses, for example, the law calls upon such enterprises to consider the interests of medium- and small-sized enterprises in order not to infringe upon them.[27] If problems concerning the adjustment of business activities occur, both parties are required to attempt to resolve the situation in an expeditious and fair manner.[28] When it is difficult for the parties to reach a voluntary solution and when it is necessary to secure business opportunities for medium- and small-sized enterprises, the minister responsible for such enterprises can recommend, based upon the application from medium- and small-sized enterprises, that the large enterprise postpone commencement or expansion of the business or reduce the size of business.[29] If necessary, the minister can take the opinion of a special council, the *Bunya-tô Chôsei Shingikai* council[30], into consideration.

This law clearly expects the administration to play a role as "arbitrator". In practice, the *Bunya-tô Chôsei Shingi-kai* is convened only once per year. However, this council has not handled a single case since the enactment of the law in 1979. This law has not, in fact, been applied to any case to resolve

---

24 Phone interview with an assistant director of the Commerce and Industry Department at Shizuoka City government on September 15, 1995.

25 The abbreviation stands for the *Chûshô kigyô no jigyô katsudô no kikai no kakuho no tame ni dai-kigyô-sha no jigyô katsudô no chôsei ni kansuru hôritsu* [Law to Adjust Business Activities of Large Enterprises to Secure Business Opportunities of Medium- and Small-Sized Enterprises], Law No. 74 of 1977 as amended by Law No. 78 of 1983.

26 Article 1 of the *Bunya-tô chôsei-hô*.

27 Article 3 of the *Bunya-tô chôsei-hô*.

28 Article 4 of the *Bunya-tô chôsei-hô*.

29 Article 7 of the *Bunya-tô chôsei-hô*.

30 The abbreviation stands for *Chûshô Kigyô Bunya-tô Chôsei Shingikai* (Council to Adjust the Business of Medium- and Small-Sized Enterprises).

disputes between big enterprises and medium- and small-sized enterprises.[31] While under *Daiten-hô*, one can detect, in light of the law's reporting procedure, the mechanisms for dispute resolution, the *Bunya-tô chôsei-hô* is applicable only when a group of medium- and small-sized enterprises apply for the minister's recommendation for adjustment of the business of large enterprises. If the parties "voluntarily" arrive at a solution, neither the recommendation of the minister nor the opinion of the *Bunya-tô Chôsei Shingi-kai* is necessary. The minister can, however, "support" the efforts of the parties to find a "voluntary" solution by offering "guidances." The number of guidances so issued thus far has not been made public.[32] It is therefore difficult to ascertain how the practice of this law has been undertaken. One recently reported example, however, sheds some light on the practice:

Morinaga Nyûgyô, a large food producing company, intended to produce a long-life bean curd (*tôfu*). The League of Commerce and Industry Partnership for *Tôfu* Makers opposed this plan. They negotiated and "voluntarily" agreed that in the Japanese market, Morinaga would produce no more than 50,000 units of long-life bean curd per year. This agreement remains valid today. The vice-president of the league admits that the *tôfu* makers have been protected, albeit indirectly, by this law.[33] Newspaper reports, moreover, have implied that the Ministry of Agriculture, Forestry, and Fisheries led the two parties to the "voluntary" solution.

Chûshô kigyô dantai-hô[34] has a very similar system to that of the *Bunya-tô chôsei-hô*. Under the *Chûshô kigyô dantai-hô*, medium- and small-sized enterprises can establish commerce and industry partnerships (*shôkô kumiai*) in each prefecture when more than half of the enterprises in a certain field become members.[35] In certain circumstances, the partnership may form a kind of cartel.[36] If problems concerning the cartel arise between non-member enterprises and member enterprises, the minister responsible is required to mediate or arbitrate the dispute.[37]

---

31 Phone interview with an assistant director of the Business and Distribution Department at the Agency of Medium- and Small-Sized Enterprises on September 8, 1995.

32 *Id.*

33 *See* NIHON KEIZAI SHINBUN, July 8, 1995.

34 The abbreviation stands for *Chûshô kigyô dantai no soshiki ni kansuru hôritsu* [Law on Organizations of Groups of Medium- and Small-Sized Enterprises], Law No. 185 of 1957 as amended by Law No. 91 of 1989.

35 Articles 9 and 12 of the *Chûshô kigyô dantai-hô*.

36 Article 17 of the *Chûshô kigyô dantai-hô*.

37 Article 30-3 of the *Chûshô kigyô dantai-hô*.

3. *Kensetsu Kôji Funsô Shinsa-kai*[38]

Based on *Kensetsugyô-hô*[39], the *Chûô Shinsa-kai* (Central Examining Committee) in the Ministry of Construction and the *Todôfuken Shinsakai* (Local Examining Committee) in each prefecture were established in 1949. These examining committees are official organizations engaged in alternative dispute resolution (ADR) sponsored by the administration.[40] These committees are entitled to mediate or arbitrate disputes concerning construction. This law does not urge parties to find a "voluntary" solution. In addition, the committees publicize this ADR system and recommend construction companies to use the system by, for example, inserting an arbitration clause into their standard contract forms.[41] The total number of applications for dispute resolution accepted by all committees in Japan in 1994 was only 261. Of these, the Central Examining Committee accepted 44, and Local Examining Committees accepted 217.[42] The committees handled disputes arising from defective construction, delay of construction, payment disputes, cancellation of contracts, etc. If one excludes cases in which one party is an individual, the number of cases decreases to 62, of which the Central Committee accepted 22 and Local Committees accepted 39.[43]

Although these committees are considered to be a functioning part of Japan's ADR system,[44] the above figures appear to be rather low. This is probably not because there were few disputes in the reported years. If a department in the Ministry of Construction responsible for a certain type of construction gives both parties some guidance to find a "voluntary" resolution, they will follow the guidance. The Central Examining Committee is completely separated from other departments of the ministry. They do not exchange information or personnel. Therefore, even secretariat members of the Central Examining Committee are unaware of the actual nature of a given "voluntary" resolution. The secretariat member may, however, assume that only those cases that could

---

38 Examining Committee for Construction Disputes, hereinafter *Shinsa-kai* in Japanese or Examining Committee in English.

39 Law of the Construction Industry, Law No. 100 of 1949 as amended by Law No. 69 of 1987.

40 *See* S. ÔTA, *Saiban-gai funsô kaiketsu seido no shisutemu sekkei to unyô* [Designs of ADR Systems and Their Practices] *in* Festschrift Kigawa Vol. 1, 61 (1994); T. YAMASHITA, Zivilrechtliche Einigungs- und Schlichtungsmodelle aus japanischer Sicht [Civil Law Models of Mediation and Conciliation from the Japanese Perspective], *in* Außergerichtliche Streitbeilegung [Out of Court Dispute Resolution] 12 (W. Röhl & M.K. Scheer, eds. 1993).

41 ÔTA, *id.*

42 From the annual statistics made by the Central Examining Committee. Since 1980, this number has remained almost the same.

43 *Id.*

44 YAMASHITA, *supra* note 40.

not be resolved by administrative guidances of the department responsible have been brought to the examining committee. As a result, all cases brought before the committee have been extremely complicated and the parties have often been very emotional.[45] In addition, given the fact that almost 80% of the cases handled by the examining committee involve at least one individual as a party, the administration seems to "mediate" disputes between enterprises outside of the purview of the administration's own ADR system.

4. *Toshi keikaku-hô*[46] *and Kaihatsu shidô yôkô*[47]

When a construction company plans to build an apartment building, it must obtain a construction permit from the governor responsible for the area of the construction. For this purpose, the *Toshi keikaku-hô* requires the company to get permission from the administrators of certain public facilities.[48] In addition, most municipalities regulate construction through the use of local regulations known as *Kaihatsu shidô yôkô* (outlines).[49] In Fukuoka prefecture, for example, 33 of the area's 35 municipalities maintain their own outlines as additional regulations. These outlines are very different in each municipality.[50] Most of the outlines require deliberations with certain local groups, for example with *Suiri Kumiai*, prior to construction.[51]

According to *Suibo-hô*,[52] partnerships can be established to administrate facilities such as embankments, lock gates, etc.[53] These partnerships normally have nearly a century of historical background as local groups commissioned by the state to regulate certain facilities. Due to their longstanding regulation of the facilities, these partnerships have developed their own concerns about aspects of development that might affect the flood control, etc. In addition, there are often many partnerships of this kind along a river and it is generally

---

45 Phone interview with a secretariat member of the Central Examining Committee on September 17, 1995.

46 City Planning Law, Law No. 100 of 1968 as amended by Law No. 79 of 1991.

47 Outlines of Instructions for Development, (issued by the various prefectures and cities).

48 The administrators of elementary- and junior high schools, gas facilities, electric facilities, and railways. Article 23 of the City Planning Law, Article 23 of its enforcement order, *supra* note 46.

49 *See* NIHON KEIZAI SHINBUN, September, 14, 1995.

50 *See* a research paper by *Kyûshû Tatemono Takuchi Kensetsu Keiei Kyôkai* [Kyûshû Management Association for Building and Residential Land Construction] which investigated 35 municipalities in Fukuoka prefecture. This paper, which was distributed to some newspapers, was offered to me by the secretariat of the association.

51 Partnership of Water Supply.

52 Flood Control Law, Law No. 193 of 1949 amended by Law no. 69 of 1995.

53 Article 1, Article 2 of that law.

quite complicated to accommodate the interests of the partnerships and those developers. The outlines often require, therefore, the permission of the partnerships of the flood control zone prior to the initiation of construction.

If the developer fails to obtain the flood control partnership's permission and nevertheless applies for the governor's construction permit, what would happen? Provided that the requirements of the outlines are not similarly required by the City Planning Law, the governor generally gives permission for construction to begin. In such an event, the developer's application for permission must first be provided to the lower municipality. The request for permission is then transmitted to the governor. If the permission of the partnership is not attached when the documents are forwarded to the lower municipality, the inferior municipality is likely to decide that the "deliberation" requirement is not yet fulfilled. Thus, the municipality would not accept the application nor transmit it to the governor. Such a response on the part of the municipality might well lead to enormous delays in construction. This, in turn, would increase the developer's interest payments, thus inflicting financial problems upon the developer. In order to avoid this situation, developers tend to offer some pecuniary incentive to encourage a "voluntary" resolution of any conflicts. In 1994, for example, a developer paid ¥2 million to a flood control partnership in order to construct only nine houses.[54]

5. *Consumer Protection and Product Liability*

In addition to disputes between enterprises, disputes between enterprises and consumers may influence the performance of enterprises. The *Shôhi-sha kihon-hô*[55] includes a fundamental provision on this point. Article 15 of the law states that municipalities shall try to mediate claims arising from transactions between enterprises and consumers and that the state and prefectures shall take appropriate measures in support of this process. A good illustration of this provision involves Japan's former product liability resolution system before the enactment of the recent Product Liability Law which went into effect in July 1995[56]. Under the former system, most prefectures maintained a *Shôhi Seikatsu Senta* (center).[57] The center's function was to hear claims, including those concerning product liability, from consumers and to give them advice accordingly. The centers did not mediate or arbitrate. No professional lawyer is involved with official activities of the center.

---

54 *Supra* note 49.

55 Fundamental Law of Consumer Protection, Law No. 78 of 1968 amended by Law No. 78 of 1983.

56 *Seizô-butso sekinin-hô*, Law No. 85 of 1994.

57 Consumer Life Center. There are 315 centers in Japan.

In addition to the center, each prefecture can establish a *Kujô Shori Iinkai* (committee).[58] In many cases, the relationship between the center and the committee was not clear. However the center was often able to transmit some cases to the committee, providing that the cases were concerned with "public interest." In other words, only those cases which were extremely difficult to resolve with the advice of the center or those cases which may have a great impact upon consumers' lives could be transmitted to the committee.[59]

Under the former system, each prefecture could require some additional steps prior to transmitting cases to the committee. In Fukuoka Prefecture, for example, the committee was a section of the Consumer Life Council. In order to transmit a case from the center to the committee, a case would have to first be sent to the council by the governor. When the council decided that a case was to be mediated by the committee, the committee could start its work. The work of the committee could only be undertaken, however, if all 10 members of the committee were in attendance.

In practice, the Fukuoka Prefecture Committee was not very active at all. Since 1977, only one case was transmitted to the committee. This case was, moreover, resolved before the mediation of the committee.[60] The situation was similar in other prefectures. Since 1991, the committees have convened at least once in only 24 prefectures. Two of these cases were concerned with product liability claims.[61] According to a 1991 survey, consumers presented their product liability claims directly to manufactures or retailers in 241 of 331 cases.[62] The product liability dispute resolution system established by the administration seems to have been largely unused.

6. *A Hypothesis*

From the above discussion, one can see that Japanese administration tends to establish "forums" for dispute resolution, especially when the gap between the relative power of the parties is wide. Examples of such forums include the *Shôchô-kyô* meeting of the *Daiten-hô*; the *Bunya-tô Chôsei Shingi-kai* Council of the *Bunya-tô chôsei-hô*; and the *Kyujô Shori Iinkai*. The administration often

---

58 Troubleshooting Committee. There are 52 committees in Japan.

59 *See*: *Kujô shori iinkai no arikata ni kansuru kenkyû-kai hôkoku-sho* [Report of the Research Group on the Ideal Troubleshooting Committee] commissioned and published by the Economic Planning Agency (1995).

60 Phone interview with a director of the Consumer Life Department of the Fukuoka Prefectural Government on September 9, 1995.

61 *Supra*, note 59.

62 *Tsûsho Sangyo-shô, Sangyo Seisaku-kyoku, Shôhikeizai-ka* (MITI, Industrial Policy Department, Consumer Economy Division] (ed.), *Purodakuto raiabiritsi taisaku handobukku* [Handbook for Product Liability Control Measures] 52 (1994).

urges the parties to find a "voluntary" solution (as in the case of the *Bunya-tô chôsei-hô* and the *Kaihatsu shidô yôkô* (outline)). Even if a given law neither requires nor anticipates "voluntary" resolution, the administration tends to urge parties to do so. The administration is not, however, willing to mediate or arbitrate. They simply take no action, or refuse to accept reports or to transmit applications. In this sense, the administrators remain "motionless." Although the administrators may issue some "guidances," these actions have neither any binding power nor legal basis. These are simply suggestions on how possibly to find a solution. Upon receiving such guidances, the parties try to find a solution voluntarily through negotiation and deliberation. If all parties to a dispute are satisfied with the solution, it is not necessary for them to use the court system or to consult lawyers. Only when the cases cannot be resolved through this process (namely when the size of damages, the number of the parties, the social resonance, the emotional reaction of the parties, etc., are problematic) are these cases brought to the court. The famous pollution cases of *Minamata* and *Kanemi Oil* might be understood in this context.

7. How Has the Dispute Resolution System Operated by the Administration Contributed to the Japanese Economy?

a. Through the mediation of the administration, enterprises often try to resolve their disputes by themselves. By doing so, enterprises can save litigation costs. Taking a lesson from the dispute between *Morinaga Nyûgyô* and the League of *Tôfu* Makers, one could also say that the parties can obtain benefits that are unavailable through litigation. For example, while it is true that Morinaga agreed to limit the production of long-life bean curd up to 50,000, thereby losing product sales, the company is able to recoup its losses through sales of other products. Morinaga, for example, sells not only long-life bean curd, but also milk products and candies. These products have been protected from foreign competition by the import tax. As a result of its cooperation with the League of *Tôfu* Makers, Morinaga may expect some further support from the Ministry of Agriculture, Forestry, and Fisheries. Morinaga may at least avoid strict administrative guidances from the ministry in the future.

One can assume the similar situation in the case of construction disputes. It is important for construction companies to obtain construction permits in an expedited and trouble-free manner and to maintain good relations with the Ministry of Construction. In other words, the enterprises may anticipate future benefits in return for current short-term losses.

When large enterprises accept losses in this way, medium- and small-sized enterprises can minimize their losses. *Toshiba*, for example, never required compensation from its subcontract manufacturers, even if the defective parts of these subcontract companies caused product liability claims and Toshiba paid the damages of the consumer.[63] As long as large companies maintain steady development, they can afford to accept losses.[64] This, in turn, has reduced burdens of medium- and small-sized companies, thereby allowing smaller companies to develop. In order for enterprises to determine if they can accept short-term losses, how they can obtain some more benefits in the future, how they can satisfy consumers' claims, etc., deliberation is the most flexible and appropriate means of dispute resolution. Through this method, all parties can be more or less satisfied and every sector of the Japanese economy can develop and expand.

b. I assume from statistics on legal aid that Japan chose that as its state policy.

Table 4

	UK	USA	Germany	France	Korea	Japan
Legal Basis since:	1988	1974	1980	1991	1986	none
Disbursment	190*	48.3*	26.2*	8.2*	0.9*	1.4*
	(1992)	(1990)	(1990)	(1992)	(1993)	(1992)
State Subsidy	156*	32.8*	26.2*	8.2*	0.64*	0.16*
	(1992)	(1990)	(1990)	(1992)	(1993)	(1992)
State Subsidy per person	2851¥	131¥	326¥	145¥	15¥	1¥

* billions of yen. Exchange rate: 1 Sterling = 170 ¥: 1 U.S.$ = 110 ¥; 1 DM = 65 ¥; 1 Fr = 20 ¥; 100 wong = 15 ¥.

Source: Annual report of Legal Aid Association 1994, p. 76.

As the above table indicates, Japan is quite reluctant to support the use of litigation.

63 Information provided by *T. Kitagawa* (*cf. supra* note 19).

64 Since Japan has no punitive damage system, the actual damages awarded are comparatively low and therefore it has been much easier for larger enterprises to accept losses.

Table 5

	State Subsidy in ¥ Million	Percentage of State Subsidy in the Annual Budget of the Legal Aid Association in %	Budget of the Ministry of Justice in ¥ Billion
1969	80	51.3	15.4
1970	85	48.0	18.6
1971	85	40.4	21.7
1972	82	35.7	25.4
1973	79	34.1	31.0
1974	79	32.7	38.3
1975	79	30.2	48.1
1976	64	23.5	54.8
1977	64	21.0	60.9
1978	64	22.3	67.0
1979	64	20.9	78.4
1980	64	19.0	78.5
1981	68	20.8	80.1
1982	72	19.9	79.6
1983	72	22.3	82.0
1984	72	22.5	92.5
1985	72	19.4	130.1
1986	72	16.3	143.2
1987	72	17.4	155.4
1988	72	15.7	156.9
1989	72	14.7	164.3
1990	104	15.2	174.9
1991	127	14.3	180.6
1992	150	14.1	191.3
1993	170	17.7	201.4
1994	191	18.7	-------

Source: Annual report of Legal Aid Association 1994, p. 57 and information collected by the author.

Two observations may be gleaned from the above table. First, the management of the legal aid system depends on resources other than the state subsidies. Second, the state has seemed uninterested in subsidizing the legal aid system. The subsidy is provided from the budget of the Ministry of Justice and this budget has constantly increased, while the subsidy remained virtually unchanged until 1989.

In addition, the fact that the number of Japanese judges in the last 15 years has remained almost unchanged relates to the issue of mediation[65]. Since the administration takes over the job of mediation and since it has become *de facto* state policy, the courts could perhaps remain small. The negative attitude of the Japanese court toward the Japanese administration might accelerate this tendency.[66]

8. *The Future of the Administration as Mediator?*

The forums established by the administration are closely connected with administrative regulations of the government. If the administration were to lose its power over the granting of permission or authorization under the current trend of deregulation, an important basis of the forums would be lost. If this were to occur, possible future benefits for enterprises would be lost.

Under the current tight economy, Japanese enterprises are losing the power to internalize short-term losses. As a result, cases such as those of the *Kaihatsu shidô yôkô* (*supra* 4) have been made public. This is so because the construction companies do not want to assume the costs for "pecuniary compensation" anymore. In addition, since the enactment of the new product liability law, product liability insurance is becoming popular. When harm is caused by

---

65

year	number of judges
1981	2761
1982	2767
1983	2774
1984	2783
1985	2792
1986	2800
1987	2808
1988	2813
1989	2818
1990	2823
1991	2828
1992	2835
1993	2842
1994	2852
1995	2864

Information provided by the Supreme Court.

66 *See* ASAHI SHINBUN (ed.), *Kokô no ôkoku, saibansho* [The Court as a Kingdom Keeping Itself Above All the Vulgarity], 218. (1991). Also *see*, J.O. HALEY, Japanese Administrative Law: An Introduction, *in* Law and Society in Contemporary Japan 31 (Haley, ed. 1988).

products of medium- and small-sized manufacturers, and when the damages are covered by the product liability insurance, the victim's insurance company will most likely require compensation from the manufacturers. In this event, the medium- and small-sized manufacturers must take these costs into consideration.[67] The insurance company may file suits against the manufacturers if manufacturers are reluctant to compensate victims.

In addition, the growing frequency of derivative suits will lead to the reluctance of executive directors to resolve disputes within the framework of business judgments. They will be required to find a clear and persuasive solution. In this context it is not surprising that one of Japan's three major business leagues is calling for reform and improvement of the Japanese court system.[68] Despite the remaining difficulties with regard to access to courts, the demand for court intervention and legal service will increase.

Despite the growing importance of the court system, the administration will likely still try to act as mediator. Depending upon how the administration approaches the situation, it may change from *de facto* to *de jure* mediator. Their reaction to the new product liability law is a good illustration of this potential. The new product liability law is based on the principles in the report of *Kokumin Seikatsu Shingi-kai*[69] published in 1993. This report also recommends reactivating the as yet largely unused Troubleshooting Committee as an ADR system for product liability cases. Many prefectures have started to follow this recommendation. In fact, Fukuoka Prefecture amended its regulations in September 1995 in order to ease the complicated procedures. As a result, the Consumer Life Council does not have to decide in each case if the case is to be mediated by the Troubleshooting Committee. The council may issue a comprehensive permit in advance. Finally, the committee can convene when at least three members attend.[70]

Since these prefectures did not use this committee as a product liability dispute resolution system, the Japanese government has tried to support its use by issuing model rules for use in the system. A report commissioned and published by the Economic Planning Agency includes many concrete and practical guidelines for using the committee as an ADR system, and also provides many examples of document forms. The report is expected to be used as a guidebook for prefectures. Most of the prefectures will adopt it as a model, and the ADR procedures in the committees will be more or less unified.

---

67 This does not necessarily mean that the amount of litigation will increase, because insurance companies and manufacturers may find solutions through settlement.

68 *See: Gendai nihon shakai no byôri to shohô* [Sickness of Contemporary Japanese Society and Prescriptions], a report edited and published by *Keizai Doyu-kai,* 8 (1994).

69 Council of National Life.

70 *Supra*, note 58.

D. Summary

Large Japanese enterprises try to resolve disputes through deliberation. When the parties cannot afford deliberation, the administration establishes forums for dispute resolutions. Since, however, the administration remains "motionless," the parties often try to arrive at a voluntary resolution. As a result of this process, each sector of the Japanese economy has been able to develop, leading ultimately to economic success. Only those disputes that could not be resolved in this way have been brought to the court.

However, some fundamental aspects of this system are being lost. In addition, reliance upon the court system is growing, while at the same time the administration is asserting its status as mediator. A turning point in the area of dispute resolution mechanism seems to be coming to Japan.

Chapter Three

Historical Trends of Civil Litigation in Japan, Arizona, Sweden, and Germany: Japanese Legal Culture in the Light of Judicial Statistics

*Christian Wollschläger**

Contents

---

* The author is indebted to many scholars who helped to collect and translate Japanese sources. Heartfelt thanks go to Professors *Setsuo Miyazawa* and *Tamotsu Isomura* (Kobe Univ.), *Kahei Rokumoto* (Tokyo Univ.), *Takao Tanase* (Kyoto Univ.), *Ryuichi Tsuno* (Chuo Univ.), *Shigeo Nishimura* (Kyushu Univ.), *Iwao Sato* (Osaka City Univ.), Dr. *Wilhelm Röhl* and Dr. *Harald Baum* (Hamburg), Dr. *Petra Schmidt* (Kobe), Ms. *Angelika Gruber* (Freiburg) and Mr. *Arnd Hafner* (Kyoto). The paper has been substantially revised since the oral presentation at the Berlin conference. *Cf. infra* note 112.

INTRODUCTION

The avoidance of litigation is a central element of the Japanese legal culture, perhaps its best-known feature. Judicial statistics have been presented as a standard piece of evidence since *Kawashima* introduced his ideas of Japanese legal consciousness to Western audiences.[1] His critics contended on the same basis that courts were used as frequently in Japan as in other industrialized nations.[2] Litigation rates were calculated which are notoriously low. Rising rates were seen as proof of increasing rights consciousness.[3] Judicial statistics were often used in a perfunctory manner, however. Their technical pitfalls -

---

1 *See* the tables in T. KAWASHIMA, Dispute Resolution in Contemporary Japan, *in* Law in Japan: The Legal Order in a Changing Society, 41, 60-72 (A. Van Mehren, ed. 1963).

2 J.O. HALEY, The Myth of the Reluctant Litigant, 4 J. JAP. STUD. 359, 364 (1978). *See* also J.M. RAMSEYER & M. NAKAZATO, The Rational Litigant: Settlement Amounts and Verdict Rates in Japan, 18 J. LEG. STUD. 263, 267 footnote 15 (1989); D.T. JOHNSON, Authority with Power: John Haley on Japan's Law and Politics, 27 L. & SOC. REV. 619, 623 (1993). But *see infra* note 23.

3 T. KAWASHIMA, The Status of the Individual in the Notion of Law, Right and Social Order in Japan, *in* The Status of the Individual in East and West 429, 440 (C.A. Moore, ed. 1968).

particularly dangerous in international comparison - were not avoided.[4] Usually data for single years were compared, neglecting large cyclical fluctuations over time.[5] Japanese historical statistics of civil justice have not been studied in full length, although retrospective data have been available for many years.[6]

This paper presents a systematic exploration of these sources. It attempts to establish historical roots of the avoidance of litigation on an empirical basis. The civil business of courts of first instance is analyzed as far back as possible. Japanese legal consciousness and legal culture are thus viewed from the perspective of quantitative history and international comparison.

At the outset, Japan's contemporary litigation rate per capita will be contrasted with other nations (part I). The historical analysis starts with an overview of the civil business of Japanese courts since the beginning of statistical reporting in 1875 (part II). Distinct phases of the development will be identified which require separate explanations. Scanty data on litigation in the 18th century will further be examined to trace possible continuities back to pre-modern Japan (part III). In general, longitudinal studies like the present reveal how structural factors in the causation of lawsuits operate in the historical dimension.[7] These include legal consciousness and legal culture because social values and attitudes towards law persist over generations.

Secular time series of three other countries will be presented in international comparison (part IV). Distinct historical growth patterns show that the demand for civil justice has reacted quite differently to urbanization and industrialization since the 19th century. Arizona represents the U.S., where civil caseloads have risen so high that a "litigation explosion" is seen by many.[8] Among European nations, Sweden offers the reverse development. In this country, litigation declined for more than a century after 1830. Reaching still farther back to the 18th century, German and Prussian time series combine elements of both secular patterns. They illustrate how the wide gap between Japanese and Western litigation rates emerged.

---

4 *See* text accompanying note 19 *infra*.

5 *See*text accompanying note 29 *infra*.

6 SAIKÔ SAIBANSHO JIMU SÔKYOKU [Supreme Court. General Secretariat], *Meiji i-kô saiban tôkei yôran* [Synopsis of Post-Meiji Judicial Statistics] (1969). HALEY, *supra* note 2, at 363 overlooked the official source and the earliest period. *Cf.* also M. KATO, The Role of Law and Lawyers in Japan and the United States, BRIGHAM YOUNG U.L. REV. 627, 664 (1987). The standard source book of general historical statistics presents incomplete and misleading data; *see* appendix.

7 *Cf.* the special issue on longitudinal studies on litigation in 24 L. & SOC. REV., No. 2 (1990) with references at 619-642.

8 W. OLSON, The Litigation Explosion (1991). *Cf.* M. GALANTER, Reading the Landscape of Disputes: What We Know and Don't Know and Think We Know About Our Allegedly Litigious Society, 31 UCLA L. REV. 4, 6-11 (1983).

In 1990, the German rate per capita was sixteen times as high as the Japanese rate. The two countries occupy opposite ends of the scale: Germany ranks in the top group, whereas contemporary Japan has the lowest position among industrialized nations. The contrast exists in spite of many parallels in law and modern civilization. Japanese civil procedure was modeled after the German *Civilprozessordnung* of 1877. The institutional framework of judicial dispute resolution is nearly identical, providing a reliable basis for international comparison. Both nations are among the richest in the world. But why does prosperity produce a high level of litigation in one country and not in the other?

Answers will be sought in the last part of the paper (part V). Contemporary avoidance of litigation is best understood as the result of effective social means of extra-judicial dispute resolution, notably negotiation and private conciliation in a network of close personal relations. The historical origins of these attitudes are ably presented in *Haley's* latest book.[9] In this volume, *Henderson* provides the most recent and convincing arguments in support of this view.[10] The latter must be reconciled with the fact, however, that litigation was more frequent in the Japanese past, including the late 19th century and the Edo period. Hence doubts arise as to the historical origins of Japanese legal consciousness. Is the avoidance of litigation really pre-modern, as Kawashima suggested?[11] Or did it rather develop in our century, as his critics argue?[12]

This paper suggests that the avoidance of litigation is indeed rooted in the feudal period. The long-term stagnation of litigation rates on a low level is presented as evidence of stable social means to enforce private rights and solve disputes with a minimum of lawsuits.

Looking towards the future, Kawashima expected that the traditional reluctance to sue would fade in the course of further modernization. He even predicted that the Japanese would resort to courts more frequently to demonstrate more rights consciousness.[13] This part of his thesis, too, has been

---

9 J.O HALEY, Authority Without Power: Law and the Japanese Paradox, ch. 3, 5, 8 (1991).

10 See *supra* Chapter One.

11 *Kawashima's* writings are summarized *in* K. ROKUMOTO, Problems and Methodology of the Study of Civil Disputes. Part I, 5 LAW IN JAPAN 97, 101-113 (1972). *See* also G. RAHN, Rechtsdenken und Rechtsauffassung in Japan [Legal Thought and Conceptions of Law in Japan] 216-239 (1990); S. MIYAZAWA, Taking Kawashima Seriously, 21 L. & SOC. REV. 219 (1987).

12 HALEY, *supra* note 2 is the "classic"; J.M. RAMSEYER, Reluctant Litigant Revisited: Rationality and Disputes in Japan, 14 J. JAP. STUD. 111 (1988); T. TANASE, The Management of Disputes: Automobile Accident Compensation in Japan, 24 L. & SOC. REV. 651, 665 (1990). For a recent review of the debate, *see* D.H. FOOTE, Resolution of Traffic Accident Disputes and Judicial Activism in Japan, 25 LAW IN JAPAN 19-23 (1995).

13 "In the long run people will develop a keener rights consciousness and assert their rights more vigorously. As a means of doing this, they will resort to the formal

met with disbelief in the literature.[14] Here a forecast will be offered to the effect that the Japanese demand for civil justice will indeed rise to higher levels in the long run. Whether this really confirms Kawashima remains to be seen.

The present study is severely limited by the author's ignorance of the Japanese language. He has been attracted by the abundance and technical excellence of Japanese judicial statistics. Originally, the research was not designed to test hypotheses in the vast literature on Japanese legal consciousness. Since the findings contradict much of what has been written in this field, a thorough discussion would be necessary. Regrettably, brief concluding remarks must suffice. An attempt to overcome the language barrier still seemed to be worth the risk. Geographically, Japan is located at even distances between the U.S. and Germany. The case of Japan is of prime value in the comparison of Eastern and Western legal cultures. The paper therefore relies on Western-language literature (with the exception of the statistical sources, of course) and focuses on quantitative issues in the macro-social or macro-economic perspective.[15]

PART I: LITIGATION RATES IN INTERNATIONAL COMPARISON

1. *Contemporary Litigation Rates*

Japan's rank on a scale of contemporary litigation rates is illustrated by figure 1. The total rate of 6.4 cases per 1,000 total population in 1990 includes ordinary lawsuits (*soshô*) and, in addition, dunning procedure (*tokusoku*), general conciliation (*chôtei*), and conciliation in the family court. It must be multiplied many times to reach Western levels. Factors of 15 and 16 are necessary to reach the top group of Israel, Germany, and Sweden. Contrary to widespread beliefs, the highest position is *not* occupied by the U.S., where claims to be "the most litigious nation in the world" have been made.[16] Nevertheless, 18 million civil cases filed in American state courts of first

procedure of lawsuit or trial more frequently." *Nihon-jin no hô-ishiki* [Legal Consciousness of the Japanese], Vol. 2, p. 202 (1967), transl. ROKUMOTO, *supra* note 11, at 106. *See* also *id., supra* note 1, at 57-59, *id., supra* note 3 at. 440.

14 HALEY, *supra* note 9, at 175.

15 Limited space prohibits a discussion of sources and methodology. *See* C. WOLLSCHLÄGER, Die Arbeit der Zivilgerichte im historischen und internationalen Vergleich [The Work of Civil Trial Courts in Historical and International Comparison], *in* Prozeßflut? Studien zur Prozeßtätigkeit europäischer Gerichte in historischen Zeitreihen und im Rechtsvergleich [Floods of Litigation? Studies on the Activities of European Courts in a Historical and Comparative Perspective] 21-114 (E. Blankenburg, ed. 1989).

16 *Cf.* the literature cited by GALANTER, *supra* note 8.

instance[17] tower above the total Japanese caseload of about one million during recent years. Reduced to the size of population, a median of 68 cases per 1,000 population of American states in 1990 still exceeds Japan by more than tenfold. Judicial statistics safely establish the wide distance from Western industrial nations. Contrary to what has been written, the Japanese demand for civil justice is clearly below all European and U.S.-American levels, even if more types of cases are counted here than usual.[18]

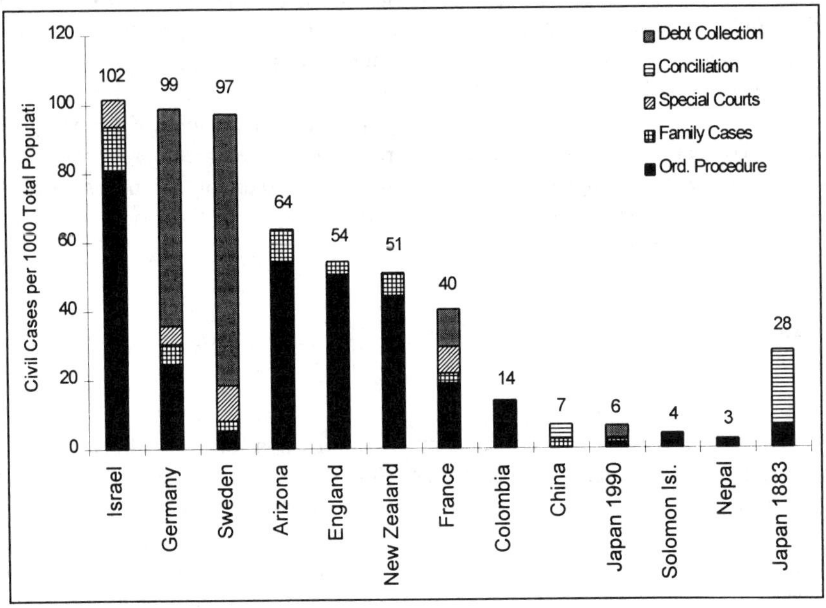

Figure 1: International Litigation Rates 1990

On the other hand, figure 1 shows that the rare use of civil courts is not unique to Japan. Seven million civil cases before the Chinese People's Mediation Committees yield a rate of 6.4, which is as low as the Japanese. Judicial statistics of third-world countries offer even less: 4.2 in the Solomon Islands, e.g., or 2.6 in Nepal. At first glance, these low rates might be attributed to economic underdevelopment. This explanation obviously would not fit the case of prospering Japan. The latter suggests indeed that social attitudes and cultural values may influence the demand for civil justice even more strongly than the economy.

17 Source: State Court Caseload Statistics: Annual Report 1990, 4, 14 (1992).

18 *See* text accompanying note 23 *infra*.

Table 1: International Litigation Rates 1990 Civil Cases Filed in Courts of First Instance per 1000 Total Population

Country	Total	Ordinary Procedure	Family Cases	Special Courts	Con-ciliation	Debt Collection
Israel[a)]	101.5	81.0	12.7	7.8		
Germany[b)]	*98.5*	24.6	5.8	5.2		*63.0*
Sweden[b)]	*97.3*	5.5	2.6	10.2		*79.0*
Arizona	63.7	54.4	9.2			
England	54.2	50.5	3.6			
France 1988	40.3	18.8	2.9	7.7		11.0
New Zealand 1987	50.8	44.2	6.6			
Colombia	13.8	13.8				
China	6.7		2.6		4.1	
Japan 1990	6.4	1.6	0.7		0.5	3.6
Solomon Islands 1985	4.2	4.2				
Nepal	2.6	2.6				
Japan 1883	28.0	6.3			21.7	

a) Family Cases = Religious Courts, b) Dunning cases reduced by estimated 12% for double counts (estimated figures in italics). *Sources*: *see* appendix.

2. *Counting Cases in Historical and International Comparison*

The historical Japanese litigation rate of 1883 raises methodological issues. How can data on civil litigation be interpreted meaningfully over time and between different legal orders?

a. Functional Approach

The problem of historical comparison is presented by the different types of cases which were counted for 1883 and 1990. In addition to ordinary lawsuits (*soshô*), these were cases of successful *kankai* conciliation before 1891 when the Code of Civil Procedure came into force.[18a] The latter abolished *kankai* and introduced dunning (*tokusoku*). Are statistical results really comparable in spite of the different categories?

The same question arises in international comparison. The rank order would be quite different if ordinary lawsuits before regular courts were counted. Due to the large share of debt collection cases, Sweden would drop from the top to near the bottom, and Germany would take on a middle position. Japan would

18a *Minji soshô-hô*, Law No. 29 of 1890 as amended by law No. 66 of 1994. For an English translation, *see* EIBUN-HOREI-SHA, EHS Law Bulletin Series, Vol. II., FA, No. 2100.

rank absolutely lowest, whereas Israel would remain the leader - exceeding Japan by a factor of 50 (instead of 16 on the basis of the total). So what is the adequate unit of counting in international comparison of judicial statistics?

Whereas the literature counts ordinary cases as they are found in national statistics, this study uses a functional approach.[19] All types of civil procedure in which judicial functions are performed are included, regardless of their qualification under national law. Conciliation is counted because consensual settlement of disputes is the duty of judges as well as the adjudication of contradictory cases in ordinary procedure. The same applies to dunning and administrative debt collection because the courts have to enforce uncontested money claims.

Historical and international comparison requires a functional approach because the various means of judicial remedies substitute for one another. As a rule, creditors may choose between ordinary and special types of procedure. For this reason, the number of regular civil cases is determined by the availability of procedural alternatives.[20] The societal demand for civil justice has to be measured by the total input into the court system. Only the sum of different case types represents all incidents in which private citizens submit particular facts to the judicial branch of government asking to enforce their claims. This macro-variable can be meaningfully compared between nations and over time as an object of sociolegal inquiry.

If the criteria of national law were applied instead, China would disappear from table 1. The People's Mediation Committees do not constitute formal courts at all. They were included, though, because mediation is *de facto* mandatory. The regular courts reject cases which have not been processed by the committees,[21] so the business of the latter represents the Chinese demand for civil justice.

The usual method of counting necessarily ranks Anglo-American jurisdictions ahead of continental European nations. As a rule, only the standard type of civil procedure is available in the U.S., whereas dunning and conciliation are unknown.[22] Excluding the latter systematically distorts the comparison

19 For details, *see* WOLLSCHLÄGER, *supra* note 15, at 30-43. *Cf.* KATO, *supra* note 6, at 657. In this volume, HENDERSON (*supra* Chapter One) uses a functional approach. He counts lawyers including paralegal personnel in addition to the organized bar.

20 *See* E. BLANKENBURG, The Infrastructure for Avoiding Litigation: Comparing Cultures and Legal Behavior in the Netherlands and West Germany, 28 L. & SOC. REV. 789 (1994).

21 Legally, conciliation is voluntary. *See* D. XICHUAN & ZH. LINGYUAN, China's Legal System: A General Survey 209 (1990). The authors' emphasis on the constitutional right to litigate raises skepticism, however. A different actual practice was suggested by Professor *R. Berring*, a teacher of Chinese law.

22 For an overview, *see* C. WOLLSCHLÄGER, Bagatelljustiz? Eine rechtshistorische, rechtsvergleichende und empirische Untersuchung des vereinfachten Verfahrens am Amtsgericht [Petty Justice? Simplified Procedure in Lower Courts in Historical,

with continental European systems, because civil procedure is more diversified there.

The correct method of counting is essential in determining Japan's international rank. Haley's critique of Kawashima was based on the assumption that litigation was on a normal level and even more frequent than in some other industrialized nations. This was erroneous because he omitted debt collection cases and relied on political scientists who had overlooked a whole branch of the Norwegian court system.[23] The reluctant litigant is a reality, not a myth.

b. Double Counts

Including alternative types of civil procedure raises the statistical problem of double counts.[24] The same case is reported twice in judicial statistics when it is transferred from one type of procedure to another. In the dunning procedure, the objection of the debtor initiates a new ordinary lawsuit. If conciliation is unsuccessful, the dispute is continued in the regular procedure. The number of these cases must be deducted in order to obtain only those cases which have been finally disposed of by dunning procedure or conciliation. Adding the result to the regular cases yields the "adjusted total" of civil filings. This variable is an appropriate measure of the demand for civil justice. It is used in this paper for the Japanese series.[25]

Often libraries or the sources themselves do not allow the fulfillment of the theoretical requirements. Most special series of judicial statistics are rare books. Statistical yearbooks do not contain the necessary procedural details, if

---

Comparative and Empirical Perspective], *in* Neue Methoden im Zivilverfahren [New Ways in Civil Procedure] 13-108 at 36-44 (E. Blankenburg *et al.*, eds. 1991).

23 HALEY, *supra* note 2, at 364 ranked Scandinavian nations below Japan citing A. SARAT & J. GROSSMAN, Courts and Conflict Resolution: Problems in the Mobilization of Adjudication, 69 AM. POL. SCI. REV. 1200, 1208 (1975). The latter placed Norway below Japan because local conciliation boards were omitted. The boards make final decisions in spite of their historical name. They handled 91% of all civil cases in 1985; [Norway] Statistik Sentralbyrå. Statistisk Årbok [Statistical Yearbook], Vol. 106, 1987, p. 130. *Cf.* also RAMSEYER & NAKAZATO, supra note 2; HALEY, *supra* note 9, at 110 footnote 118, 216, and most recently JOHNSON, *supra* note 2, at 623. KATO, *supra* note 6, at 656-658 reproduced *Sarat & Grossman's* list, but cautiously arrived at the position of the text.

24 The literature ignores the problem. *Cf.* the list of nations in GALANTER, *supra* note 8, at 52-54. Various types of procedure are added indiscriminately and inconsistently. Debt collection cases, e.g., are included for Sweden but not for Germany.

25 The data on new cases are taken from the official retrospective until 1967 (*supra* note 6 tables 9-11; 23-25, 36-37; 70-79; 83-86, 93, 94). Later years and data on the disposition of conciliation and dunning cases are based on the original series; *see* appendix. Missing years were estimated.

they report dunning cases at all. Estimates must then fill the gap. If the gross total is used for lack of precise data (as, e.g., for Germany and Sweden), the analyst must be aware that the input into the court system is overstated. Like most statistics of the economy, judicial statistics contain a considerable margin of error. They measure judicial activity only approximately. This is no reason to ignore the empirical data, however. No alternative source permits a comprehensive view of the real functioning of courts in the macro-perspective.

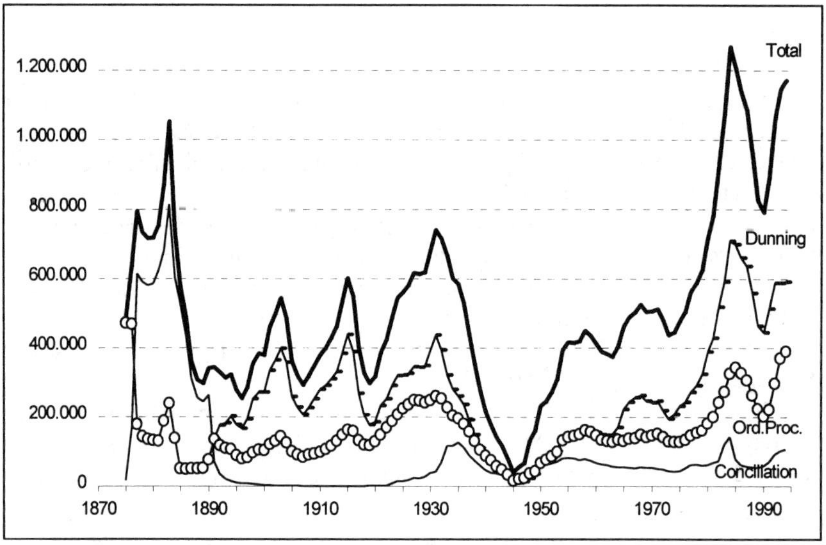

Figure 2. Japan: Civil Cases in Courts of First Instance 1875-1994

PART II: 120 YEARS OF CIVIL CASES IN JAPANESE COURTS OF FIRST INSTANCE

Figure 2 illustrates the civil business in courts of first instance for more than a century. The graph presents the adjusted total of new civil cases (exclusive of double counts).[26] Ordinary lawsuits in first instance (*dai-isshin soshô*) have existed over the whole time span. Other case types vary according to the changing law of civil procedure. *Kankai* conciliation cases dominated the caseload during the initial phase of the modern court system (1875-1890). In 1891 the Code of Civil Procedure introduced dunning (*tokusoku*), provisional

26 *See* text accompanying note 25 *supra*. For sources and data, *see* appendix.

injunction, and provisional attachment (*kari-shobun, kari-sashiosae*).[27] A new type of conciliation (*wakai*) was provided, but it disappeared practically after a few years. Due to the tiny share of the total (< 1%), the line is hardly visible in the graph for the following 30 years. Beginning in 1922, special conciliation procedures (*chôtei*) were successively enacted. The Conciliation Law of 1951 later provided a uniform procedure which appears in the graph as the lowest line.[28]

The graph looks bewildering at first sight. The time series reveals large litigation waves which mean a doubling or tripling of the caseload within few years.[29] They characterize the series until World War II, which is marked by a deep trough. During the postwar decades, comparatively moderate undulations prevailed. But starting in 1973, a litigation explosion erupted again. The filings tripled in ten years until 1984. The outburst collapsed until the next trough in 1990. The most recent statistical data indicate by their upward direction that the pattern will be repeated. The economic problems of the early 1990s are likely to produce a new peak of judicial business.

How can we interpret the erratic long-term development?

1. Phases of Civil Litigation

The irregular shape of the time series suggests that different explanations are applicable for single time spans. Separate phases can be isolated by computing a long-term trend. Two breaks are identified by different methods.[30] The first occurred in or about the year 1889, during the transition from the climax of 1883 to the cyclical wave pattern of the prewar phase; the second occured in or about 1973, before the historical maximum in 1984. World War II presents the third discontinuity. As a result, five phases of Japanese civil litigation emerge on the whole:[31]

---

27 Both types of summary procedure have been combined with the dunning cases in the graph. Actions for checks and bills (*tegatta, kogitte soshô*) were also added since 1965, due to the summary nature of the procedure.

28 Family courts were established as a mediation institution in 1939. Their conciliation cases have been counted in the total, but have been omitted from the graph for visual clarity.

29 The common use of data for single years in the literature is quite unreliable for this reason.

30 A moving average of five years exhibits 1889 and 1973 as precise turning points. These years are consistent with a fourth-order polynomial which runs straight before and after World War II. It was computed in the graph for the whole time span, yielding a significant fit of r_ = 0.588 for N = 120. See also fig. 10 (*infra* sec. V.1) where trend lines of the litigation rate are shown for single phases.

31 Note that the phases are based on breaks in the causation of lawsuits which is mainly economic in nature. *Henderson's* phases in the development of conciliation

A: The Start of Modern Courts 1875-1889;
B: Imperial Japan 1889-1937;
C: War and Recovery 1938-1953;
D: Postwar Economic Expansion 1954-1973;
E: Contemporary Development 1974-1994.

2. *Phase A: The Start of Modern Courts (1875-1889)*

The initial phase of the modern courts was characterized by a stepwise adaptation from the old system of justice to the new.[32] Civil procedure was not yet codified. The Ministry of Justice instead directed judges how to proceed and to decide cases according to the time-honored principle of sound reason (*jôri*).[33] Judicial statistics display perhaps the most salient aspect of transition: the continuance and prevalence of conciliation. The latter had been the dominant mode of disposition in the Edo period (1603-1868), when the parties were more or less involuntarily brought to settle their disputes before the Shogunal authorities.[34] After the new court system had been established by the law of 1872, no formal conciliation procedure seems to have existed initially. The courts soon resorted to former practice, however, demanding an attempt of conciliation between the parties as a prerequisite to adjudication. In 1876, *kankai* procedure was prescribed as mandatory by the Ministry of Justice. The measure was enormously successful: 80% of all cases and more were settled in *kankai* as long as it was available.[35]

The peak of litigation in 1883 strikes the eye as the most conspicuous feature of this phase. After 1875, filings doubled within eight years. At the climax, the courts of first instance had to process over one million cases (double counts eliminated). Afterwards the litigation explosion collapsed in the six years until 1889. The extreme movement occurred during the so-called *Matsukata* finance in the first half of the 1880s.[36] This coincidence gives clear

---

use legal criteria, yet the result is similar. *Cf.* D.F. HENDERSON, Conciliation and Japanese Law: Tokugawa and Modern, VOL. 2, p. 208 (1965).

32 *See* R. ISHII, Legislation in the Meiji Era 295-320 (W. Chambliss, transl. 1958). For an overview *see* RAHN, *supra* note 12, at 85-91.

33 *See* W. RÖHL, Rechtsgeschichtliches zu *jôri* [*Jôri* from a Historical Perspective], *in* Das Japanische im japanischen Recht [The "Japaneseness" of Japanese Law] 49 (H. Menkhaus, ed. 1994).

34 *See* HENDERSON, *supra* note 31, Vol. 1, at 127-171; C. STEENSTRUP, A History of Law in Japan until 1868, 157-158 (1991); HALEY, *supra* note 14, at 57-58.

35 *See* also fig. 3 and appendix table 3 for the share of *kankai* cases.

36 *See* ERICSON, Matsukata fiscal policy, *in* Kodansha Encyclopedia of Japan, Vol. 4, p. 133 (1983); E.S. CRAWCOUR, *in* Cambridge History of Japan, Vol. 5, p. 608 *et seq.* (1989).

indications of the economic origins of the litigation wave. The *Meiji* reforms of land ownership and agrarian taxation after 1868 had caused a monetary crisis which was followed by inflation during the *Satsuma* wars. As the finance minister drastically shortened the supply of money, civil filings rose. When the measures became effective after 1883, the economy recovered and litigation decreased. Debt collection cases were obviously responsible for the flood of litigation. The shortage of money caused the defaults of debtors and at the same time prompted creditors to sue. Economic recovery later reduced judicial business.

The extreme size of the litigation wave as well as its causes illustrate the specific problems of the Meiji reform phase. The modern courts were established under extraordinary economic conditions which were not repeated later. In the long run of history, phase A has to be considered as a singular event. As such it is not representative of normal economic and social situations. For this reason, the frequent use of courts before 1889 does not provide evidence against the Kawashima thesis. These 15 years are irrelevant because social attitudes towards litigation persist over generations.

3. Phase B: Imperial Japan (1889-1937)

The Code of Civil Procedure went into force in 1891, two years after the break in the long-term trend. The short time interval is important to note that the new law had no immediate effect on the demand for civil justice. The litigation rate had reached its minimum under the old law. The lower volume of the following years had purely economic reasons: crisis was over.

Later crises had a different impact on the litigation waves. Figure 2 exhibits a new form which is more even in shape. The crisis of the Meiji reforms induced a relatively short explosion of caseloads in an economy which was still basically agrarian. Later cyclical fluctuations successively increased in amplitude until they reached the peak in 1931. Just as in earlier times (and everywhere), the causal force behind the ups and downs was the business cycle. The new pattern indicates more regularity as a result of industrialization which progressed steadily after World War I.

The big waves make it difficult to detect the upward long-term trend. Visual inspection of the graph may be oriented by the peaks (1903, 1915, 1931) and troughs (1896, 1907, 1919). In 1937, the caseload had risen by 73% over 1896, representing a modest average increase of 1.7% in 42 years. Computing a linear trend function secures that the growth of civil business was in fact nearly precisely limited to the growth of total population. The mean litigation rate remained constant at a stable value of 8.0 cases per 1,000 total population over half a century between 1889 and 1938.[37]

This means that, in spite of the large fluctuations of the caseload, the whole generative system of civil litigation returned to a constant equilibrium path, merely adapting to the increase of population. Either the growth of the economy had no impact - or, if it had, its effect must have been balanced by factors which operated in the opposite direction. In the net result, civil litigation remained immune against an obvious consequence of economic growth. The data thus illustrate social stability for an important period of Japanese modernization. Since the phase of imperial Japan (B) extended over half a century, it is safe to conclude that permanent causal structures of litigation persisted which are representative for earlier and later phases. This hypothesis requires closer scrutiny, of course.[38]

In this decisive stage of modernization, Western law and the modern courts achieved a firm hold in Japan. As industrialization progressed, the legal profession expanded and the courts were gradually used more frequently. Contrary to Haley's earlier conclusions, however, the long-term development of civil litigation had nothing to do with the number of lawyers.[39] The lawyer population expanded rapidly (449% between 1896 and 1934 = 11.5% p.a.), whereas adjusted filings only grew at the slow pace of the population (1.7% p.a. as mentioned). The size of one growth process (lawyers) was seven times as large as the other (litigation). The different dimensions of the change exclude the possibility that the two processes were causally related.[40] Lawyers were highly concentrated in Tokyo, leaving large parts of Japan bare of professional

---

37 Due to the large fluctuations, precise values depend on the base year and the computational method. A first measure is to follow the troughs. The litigation rate was 7.5 cases per 1,000 total population in 1889; 6.1 units in 1896; 6.2 units in 1907; 5.4 units in 1919; 6.2 units in 1937. The text uses the linear trend as a more reliable tool of time series analysis. *See infra* fig. 10 and *note* 111. The same per capita rate is computed on the basis of the adult population (20 years and over). Changes in the age structure of the population were irrelevant.

38 *See infra* sec. III. and V.1.

39 HALEY, *supra* note 2, at 383-385. But *see id. supra* note 9, at 99-100.

40 The conclusion of the text is based on plain inspection of absolute numbers. This may be surprising since *Haley* presented statistical evidence for a causal relation between lawyer population and litigation. His methodology was unsuited, however. Size effects were eliminated by regression equations. Using annual rates of change for new civil cases as the dependent variable eliminated the long-term trend. The result therefore proves a middle-term causal relation only. The latter is obvious during the Great Depression (*id.* at 372 fig. 2). *Haley's* significant correlation coefficients are probably an artefact created by the numeric weight of these few years. This confirms the historical criticism raised by TANAKA, 42 HIKAKU-HÔ KENKYÛ 46, 61 (1982); cited from KATO, *supra* note 6, at 665.

legal counsel until today.[41] This small group was not relevant for the size of everyday civil business in courts. The demographic factor alone explains the increase of litigation.

The data before and after 1891 illustrate how the Code of Civil Procedure, which came into effect that year, changed the composition of the caseload. Japanese judicial statistics offer one of the rare cases where the transition can be observed with accuracy.[42] As conciliation nearly disappeared, the number of ordinary civil cases leaped upward by 49% from 1890 to 1891. In spite of the new law, the adjusted total remained nearly unchanged (+ 1%). The dunning procedure filled the gap which was left by the *de facto* abolition of *kankai*. Societal demand for civil justice thus developed continuously according to the conditions of the economy, while the forms of supply were changed by the new law of civil procedure. Dunning and conciliation proved to be functionally equivalent as the primary means of debt collection.

The tradition of informal civil justice was effectively discontinued. With quite similar political intentions, the German Code of Civil Procedure of 1877 had abolished lay judges and decision making by equity, which had been common in many German territories.[43] The idea of *Rechtsstaat* (due process) instead required adjudication by professional judges who applied written law. These liberalistic principles were readily accepted by the Meiji reformers. They remained unchallenged in Japan for the next three decades.

Later in the *Taisho* era, judicial policy reverted to the Japanese tradition. The idea of informal justice was revived by special conciliation procedures (*chôtei*). They were successively instituted to solve sensitive social problems such as landlord-tenant relations and insolvency.[44] The measurable effect was marginal, however, as the lowest line in figure 2 shows. The political aspirations were not fulfilled.[45]

4. *Phase C: War and Recovery (1938-1953)*

The continuous decline of civil caseloads after 1931 makes it difficult to determine the precise year in which the impact of war became effective. The

---

41 *See* HENDERSON, *supra* Chapter One. Recent research shows that civil filings depend on the frequency of *pro se* litigation (i.e., without attorneys). T. TANASE, *Gendai shakai to bengoshi* [Modern Society and Lawyers] ch. 1 (1987).

42 *Cf.* WOLLSCHLÄGER, *supra* note 15, at 38-41 for Prussia 1833, 1846 and Sweden 1948.

43 *Cf.* DAHLMANNS *in* Handbuch der Quellen und Literatur der neueren europäischen Privatrechtsgeschichte [Handbook of Sources and Literature of Modern European History of Private Law], VOL. III/2, p. 2672 *et seq.* (H. Coing, ed. 1982).

44 HALEY, *supra* note 2, at 373-378; *id., supra* note 9, at 85-96.

45 *See infra* text accompanying note 61.

business of courts gradually came to a halt. The causes are extraordinary in nature and need not be discussed here in detail for the moment.[46]

During the years of recovery, civil caseloads climbed steeply until 1953. The end of this process is marked by a bend in the curve which again signals a break in the long-term trend.[47] The postwar phase therefore requires separate examination.

5. *Phase D: Postwar Economic Expansion (1954-1973)*

After 1954, characteristic features of the prewar development returned for two decades. Ordinary civil cases had about the same volume as in the trough of 1919. Conciliation gradually declined until 1974, returning to the level of 1930. Dunning cases rose in unspectacular dimensions. The slight upward direction of the adjusted total continued the tendency of the phase of imperial Japan (B) and - more surprisingly - the increase of civil caseloads was again limited to population growth until the next trend break in 1973.[48] A stable generative process of litigation continued for over two decades, just as before the war.

Figure 2 also exhibits two novel elements of the postwar phase.

The big litigation waves of imperial Japan (phase B) had disappeared. A smoothly undulating pattern instead characterizes the phase of postwar economic expansion (D). It is quite similar to the fluctuations which civil courts experience in other industrialized nations. Japan had undergone a transition to a modern cyclical pattern and left behind a pre-modern wave type. The latter has been observed in Scandinavian countries during the 19th century and in a German time series of the 17th century.[49] In pre-modern agrarian economies, creditors seem to have reacted more sensitively to economic crises, whereas the business cycle had less impact in the progress of industrialization. Emerging mass prosperity presents the most obvious difference between prewar and postwar Japan. It was more profitable for creditors to drop claims and seek new customers rather than risking time and money in lawsuits.

The second structural change concerns both the volume of civil cases and the litigation rate. The average adjusted total of new civil cases was one quarter

---

46 *See infra* sec. IV.3 for German parallels.

47 The break is revealed by the abrupt decline of the annual percentage of change. Between 1948 and 1954, rates ranged from 15% to 55% for ordinary lawsuits and 6% to 44% for the adjusted total. Later they ranged between 9% and 8% only.

48 Caseloads rose by 39% from 1954 to 1973, parallel to the growth of population (*infra* sec. V.1).

49 For Sweden, *see infra* sec. IV.2 fig. 6; in general C. WOLLSCHLÄGER, *supra* note 15, at 99, *id.*, Civil Litigation and Modernization: The Work of the Municipal Courts of Bremen in Five Centuries, 1549-1984, 24 L. & SOC. REV. 261, 269-271 (1990).

less than in 1935.[50] The litigation rate dropped by about one half from an average rate of 8.0 cases per 1,000 population in imperial Japan (phase B) down to 4.5 units between 1954 and 1973.[51] A downward shift in the long-term development thus constitutes the most remarkable feature of the postwar phase (D). Civil litigation stagnated at the 1954 level for two decades, adapting only to population growth. The demand for civil justice was saturated. Since the ceiling was below the prewar level, there must have been a causal event in the meantime which obstructed a return to previous conditions.

Was this the early *Showa* judicial policy which Haley held responsible for the rare use of courts?[52] The regulation of legal education in 1930 had restricted the number of judges and attorneys to the capacity of post-university legal education (the Legal Training and Research Institute). The supply of manpower available for judicial and other legal services was thus structurally limited. In Haley's view, this made the courts less effective to the extent that the overburdened court system itself became a deterrent to litigation.

Although the statistical data are compatible with the institutional explanation of the avoidance of litigation, they do not provide positive proof. Other causes may have worked to the same effect. The Japanese economic expansion after the Korean War could have reduced the demand for judicial dispute resolution and debt collection. Besides, it is still an open question whether civil justice has become less efficient. Rational choice theory attributes low litigation rates to the superior quality of the Japanese courts, particularly to the predictability of decisions.[53] As long as alternative causes are not excluded, the institutional approach is a conclusive hypothesis only.[54]

6. *Phase E: Contemporary Development (1974-1994)*

The most recent development offers a new pattern which comes closer to Kawashima's expectations of a rising demand for civil justice.[55]

---

50 The arithmetic mean for 1954 to 1975 is 24.5% lower than the adjusted total of 1935 (a midpoint year in the wave, situated at the intersection of a linear trend with the serial value).

51 Both values are obtained from computation of linear trends of the adjusted total for the years 1889-1937 (B) and 1954-1975 (D). These years have been selected to measure from midpoint to midpoint in the wave. Using the trough of 1973 would have tilted the trend.

52 HALEY, *supra* note 2; *id. supra* note 9, at 110 and the literature cited *supra* in note 12.

53 *See* RAMSEYER & NAKAZATO, *supra* note 2, at 263. *See* also FOOTE, *supra* note 12, who emphasizes judicial activism.

54 For further discussion, *see* text accompanying note 131 *infra*.

55 *Supra* note 13.

The year 1984 exposed Japanese courts of first instance to their largest burden in history. Figure 2 exhibits a litigation wave of prewar dimensions, even higher than the peak of 1883. The extreme movement occurred after the break in the long-term trend which can be dated to the years 1973-1975.[56] The structural nature of the change is established by the fact that the following trough in 1990 was 88% above the preceding trough in 1973.

Judicial observers attributed the peak of litigation in 1984 to the expansion of small-scale loans and consumer credit. Kato saw changes in the financial market after the oil crisis when new types of consumer credit became popular.[57] His explanation seems to be plausible, since other nations offer examples of similar developments.[58]

The trend break thus signals an increase in the future volume of litigation. It raises new questions as to whether the avoidance of litigation will continue in Japan. But the apparent economic causes exclude the theory that the latest development has anything to do with more rights consciousness or an increasing need for normative rationality as Kawashima expected.

7. *The Composition of Civil Caseloads*

a. Money Claims in Ordinary Procedure

Looking at the time series as a whole, the large litigation waves of imperial Japan (phases A and B) and of the contemporary phase (E) stand out as distinctive elements. Economic crises were the underlying causal mechanism. The wave pattern pervades all lines in figure 2. No type of civil procedure escaped the forces of the business cycle. While this is obvious for the dunning cases, which are restricted to money claims by law, it must be emphasized that the same holds true for conciliation and ordinary lawsuits. The parallel movement indicates that the same causal explanation applies for all types of procedure. There is no essential difference between debt collection and ordinary lawsuits as far as the middle-term effect of business cycles is concerned.

---

56 1973 marks the minimum of the adjusted total. New ordinary civil cases reached a minimum in 1975. The text uses 1973 for convenience. In reality, structural changes may extend over several years. Figure 10 (*infra* sec. V.1) exhibits the break in the trend-line of the litigation rate.

57 KATO, *supra* note 6, at 664 citing 27 HOGAKU SEMINA. *Zôkan Gendai no Saiban* [Special Edition: Contemporary Justice] 27 (1984).

58 For Germany, *see* C. WOLLSCHLÄGER, Rechtstatsachenforschung: Konjunkturprognose für die Zivilgerichte [Empirical Legal Research: Forecasting the Business of Civil Courts], 29 JURISTISCHE SCHULUNG 684-686 (1989); for New Jersey *see id.*, Historical Trends of Civil Caseloads in State Trial Courts 1900-1990: The Protracted Litigation Explosion. Paper presented at the Annual Meeting of the Law & Society Association, Philadelphia, fig. 3. (1992).

Additional evidence is available from an analysis of the type of cases in ordinary lawsuits. The time series in figure 3 displays what is perhaps the most valuable asset of Japanese judicial statistics. No other nation offers a similar overview of the objects of litigation for more than a century. The broad categories of cases were kept constant in the frame that had been set by the Meiji statisticians.

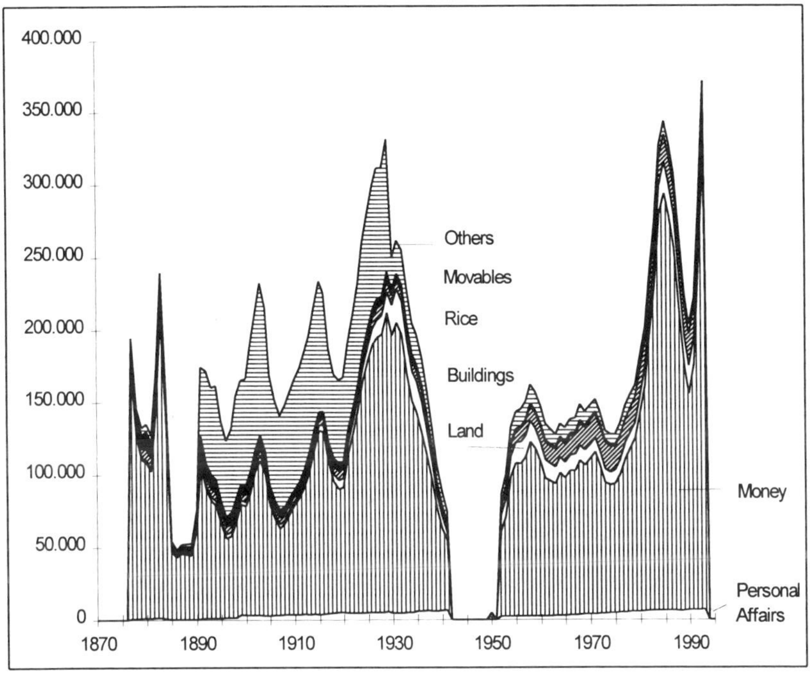

Figure 3. Japan: Type of Cases in Ordinary Procedure (soshô) 1877-1993

Money suits always dominated the caseload. Their changing volume caused the litigation waves. The rest of the case types are hardly visible. Personal affairs (including divorce), buildings, land, the delivery of rice in kind, and movable property each constitute a small percentage of ordinary lawsuits. They appear as a narrow ribbon which is too small to influence the line of the total. The composition of the caseloads thus underlines that the overall pattern has to be explained mainly from the viewpoint of credit relations.

b. The Decline of Conciliation (*kankai* and *chôtei*)

The role of single types of civil procedure underwent significant changes in the course of 120 years. The percentage of ordinary lawsuits, conciliation, dunning, and provisional injunction in figure 4 illustrates to what extent plaintiffs preferred procedural alternatives. Under theoretical aspects, conciliation is most interesting, since Kawashima relied heavily on its importance.[59]

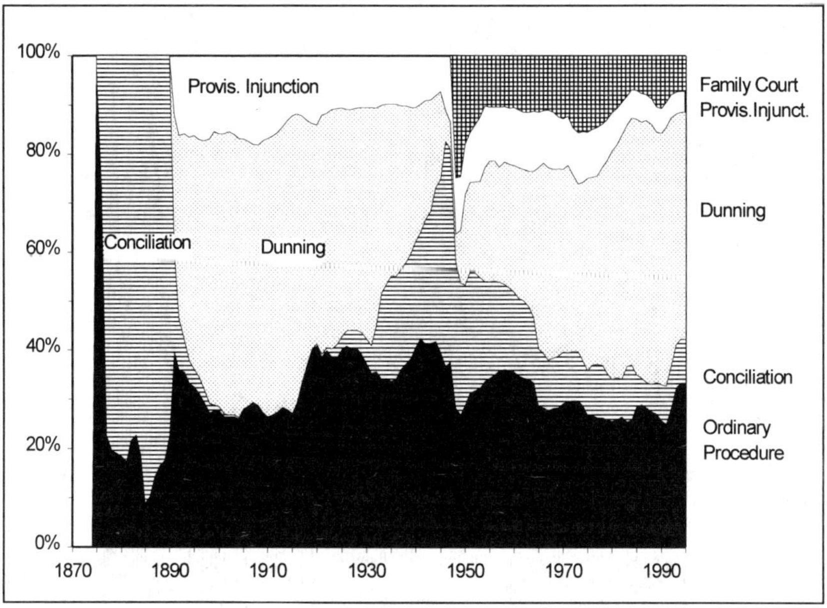

Figure 4: Percentage of Single Types of Civil Procedure 1875-1994

The left part of the graph recalls the initial phase of the modern court system when *kankai* conciliation dominated. The impact of the Code of Civil Procedure is visible at the start of phase (B). In the year 1891, a remarkable exchange happened. Conciliation was replaced mainly by the dunning procedure and, to a lesser extent, by provisional injunction and provisional attachment. As the traditional means of dispute resolution had been abolished, the demand for ordinary procedure increased immediately. The share of *soshô* doubled immediately, as the upward jump from 23% to 40% shows. The substitution effect between all four types of procedure is demonstrated clearly by figure 4. It underlines the necessity of including all procedural alternatives in historical comparison.[60]

59 *Supra* note 1.
60 *See* text accompanying note 19 *supra*.

The revival of conciliation in the *Taisho* era (1912-1926) had initially modest results. During the early *Showa* era (1926-1989), the share of *chôtei* grew rapidly in the political climate of nationalism which heightened during the war years. The relative expansion took place at the expense of the dunning procedure. The substitution effect between *kankai* and *tokusoku*, which had been caused by the Code of Civil Procedure in 1891, was repeated in reverse order. The share of ordinary civil cases (as well as their absolute number) was not affected, however. *Chôtei* did not reduce the need for contradictory procedure, as its political proponents had hoped.[61] Conciliation mainly functioned as a means of debt collection rather than a way of restoring harmony between estranged parties.

After the war, *chôtei* gradually lost its influence as the share shrunk from 46% in 1946 to a minimum of 5% in 1987. Conciliation in the family courts developed in parallel ways. Its portion decreased from 24% to 7% over 47 years. Nowadays, formal conciliation still presents an alternative to the regular procedure, but its significance is ebbing away. It is no longer a dominating or central means of dispute resolution as it had been in the early history of Japanese civil procedure.

c. The Rise of Dunning Procedure (*tokusoku*)

Dunning cases show opposite tendencies before and after World War II.[62] After a maximum of 58% about 1900, their share decreased continuously to 37% in 1937. The need for routine debt collection diminished as industrialization improved the situation of debtors. The tendency reversed after the war. From a modest share of 23% in 1954, dunning expanded strongly. After the litigation explosion of 1984, every second case was finally disposed of in this procedure. The postwar phases (D and E) are thus characterized by an increasing role of routine debt collection cases.

At the same time, the frequency of objections in dunning cases underwent a remarkable change.[63] Objections remained at a high level of 32% for 15 years until 1963. Over the next two decades, the rate fell continuously to a new level of 8.5%, where it has stabilized since 1982. The decline attests to structural changes in the overall demand for civil justice in the contemporary phase (E). Expanding consumer credit caused a higher demand, as the increase of total

61 *See* HALEY, *supra* note 9, at 96.

62 The following data refer to number of petitions adjusted for double counts (*supra* sec. I.2). They do not include provisional injunction and provisional attachment (*kari-shobun, kari-sashiosae*) as in the graphs. The latter type has declined steadily since 1915 from a level of about 17% to merely 4% in 1994. This attests to structural changes in procedural habits which need further study.

63 *Cf.* text accompanying note 24 *supra* for the problem of double counts.

filings showed.[64] More and more uncontested claims are raised because debtors fail to perform because of simple lack of money. The role of Japanese civil courts has thus shifted from adjudication and conciliation of real disputes to the routine enforcement of money claims. This is a clear parallel to developments in the U.S. where modernity seems to progress most quickly.[65]

8. *Interim Questions*

After a lengthy exploration of historical caseload data, the basic questions of Japanese avoidance of litigation return. Does the secular development confirm Kawashima's traditionalistic explanation, and does it correspond to what he envisaged as a corollary of modernization?

Only few observations fit into his expectations. The shrinking share of conciliation cases during the postwar phases (D and E) may fit the assumption that informal dispute resolution fades away as personal relations become estranged. The upward trend of the contemporary phase (E) gives no support because of its economic causes. The increase of debt collection was obviously not what Kawashima had in mind.

If rights consciousness were a direct corollary of societal modernization, the demand for civil justice should have already increased in imperial Japan (phase B). At that time, urbanization was continuing and the expanding legal profession could have educated citizens to use courts more freely. Instead, the data show litigation rates which stagnated in the long run, immune to societal changes. The flat course of the litigation rate during the phase of postwar economic expansion (D) exhibits the same pattern on an even lower level of litigation.

As a whole, the first century of modern courts can be briefly described by three average litigation rates: 16.6 units between 1875 and 1889 (phase A), 8.0 units from 1889 to 1937 (phase B), and 4.5 units from 1954 to 1973 (phase D).[66] The Japanese secular pattern since 1875 is thus marked by a stepwise descent from ever higher levels of the demand for civil justice. It is quite contrary to evolutionary notions of how legal consciousness gradually modernizes and thereby raises litigation. Kawashima's views on changing mentalities and his Weberian desire for more rationality through law[67] find no support in judicial statistics.

---

64 *See* text accompanying note 57 *supra*.

65 *See* D. CLARK, Adjudication to Administration: A Statistical Analysis of Federal District Courts, 55 SO. CAL. L. REV. 65 (1981) for federal district courts of the U.S.

66 *See* figure 10 *infra* sec. V.1.

67 *Supra* note 13.

Kawashima also affirmed the continuity of patriarchal social structures and social patterns of dispute resolution from rural milieus of feudal times into the present.[68] This aspect of the thesis is indeed confirmed by the stagnation of the mean litigation rate over long time spans, though not by the sequence of the downward shifts.

However, are the latter really relevant? Or is the shift from 8 units down to 4.5 units within the limits of normal irregularities? Was the litigation rate in prewar Japan "high" or "low"? What do longitudinal patterns look like in countries where contemporary litigation rates are high? These questions require an analysis of the Japanese time series in a wider comparative outlook.

In the Japanese context, phase A presents the question of whether the earliest high litigation rates can be related to the pre-modern demand for civil justice. The stability of phase B leads us to hypothesize that no basic change occurred in the transition from feudal Japan.[69] A few surviving data from this period permit a cautious test.

PART III: PRE-MODERN JUDICIAL BUSINESS IN EDO AND OSAKA

1. Civil Justice Under the Shogunate

Legal history and social history depict an active and well-frequented metropolitan civil justice in the *Tokugawa* period (1663-1868).[70] *Kobayakawa* reports figures on the size of judicial activity of the town commissioners (*machi bugyô*) of Osaka and Edo (the former name of Tokyo) in the 18th century.[71] The data exhibit a sizable volume of business which was handled by the judicial officers. Annual caseloads ranging from 10,000 to 60,000 were as high as in metropolitan courts today. A task of this size required a permanent organization. Several judicial officers pronounced the authoritative final decision, whereas registrars and clerks, who formally "prepared" the decision, actually made it in most cases. Buildings existed in Edo with a capacity for crowds of 300 petitioners waiting to be heard by the officers. The nucleus of a legal

---

68 *See* ROKUMOTO, *supra* note 11, at 104.

69 *See* text accompanying note 38 *supra*.

70 *See* STEENSTRUP, *supra* note 34; HALEY, *supra* note 9, at 57-65; HENDERSON, *supra* note 31, Vol. 1, at 99-169; K. KUKITA, *Naisai to kuji yado* [Settlement and Suit Inn], *in*: *Nihon no shakai-shi* [Social History in Japan], Vol. 5, *Saiban to kihan* [Court and Norms] (1987).

71 K. KOBAYAKAWA, *Kinsei minji soshô seido no kenkyû* [Study of the Procedural System in the Recent Era] 8-10 (1957). Data for Osaka are found in G. HARUHARA, *Osaka no machi bugyô-sho to saiban* [The Osaka Town Commission and Litigation] 12-13 (1962). *See* HENDERSON, *supra* note 31, Vol. 1, at 107. Data and translation of the procedural terms have been kindly provided by *Dr. Wilhelm Röhl*, Hamburg.

profession developed from the keepers of about 200 specialized "suit inns" (*kuji yado*) where nonresident plaintiffs found shelter and advice on how to succeed before the authorities. The metropolitan centers were far from being non-litigious societies.[72]

Was this "civil justice", comparable to the business of modern courts?

Whereas legal history and social history have no problems with this qualification,[73] *Henderson* sees it rather as mere administration, drawing a strict line between the application of modern justiciable law and administrative maintenance of order and dispute resolution.[74] His terminology unnecessarily blurs the distinction between law as governmental social control and extralegal (private or informal) social control.[75] It disregards the fact that the doctrine of separation of powers was not applicable (just as in Europe at that time). The Shogunal officers enforced norms and settled disputes by virtue of their position in the feudal government. Their activity was attributable to the Shogun who incorporated government or "the state" in his person. According to the historical Chinese concept of law, this did not apply to institutions which enjoyed autonomy from centralized government: the village elders, the heads of commercial guilds, or the five-household units. Their ordering of private affairs was not attributable to the feudal state. Consequently, judicial authorities of the Shogunate rendered civil justice. Their cases are comparable to ours.

2. *Quantitative Evidence*

The earliest results of judicial statistics for the year *Meiji 8* (1875) provide a link between modern and pre-modern demand for civil justice.[76] They can be related to the volume of judicial business in Edo and Osaka as shown in table 2. The Edo rates of 75 cases per 1,000 population in 1718 and 100 units in 1719 precisely correspond to the Tokyo rate of 84 units in 1875. The same applies to Osaka, where the lowest rate of 26 units in 1786 nearly equals the rate of 29 units in 1875.

---

72 *See* M. OKI, Schlichtung als Institution des Rechts [Conciliation as a Legal Institution], 16 RECHTSTHEORIE 151 at 160-161 (1985).

73 *See* STEENSTRUP, *supra* note 34; HALEY, *supra* note 9, at 57, 64; KUKITA, *supra* note 70.

74 *Supra* in this volume Chapter One, where "justice" is referred to in quotation marks only. In his 1992 article (cited *ibid.* at note 40), *Henderson* develops the substantive distinctions between Western and Chinese concepts of law, but avoids the less convincing terminology.

75 *See* D. BLACK, The Behavior of Law 2 (1976).

76 Professor *Aritsune Katsuta* (Tokyo) has graciously provided a copy of the rare first volume of judicial statistics, where the data are found on pp. 19, 21, 30.

Table 2: Pre-Modern Litigation Rates in Edo and Osaka Civil Cases per 1,000 Total Population

	year	*soshô* plaints*	*kuji* suits	*tôza soshô* **)	1875	*soshô* formal trial	*kankai* conci-liation	total	litiga-tion rate
Edo Town	1718	47,731	35,790	11,739				59,470	100
Commissioners	1719	34,051	26,070	10,872				44,923	75
Tokyo District	1875				new	57,031	14,792	71,823	84
Court incl. ward divisions					pending	60,054	14,792	74,846	88
Osaka Town	1782	15,839	4,363					15,839	38
Commissioners	1783	22,258	5,613					22,258	53
	1784	18,964	5,195					18,964	45
	1785	3,570	12,715					12,715	30
	1786	10,718	2,560					10,718	26
Osaka District	1875				new	43,276		43,276	29
Court					pending	45,652		45,652	30

*) i.e., applications for admission to a hearing by the judicial officer; counted in the total. *Kuji*, i.e., suits that have been admitted, are excluded to avoid double counts.
**) applications for provisional orders, counted in total.

The 18th-century litigation rates have to be viewed with caution, of course, since both population and caseload data contain uncertainties. Relatively safe rates can be obtained for Osaka.[77] These refer to the city in the 18th century and to the prefecture in 1875, which also included large agrarian portions. The Edo population cannot be determined accurately. Only commoners (*chônin*) were counted, leaving the large number of resident *samurai* unknown. Two hundred "suit inns" could accomodate thousands of nonresident litigants per year. So the relevant population which generated the lawsuits must be estimated.[78] Nevertheless, the litigation rates are still reliable. The margins of error do not exceed the normal fluctuations of the caseloads themselves. These could be twice as high in one year as in the other, as Osaka shows. The data thus give clear evidence that the civil business of the modern metropolitan courts continued in the same size as in feudal times.

77 Osaka 1782-86: 420,000 population reported for 1765. Osaka prefecture 1875 (incl. Nara): 1.50 million population estimated from 1.63 million reported for 1884. Source: *Nihon-shi dai-jiten* [Grand Dictionary of Japanese History], Vol. 1 (H. Shimonaka, ed. 1992); Historical Statistics of Japan, Vol. 1, table 2-12 (1987).

78 Edo 1718-19: 600,000 estimated from reported 500,000 commoners (*chônin*) for 1721; missing *samurai* and nonresidents estimated at 100,000. Tokyo 1875: 850,000 estimated from reported 1.15 million for 1884.

The wide fluctuations are a second pre-modern parallel to later caseload patterns in imperial Japan. Floods of litigation could pour in during years of economic crises or as an antecedent to peasant uprisings. The Osaka figures exhibit the characteristic shape of a litigation wave in its final stage. It can be detected from the continuous downward slope from 1783 to 1786. The caseload shrunk by one half in three years - quite congruous to the pre-modern type of litigation waves of later Japan (phases A and B) or of 19th-century Sweden.[79] The Edo data for 1718 and 1719 show an even steeper annual decrease of 24% in one year.

The litigation waves were obviously caused by money suits (*kane-kuji*) which dominated the caseload with a share of 93% - just as in *kankai* conciliation cases of phase A and in later times.[80] The same economic necessities of debt collection caused the bulk of pre-modern lawsuits. The objects of litigation were not qualitatively different from the initial phase of the modern courts.

On the other extreme, litigation was repeatedly suppressed. Reacting to the overburdening of civil justice, the Shoguns simply declined to accept money suits (*kane-kuji*) or other specified types of cases. The data do not seem to be distorted by such restrictive measures, however, as the mere size of the caseloads attests.

The evidence directly refers to the biggest metropolitan centers with only 4% of the total Japanese population of 26 million. Although no information is available on the volume of litigation in the middle-sized castle towns, there is no reason to believe that the transition from feudal to modern times developed differently there. No civil justice existed in rural Japan where 80% of the population lived,[81] so the problem of continuities in the later use of courts is not applicable. But it is safe to assume that disputing and extra-judicial dispute resolution remained stable in the rural sector as well.

Quantitative evidence thus establishes a decisive link between the statistical and the pre-statistical eras of Japanese civil justice. The pre-modern wave type and the dominance of money suits present additional parallels to early 20th-century litigation. For these reasons, the long-term trend of imperial Japan (phase B 1889-1937) can be safely prolonged backwards into the feudal era. As far as urban litigation is concerned, the demand for civil justice can be assumed to have been same in Tokugawa period as after the Meiji reforms. The traditional roots of its low level are more clearly visible in the decisive transition from feudal to modern times.

---

79 *See* text accompanying note 93 *infra*.

80 KOBAYAKAWA reports 33,037 *kane-kuji* cases for 1718 and 24,304 for 1719 (*supra* note 71). *Cf. supra* sec. II.7.a. with fig. 3.

81 *See* HALEY, *supra* note 9, at 57-61.

This adds further support for the historical centerpiece of the Kawashima thesis. International comparison will then have to answer the additional question of whether Western countries offer similar developmental patterns.

PART IV: AMERICAN AND EUROPEAN HISTORICAL TRENDS OF LITIGATION

1. *Exponential Growth of Litigation: Arizona 1912-1990*

Arizona is one of the few states of the U.S. where the business of trial courts has been reported continuously during the prewar period. Data on the superior courts, which have general jurisdiction similar to the Japanese district courts, are available since 1912, when the state was incorporated in the U.S.[82] The lower courts (of limited jurisdiction) are missing until 1963. Since the business of the justices of the peace was small until then (17% of the total), the gap is negligible. The historical development is typical for other American states.[83]

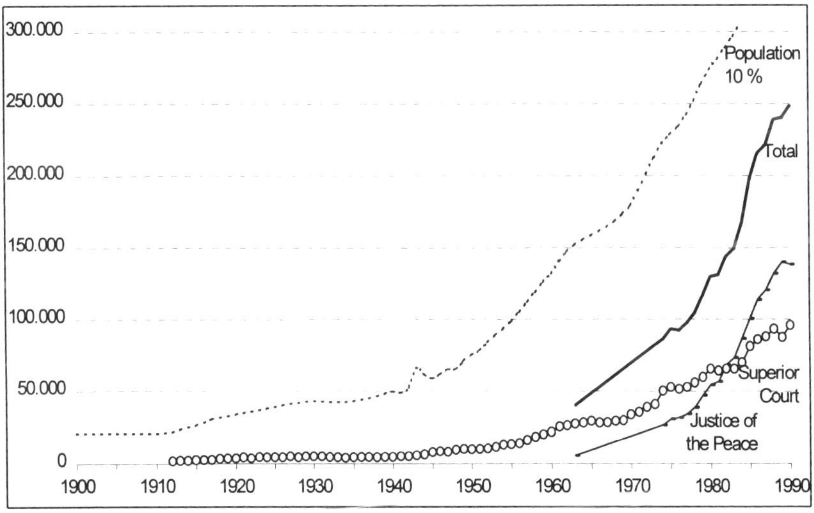

Figure 5. Arizona: Civil Cases Filed in State Trial Courts 1912-1990

82 For sources which have not been analyzed in the literature, *see* appendix. The total has been computed from time series for 15 superior courts. A few missing data have been estimated. Superior court data comprise regular civil cases only. Domestic relations cases are included in the total, but have been omitted in fig. 5 for visual clarity. Probate and mental health cases were omitted because of their non-litigious nature.

83 *See* WOLLSCHLÄGER, *supra* note 58.

Figure 5 exhibits an exponential growth both of litigation and population.[84] By its mathematical form alone, the graph indicates that the use of courts was determined by the expansion of population and economy. The time series of litigation has the same shape which is typical for demographic and macro-economic variables. (This could be further demonstrated by direct correlation with population and personal income data.) Lawsuits have steadily increased in absolute numbers with few exceptions (e.g., after the Great Depression). There were 100 times as many filings in 1990 as can be estimated for 1912.[85] The litigation rate multiplied more than fourfold, from approximately 14 cases per 1,000 total population to 67 in 1990.

This development characterizes the ever rising demand for civil justice in the U.S.[86] The permanent increase of the workload of federal courts as well as of state courts, the expansion of the legal profession, and the public awareness of law all fit into the same pattern of "total justice". Arizona presents a model of the so-called "litigation explosion", which has been denied by prominent American sociolegal scholars.[87]

On the other hand, the data do not support conservative voices who suspect that American virtues of good personal and business relations have been corrupted by litigiousness. The economy expanded simultaneously with the population. Consequently, the total potential of legal relations, from which lawsuits arise, multiplied, too. It is premature to conclude that, in relation to the total potential of economic transactions, courts are used more frequently than in earlier times. The rising caseload alone is no proof of a rising propensity to sue.

The latter cannot be excluded, though. A higher litigation rate means that more people are personally involved in court procedures. Psychological barriers may be removed as litigation becomes a normal reaction to problems. The broad media coverage of courts supports and accelerates this process. Thus the ability for private resolution of conflicts may have suffered in the long run. This cannot be ruled out by statistical data either.

In this respect, the exponential growth pattern supports Kawashima's anticipation of a fading avoidance of courts in Japan. He viewed it as a con-

---

84 An exponential trend yields a highly significant fit of r_ = 0.965 for superior courts 1912-1990 (N=79) and r_ = 0.968 for the total 1963-1990 (N=13).

85 2047 filings in the superior courts and approximately 400 cases before the justices of the peace, who handled small claims. Prior to 1963 no data are available for the latter. Their share of the total was estimated for 1912 on the 1963 basis. This seems to be admissible because justices of the peace still had less business than the superior courts during the following 20 years.

86 *See* WOLLSCHLÄGER, *supra* note 58.

87 L.M. FRIEDMAN, Total Justice (1985) correctly described the societal trend although he denied the rise of caseloads (*ibid.* at 5) following GALANTER, *supra* note 8.

sequence of industrialization, following Weberian notions that law and litigation are necessary and useful corollaries of economic growth.[88] This developmental model could be confirmed indeed by a number of European nations, such as Belgium, the Netherlands, and Denmark. In these countries, the use of courts has increased permanently since the 19th century.[89]

Compared to Japan, the case of Arizona and the latter group of countries negatively demonstrate what has been absent: the gradual rise of litigation rates. The consecutive surplus of lawsuits over time, which makes the exponential function rise ever steeper, did not occur. The contrast underscores that Japan has been essentially different because social patterns and attitudes toward law have remained unchanged.

The exponential growth pattern is by no means universal, however. The reverse effect can be observed, too.

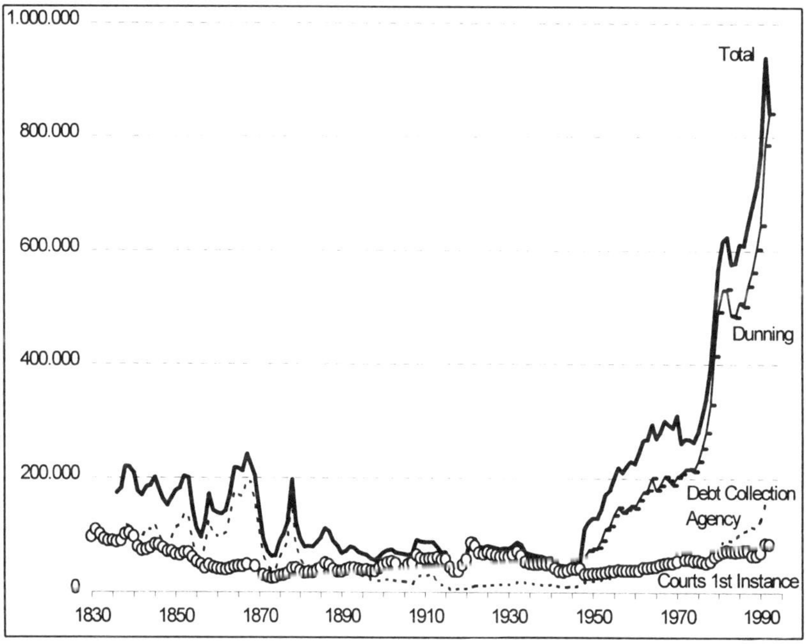

Figure 6. Sweden: Civil Cases in Courts of First Instance and Debt Collection Cases 1830-1992

88 KAWASHIMA, *supra* note 3, at 440.
89 WOLLSCHLÄGER, *supra* note 15, at 55-61.

2. *Agrarian Poverty and Consumerism: Secular Decline and Rise of Litigation in Sweden 1830-1994*

Sweden is one of those countries or regions where economic growth reduced the volume of litigation for more than a century. In fact, the Swedish time series in figure 6 presents both effects.[90] The postwar phase after 1948 gives the impression of a Swedish "litigation explosion" similar to American dimensions. The total caseload of ordinary lawsuits and debt collection cases has risen eightfold.[91] The civil business of ordinary courts has risen by a factor of 2.5 only, which means a modest increase over 45 years. The rise of the total is thus mainly caused by debt collection. The very nature of these cases suggests that the permanent increase after World War II was caused by the expansion of consumer credit as a corollary of prosperity.

Credit relations also provide the clue to understanding the secular downward trend of litigation between 1830 and 1917. Over decades, civil cases declined in absolute numbers, though fluctuating in huge litigation waves. In the long run, the growth of population and economy had a negative combined effect on the use of courts. Agrarian poverty was the dominant cause behind this development which has been observed in other European regions, too.[92] Swedish judicial statistics offer the safest evidence for the rural origin of these floods of litigation. The court organization provided for separate courts in villages (*häradsrätt*) and towns (*radstufrätt*) until 1974. Distinct litigation rates can be computed to observe the crucial boundary between agrarian and urban sectors of society over a period of 130 years.

Figure 7 presents the data for ordinary civil procedure (*tvistemål*). (The national total includes debt collection cases where the urban-rural distinction cannot be made.) At the start of the time series in 1830, Sweden was purely agrarian; 90% of the population lived in villages. During the first decades, rural and urban litigation rates were roughly the same. Regional analysis, in fact, reveals provinces where rural rates exceeded urban rates. When industrialization began after 1850, a gap opened between rural and urban rates. During the next five decades, the well-known effect of urbanization emerged. A clear and stable distance continued until World War I. The average urban litigation rate was four times as high as the rural average. In the course of 44 years, the rural rate stagnated on a low level (5.4 ordinary cases per 1,000 population in 1872; 5.7 units in 1915). Nothing happened which could have

90 Fig. 6 is an improved version of a first attempt *in* WOLLSCHLÄGER, *supra* note 15, at 72. The literature on Swedish historical statistics has not taken notice of civil judicial statistics.

91 Due to double counting of the debt collection cases, the figure may overstate the filings although it has been reduced by an estimated 12%.

92 WOLLSCHLÄGER, *supra* note 15, at 86.

disturbed the litigating habits among Swedish peasants and farm workers. The dynamics of litigation progressed in the commercial milieu of towns and cities, as the large fluctuations in the urban series show.

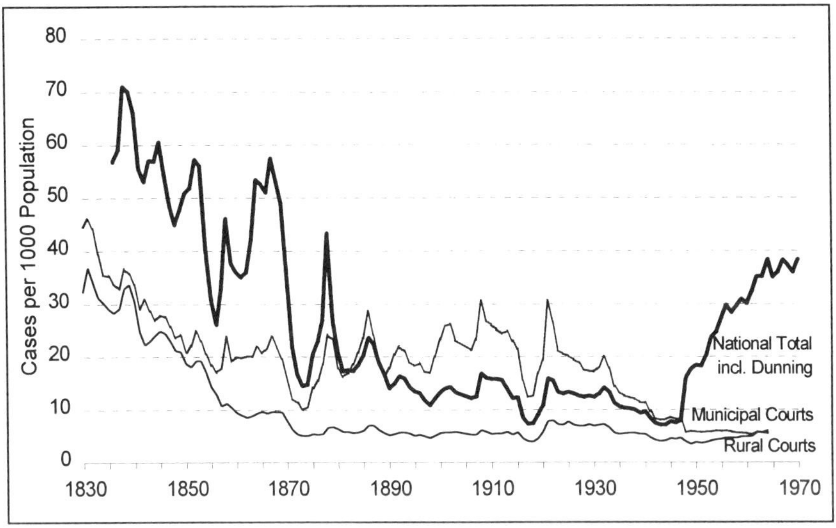

Figure 7. Sweden: Urban and Rural Litigation Rates 1830-1964

For an explanation of the secular decline, the mechanism of the business cycle may be recalled from the Japanese time series.[93] Here its operation during the phase of recovery from the crisis matters. As the economic situation improved, the need for borrowing became less for farmers and workers, because sufficient income for subsistence was available. The number of credit contracts was thus reduced. Debts could be repaid more easily, thus lowering the rate of default. Creditors were more willing to grant deferment of payment instead of suing. Hence the propensity to sue was lowered. In the end result, lawsuits declined as prosperity spread.[94] Economic growth had a negative combined effect on the demand for civil justice. Sweden illustrates that this mechanism is not confined to the cyclical fluctuation of caseloads. It also works in the long run, reducing litigation over decades.

93 *Supra* sec. II.2.

94 For parallel observations for working class households, *see* P. JOHNSON, Small Debts and Economic Distress in England and Wales, 1857-1913, 26 ECONOMIC HISTORY REV. 65-87 (1993).

The magnitude of the litigation waves during the 19th century offers another parallel. The pre-modern pattern of the fluctuations attests to a similar impact of the business cycle in both nations.[95] Seeking judicial enforcement of claims, creditors reacted more "nervously" to bad times than today. An inconspicuous feature of the time series may provide an important clue to understanding the Japanese development The stagnation of Swedish rural litigation rates in the five decades before World War I parallels the horizontal long-term trend in the prewar and postwar phases of Japan (B and D). This requires closer analysis.[96]

Differences should also be noted. Whereas Swedish litigation declined in absolute numbers for nearly a century, the decrease can be observed in Japan for middle-term fluctuations only, particularly for the litigation wave of the Meiji reforms (Phase A). Japanese caseloads showed instead a modest mean increase between 1889 and 1937 (Phase B). The combined effect of economic growth was positive in Japan. Hence the dominant forces in the causation of lawsuits must have had different weight. The relation between urban and rural regions has not been studied for Japan. Agrarian poverty may have influenced the demand for civil justice in different ways.

3. Litigation Explosion and Long-Term Stability: Germany 1880-1991

Though German judicial statistics are available for the nation since 1881, political history makes it difficult to analyze civil litigation on a homogenous data base. Many territorial changes require computation from disparate sources and occasional estimations. Based on the statistical results for single districts of appellate courts (*Oberlandesgerichte*), a time series has been construed for the combined filings in the two courts of first instance (*Amtsgericht* and *Landgericht*) for the area of the Federal Republic before unification in 1990.[97]

The development of the litigation rate since 1880 strikes the eye by the erratic movement of the curves between the two world wars (figure 8). The wars appear as deep troughs because civil litigation was suppressed. In between, the peak of 1931 jumps out during the Great Depression. The litigation explosion climbed to a record high of approximately 200 cases per 1,000 total population. In single cities such as Bremen, even values of 600 were

95 *Supra* sec. II.2.

96 *Infra* sec. V.1 b.

97 The new data base improves an earlier first attempt; *cf.* WOLLSCHLÄGER, *supra* note 15, at 62. Regional differences of litigation rates are now taken into account. These were also neglected by H. ROTTLEUTHNER, Aspekte der Rechtsentwicklung in Deutschland - Ein soziologischer Vergleich deutscher Rechtskulturen [Aspects of Legal Development in Germany: German Legal Cultures in Sociological Comparison], ZEITSCHRIFT FÜR RECHTSSOZIOLOGIE 235-239 (1985).

reached.[98] In these years of economic and political crisis, the German courts were burdened by the highest civil caseloads in their history.

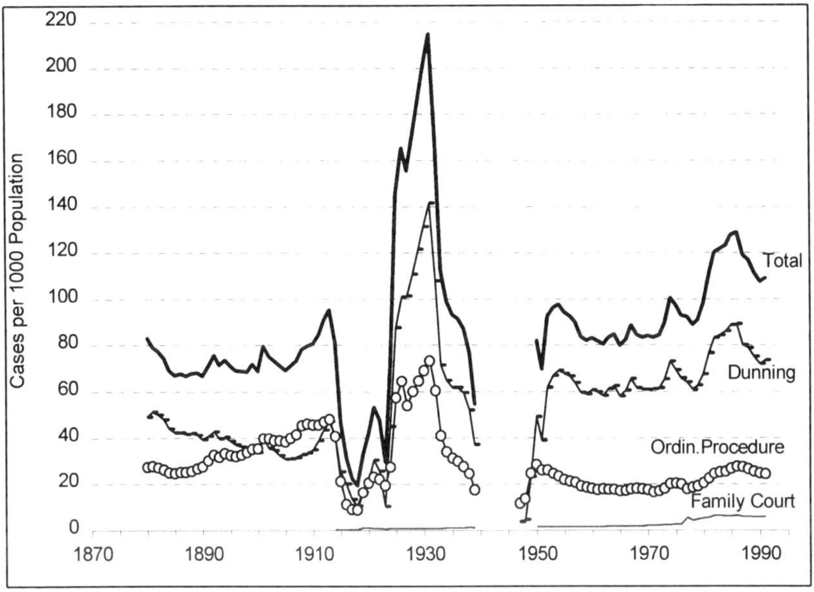

Figure 8. Germany: Litigation Rates 1880-1991 (Area of the Federal Republic Before Unification)

The interwar period between 1914 and 1945 presents abnormal economical and political conditions. In spite of these, the erratic pattern illustrates how the same mechanisms which determine civil judicial business under stable circumstances operated.

During war times, civil litigation declines because military service draws parts of the male populations away from their homes, thereby reducing the number of potential plaintiffs. Moreover, the volume of private contractual relations decreases as the economy turns to military objectives. This illustrates how the caseload depends on the total potential of normal, undisturbed legal relations by which economic production is distributed. This universal mechanism makes the litigation rate drop when war begins and rise when it is over.

98 *See* WOLLSCHLÄGER, *supra* note 49. Due to double counts of dunning cases, approximate figures can be given only.

The peak of litigation in 1931 during the world economic crisis demonstrates how the rate of injury operates as a causal factor when the frequency of default increases. The extraordinary movement up and down displays the same crisis effects which have been observed in Japan and in Sweden.

The full length of the time series is most surprising in the continuity between 1880 and 1991. After 1945, the line of the total follows the direction of the long-term trend which prevailed before World War I. It started at a level of about 67 cases per 1,000 total population after 1885 and increased to only 80 in the following 25 years. After the two wars, the lowest rates range between 70 in 1951 and 107 in 1990. This pattern stands in sharp contrast to Arizona, where the litigation rate rose fourfold during the last eighty years. Just as in Japan, the question arises of why the upsurge of the German economy since the late 19th century was *not* reflected in the use of civil courts.

Closer analysis reveals distinct courses for single types of procedure. Until World War I, economic growth contributed to an increase in the number of ordinary lawsuits, whereas it made the dunning cases go down. As commerce and industry expanded, more contracts were made which raised serious disputes; these were fought out in ordinary procedure. Simultaneously the need for simple debt collection declined as the economic conditions of debtors improved. In the late 19th century, economic growth thus had an ambivalent combined effect on the total demand for civil justice.

Opposite movements also prevailed during the postwar period after 1945. The absolute number of ordinary lawsuits remained fairly stable until 1970. The rate per capita declined as the population increased. During the phase of reconstruction, the so-called "economic miracle" reduced ordinary civil litigation. Either the need for debt collection became less or the dunning procedure replaced regular procedure to a larger extent. Dunning cases, on the other hand, have continued to increase both in absolute numbers and per capita since the mid-fifties.

Around 1970, however, this pattern basically changed as the present upward direction began to emerge. A break occurred in the long-term trend.[99] Civil caseloads have increased in the long run since then. The overburdening of courts became a standard concern in the German literature. Legislation repeatedly simplified civil procedure and shifted workloads from the upper courts of first instance (*Landgericht*) to the lower courts (*Amtsgericht*) by raising the jurisdictional amount.

The reasons for the trend break are still unclear. The years of rapid economic growth were over. The oil price shocks of preceding years had

---

99 *See* WOLLSCHLÄGER, *supra* note 58.

sharpened the awareness of crisis. Creditors were possibly less inclined to compromise or to extend credit. Consequently they went to court more often. Student unrest and political dissatisfaction may have had an impact, too. Whatever the exact causes, the effect is clearly visible in the time series of Germany as well as of Japan, Sweden, and certain states of the U.S. The international dimension of the trend break strongly suggests that economic causes were effective.

With a view to Japan, the most important question seems to be why the German litigation rate is so remarkably high. In this respect, figure 8 shows that the present level already existed at the end of the 19th century. Consequently, the frequent use of civil courts in Germany must be the result of a historical evolution which took place earlier during the process of industrialization.

The development cannot be traced backward for the whole of Germany. National data are not available prior to the unification of the court system in 1879. In a few territories, data on civil caseloads have been preserved since the 18th century. One has to look back in German history over 200 years, indeed, to observe litigation rates which are as low as those in present-day Japan.

4. *Urbanization, Industrialization, and the Rise of Litigation: Berlin and Brandenburg, Prussia 1773-1913*

Total civil filings per capita can be computed since 1773 for the district of the *Kammergericht*, which resided in the City of Berlin.[100] The jurisdiction of this appellate court included the present federal state of surrounding Brandenburg (comparable to the size of a Japanese prefecture). The complexity of the Prussian court system was reduced in figure 8 as far as possible. Total filings in first instance were added from a variety of up to four courts and six types of proceedings at certain periods.

Although basically agrarian, the district of the Kammergericht had been most strongly affected by urbanization since the 18th century. In about 1784, 145,000 people lived in the residential city of the Prussian kings (one third of Osaka at the same time). By 1900, the city had expanded to two million inhabitants and was heavily industrialized; it was a center of German modernization.

---

100 For details and sources, *see* WOLLSCHLÄGER, Zivilprozeß-Statistik und Wirtschaftsentwicklung in Preußen im 18. und 19. Jahrhundert [Civil Judicial Statistics and Economic Development in Prussia During the 18th and 19th Centuries], ZEITSCHRIFT FÜR NEUERE RECHTSGESCHICHTE 16-27 (1981).

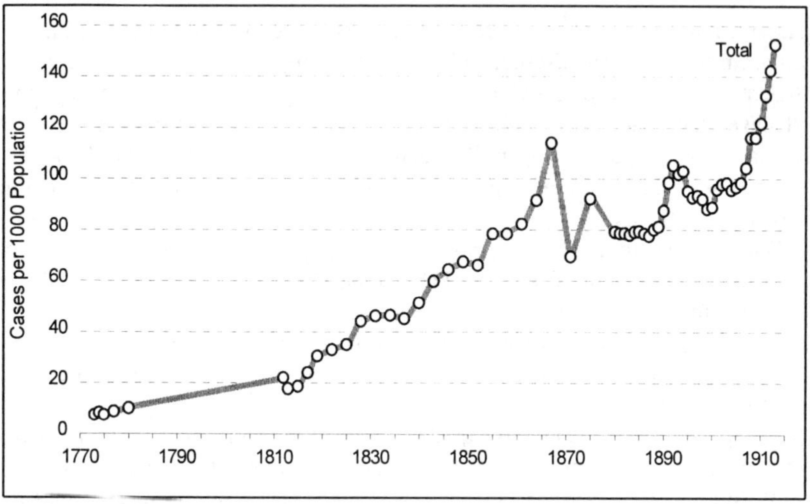

Figure 9. Prussia: District of the Kammergericht (Berlin and Brandenburg): Litigation Rates 1773-1913

The series of the Kammergericht extends from 1773 to 1913. During these 140 years, the absolute number of filings rose by a factor of 126 while the litigation rate increased twentyfold from about 7.5 cases per 1,000 population to 153 units. The activity of civil courts grew into new dimensions as Berlin became an industrial and commercial metropolis. This was the same structural change as occurred in Arizona after 1912, though one century earlier. The time series of the Kammergericht illustrates how Germany reached its high level of civil litigation in a secular economic rise which began in the 18th century.[101]

As noted before, the upward historical trend alone is no definite proof that the propensity to sue rose. The increase of social mobility during the 19th century,[102] however, indeed suggests that social attitudes towards the use of courts changed. As people migrated from villages and small towns into anonymous cities, the close social ties of intimate communities became lost. Personal relations and the informal control of neighborhood and family mattered less. Recourse to legal norms and judicial dispute solution became more frequent in this process.

The expansion of consumer credit offers an additional explanation. The business community seems to have profited most from civil justice in the 19th century (just as in our times). Businessmen were politically active in demanding

---

101 The Prussian series is typical for the majority of German territories, although the development was not uniform.

102 *See* H.U. WEHLER, Deutsche Gesellschaftsgeschichte [German Social History], Vol. 2, p. 8-18 (1987), Vol. 3, p. 7-28 (1995).

unification and modernization of the law of civil procedure.[103] "*Keine Justiz, kein Kredit*" (No civil justice, no credit) was a pertinent observation on the relation of law and economy. Merchants were interested in extending credit in order to raise their sales. They needed speedy justice to enforce claims against customers.

Economic history and legal history show that the volume of credit expanded during industrialization. Whereas commercial banks served industry, credit for private individuals was provided by municipal savings banks. Their growth in number and size indicates an expansion of consumer credit.[104] The Installment Purchase Law[105] of the end of the century indirectly attests to the large volume of installment sales. It was enacted to protect consumers against unfair clauses in sales contracts. Abuses had become notorious and prompted legislative action. A rising number of credit contracts had thus enlarged the total potential of civil litigation as industrialization reached an advanced stage.

Consumer credit also provides a link to the high level of civil litigation in contemporary Germany. Although a century has passed, parallels can be drawn because the present litigation rate (approximately 100 units) is in the same order of magnitude as about 1885 (71 units). Research on small claims litigation reveals an enormous share of consumer relation cases in the business of lower courts. It has been observed in Germany as well as the U.S., Sweden, and Australia.[106] German judicial statistics report a high portion of corporate plaintiffs suing private individuals: 79% in the lower courts and 72% in both courts of first instance in 1984.[107] An even larger share can be presumed for the millions of dunning cases. Consumer cases thus constitute by far the majority of civil litigation. The national total is determined to the largest extent by the frequent use of courts by business enterprises. Historically, the dominant function of German civil courts of first instance emerged during the 19th century as a result of expanding consumer credit. Germany's high litigation rate is largely determined by this field.[108]

---

103 *Cf.* DAHLMANNS, *supra* note 43.

104 *See* Handbuch der Wirtschafts- und Sozialgeschichte [Handbook of Economic and Social History] Vol. 2, p. 591-592 (H. Aubin & W. Zorn, eds. 1975); Article *Sparkassen* [Savings & Loan Associations], *in* Handwörterbuch der Staatswissenschaft [Handbook of Political Science], Vol. 7, p. 684-691 (Elster *et al.* eds., 4th ed. 1926).

105 *Gesetz betr. die Abzahlungsgeschäfte* of May 16, 1894, REICHSGESETZBLATT 1894, p. 450.

106 *See* for the U.S.: B. YNGVESSON & B. HENNESSY, Small Claims, Complex Disputes: A Review of the Small Claims Literature, 9 L. & SOC. REV. 219-274 (1975).; for Germany: WOLLSCHLÄGER, *supra* note 22, at 56-60 with further references.

107 Justizstatistik-Informationssystem (JUSTIS). Electronic data base of the Federal Ministry of Justice. Table C.1.3.

108 For parallel recent observations, *see* BLANKENBURG, *supra* note 20.

PART V: THE HISTORICAL CONTINUITY OF THE AVOIDANCE OF LITIGATION

Two characteristics of the Japanese development stand out more clearly against the background of European and American time series of civil litigation:

— the long-term stagnation of the mean litigation rate on low levels during the phases of imperial Japan (B) and postwar economic expansion (D);
— the downward shift of civil litigation between the two phases.

The first is essential to understanding the historical roots of Japan's legal culture. A stability of this kind has no parallel in Western national patterns. The structural drop between the two phases is equally unique. A similar development has not been observed in the literature; it presents a novel formal component in time series of litigation.[109]

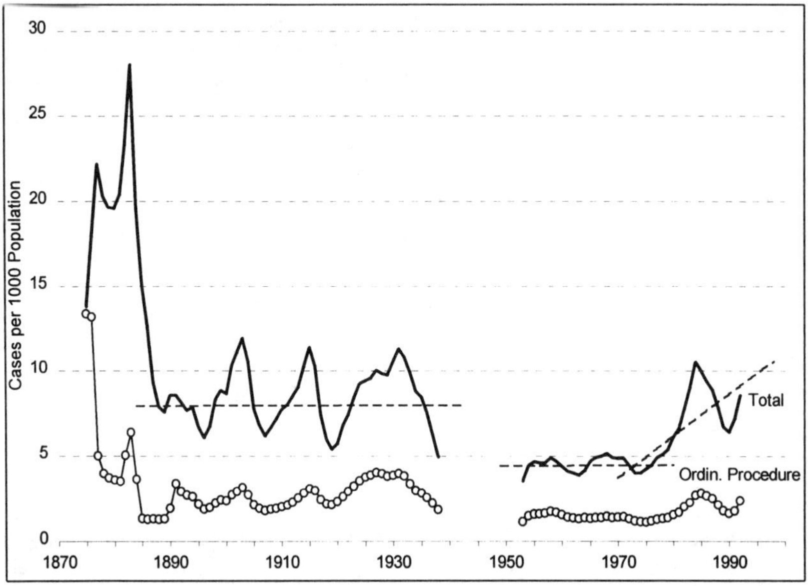

Figure 10. Japan: Litigation Rates 1875-1994

Figure 10 summarizes the secular pattern. It presents litigation rates for the adjusted total and for ordinary civil cases. The distinct features of single phases have been visualized by linear trends which were computed separately. The

109 *Cf.* WOLLSCHLÄGER, *supra* note 15, at 83-85; *id. supra* note 58.

horizontal course is the same for ordinary civil cases[110] and the adjusted total.[111] No matter how the litigation rate is defined, the trend remained constant during the crucial phases B and D.[112]

1. The Secular Pattern: Stagnation on Low Levels

a. Stability: The Japanese Element in Civil Litigation

Horizontal trend lines of the prewar and postwar phases (B and D) illustrate that the average litigation rate remained constant in the cyclical movement. This means that the complex causal process which generated litigation yielded stable results in the long run. In spite of the large litigation waves, the underlying socioeconomic system fluctuated around an equilibrium path which was determined by the size of the population. All other causal factors of litigation must have compensated each other. If a rising economy produced more contracts, more traffic, and more legal relations in general, prosperity must have lowered the incidence of breach of contract at the same time. While the total potential for litigation increaded, balancing counter-forces must have operated in the opposite direction. Otherwise the total number of lawsuits could not have remained constant. If injury and disputes became more frequent, a higher willingness to settle disputes out of court or a lower willingness to assert one's rights may have reduced the probability of lawsuits. The court system may have deterred potential litigants, and litigation may have become more expensive.

It is idle to speculate about the relative strength of the many factors which are put forward by litigation theories.[113] The multi-causal nature of the genesis

---

110 The equations for the crucial phases B and D are: B (1889-1938) y = 0.023x + 1.67. The mean litigation rate was 2.7 cases per 1,000 population. The annual increase of 0.02 is negligible. Phase D (1953-1975): y = - 0.015x + 2.82; mean litigation rate: 1.4 units; negligible annual decrease.

111 The equations are: A (1875-1889): y = - 0.588x + 23.9;B (1889-1938) y = 0.01x + 7.92 (mean rate: 8.0 units; negligible annual increase of 0.01 units.). Phase D (1953-1975): y = - 0.0016x + 4.3 (mean rate 4.5 units; almost perfectly horizontal);F (1970-1992) y = 0.2446x + 21.0. End years deviate from the phases to avoid troughs or peaks. World War II is omitted.

112 *See* text accompanying notes 24 and 62 *supra*. Constant trends result from the elimination of double counts. Earlier versions of this paper erroneously saw a decreasing trend; *cf.* C. WOLLSCHLÄGER, Die historische Entwicklung der Zivilprozeßhäufigkeit in Japan und Europa seit dem 19. Jahrhundert [Historical Development of Civil Litigation in Japan and Europe Since the 19th Century], 37 COMP. L. REV. CHUO UNIVERSITY 1-33 (1993).

113 *Cf.* E. BLANKENBURG, Mobilisierung von Recht [Mobilizing Law], 4 ZEITSCHRIFT FÜR RECHTSSOZIOLOGIE 34-64 (1980); W. FELSTINER, R. ABEL, & A. SARAT, The Emergence and Transformation of Disputes: Naming, Blaming, Claiming, 15 L & SOC. REV. 615-654 (1981); WOLLSCHLÄGER, *supra* note 15, at 45-53.

of lawsuits permits only one safe conclusion: the demand for civil justice as a whole remained stable, adapting only to the growth of population. As long as we do not know more about single causes of litigation, a constant relative weight must be assumed. Changes in the propensity to sue, in particular, are improbable. Society reproduced itself as a whole; the causal structure of litigation remained permanent. This includes the ways and means of how legal relations and violation of norms arise, how disputes are created and settled, and how the courts are called to intervene.

The stable demand for civil justice, which is directly proven by judicial statistics, thus confirms the historical core of Kawashima's thesis: the permanence of social structures and of mechanisms of extra-judicial dispute resolution.

b. The Rural Character

The Swedish time series gives evidence of the essentially rural nature of the Japanese development. As mentioned, the long-term stagnation on low levels has no parallels in European national totals. Similar stability can be observed, however, for Swedish *rural* litigation rates between 1872 and 1915. These remained nearly constant over four decades after agrarian poverty had been overcome.[114] The dynamics of an increasing demand for civil justice were thus equally absent in rural Sweden as well as in the whole of Japan. There were obviously no new social or economic fields where judicial dispute resolution was needed. This concerns the long-term development only. Japanese middle-term fluctuations correspond to the shape of *urban* litigation rates in Sweden during the same period. In figure 7, the typical wave pattern of the urban series contrasts with the flat rural course. The middle-term parallelism is no surprise since Japan's national total comprised metropolitan centers with populations of millions. Evidently the business cycle had stronger effects in cities than in agrarian regions. The development of civil litigation in imperial Japan was thus composed of two elements: it was urban in the middle-term perspective and rural in the long-term perspective.

This observation further supports Kawashima's assumption that attitudes of a rural society survived in contemporary Japan. Patriarchal social structures persisted in spite of industrialization and urbanization. The avoidance of courts continued as a specific feature of rural social patterns.

---

114 *Supra* sec. IV.2.

c. The Low Level of Demand for Civil Justice

Comparative analysis further shows that, except for the litigation wave of the Meiji reforms, Japan's litigation rate was in fact always low by historical and international standards. The level of 8.0 civil cases per 1,000 population in the phase of imperial Japan (B) corresponds exactly to those 7.5 units from where the Prussian time series started in the late 18th century.[115] The Japanese demand for civil justice between 1889 and 1937 and in the postwar decades was in an order of magnitude which prevailed in agrarian pre-modern Europe. It was also close to U.S.-American litigation rates which can be estimated for the beginning of the 20th century.[116]

As the data show, the wide distance from Western levels of civil litigation reaches back in history. Throughout the 20th century, the German rates were at least ten times higher than the Japanese. Theories which try to attribute the avoidance of litigation to modern phenomena, such as the deficiencies or advantages of contemporary civil justice,[117] miss the essential point.

The historical data, on the other hand, reveal that the low level of litigation which existed in the past was common to Japan and Western nations. This raises the question as to which social and economic changes have caused the present distances.

d. Social Mobility

The time series of Arizona and Prussia point to social mobility as a crucial process in social and economic history. Both exhibit the secular growth pattern of civil litigation. It took a century for both countries to progress to those high levels which contemporary Japan fails to reach.

Situated in the sunny Southwest of the U.S., Arizona has been the destination of continuous domestic migrations in our century. Americans moved to the "sunbelt" to find jobs and income. A close interrelation between demographic and economic developments has been observed in the U.S.[118] (and elsewhere). The total potential of civil litigation was thereby increased. Personal relations remained anonymous, be it in the metropolitan centers of Phoenix and Tucson or in the wide arid rest of the thinly populated state. An

115 *See* text accompanying note 100 *supra*. The precise fit in one year is accidental, of course, because it is just one point in a long-term upward trend. What matters is the order of magnitude.

116 14 units in Arizona in the year 1912 (*supra* text after note 85) and 10 units in New Jersey about 1900; *see* WOLLSCHLÄGER, *supra* note 58.

117 *Cf.* HALEY, *supra* note 2; RAMSEYER & NAKAZATO, *supra* note 2; TANASE, *supra* note 12.

118 *See* R.A. EASTERLIN, Population, Labor Force, and Long Swings in Economic Growth: The American Experience (1986).

efficient network of dense social relations, which is essential for private dispute resolution and norm enforcement, could not evolve in either environment.

Increasing social mobility also characterized 19th-century Germany where urbanization was similarly fostered by internal migrations. Rural population poured into towns and cities to find job opportunities in industry and trade.[119] In the 20th century, millions of refugees and immigrant workers were absorbed by the West German population after World War II. All of these developments dissolved the intimate social relations which had prevailed in agrarian periods.

The Japanese system of life-long employment seems to be a main reason for the absence of comparable social mobility. Stable neighborhoods are the basis of efficient private social control. They are an evident precondition for the avoidance of litigation. Traditional values and attitudes are passed from one generation to the next in an environment where social learning by doing persists. Social structures can remain untouched over time.

e. Consumer Relations

The Prussian and the German time series also point to consumer relations as another field where essential differences exist in relation to Japan. Expanding consumer credit was a major cause of increasing judicial business in the 19th century.[120] If consumer problems were resolved more effectively by private negotiation and mediation as in Japan, a large source of litigation in Western countries would be decisively smaller, if not absent. This again is closely related to social mobility and the intimacy of personal and business relations. Creditors who know that they depend on the future goodwill of their debtors will be cautious to risk continuing relationships by judicial intervention.

2. *Pre-Modern Metropolitan Litigation*

Litigation rates were traced back to the feudal era for the judicial authorities in Edo and Osaka.[121] In both metropolitan jurisdictions, the pre-modern demand for civil justice had the same size as in 1875. Fragments of litigation waves and the dominance of money suits gave further evidence of continuity with later developments. The Western-style courts were neither rejected nor did they attract more lawsuits than their feudal predecessors. The evidence of the two cities underlines that the stable litigation patterns of imperial Japan extend farther back in history. Needless to say, the traditionalist explanation of court avoidance alone captures this point.

---

119 *See* WEHLER, *supra* note 102.
120 *See* text accompanying note 103 *supra*.
121 *See* text accompanying note 76 *supra*.

Among European cities, Bremen offers a sharp contrast in the transition from a pre-industrial to a modern litigation pattern. Bremen was a German commercial center, a port like Osaka, though not quite as populous. In about 1780, the litigation rates were quite similar in both cities.[122] Within the next 100 years, the rate rose threefold in Bremen. This fits into the general pattern of urbanization in Europe, where civil litigation, divorce, and criminality increased in the expanding cities. These effects were absent in Osaka, where the litigation rate was nearly the same in 1875 as it had been in 1786.[123] The contrast illustrates once more that the continuity of pre-modern social patterns of dispute resolution constitutes the specific element of the Japanese legal culture.

3. *The Litigation Wave of the Meiji Reforms*

The litigation wave of the Meiji reforms during phase A proved to be a singular event which was caused by the *Matsukata* finance crisis.[124] As such it is no evidence for permanent changes in the demand for civil justice. Its exceptional nature is underlined by the clear parallel in the German time series. The litigation explosion which occurred during the Great Depression in 1931 had no historical counterpart earlier or later.[125] Its short-lived effects are not representative of normal attitudes towards courts.

4. *The Insignificance of Formal Conciliation (chôtei)*

Formal conciliation procedures have become nearly extinct in continental Europe;[126] they are unknown in Anglo-American jurisdictions. Hence Kawashima could justly present *chôtei* as a specific form of Japanese dispute resolution.[127] However, he misconceived the nature of formal conciliation as a way of establishing harmony between the parties. Judicial statistics rather show that conciliation was mainly used for debt collection. This was demonstrated by the substitution of dunning for *kankai* in 1891 and by the reverse process

122 23 cases per 1,000 population in Bremen and 26 to 53 in Osaka. Bremen's population grew from 33,000 in 1780 to 143,000 in 1875. The litigation rate rose to 76 units. *See* WOLLSCHLÄGER, *supra* note 49, at 268.

123 *See* text accompanying note 77 *supra*.

124 *See* text accompanying note 36 *supra*.

125 *See* text accompanying note 98 *supra*.

126 *See* WOLLSCHLÄGER, *supra* note 15, at 30-41; *id. supra* note 22, at 20-26.

127 *Supra* note 1.

between *chôtei* and dunning in the early Showa era.[128] The history of Italian civil procedure offers a clear parallel here.[129]

Kawashima also overstated the role of formal conciliation as an explanation for the avoidance of litigation. The share of *chôtei* cases had reached a climax before, during, and after World War II. The abnormal political and economic conditions do not allow the conclusion of genuine preferences for conciliation. After the following decline, only 0.5 conciliation cases per 1,000 population remained in 1990. This quantity is negligible in international comparison. The distance between contemporary Japanese and Western levels is by far too big to be explained by *chôtei*. While conciliation continues to be an essential element of the Japanese legal culture, this is true nowadays for private conciliation only.[130]

5. *The Downward Shift from Imperial Japan to Postwar Japan*

The "structural drop" between the mean litigation rates before and after World War II has no European or American parallel. This circumstance alone suggests that the unique phenomenon might be irrelevant in international comparison. In the earlier discussion, Haley's assumption that deficiencies of the court system were responsible for the lower demand for civil justice was seen as a conclusive hypothesis so far.[131] Longitudinal international comparison suggests a complete dismissal of the institutional explanation. During the whole 20th century, the distance between Japanese and German litigation rates was so wide that the downward shift did not matter. German rates ranged at about 80 units after the Korean crisis. Japan's "structural drop" from the average prewar rate of 8.0 down to 4.5 units between 1954 and 1973 widened the distance to Western nations to some minor extent. The basic difference in the demand for civil justice was not affected.

If deficiencies of the court system exist at all, they may have exercised an additional causal effect at best. Even the latter has not been proven systematically. The downward shift of civil litigation constitutes an interesting phenomenon in the history of postwar Japan which still awaits a satisfactory explanation. But its significance does not reach farther.

The institutional explanation thus missed the essential historical foundation of Japanese avoidance of litigation. These are convincingly described in Haley's

128 *See* text accompanying note 61 *supra*.

129 *See* WOLLSCHLÄGER, *supra* note 15, at 71. The same can be presumed for France, although no data are available after the introduction of the dunning procedure.

130 *See* also D.F. HENDERSON, Dispute Resolution Systems Other Than Litigation, *in* 2 Kodansha Encyclopedia of Japan 117 (1985).

131 *Supra* sec. II.2.

later book which returned to the historical core of Kawashima's thesis.[132] The distance from Western nations arose out of the absence of expansive growth processes, which lasted over generations. Social structures of norm enforcement and informal dispute resolution, which remained stable for centuries, are the decisive factor which explains Japanese legal culture.

6. *The Trend Break After the Oil Crisis and Future Development*

The upward direction of the contemporary trend constitutes a novel feature in the secular development. For the first time in history, Japanese civil caseloads are taking the same course as in Western nations.[133] Whereas the adjusted total of filings had been limited to population growth in the preceding phase of economic expansion (D), this limitation seems to have been removed. Litigation rates rose between the troughs of 1973 and 1990 just as they did in Arizona, Germany, Sweden, and all other industrialized nations.

The size of the economy seems to emerge as the new dominant factor which determines the demand for civil justice. The impact of economic growth on litigation thus differs essentially from past patterns. The post-Korean War expansion since 1953 was neutral in its effect on the use of courts until 1973. The increase of the adjusted total between the troughs (88%) roughly corresponds to the growth of gross national product (108%). This indicates a new power balance among the many determinants of litigation. A new causal structure underlies the trend break. Consequently, higher caseloads can be predicted for the future. Economic growth will add to judicial business in the long run. The Japanese justice system will have to face higher burdens, mitigated only by middle-term fluctuations in the business cycle.

The causes of the trend break which occurred in or around 1973 are still unclear. Similar observations in other states, such as Germany, Austria, Sweden, and New Jersey, suggest that the underlying forces have international dimensions. The years of "economic miracles" were over. National economies shrunk or grew at modest rates only. The oil price shock may have been the event that initiated structural changes in the fabric of the many determinants of civil litigation.[134] A new generation, born after the war, took over active roles. Social unrest and student movements of the preceding years may be alternative (or interrelated) explanations.

Whatever the causes, they are not specific for Japan. Moreover, the distance from Western litigation rates will remain in the future. Even the peaks of the

---

132 HALEY, *supra* note 10, ch. 3, 5, 8. A reviewer noted a "retreat", JOHNSON, *supra* note 2, at 622.

133 The steep rise during the recovery phase after World War II is not comparable.

134 *See* KATO, *supra* note 6, at 664; WOLLSCHLÄGER, *supra* note 58.

litigation waves in 1984 (10.5 units) and 1994 (9.4 units) were only one tenth of German, Swedish or Israeli values.[135] To reach the high Western levels, the demand for civil justice would have to change in quite unprecedented ways. The activity of courts would have to expand into new fields of mass litigation such as consumer credit or landlord-tenant relations, e.g. In the foreseeable future, the avoidance of litigation will continue as a distinctive element of the Japanese legal culture.[136]

CONCLUSION: THEORIES AND HISTORICAL JUDICIAL STATISTICS

The present study could not exhaust the wealth of historical information which is offered by Japanese judicial statistics. Only basic data were analyzed over time: the national totals of the civil business of the courts of first instance, the composition of caseloads, and the object of litigation. Stable mean litigation rates per capita in imperial Japan and in the postwar phase of economic expansion were the main findings. They showed the historical origins of the avoidance of litigation as well as the continuity of effective private means of dispute resolution and norm enforcement. The low demand for civil justice could be traced back to the 18th century for metropolitan courts.

The findings confirm the traditionalist explanation of the avoidance of litigation as it was laid down in Kawashima's historical studies and which is now followed by Henderson and Haley in their recent writings.[137] Social attitudes towards law which continue from an agrarian feudal state are indeed the only basis for explaining the stable secular development of litigation in Japan as well as the wide distance from Western nations. The low demand for civil justice is a genuine element of legal culture insofar as it distinguishes the practical operation of law from Western nations. It is the Japanese aspect of Japanese law which otherwise comprises many foreign imports.

Concurring theories are hardly compatible with the conclusions which were drawn from judicial statistics here. Few studies provide comparative empirical evidence at all, simply asserting different notions of legal consciousness between Japan and the West. Opinion polls among Japanese citizens provide basically the same answers as in Western nations, namely that litigation is an unwelcome and ineffective means of dispute resolution. This is by no means specific for Japan. Cultural properties cannot be proven by unilateral national research.

---

135 *Cf. supra* sec. I. table 1.

136 For mathematical entertainment: if the linear trend of the contemporary phase E (*supra* note 111) were extended into the future, it would take 400 years to reach the level of 100 units in the top group.

137 *Supra* notes 9-10.

Hard evidence of different national propensities to sue has been established in the field of automobile tort litigation.[138] The latter constitutes only a fraction of the whole civil business of courts, however (0.8% of the adjusted total of filings in 1990). The various explanations which are suggested in these studies are therefore valid for a small sector only, not to mention their lack of historical relevance. The predictability of judicial decisions, e.g., certainly matters for attorneys, insurance agents, and other professionals who process traffic accident cases. The explanation does not fit the mass of contract cases, most of which are initiated without attorneys. It is in this field of business and consumer relations that the Japanese abilities of consensual dispute resolution become most relevant. Judicial statistics, which measure litigation as a whole, ensure that the traditionalist explanation is valid in the broadest and most important field of civil justice.

Kawashima himself emphasized mentalities. He contrasted the spirit of social harmony with Western rights consciousness. This aspect of his thesis, which has been carefully distinguished from his description of traditional social structures,[139] has found more attention than his historical studies. It has been simplified quite often. It has been criticized as a "myth", an ideology of the rulers rather than a correct historical or empirical description. Indeed, the underlying evolutionary notion of a progressive parallel rise of litigation rates and rights consciousness finds no support from historical judicial statistics. Time series of four nations instead show individual national patterns on the way to modernity. Kawashima's view of formal conciliation could not be confirmed either. Historical mentalities are difficult to prove. Whether social harmony is wishful thinking on the part of the rulers or an effective means of problem solving in everyday life is a question that needs further discussion. Whatever the answers, the historical origins of the avoidance of litigation should be safe grounds for ongoing research.

---

138 TANASE, *supra* note 12. *See* also RAMSEYER & NAKAZATO, *supra* note 2 and FOOTE, *supra* note 12. Though not strictly comparative in the research design, both show plausible contrasts to the jury system of the U.S.

139 ROKUMOTO, *supra* note 11.

APPENDIX

Sources of Judicial Statistics

A. *Japan*

1. NIHON TEIKOKU SHIHÔSHO [Ministry of Justice of the Empire of Japan], *Minji Tôkei Nenpô* [Annual Report on Civil Case Statistics.] Vol. 1 Meiji 8 (1875) - Vol. 67 Showa 16 (1941).
2. SAIKO SAIBANSHO JIMU SÔKYOKU [Supreme Court. General Secretariat], *Shôwa 25: Nen Shihô Nenpô 1 Minji Hen* [1950 - Annual Reports of Judicial Statistics, Book 1 Civil Cases].
3. SAIKÔ SAIBANSHO JIMU SÔKYOKU [Supreme Court. General Secretariat], *Meiji i-kô saiban tôkei yôran* [Synopsis of Post-Meiji Judicial Statistics] (1969).
   Complete retrospective of national data 1875-1967. With annotations on systematic changes.
4. *Nihon chôki tôkei sôran / Historical Statistics of Japan*, Tokyo 1987. Vol. 5 Table 24-7.
   Incomplete and misleading. Data for 1875-1890 and 1942-47 are missing. The systematic change of the year 1930 is ignored, causing an artificial discontinuity in the series.

B. *Arizona*

5. ARIZONA. ADMINISTRATIVE OFFICE OF THE COURTS, *The Superior Court in Arizona 1912-1984. A History of the Court in Each County Since Statehood.* Phoenix AZ, Supreme Court. 1985.
6. ARIZONA. ADMINISTRATIVE OFFICE OF THE COURTS, *The Arizona Courts. 1977* (...) *Annual Judicial Report.* Phoenix AZ, Supreme Court. 1978 (continued).
7. NATIONAL CENTER FOR STATE COURTS, *State Court Caseload Statistics. Annual Report 1990*, Williamsburg, Va. 1992.

C. *Sweden*

8. *Bidrag till Sverige's officiela statistik. B) Rättsväsendet. Ny följd* [Contribution to Sweden's Official Statistics. Justice. New Series] I 3a., N. F. 1 - 55. 1860-1913.
9. STATISTISKA CENTRALBYRÅN [Central Statistical Office], *Statistisk Årsbok* 1913-1974 [Statistical Yearbook] Stockholm.
10. STATISTIKA CENTRALBYRÅN [Central Statistical Office], *Rättsstatistik Årsbok* 1975-1993 [Yearbook of Judicial Statistics] Stockholm.

D. *Germany and Prussia*

District of the Kammergericht Berlin: General legal periodicals, official serial publications, and archival records of the Ministry of Justice. Cf. *supra* note 100.

German data for 1880-1939 have been computed using published and archival sources of federal states and the nation. Postwar data are based on the literature, publications of the ministries of justice of federal states, statistical yearbooks, special series of the Federal Statistical Office, and the electronic data base of the Federal Ministry of Justice. *Cf.* WOLLSCHLÄGER *supra* note 15, at 105.

E. *International (Figure 1)*

11. [People's Republic of China] STATE STATISTICAL BUREAU. *China. Statistical Yearbook* 1990. Beijing.
12. [Colombia] DEPARTAMENTO ADMINISTRATIVO NACIONAL DE ESTADÍSTICA, *Colombia Estadística.* 1990. Vol. 1 Nacional. Bogotà.
13. [England & Wales: United Kingdom] LORD CHANCELLOR'S DEPARTMENT, *Judicial Statistics. Statistics Relating to [. . .] Civil Courts for the Year 1990.* London 1992.
14. [France] MINISTERE DE LA JUSTICE, *Annuaire Statistique de la Justice. 1992.* Paris.
15. [Nepal] NATIONAL PLANNING SECRETARIAT. CENTRAL BUREAU OF STATISTICS, *Statistical Yearbook of Nepal.* 4th ed. 1993. Kathmandu.
16. [New Zealand] Law Commission. Report No. 7. *The Structure of Courts.* Wellington 1989, p. 234.
17. [Solomon Islands] STATISTICS OFFICE, *Statistical Yearbook.* Vol. 7. [s. l., s. d., Honiara 1987?].

Table 3: Comparative Litigation Rates 1773-1990
Civil Cases Filed in Courts of First Instance per 1000 population

Year	Germany		Sweden			Arizona		Japan	
	Total	Ordi nary Proce dure	Total	Muni cipal Court O. P.	Rural Court Ord. Proc.	Total	Sup. Court	Total	Ordi nary Proce dure
	Berlin								
1773	7.5								
1780	10.0								
1815	18.7								
1822	32.9								
1831	46.2			46.0	36.9				
1837	45.1		59.1	32.9	29.1				
1840	51.4		66.1	33.7	30.4				
1846	64.4		54.3	27.5	24.4				
1852	66.1		57.2	24.8	19.2				
1855	78.5		30.9	18.4	14.3				
1861	82.3		35.1	19.8	9.0				
1867	114.0		57.4	23.8	9.6				
1875	92.0		20.4	14.2	5.3			13.8	13.4

continues on next page

Table 3: Comparative Litigation Rates 1773-1994 (continued)

Year	Germany		Sweden			Arizona		Japan	
	Total	Ordinary Procedure	Total	Municipal Court O. P.	Rural Court Ord. Proc.	Total	Sup. Court	Total	Ordinary Procedure
	Germany								
1880	83.2	27.3	20.8	17.8	6.3			19.6	3.6
1883	74.3	26.3	17.3	18.5	5.6			28.1	6.4
1885	67.2	24.7	20.2	23.5	6.0			15.1	1.4
1889	68.1	26.8	16.9	16.5	5.6			7.5	1.3
1890	66.8	27.6	14.1	17.7	5.1			8.6	1.9
1891	71.1	30.2	14.9	20.4	5.4			8.6	3.4
1895	71.1	32.5	13.5	18.3	5.0			6.7	2.2
1896	69.0	32.0	13.1	18.7	5.2			6.1	1.9
1900	69.0	35.3	13.4	23.3	5.6			8.7	2.4
1903	73.3	38.8	13.2	23.1	5.7			11.9	3.2
1905	69.2	38.4						7.7	2.2
1907	73.2	41.6	12.5	23.2	5.2			6.2	1.8
1910	80.7	45.7	15.8	26.1	5.4			7.7	2.0
1913	95.2	48.0	13.9	24.8	5.7		9.7	9.0	2.5
1915	46.6	21.3	12.3	21.5	5.7		9.7	11.4	3.1
1919	32.8	16.2	9.1	16.9	4.5		11.5	5.4	2.2
1920	41.9	20.6	10.8	19.3	5.8		11.6	5.7	2.3
1925	145.0	57.4	13.4	20.2	7.7		11.7	9.4	3.8
1929	186.4	64.7	12.6	17.3	7.2		12.1	9.8	3.8
1930	200.4	69.0	12.4	17.3	6.8		12.0		3.9
1931	214.8	73.3	13.1	18.1	7.1		11.6	11.3	4.0
1935	93.1	31.2	10.6	13.2	5.4		10.5	8.4	2.8
1938	76.6	24.4	9.9	12.0	5.6		9.8	5.0	1.9
1940			9.6	11.2	5.4		9.3	3.0	1.2
1945			7.7	8.5	4.5		13.3	0.6	0.2
1948		13.7	16.1	5.7	3.8		14.7	1.6	0.5
1950	82.1	28.4	18.4	5.8	3.7		13.3	2.8	0.8
1952	92.5	26.1	20.3	5.7	3.8		12.6	3.2	1.0
1954	97.5	23.5	24.7	6.0	4.2		14.0	4.5	1.5
1955	94.2	21.8	27.4	5.9	4.4		13.5	4.7	1.6
1960	83.3	18.2	30.0	5.4	4.8		16.5	4.4	1.6
1963	83.5	17.8	35.0	5.6	5.6	21.8	18.2	3.9	1.3
1965	79.8	17.0	35.0	5.9			18.8	4.7	1.3
1970	84.0	17.5	38.3	6.8			19.1	4.9	1.4
1974	100.4	20.1	32.3	6.7		34.6	22.6	4.0	1.2
1975	97.0	20.2	34.3	6.8		36.8	23.2	4.3	1.1
1980	98.2	20.5	68.5	8.1		43.9	24.0	6.1	1.6
1984	123.4	25.3	69.5	8.5		51.2	22.8	10.5	2.7
1985	127.7	26.7	73.2	8.6		57.0	25.5	10.0	2.8
1990	107.4	24.6	90.0	8.2		63.7	26.0	6.4	1.6
1994								9.4	3.1

Table 4: Japan: Civil Cases in Courts of First Instance 1875-1994
Definitions: Supra text accompanying note 25

Year	Cases in 1000		*Index Values 1952 = 100*		Percentage of Adjusted Total			
	Adjusted Total	Ordinary Procedure	*Adjusted Total*	*Ordinary Procedure*	Ordinary Procedure	Conciliation adjusted	Dunning adjusted	Provisional Procedures
1875	489	473	*180*	*548*	97%	3%		
1876	638	470	*246*	*544*	74%	30%		
1877	795	180	*293*	*208*	23%	77%		
1878	735	145	*270*	*168*	20%	80%		
1879	717	136	*264*	*158*	19%	81%		
1880	718	132	*264*	*153*	18%	82%		
1881	755	131	*278*	*152*	17%	83%		
1882	870	189	*321*	*218*	22%	78%		
1883	1,054	240	*389*	*278*	23%	77%		
1884	742	139	*273*	*161*	19%	81%		
1885	580	52	*213*	*60*	9%	91%		
1886	489	50	*180*	*58*	10%	90%		
1887	361	51	*133*	*59*	14%	86%		
1888	307	51	*113*	*59*	16%	84%		
1889	298	52	*110*	*60*	17%	83%		
1890	341	77	*126*	*90*	23%	77%		
1891	345	137	*127*	*158*	40%	20%	28%	12%
1892	330	118	*121*	*137*	36%	10%	37%	16%
1893	314	111	*115*	*129*	35%	7%	42%	16%
1894	323	107	*119*	*124*	33%	4%	46%	17%
1895	278	90	*102*	*105*	32%	4%	48%	16%
1896	255	80	*94*	*92*	31%	3%	48%	17%
1897	285	84	*105*	*97*	29%	3%	51%	17%
1898	356	97	*131*	*113*	27%	2%	54%	17%
1899	384	106	*141*	*123*	28%	1%	56%	15%
1900	380	105	*140*	*121*	28%	0%	56%	16%
1901	459	121	*169*	*141*	26%	0%	57%	16%
1902	498	132	*183*	*153*	26%	0%	58%	15%
1903	544	144	*200*	*167*	26%	0%	57%	16%
1904	487	127	*179*	*147*	26%	0%	57%	17%
1905	361	101	*133*	*117*	28%	0%	55%	17%
1906	321	91	*118*	*105*	28%	0%	54%	17%
1907	293	85	*108*	*99*	29%	0%	53%	18%
1908	318	91	*117*	*105*	28%	0%	53%	18%
1909	347	94	*128*	*109*	27%	0%	55%	17%
1910	380	100	*140*	*116*	26%	0%	57%	17%

continues on next page

Year	Cases in 1000		*Index Values 1952 = 100*		Percentage of Adjusted Total			
	Adjusted Total	Ordinary Procedure	*Adjusted Total*	*Ordinary Procedure*	Ordinary Procedure	Conciliation adjusted	Dunning adjusted	Provisional Procedures
1911	399	106	*147*	*123*	27%	0%	57%	16%
1912	429	117	*158*	*136*	27%	0%	57%	16%
1913	463	131	*170*	*151*	28%	0%	57%	14%
1914	534	148	*196*	*172*	28%	0%	59%	13%
1915	601	163	*221*	*188*	27%	0%	61%	12%
1916	549	159	*202*	*185*	29%	0%	59%	12%
1917	401	133	*148*	*154*	33%	0%	55%	12%
1918	328	121	*121*	*140*	37%	0%	50%	13%
1919	298	119	*110*	*138*	40%	0%	46%	14%
1920	316	129	*116*	*150*	41%	0%	45%	14%
1921	384	149	*141*	*172*	39%	0%	49%	12%
1922	424	169	*156*	*196*	40%	0%	48%	12%
1923	487	188	*179*	*218*	39%	2%	49%	11%
1924	544	209	*200*	*242*	38%	3%	48%	11%
1925	562	225	*207*	*261*	40%	3%	47%	11%
1926	581	237	*214*	*275*	41%	3%	45%	11%
1927	619	249	*228*	*288*	40%	4%	45%	11%
1928	615	248	*226*	*288*	40%	4%	45%	11%
1929	619	243	*228*	*281*	39%	4%	46%	11%
1930		250		*290*				
1931	741	262	*272*	*303*	35%	6%	49%	10%
1932	717	255	*264*	*296*	36%	9%	44%	11%
1933	667	228	*245*	*264*	34%	17%	38%	10%
1934	600	205	*221*	*237*	34%	19%	37%	10%
1935	584	197	*215*	*228*	34%	22%	35%	10%
1936	530	180	*195*	*209*	34%	21%	35%	10%
1937	441	159	*162*	*184*	36%	20%	33%	10%
1938	354	132	*130*	*153*	37%	21%	32%	10%
1939	276	106	*102*	*123*	38%	21%	30%	10%
1940	217	88	*80*	*102*	41%	22%	27%	11%
1941	178	76	*66*	*88*	42%	22%	26%	10%
1942	142	58	*52*	*67*	41%	26%	24%	9%
1943	117	48	*43*	*56*	41%	27%	23%	9%
1944	79	33	*29*	*38*	42%	31%	19%	8%
1945	40	16	*15*	*18*	39%	35%	18%	7%
1946	55	20	*20*	*23*	37%	46%	6%	11%
1947	65	25	*24*	*28*	38%	43%	6%	13%
1948	131	37	*48*	*43*	28%	30%	6%	12%
1949	160	43	*59*	*50*	27%	27%	11%	11%

continues on next page

Year	Cases in 1000		*Index Values 1952 = 100*		Percentage of Adjusted Total			
	Adjusted Total	Ordinary Procedure	*Adjusted Total*	*Ordinary Procedure*	Ordinary Procedure	Conciliation adjusted	Dunning adjusted	Provisional Procedures
1950	232	67	*85*	*77*	29%	25%	18%	10%
1951	245	77	*90*	*89*	31%	25%	18%	10%
1952	272	86	*100*	*100*	32%	24%	19%	12%
1953	309	100	*114*	*116*	32%	23%	20%	13%
1954	394	132	*145*	*154*	34%	20%	23%	13%
1955	417	143	*153*	*166*	34%	20%	25%	11%
1956	415	145	*152*	*168*	35%	19%	24%	11%
1957	419	150	*154*	*174*	36%	18%	23%	12%
1958	449	162	*165*	*188*	36%	17%	25%	11%
1959	435	156	*160*	*181*	36%	17%	25%	11%
1960	413	147	*152*	*170*	36%	16%	26%	12%
1961	388	135	*143*	*156*	35%	16%	27%	12%
1962	383	131	*141*	*152*	34%	16%	27%	12%
1963	375	128	*138*	*148*	34%	15%	28%	12%
1964	404	135	*149*	*156*	33%	13%	30%	12%
1965	461	132	*170*	*153*	29%	12%	31%	11%
1966	488	138	*180*	*160*	28%	11%	33%	11%
1967	502	139	*185*	*161*	28%	10%	33%	12%
1968	525	148	*193*	*172*	28%	10%	32%	12%
1969	505	143	*186*	*166*	28%	10%	33%	11%
1970	506	148	*186*	*171*	29%	10%	32%	10%
1971	512	152	*188*	*176*	30%	10%	33%	10%
1972	481	143	*177*	*166*	30%	10%	31%	10%
1973	438	130	*161*	*151*	30%	10%	30%	10%
1974	445	128	*164*	*148*	29%	9%	32%	10%
1975	477	128	*175*	*148*	27%	9%	35%	9%
1976	505	135	*186*	*157*	27%	10%	33%	10%
1977	562	148	*207*	*171*	26%	11%	33%	10%
1978	590	155	*217*	*180*	26%	11%	36%	9%
1979	626	162	*230*	*187*	26%	9%	40%	8%
1980	716	183	*263*	*212*	26%	8%	43%	8%
1981	782	202	*288*	*233*	26%	9%	45%	7%
1982	920	243	*338*	*282*	26%	8%	47%	7%
1983	1,074	273	*395*	*317*	25%	11%	48%	6%
1984	1,267	327	*466*	*379*	26%	11%	49%	6%
1985	1,207	344	*444*	*398*	28%	6%	51%	6%
1986	1,138	329	*419*	*381*	29%	5%	51%	6%
1987	1,085	308	*399*	*356*	28%	5%	52%	5%

continues on next page

Year	Cases in 1000		*Index Values 1952 = 100*		Percentage of Adjusted Total			
	Adjusted Total	Ordinary Procedure	*Adjusted Total*	*Ordinary Procedure*	Ordinary Procedure	Conciliation adjusted	Dunning adjusted	Provisional Procedures
1988	961	264	*353*	*306*	28%	6%	52%	5%
1989	826	223	*304*	*259*	27%	6%	50%	5%
1990	792	204	*291*	*236*	26%	7%	51%	5%
1991	891	223	*328*	*258*	25%	8%	52%	5%
1992	1,063	298	*391*	*345*	28%	9%	50%	5%
1993	1,146	371	*422*	*430*	32%	9%	46%	4%
1994	1,173	391	*431*	*452*	33%	9%	45%	4%

Part Two:
Law and Contract in Japanese Businesses

Chapter Four

Use and Non-Use of Contracts in Japanese Business Relations: A Comparative Analysis

*Zentaro Kitagawa**

Contents

---

* The author wishes to thank *Mr. Andrew H. Thorson*, Esq., graduate student at the Faculty of Law, Kyoto University, who kindly read my manuscript and corrected the English with valuable suggestions. Of course the author is solely responsible for the contents of this paper.

A. Is Japanese Contract Law Pre-Modern?

1. The Modernist View of Japan

Japan "modernized" her law more than one century ago by receiving Western legal systems[1]. After World War II, Japan again experienced "modernization" of her law by the introduction of the U.S. legal system[2]. While it would certainly be correct for many of us to refer to these changes as "modernization" of law in Japan, and to these periods of transition as "periods of modernization", such descriptions of legal transitions without reservations may mislead us in understanding the comparative differences between the Japanese legal system and Western legal systems.[3]

During Japan's postwar development period, leading Japanese scholars such as *Kawashima*[4] stressed the uniqueness of Japanese legal thinking, most impressively in the field of contract law and the pre-modern attitude of Japanese toward contracts. They raised such questions as: [1] why do Japanese not usually produce written contracts, and even if they do, why are such contracts drafted without detail? and [2] why do Japanese not feel bound by their contractual commitments? For instance, these scholars critically compared the careful and detailed drafting of contracts and strict insistence on contract rights found in the U.S. with the Japanese preference for informality and simplicity in contract drafting and the tendency toward accommodation and compromise. They contended that these unique features of the Japanese legal attitude toward contracts are the residue of traditional and pre-modern ways of thinking, the implication being that Japan should be "modernized" in the mold of the Western legal mind. Theories of this nature, which I characterize as the moder-

---

1 *See* Y. NODA, Introduction to Japanese Law, 41 (A. Angelo trans., 1976); Z. KITAGAWA, Rezeption und Fortbildung des europaischen Zivilrechts in Japan [The Adoption and Development of the European Civil Law in Japan] (1970); Z. KITAGAWA, *Nihon hôgaku no rekishi to riron - minpô-gaku wo chûshin to shite* [History and Theory of Japanese Jurisprudence: Focusing on Civil Law] (1968).

2 A. VON MEHREN, Law in Japan: The Legal Order in a Changing Society (1963).

3 The issue of modernization of Japanese law is, domestically and internationally, an old but still current one. With regard to this issue, I myself have recently published, among others, *Kokusai masatsu no naka no nihon-hô* [Japanese Law Amidst International Frictions - Part 1-3], NBL No. 500, No. 501, No. 502 (1992); Modernization and Japanese Law: A Thought on "Another Modern", presented at the Symposium on "Law and Modernization" of the 1995 Annual Meeting of the Research Committee on Sociology of Law, International Sociological Association, Tokyo.

4 *See* T. KAWASHIMA, *Nihon-jin no hô-ishiki* [Japanese Legal Consciousness] (1967); *id.*, Dispute Resolution in Contemporary Japan, *in* A. von Mehren, *supra* note 2, at 41; *id.*, The Legal Consciousness of Contract in Japan, 7 Law in Japan 1 (Stevens trans., 1974); W. GRAY, The Use and Non-Use of Contract Law in Japan: A Preliminary Study, 17 LAW IN JAPAN 103 (1984).

nist view,[5] have exercised a serious impact not only upon Japan's postwar ideology, but also upon the way that Japanese law is observed abroad. Even today, U.S. attorneys who are hired by U.S. clients to negotiate with Japanese firms often believe, in accordance with this modernist view, that Japanese do not observe what they promise in their contracts.[6]

2. *Some Critical Observations*

This modernist view, however, has long been criticized both from inside and outside Japan. Some critics maintain that distinctive features of Japanese contract making should not be attributed to general legal consciousness (*hô-ishiki*), that American and Japanese businesspersons observe contracts similarly, and that a comparison at the level of lawyers in the two countries does not indicate the existence of any significant gap with respect to contractual consciousness. These three points are worthy of further discussion and study. First, with regard to comparing the general legal consciousness of Japanese and non-Japanese businesspersons, critics have pointed out that modernist views of Japan usually focus upon the attitudes of different groups in the two countries: namely, U.S. lawyers and Japanese businesspersons.[7] Thus, there is sometimes a mismatch in the target groups compared. Lawyers and businesspersons are significantly different target groups. Second, comparative studies which do not compare the appropriate target groups could mislead us into believing in gaps which do not actually exist. In fact, such may be the case with regard to the alleged gap between Japanese and U.S. general legal consciousness. Insofar as *Macaulay's* empirical research indicates that U.S. businesspersons cannot utilize legal rules which oppose their own common sense,[8] a character trait

---

5 Z. Kitagawa, Resonance Theory: A Tentative Approach to the Dispute Settlement Mechanism, *in* Commemorative Work for Constantinesco, 394 (1983).

6 This is an episode a Japanese professor experienced as a visiting professor at a U.S. law school. *See* S. Michida, *Keiyaku-shakai: Amerika to nihon no chigai wo miru* [Contractual Society: Observing Differences Between the U.S. and Japan] 1 (1987).

7 Gray, *supra* note 4, at 101.

8 S. Macaulay, The Use and Non-Use of Contracts in the Manufacturing Industry, 9 The Practical Lawyer 13 (1963); *id.*, Non-Contractual Relations in Business: A Preliminary Study, 28 Am. Soc. Rev. 55 (1963). A similar attitude is also found among business people in the United Kingdom. *See* W. Howarth, Contract, Reliance and Business Transactions, Journal of Business Law 122 (1987); Gray, *supra* note 4, at 101.

S. Macaulay's empirical surveys revealed U.S. businessmen's negative attitude towards contracts: "Contracts are a waste of time. We've never had any trouble, because we know our customers and our suppliers. If we needed a contract with a man, we wouldn't deal with him." "Lawyers are overprotective and just get in the way of buying or selling. If business had to be done by lawyers as buyers and sellers, the economy would stop. No one would buy or sell anything; they'd just negotiate for ever." (The Use and Non-Use of Contracts, p. 17.) According to

which scholars have found to exist among Japanese businesspersons as well, this is an indication that the differences between the attitudes of U.S. and Japanese businesspersons toward contracts are not fundamentally different.[9]

Critics of the modernist view also maintain that a comparison of the attitudes of lawyers in the two countries does not indicate the existence of a significant difference in contractual consciousness. It is true that lawyers in Japan and the U.S. view contracts similarly, even though U.S. lawyers are more knowledgeable about business practices and more likely to participate regularly in the negotiating and drafting process.[10]

Furthermore, and in addition to the above, special attention should be drawn to structural and theoretical differences between Japanese and U.S. contract law. Such differences influence contract practices but have not received adequate attention. For example, in the U.S. the choice of law rules in interstate transactions is uncertain, and more generally, spelling out the precise rules of case law is often difficult. Common law itself necessitates long, detailed, and self-sufficient contract documents. Common law concepts such as consideration, the parole evidence rule, or the Statute of Frauds make drafting enforceable contracts a difficult task. Thus, forming an enforceable contract in the U.S. sometimes necessitates the employment of skilled and technical lawyers in the drafting stage in order to make certain the contract is enforceable at law. Because the Japanese civil law, as in other civil law systems, does not recognize such common law concepts, forming contracts under Japanese law and in other civil law jurisdictions is a relatively simple affair. The law of conditions, which creates subtle and tricky loopholes that can make even a detailed contract inoperable in a common law jurisdiction, is a negligible matter in Japanese and European contracts because under the civil law it has a different meaning and operation.[11] In some circumstances, a comparatively brief Japanese contract may therefore function as effectively as its lengthy U.S. counterpart. These and other legal factors figure prominently in the tendency of civil law contracts to be less self-sufficient than common law contracts.

We must consider each of the above factors when discussing the use and non-use of contracts in business relations. When negotiating contracts, Japanese

---

Macaulay, his survey has not been reflected yet in books on contract law in the U.S. This comment was in response to this author's personal question in August 1995 on the occasion of the Annual Meeting of the Sociology of Law Association.

9 GRAY, *supra* note 4, at 104.

10 GRAY, *supra* note 4, at 101.

11 GRAY, *supra* note 4, at 102: ". . . a fact which is often overlooked in comparing long contracts used in the United States with shorter Japanese agreements in similar situations is the inherent uncertainty of the rules of law in the United States." As to a comparative analysis of these differences, *see* the detailed discussions *in* W. SHATTUCK & Z. KITAGAWA, United States/Japanese Contract and Sale Problems (Univ. of Washington, 1973).

as well as non-Japanese, particularly Americans, need to keep these comparative differences in mind. Japanese should also explain to their counterparts the operation of the pertinent provisions of Civil and Commercial Codes that supplement their short and simple contracts. Likewise, U.S. lawyers should refrain from interpreting the short and simple Japanese contract in accordance with common law traditions.

B. Development of the Problem: The Characteristics of Japanese Contracts

1. Need for a Renewed Questioning

We have just finished a brief examination of the modernist view, which stresses Japanese contract law's pre-modern tendencies and the alleged differences between the general contractual consciousness of Japanese and non-Japanese. We also discussed some criticism directed at the modernist view. While it is true that the views of both businesspersons and lawyers in the U.S. and Japan regarding contracts are similar, a series problems continue to exist and need to be addressed, for Japanese contracts, in my view, still differ from U.S. and European contracts. The drafting technique of contracts, the contract negotiation, the contract dispute resolution, the interpretation of contracts, etc., are some examples of instances where an in-depth analysis is needed for locating such differences. Thus, we must reexamine the question of what the characteristics of Japanese contracts are when compared to the contracts of the U.S. and Europe in relation to such issues.

The question, "What are the characteristics of Japanese contracts when compared with U.S. and European contracts?" holds great meaning not only for Japanese law but also for comparative law in general. This question was originally put to us by supporters of the modernist view, albeit with a special accent toward the pre-modern concept. In recent years, with Japanese economic clout and its international presence increasing, the question has not been posed very often and Japanese interest in such question, has decreased. However, the problem must now be pursued from a different angle. Adequate investigation has not yet been conducted into whether outwardly similar legal concepts, forms, and institutions fulfill the same functions in Japan, the U.S. and Europe.[12] For example, the legal structure of the competitive order in Japan seems to differ from those in the U.S. and Europe, even though it is outwardly identical with regard to its legal concepts, forms, and institutions, and is based

12 This issue is raised by Z. KITAGAWA, *Kokusai masatsu no naka no nihon-hô* (2) [Japanese Law Amidst International Frictions], 501 NBL 27 (1992) ("the first research area").

largely on the basic doctrine of private autonomy. This problem stands at the core of many recent bilateral issues, among which we can count U.S.-Japan trade frictions. The view that Japan is somehow different is just an international version of the modernist view's central question.[13]

From this perspective, my presentation today seeks to comparatively analyze the characteristics of contracts and contract law in Japan in relation to the U.S. and Europe. First, as my focal point for comparison, I will examine contract documents, terms, functions, and the standards used to resolve contract disputes. After building an analytical framework, I will go on to discuss the use and non-use of contracts in Japan. I will also touch upon what I call the phenomenon of "contractualization" - the extraordinary development of the contract area in our society today. This last item will enable us to set a more realistic perspective in our comparative look at contracts. Finally, a brief remark on the quality of contracts will be made for further considerations of the comparative law of contracts.

2. *What Should be Compared?*

It has often been said that Japanese contracts are both shorter and simpler than U.S. contracts. I would like to explore the validity of comparative studies which focus on the level of detail found in written contracts or the structure of the contract terms set forth in a written contract. A comparison of these factors which are simply taken from the face of written documents will not lead to an understanding of the actual workings of the contractual relationship. For example, even a contract document which appears at face value to be perfectly complete cannot be said to reflect the participants' relationship as long as the contracting parties' business relationship is based on some other standard. The opposite also holds true - even if a contract document is short and simple, the contract document is only practically relevant to the relationship as long as its basic ideals are reflected in the business relationship. Thus, we cannot understand a contract without understanding the function that it plays in the parties' relationship. In pursuing the comparative characteristics of Japanese contracts, we must expand our horizon by including in our analysis a study of the contract's function in relationships and in action. There are situations in which a contract term that is different from the written term will be operative between the parties, and in such a case we must compare the contract terms in action, not the contract terms in writing.

13 It is well known in comparative law that the same theory functions differently from country to country. But it is quite a difficult task to precisely identify how and why.

C. A Legal Framework for Comparison

1. Seven Different Cases of Dispute Resolution

Freedom from form in the area of business transactions is widely recognized under the Civil and Commercial Codes of Japan; i.e., contracts that do not take a written form are still enforceable.[14] Also, in Japanese contract practice, the parties do often conclude oral contracts. Thus, we must begin by ascertaining whether or not a written contract document exists. By individually examining whether a contract problem is being solved according to the contract terms set forth in the contract document, according to the will of the parties in a collateral agreement, according to some other legal standards, or according to extra-legal standards, we can come up with the following seven cases:

Group I

(1) when a written contract exists and the contract dispute is being resolved in accordance with the written terms, we say the "contract is functioning";

(2) when a written contract exists but the contract dispute is being resolved in accordance with a collateral agreement between the parties, we say the "contract is functioning";

(3) when a written contract exists but the contract dispute is being resolved in accordance with legal yielding statutory standards, such as supplementary Civil and Commercial Codes provisions[15] or good faith principles or otherwise implied terms (i.e., course of performance, trade customs), we still say the "contract is functioning";

(4) when a written contract document exists but the contract dispute is being resolved in accordance with mandatory statutory standards or extra-contractual standards (such as administrative standards, political standards,

---

14 Even compared to many civil law systems in Europe, freedom from form is most widely assured in Japanese contract law. See a brief note *in* SHATTUCK & KITAGAWA, *supra* note 11, at 208: "Japan is notable among Civil Law countries in that it provides a legal system which has the least extrinsic legal requirements for accomplishing an enforceable agreement."; Z. KITAGAWA, Doing Business in Japan, Vol. 3, Part II, Ch. 1 [Contract Law in General] § 1.07[3].

15 See the distinction of code provisions between jus cogens and jus dispositivum, SHATTUCK & KITAGAWA, *supra* note 11, at 133-134: Cogent or required or mandatory provisions deprive the contract parties of power to deviate from them. Optional or yielding provisions are subject to modification by the contract parties.Where express or implied declarations of intention are put into the agreement, divergent code provisions yield to them.

economic standards) or by violence, we say the "contract is not functioning";[16]

Group II

(5) when no written contract exists but the contract dispute is being solved in accordance with the agreed-upon contract terms, we say "the contract is functioning";

(6) when no written contract exists and the contract dispute is being solved in accordance with yielding statutory standards, such as supplementary Civil and Commercial Codes provisions or good faith principles or otherwise implied terms (i.e., course of performance, trade customs), we say "the contract is functioning";

(7) when no written contract exists and the contract dispute is being solved in accordance with mandatory statutory standards or extra-contractual standards (such as administrative standards, political standards, economic standards) or by violence, we say the "contract is not functioning".

These seven variations of dispute resolution can be thought of as reflective of contract practices which are common to many countries. These seven variations can therefore provide one basis for objective comparisons.

2. *Comments on the Seven Cases*

In the above cases, a written contract exists in cases 1-4, but not in cases 5-7. The collateral agreement in case 3 is one which is made at the time the contract is concluded. That is, collateral agreements, such as amendments or modifications, which are made after the contract is concluded are not considered here.[17] While it is logically possible to envision in group II a category in which there would be a collateral agreement separate from the concluded contract, its listing here is not significant in the pursuit of our comparative analysis.

I must briefly touch upon the formality requirement, such as the Statute of Frauds,[18] that requires writing for a contract to be enforceable. Even where

---

16 As discussed below, case 4, wherein contracts do not function, is just a combination of various types of dispute resolution which in turn require separate observation.

17 This problem of contract renegotiation or adjustment requires further inquiry, but is indirectly connected with our present subject.

18 Most of the formal requirements under the famous Statute of Frauds of 1677 were repealed in England in 1954. The contract of guarantee and the contract for sale or other disposition of an interest in land requires writing. *See* P.S. ATIYAH, An Introduction to the Law of Contract 163 (5 ed., 1995). It is to be noted that no formal requirements for such contracts are provided for under the Civil Code of Japan.

such a requirement exists, it is not uncommon for business practices to take place without contract documents being drawn up. In such a situation it is also conceivable that the business relationship may be ongoing even though the contract is unenforceable in court.[19] Group II includes such situations, and thus must be considered even under legal systems where the existence of a contract document is required for the formation of a contract.

I am differentiating between cases where a contract exists and is functioning and where it exists but is not functioning. When I say that a contract is functioning, I refer to the standard by which contract disputes are being solved. However, this assessment does not speak to the legality or illegality of the settlement (a point to which I refer later in section E). The distinction is important because, when a contract dispute arises, one party may dare to choose to perform an obligation under an unfair term without litigating. How do we evaluate such a performance? The aggrieved party may often endure the contract relationship because of the prospects of long-term benefits. We cannot simply ignore it by saying the contract is unfair and void if litigated in court. Although the existence of unfair contract terms is an undesirable reality, the reason why they are allowed to govern the parties is important from a legal standpoint too.[20]

If a contract is detailed, the chances may be greater that the contract dispute will be solved according to the contract, but this is not always true.[21] The parties may resort to a separate agreement if the terms of the contract are so detailed as to interfere with smooth development of business relations. The contract term may be judged not appropriate, or the contract term may function combined with custom and other standards to bring about a resolution that is desirable. Thus, among the cases in which the contract is functioning, if based on the principle of private autonomy, we cannot simply say whether one resolution is legally better than another.[22]

---

19 This means that a contract which violates the formal requirements under the Statute of Frauds is treated in this paper as a "functioning" contract, insofar as the contract parties perform their obligations without contending its unforceability due to lack of formality.

20 The legal framework at first tests the functional aspect of contracts in the business process.

21 An interesting result is reported in this regard by *W. Gray's* inquiry:"As to the desirability of longer or shorter contracts, 36% said that disputes have been more common under short contracts in general terms, but 64% said that in their experience they had not seen a relationship between the detailed nature of the contract document and disputes arising under it." *See* GRAY, *supra* note 4 at 111-112.

22 Nobody doubts this unified evaluation resulting from private autonomy. However, I think that contractual justice is calling for a mechanism for making value judgments which we can use to differentiate and articulate within the sanctuary of private autonomy. *See infra* at H (The Good Contract).

D. Contract Dispute Resolution in the Business Process and in the Litigation Process

The distinction between functioning and not functioning contracts refers to the contract dispute resolution in the context of the business transaction. What significance does the distinction hold when the contract dispute develops into contract litigation? For example, because contracts are functioning, case 1 might look problem-free. But appearances can be deceiving. Just think of a situation where there is an unfair standard form contract. These are often drafted to be unduly advantageous to the party that draws it up, be it a consumer or business transaction. In such a case, the unfair term may be either regulated by law or voided by a court. Thus, even if a contract is functioning between the parties (a state that remains as long as there is no litigation over the contract), legally void terms may exist in the contract. This means that in case 1, the contract certainly may be functioning in daily business practices, but this does not mean the contract is a legitimate and lawful one. Jurists usually handle contract problems without making the distinctive consideration between the function of a contract in the business process and the enforceability and validity of a contract in the litigation phase, but such a distinction can help us to better understand contract law.[23]

According to this distinction, case 4 and case 7 - where the contract dispute is resolved according to mandatory statutory standards, extra-contractual standards (such as administrative standards, political standards, economic standards), or by violence - present an interesting problem. If, for example, violence is used to resolve a contract dispute, the resolution would be voided in court as being in violation of public order and good morals. Thus the payment of money after the problem is resolved is also void and the question becomes one of restitution.[24] Essentially different from cases involving violence are those cases where the parties in dispute come to understand that contract terms violate a mandatory provision and resolve their dispute accordingly.

---

23 By definition, the contract binds the contracting parties. For example, the definition known to the common law lawyer - "contract is a promise enforceable at law" (§ 1 Restatement of Contracts) is concerned with the aspect of enforceability of contracts. However, the issue of "void" contracts or "unenforceable" contracts is an important area of contract law. A similar problem also exists in civil law contracts. In the civil law system, the contract is a juristic act (*hôritsu koi*, Rechtsgeschäft) which is defined as lawful human behavior or conduct. "Void" or "illegal" juristic acts and contracts, however, form an important chapter of the law of contracts and juristic acts. The distinction between contract in the business process and in the litigation process, as in this report, enables us theoretically as well as practically to articulate the problem areas of contracts.

24 *See* Articles 703, 708 of the Civil Code (*Minpô,* Law No. 89 of 1896 as amended by Law No. 79 of 1991; for an English translation *see* Z. KITAGAWA (ed.), Doing Business in Japan, Statute Volume I, App. 4A.

Economic, administrative, or political standards that deviate from those set forth in the agreed contract are not automatically rendered void in court. These situations cannot be looked upon favorably from a contract law standpoint, however, because the contract is not functioning. On the other hand, such manners of resolution are not always regarded as undesirable.

E. The Relationship Between Contract Function and Private Autonomy

So far under a legal framework we discussed situations in the business process wherein contracts are and are not functioning. We now need to discuss the relationship between the doctrine of private autonomy and contract functions.

Assume that the contract contains unconscionable terms, and if a party were to bring the contract to court the court might invalidate the contract. In such a case, we can say that the contract is unenforceable in court and therefore bad, but even so, the parties have a functioning contract so long as the parties perform the contract without disputing over it in court. What about cases where the contract contains unconscionable terms, but not so unconscionable that leading court cases have invalidated such terms? In the latter case we cannot say the parties have a good contract, but it is not void even in court. We cannot say that contracts in either of these cases are good. This evaluation means something different, however, in each case above. Let us consider this point in light of private autonomy and the function of contracts by analyzing it under the framework of the seven cases set out above.

We will start with case 4 and case 7 wherein the contract does not function and the described contractual practices are not legitimized under principles of private autonomy. While a contractual relationship exists in both cases, the contract disputes are resolved not according to the agreed-upon contract terms but rather in accordance with some mandatory statutory provisions or extra-contractual standards. If this extra-contractual standard is an illegal method of contract dispute resolution, there is a violation of public order and good morals, and such a dispute resolution does not fall under the domain of private autonomy. The same applies to such cases where the parties in dispute come to treat their contract as void due to the violation of a mandatory statutory provision.[25]

There are, however, other types of contract dispute resolutions under which contracts are not functioning, but which are not necessarily against the principle of private autonomy. For example, there are cases where a contract party which enjoys economically advantageous contract terms solves the contract dispute not

---

25 This may happen when a party or the parties were at the time of contract making ignorant of, but afterwards aware of, the violation of a mandatory provision.

by resorting to, but by deviating from the contract terms. The reason for such resolution may be a high-level managerial business decision in light of the long-term continuing business relationship with the defaulting party. As long as such collateral legal business standards do not violate mandatory statutory provisions and good morals, resolving contract disputes by means of economic and business standards does not violate public order and good morals. It may be one-sided decision making or another agreement based on the parties' renegotiation. Either way, such instances of contract dispute resolution do not go beyond the domain of private autonomy.[26]

We can similarly analyze methods of contract dispute resolution which employ administrative or political interference rather than agreed-upon contract terms.

Let us next examine cases 1-3, case 5, and case 6, wherein contracts are functioning. In case 3 and case 6, the yielding statutory provisions, trade customs, or good faith principles supplement the original agreement. Numerous varieties of such types of implied and supplemental terms exist and for the most part such terms are in accordance with the doctrine of private autonomy. The more problematic situations likely exist in case 1, case 2, and case 5, wherein the contract dispute resolution depends upon the contract terms. As just mentioned, where the contract is functioning we need to evaluate the dispute resolution itself according to its reasonableness and legality. Even in detailed contract documents, when a contract dispute is resolved under unfair contract terms, a court can declare the contract illegal and invalid. In some such cases a special agreement rather than the original written contract terms could appropriately resolve the contract dispute. When a contract dispute can be adequately resolved under the written contract terms, we can say that the parties have a good contract because the original contract terms anticipated the parties' business practices.[27]

F. Japanese Contracts in Action Analyzed Under the Seven Cases

1. Cases Where Contracts are Functioning

Let us examine Japanese contracts in light of the seven cases set forth above to uncover what special characteristics Japanese contracts may possess.

---

26 Thus, the domain of private autonomy is comprised of a complex system capable of recognizing different values. Even among enforceable contracts within the realm of private autonomy, one contract may be evaluated as better than another. *See* Z. KITAGAWA, Standard als Weg zur "besseren Privatautonomie" [Standards as a Way Towards "Better Private Autonomy", *in* Festschrift für Karl Larenz [Festschrift for Karl Larenz] 329 (1983).

27 *See infra* at H (The Good Contract).

First, we will begin with the cases in which the contract functions. In case 1, wherein a written contract exists, the written contract terms resolve the dispute. In such a case the contract remains functional.In Japanese business practices, a large percentage of the contracts have been written contracts for quite some time now,[28] but in many cases one cannot say that the contract terms are detailed and skillfully drafted. Recently, however, a trend of using and establishing more detailed and skillfully drafted contract documents has arisen. It seems that case 1 does, as a matter of general practice, reflect Japanese contracting practices, as in Europe and the U.S., in the sense that most contracts usually end up with performance. As a matter of law, however, and in comparison to Europe and the U.S., a special characteristic of Japanese contract law should be found in the rather loose value standards applied to judgments regarding the fairness of contract clauses under Japanese law (see below).

In case 2, even where a written contract exists it may often occur that the parties do not resolve the contract dispute under the contract terms but by means of a collateral agreement or memorandum between the parties. In this case we can say that the contract nevertheless continues to function. The use of collateral agreements or a memorandum often occurs in Japan. In some fields collateral agreements such Amendments and modifications to contracts are also not rare in the U.S. In case 3, the contract dispute is resolved by the application of not agreed-upon legal standards such as supplementary provisions of Civil and Commercial Codes[29] or good faith principles or otherwise implied terms (i.e. course of performance, trade customs). Cases 2 and 3 do not necessarily indicate the existence of any special characteristic of Japanese contracts. On these issues, the extent of the differences between the U.S. and Europe on one hand and Japan on the other hand does not appear significant.

In case 5, in which no written contract exists, agreed-upon contract terms resolve the contract dispute. In case 6, the contract is not written and the contract dispute is not resolved by the contract terms but rather by other supplementary statutory standards, trade customs or good faith principles. It is not clear to what extent these two cases reflect Japanese contract practices.

---

28 A questionnaire conducted in the early 1970s shows that only 7% of 669 Japanese companies never drafted a contract document. *See* Z. KITAGAWA, *Gendai keiyaku-hô* [Modern Law of Contracts], Vol.I, 15 (1983).

29 When original contract clauses turn out to be insufficient for handling a contract dispute, not agreed-upon legal standards, as reflected in case 3, supplement the contract. The common law tradition does not have a codified legal system which provides a series of yielding or optional provisions supplementing contractual agreements. In this situation differences exist between common law and the civil law, to which Japanese law relates. As to the distinction between required or cogent code provisions and yielding or optional provisions, *see* SHATTUCK & KITAGAWA, *supra* note 15.

Such situations can be thought to exist in a standardized business transaction for certain specific goods or in rather simple business transactions with mutual reliance between parties, but some doubt exists with regard to assertions that these two cases indicate a unique characteristic of Japanese contracts. In respect to the situations addressed in cases 5 and 6, a comparative study of foreign laws requires a better grasp of this problem area.

When we compare how contracts' contents are evaluated in Japan on one hand and in the U.S. or European countries on the other hand, we can discover some special characteristics of Japanese contracts falling under the cases 1-3 and cases 5 and 6. Some differences arise because [i] with regard to fairness in contracts, U.S. law and European laws contain significantly more strict statutory controls, while Japan has yet no general statutory rules controlling unfair contract terms or standard form contracts;, and also [ii] Japanese courts employ much looser standards with regard to fairness in contracts than one would expect of a U.S. or European court. Even with regard to one-sided contract terms which benefit only one party - usually the one who has drafted such terms - Japanese judicial practices have not developed the rules of interpretation which enable judges to reduce the operative scope of such terms to meet substantial justice in contracts. As a result, Japan has employed standards with regard to fairness in competition law and substantial contract justice which differ from the U.S. and European standards.[30]

2. *Cases Where Contracts Are Not Functioning*

I would like now to discuss those cases in which the contract is not functioning. In cases 4 and 7, a written or unwritten contract exists, but mandatory statutory standards or administrative, political, or economic standards resolve the dispute. If viewed in light of the original contract, such interference does not follow in the anticipated normal course of the business transaction. Such interference is, however, not rare. Under these situations the contract is not functioning. The method of dispute resolution employs extra-contractual standards to which the parties have not agreed.

30 There are numerous books and articles dealing with unfair contract terms or standard form contracts. A comparative study of legal standards for unfairness or fairness still needs further analysis, but two recent symposia in Japan afford us with some materials for this aspect of comparison. One is the symposium of the JAPAN ASSOCIATION OF PRIVATE LAW, *Yakkan - hô to genjitsu* [Contract of Adhesion: Theory and Practice], 44 SHIHÔ 4 (1982). The other is that of JAPAN SOCIETY OF COMPARATIVE LAW, *Keiyaku to Yakkan - Ishi to Kisei* [Contract and Standard Form Contract: Intention and Regulation], 49 HIKAKUHÔ KENKYÛ 2 (1987).

Political interference may occur when contract parties in a large business transaction are involved in a contract dispute.[31] When an aggrieved party, despite a breach of contract on the part of the other party, nevertheless continues to remain in the contract without canceling it, economic standards may be determinative.[32] In some extreme situations, it is not unheard of that a contract dispute is resolved by violence. As for these methods of settling contract disputes, one may say reluctantly that each country has such irregularities in settling contract disputes.

It may be said that the role of administrative standards is more important in Japan than in either Europe or the U.S. In Japanese contract practices, administrative guidance, which often possesses no basis in law, may display an ability to excel in dispute resolutions over agreements established between the parties involved in a business transaction. Such occurrences reflect a link between business and administration (see following section).

G. Thoughts on Japanese Contracts

1. Contractual Justice in Administrative Interference

The influence of administrative standards over the private contract relationship is an important characteristic of the Japanese law of contracts. Even when a business transaction is purely private in nature, Japanese bureaucrats often intervene in the business relationship. This matter has in the past been addressed in the context of the infamous administrative guidances by the Japanese ministries.[33] Up to now, however, the emphasis of study has been

---

31 It is not seldom reported that politicians intervene in a large scale business negotiation or the litigation process to act as go-between.

32 Parties in contract disputes may often prefer their economic and business values to legal standards. These transactional, non-legal elements offer us a variety of materials for promoting alternative dispute resolution. *See*, for example, KITAGAWA, *supra* note 1 ("Rezeption"), at 171 (with examples); *id.*, *Torihiki shakai ni okeru funsô kaiketsu* [Dispute Resolution Concerning Transactions], 75 MINSHÔHÔ ZASSHI 6 (No. 1, 1977).

33 Among others, T. FUJITA, *Gyôsei shidô no hôteki ichizuke ni kansuru ichi shiron* [A Tentative Approach to the Legal Qualification of Administrative Guidance], *in*: *Takayanagi koki kinen ronbun-shû* 167 (1991); M. YOUNG, Judicial Review of Administrative Guidance: Governmentally Encouraged Consensual Dispute Resolution in Japan, 84 COLUM. L. REV. 923 (1984); *id.*, Administrative Guidance in the Courts: A Case Study in Doctrinal Adaptation, 17 LAW IN JAPAN 121 (1984); Z. KITAGAWA, Unfair Contract Terms in Administrative Guidance, 16 RECHTSTHEORIE 181 (2/3, 1985); R. YEOMANS, Administrative Guidance: A Peregrine View, 19 LAW IN JAPAN 125 (1986); M. KLOEPFER, "Gyôsei Shidô" und das informelle Verwaltungshandeln im Umweltrecht der Bundesrepublik Deutschland [*Gyôsei shidô* and Informal Administrative Practice in the German Environmental Pro-

rather on the administrative law aspects, with contract scholars showing little interest in the problem. The influence of Japan's bureaucracies over private business transactions is, however, a major factor differentiating Japanese contracts from U.S. and European contracts. This influence may be problematic in relation to the private autonomy principle in certain cases, but should not be rejected out of hand.[34]

Next, the laxity of legislative, judicial, and executive control over unfair or unjust contract terms is another more troubling characteristic of Japanese contracts. This laxity is evident whether a written contract exists or not, and whether the contract is detailed or simple. Such different value standards in Japan may lead to the following outcome: Although identical concepts, such as "free" competition or "fair" market are used in both Japanese and U.S.-European legal terminology, they often possess different meanings in law. A study of these issues from a comparative law standpoint may yet yield some answers to the age-old question of whether Japan is a unique society or not.[35]

Here, I would like just to point out the interrelationship between the Japanese laxity toward contractual justice and the large role that administrative standards play in Japanese business practice. As a matter of fact, they are and have been closely related to each other. Whether intentional or not, bureaucratic intervention into private business does serve some positive roles. First, it serves to prevent an unfair contract term from being imposed on a weaker party. Second, if a dispute arises over unfair terms then the bureaucratic intervention can contribute to the resolution of the dispute, though in an informal and not altogether uniform fashion. We can thus identify two positive aspects of bureaucratic intervention: the prevention of an unfair contract term being forced upon a weaker party, and the securing of a certain balance between the interests of the business parties. These traits can be counted among the characteristics of Japanese contracts. Such administrative practices, continued over many years, can conceivably prevent the problems associated with an economically stronger party imposing an extremely unfair contract onto a weaker party. An additional benefit may be that when the regulatory agency for a particular industry steps in, more disputes can be resolved outside of the courtroom.[36]

---

tection Law], *in* Die Japanisierung des westlichen Rechts [The Japanization of Western Law] 83 (H. Coing *et al.*, eds. 1990).

34 This reservation is necessary in the age of globalization of law. The close relationship between administration and private business is going to be a big topic for comparative law perspectives of contracts, as administration everywhere in the world is getting more and more involved in the resolution of worldwide business disputes.

35 *See supra* note 12.

36 My essay on Unfair Contract Terms in Administrative Guidance, *supra* note 33 reports the activities of a standard form contracts committee in the Economic

Of course, intervening informal justice has its limits. For one, foreign firms, even if they have offices or subsidiaries in Japan, are outside the realm of the Japanese government-business relationship. Another limit may be that as businesses seek new opportunities across traditional regulatory jurisdictions, a friction may arise between the newer entries and those that traditionally have had relations with the bureaucracies. The more Japanese economic clout increases, the more traditional ties between business and government will be challenged. These criticisms can only increase in the face of the business slowdown now affecting the Japanese economy. As we see now in the slow progress in administrative deregulation, however, the eventual outcome of these and other issues is still uncertain. This is a problem that will affect the very future of Japan, but I will not go into it in detail here except by mentioning just two things. First, there is a new trend symbolized in a MITI research paper which intends to enlarge and strengthen the private law remedies for unfair competitive business practices.[37] The other is that Japanese experiences may provide us with hints for building a new legal order called upon as the result of globalization of economy and law.[38] In any event, Japanese contracts can be said to be caught up in these unprecedented currents.

2. *Interpretation of Contracts*

Another area for study which may indicate the existence of some characteristics of Japanese contract law in action is the Japanese judicial practice of employing a discretionary method of interpreting the parties' intent as set forth in contracts. In the litigation process, a distinction should be made between the determination of the parties' intent as a matter of fact and its legal meaning as a matter of law. This is not always the case in Japanese courts. Relying on and

---

Planning Agency. This ad hoc committee started in 1980 and existed for about ten years. It consisted of law professors, attorneys, consumer representatives, business representatives, journalists, and representatives of pertinent business associations. The committee discussed about fifteen standard form consumer contracts and published a series of recommendations. Pertinent government agencies resort to them as administrative standards for improving individually reviewed unfair contract terms. Most of the recommendations were successfully incorporated in consumer contracts. Looking back at what this committee performed, I see a typical example of how administrative guidance operates in controlling unfair contract terms.

37 MINJI KYÛSAI SEIDÔ KENKYÛ-KAI [Civil Remedy System Research Committee], *Jiritsuteki na kyôsô chitsujo no keisei ni mukete* [Toward Building a New Autonomous Competitive Order], Interim Report, May 1996.

38 With respect to the globalization of law, *see* a stimulative article by M. SHAPIRO, The Globalization of Law, 1 Indiana Journal of Global Legal Studies (1993/1) *in*: www.law.indiana.edu/glsi/vol1/shapiro.html.

referring to their competence to interpret contracts, Japanese judges sometimes impose upon the parties terms which are different from those that the parties may appear to have expressly and clearly agreed upon. In such cases, Japanese courts might interpret the contract terms to mean something different from what the parties clearly spelled out in the contract. In many legal systems, except when the meaning of a contract is expressly and clearly agreed upon, judges construe what they determine to be the parties' agreed-upon terms. However, judges may not modify the meaning of such clearly and expressly agreed-upon terms at their own discretion. If judges think such contract terms violate a good faith principle, however, they may intervene by invalidating terms. One characteristic of Japanese judicial practices may therefore be that instead of exercising this sort of judicial control, judges in Japan also construe the meaning of contractual agreements by interpretation.[39] Whether or not this method of interpretation in the Japanese court system is of any practical significance with regard to its actual effect upon Japanese contract law in action is a subject for further investigation.

3. A New Legalism

It is often said that Japanese contracts are not always drafted with strict legal precision. This may have been true in the past. There were cases where contract drafting skills in Japan were not of a high level and contract terms did not accurately reflect the true contract relationship. The legal departments of Japanese corporations were not well developed and contracts were not being used effectively in business transactions. These factors are no longer true today, however, and at least as far as the contract drafting techniques are concerned, there does not seem to be any substantial difference between Japanese contracts and those of the U.S. and Europe.[40]

In Japanese contract practices, there are instances in which those persons who actually carry out the daily business of a firm may resort to use of a not agreed-upon standard to resolve a contract dispute. In such instances, the case may be that the firm's leadership and its legal department are not interfacing properly. Although the contract drafting skill in Japanese business practices is remarkably improving, inadequate interface between corporate leaders and legal departments remains a characteristic of Japanese contract law and practice.

---

39 See T. NOMURA, *Hôritsu koi no kaishaku* [Interpretation of Juristic Acts], *Minpô Kôza* I, 291 (1984) (the interpretation of juristic acts in general with a brief case analysis).

40 *W. Gray's* interim report illustrates some of these recent traits in international legal practices in Japan, *see* GRAY, *supra* note 4, at 109.

As a result I believe that this improper "interfacing" will give rise to a new kind of legalism[41] that cannot be ignored. This will be accelerated by the fact that Japanese lawyers are usually not involved in the contract negotiation process itself (we can call this "next-door counselling"), and their clients confine their legal services to drafting only what the client businesses have previously agreed on. Consequently, the role of Japanese attorneys is often inflexible and legalistic when they are brought into business negotiations.

In an information society characterized by high technology, and with the creation of the Internet and a new world called cyberspace, the use of contracts is bound to increase even more. These contracts usually operate within a computer system and involve strictly construed technological concepts and much more detailed contract documents.[42] This phenomenon may be called the "contractualization" process and it is common to all modern information societies. In the face of such trends, the realization of substantial contractual justice and control over unfair contract terms becomes all the more important. This major task confronts the contract regimes of all countries. In the rush of contractualization, wide use of unfair contract terms must not be allowed to go on unchecked. Since these new types of contracts use difficult terms that are based on technical concepts found in computer systems, I fear the spread of a new conceptualism may pervade legal discourse. I have already pointed out that Japanese contract law and practice lag behind the U.S. and Europe when it comes to realizing substantive contractual justice, or in controlling unfair contract terms. The threat is that this trend will accelerate along with a new legalism.

H. The Good Contract

We have already seen how the notion that detailed contracts are automatically good and simple ones are automatically bad does not hold. With these and other factors in mind, it should be said that contracts must be judged in the entirety of their functions and roles. The important thing is the relationship between the contract and its actual function. Contracts must be construed to appropriately reflect the legal aspects of a business's activity. Whether a contract dispute is being resolved by using the contract in an appropriate way is an important

41 The legalism here refers to a legal attitude on the part of corporate employees who are only concerned with a legal theory that supports their own corporate interests without paying due attention to factual situations as well as their counterpart's interests.

42 There emerges, in my view, the "system contract, "a new contract type, *see* Z. KITAGAWA, Der Systemvertrag: Ein neuer Vertragstyp in der Informationsgesellschaft [The System Contract: A Type of Contract for the Information Society], *in* Festschrift für Murad Ferid [Festschrift for Murad Ferid] 219 (1988).

factor in evaluating the characteristics of a contract. It is self-evident that the new legalism today is not the right way for Japanese contract law to go in the era of contractualization.

From our comparative analysis, we can begin to see the emergence of a new issue for contract law: whether a contract is good or bad. I will end this paper by sketching the broad outlines of the problem. A contractual relationship is fundamentally one involving competition, in which the respective parties attempt to do business on terms most favorable to them; naturally a certain imbalance of interests results. This process is market competition, conducted within the framework of contract doctrine and the private autonomy principle.

My impression is that the question of whether a contract is good or bad within this framework is being asked with increasing frequency. A good contract is not necessarily one in which the interests of the contracting parties are balanced equally. Within the limits set by the principle of private autonomy, a certain amount of imbalance is to be expected under our market system of competition. Rather, a good contract is one in which the parties disclose information in good faith, one that does not include terms that are unjustly advantageous to one party, that regulates the actual business relationship in an appropriate way, and in which the ideals enumerated in the contract are used to resolve contract disputes. These factors have been realized in part, but I will leave the required empirical and theoretical inquiries for another time.[43]

I. Epilogue

My paper attempts to shed some light on the comparative legal characteristics of Japanese contracts by utilizing a framework of seven cases of dispute resolution methods. In the process, we have been able to examine from a number of perspectives the difference between a functioning contract and a non-functioning contract. We have also discussed the difference between the contract negotiation process and the litigation process, and the relationship between a contract's actual functioning and its illegality, its unfairness, and unjustness.

A contract cannot be praised for being detailed if it is not functioning. Furthermore, a functioning contract may not be a desirable contract if it imposes an unjust term on a weaker party, even if the term may be judged to be valid under the principle of private autonomy. This of course is a question of

43 Standards of various types would contribute to develop this new domain of contract law and private autonomy. In addition to unenforceability or invalidation standards, there are those standards, such as rationalization standards or correcting standards, which will work as a test for good or bad contracts; both of these standars are enforceable. *See* KITAGAWA, *supra* note 26.

degree, but at the very least we cannot accept the notion that anything is acceptable as long as it is not illegal. In our quest to identify the characteristics and problems of Japanese contracts, we have examined these and other points from various angles. One of the important points is the unique interrelationship between the role of administrative standards in resolving contract disputes and the laxity of legal control over unfair contract terms in Japanese contract law. Finally, we have touched upon the growing importance of asking whether a contract is good or bad.

Chapter Five

Relational Contracting: Does Community Count?

John O. Haley

Contents

Most business transactions occur in the context of on-going, long-term business relationships. Whether simply the product of repeated dealing or more formal, legally binding, long-term commitments, the vast majority of transactions in this sense are "relational". The predominance of relational contracting is evidenced in nearly all existing studies of contract practices in both Japan and the United States.[1] There thus appears to be at least a superficial similarity in contracting in both countries. Anecdotal data, however, continue to suggest some fundamental differences. Relational contracting and related practices are widely considered to be more pervasive in Japan than in the United States. More significant, however, prevalent relational contracting in the United States is not thought, as in Japan[2], to reduce the relevance of law and legal rules.

To be sure, in the United States no less than in Japan, the parties to on-going, long-term relationships appear to avoid both courts and the law. In both countries they tend, it seems, to deal with grievances through compromise and flexible adjustments rather than strict adherence to legal rules and "rights". Without more complete empirical data, to what extent they negotiate conflicts and disputes "within the shadow of the law" may be open to debate; nevertheless, most observers seem to agree that, until the parties envision the termination or rupture of the relationship without resort to court, lawyers are not likely to become involved and legal rules are less relevant than economic considerations to the resolution of any dispute. What appears to distinguish Japan is therefore neither patterns of contracting nor those for resolving dis-

---

1 The classic studies are T. KAWASHIMA, The Legal Consciousness of Contract, 7 LAW IN JAPAN 1-21 (C.R. Stevens, trans. 1970), and S. MACAULEY, Non-Contractual Relations in Business: A Preliminary Study, 28 AM. SOC. REV. 55-69 (1963).

2 This, of course, is *Kawashima*'s principal point. *Id.*, at 20-21.

putes. Rather, Japan seems different in the apparent ability of the parties to hold the relationship together, to avoid termination and rupture, and to deal with bad bargains and broken promises in ways that seem to make legal rules less relevant.

Under the auspices of the Center for Global Partnership Project on Civil Responsibility, a group of scholars led by *Takeshi Uchida* (University of Tokyo) has attempted to develop empirical data that would enable us to have a better grasp of the similarities and differences between relational contracting in Japan and the United States. The Japanese participants conducted extensive surveys and interviews in Japan. With the assistance of *Michael K. Young* (Columbia Law School) they also interviewed several major United States enterprises in the New York area. A similar series of interviews were conducted in Seattle. A dozen businesses were selected representing ten different fields of business. In most cases, those interviewed were managers without legal training. In one instance, a private attorney with significant experience in construction contracts was selected (Interview 12). Only one other lawyer - the general counsel for a major truck manufacturer (Interview 1) - was interviewed. The others included the managers of two retail automobile dealers (one, the owner-manager) (Interviews 2 and 3), two chain retail grocery stores (Interviews 4 and 5), a fast-food franchise (the owner-manager) (Interview 7), a public relations firm (Interview 9), a high-tech medical equipment firm (Interview 9), a software manufacturer (Interview 10), and a major commercial aircraft manufacturer (Interview 11).

The Japanese researchers are reporting the results of the surveys and interviews undertaken in both countries in forthcoming Japanese publications. Their findings confirm the conclusions of prior research that the basic patterns of relational contracting in Japan and the United States are remarkably similar. Unfortunately, the results raise as many questions as they answer. We still do not know, for example, the extent to which conduct that would be considered repeated dealing in the United States might involve both legal and socially recognized commitments to continue the relationship in Japan. The common law emphasis on a consideration-based "bargain theory" of contract may exclude from legal protection conduct that under Japanese law might be deemed as a "contract" to produce legally enforceable commitments. As detailed below, Japanese judges have not made a clear a distinction between repeated deals and long-term contracts.[3] Nor does the data deal with differences in the contracting environment. The questions of both the survey and the interviews tended to

3 One of the most thorough comparisons of "contract" in United States and Japanese law is W.L. SHATTUCK & Z. KITAGAWA, United States/Japanese Contract and Sales Problems (Seattle: University of Washington Asian Law Program Teaching Materials, 1971).

focus on the parties to the deal and their relationship in isolation from others. No one on either side of the Pacific was asked, in effect, whether community counts.

My purpose here is to set out some thoughts that relate to these still unresolved issues and the implications of relational contracting to law. The original aim was less to provide answers than to attempt to suggest what questions now need to be addressed. One result has been a hypothesis - that differences between Japan and the United States do exist and that these differences can be understood best by the communitarian orientation of Japanese society and law enforcement. In other words, despite superficial similarities, relational contracting in Japan, unlike the United States, occurs in a communitarian context that both encourages relational contracting and provides a system of ordering that effectively substitutes for the formal legal system. Although such substitution may not reduce contract rules to irrelevance, it does restrict their application and thus their role in regulating transactions and determining outcomes. Moreover, to the extent that, as a result of this orientation, potential litigants are discouraged from pursuing claims, the community may indeed retard if not preclude any expansion of the judicial system and the development of legal rules at variance with community preferences. Judicially created rules that prevent unilateral termination of commercial relationships notwithstanding, the lack of contractual commitments to continue dealing both reflect and reinforce Japan's fundamental communitarian orientation. In this respect, neither the law nor the courts are irrelevant. Rather, both play a positive role in fostering relational contracting in Japan.

A. Legal Rules and Processes

The first questions to be addressed are *how* legal rules become relevant to contracts in the first place, and *whether* differences in legal institutions or procedures or the rules themselves rather than differences in contracting determine the relative relevance of law in the two countries. We begin therefore with an examination of the legal context or environment within which business relationships are formed and agreements are performed in Japan and the United States.

Whatever differences may exist at the margins, both Japan and the United States share with all other industrial democracies a stable legal order in which rules made both by legislatures and by courts regulate agreements. At the heart of this system of regulation is the law of contract, which, simply stated, consists of a body of rules that determine (1) whether a particular transaction or agreement qualifies as a set of reciprocally enforceable rights and duties as a legally defined "contract;" (2) what legal effect as contracts the words used in agreements as well as the conduct of the parties pursuant to their agreement have; (3) what legal remedies and sanctions are available in the event of a failure of either party to perform the legal duties imposed by the contract; as well as (4) how to answer the variety of related questions related to these principal concerns, such as whether a failure to perform can be excused and what rights and duties the parties have to each other as a consequence of their transaction but in the absence of any agreement with respect to such rights and duties.

In all contemporary legal systems, Japan and the United States included, the rules of contract are for the most part optional or default rules - that is, the parties are free to modify them by agreement - enforced directly only by party-initiated and controlled lawsuits or, more importantly, indirectly through negotiated settlements in which litigated outcomes are taken into account. Even in the case of mandatory contract (or other private law) rules, however, their enforcement depends upon lawsuits initiated by a party to the contract or a third-party beneficiary. In other words, the relevance of contract law depends upon the willingness and capacity of the parties to resort to judicial enforcement.

As used here, the word "law" of course does not include all functionally equivalent rules and sanctions of a society. My definition is much more narrow. By "law" I mean simply the rules and principles established or recognized and enforced by legislatures, government agencies, and courts as agencies of the "state". The codified or judge-made rules of contract and commercial law satisfy this definition as do the rules the parties select by agreement to govern their relationship insofar as they are or can be recognized and enforced by a competent state authority. What matters, however, is not the label. Whether Japanese business enterprises play by rules categorized as "law" is significant only if consequences follow from such categorization. The difference between law rules and nonlaw rules is thus not their function or identity, but their effect and enforcement. To the extent that the parties to a contract choose not to enforce the rules that govern the transaction, it matters little what we call such rules. However, to the extent that the enforcer determines what rules are virtually controlling and thus viable, it does make a difference whether the parties choose to enforce the agreements rules through the courts or by extra-judicial or "private" means. If by "law" we mean justiciable or state-enforced rules, the distinction between law rules and nonlaw rules becomes significant.

It should also be emphasized that judicial enforcement may be rarely if ever sought. Long-term business relationships are almost by definition immune from litigation. As explained in more detail below, unless the parties are willing to end the relationship, nearly all grievances will in fact be resolved without judicial intervention. One explanation is that the parties have not made legally enforceable long-term commitments. A pattern of repeated dealings is thus distinguished from contract in that both sides recognize the freedom of the other to cease. Except for disputes related to discrete "spot" transactions, the parties do not ordinarily consider that either is obligated legally or "morally" to the other. Thus they have nothing to litigate about. Even if legally enforceable commitments are made, the continuing relationship in most cases provides sufficient incentives for compromise and settlement within the shadow of both legal rules and business considerations. The benefits of repeated dealing and the mutual trust that will usually pertain in such cases enables the parties in most cases to settle any dispute that may arise without resort to court.

Absent legally recognized contractual commitments, in these and other instances litigation is unlikely. At least contract rules cannot be assumed to apply. Thus any serious dissatisfaction that may arise other than a dispute related to a spot transaction is generally resolved by termination without reference to litigated outcomes. Less serious grievances are settled by the more dependant part "eating" a loss or by compromise based on commercial rather than legal standards.

Whether or not the parties actually litigate contract claims is not significant. So long as the parties perceive that resort to court is an available alternative, their assessment of the likely outcome of litigation in the event of a dispute will determine the parameters for negotiated settlement. The availability of judicial enforcement is therefore the critical factor for the relevance of contract law.

Whether judicial enforcement is *available* depends upon a number of discrete factors. Some can be lumped under the category of formal barriers to litigation, such as the legal requirements for capacity, standing, and the justiciability of the particular claim. Other factors relate to what I have labelled "institutional capacity."[4] Many are cost-imposing factors that preclude resort to court to enforce legal rules in cases where the amounts in controversy are less than the cost of a lawsuit. Such cost-imposing factors include attorney fees, filing fees, bond-posting requirements, pre-trial discovery, and similar direct costs that a potential litigant must bear. They also include the dearth of judges and lawyers, the complexity of procedures, and other features of the judicial process that result in delay and thus indirectly impose costs on the litigants.

Where the claims at stake exceed the threshold costs, these factors do not make litigation less available or make contract rules less relevant. They simply reduce the amount of any settlement by costs borne by potential plaintiffs or, conversely, increase settlements by costs imposed on potential defendants. Contract disputes in these cases will still be negotiated within the shadow of the law, but the settlements reached will be discounted to reflect the costs

---

4 *See* J.O. HALEY, The Myth of the Reluctant Litigant, 4 J. JAP. STUD. 359 *et seq.* (1978).

imposed.[5] As a consequence, we should expect that most contract disputes will be resolved by negotiated settlement with two factors determining the outcome. First, the commercial relationship of the parties and the extent of their mutual dependency upon a continuation of that relationship, as well, however, as the legal rules and the probable outcome of a future lawsuit.

Differences in litigation rates (based, for example, on the number of first instance filings per capita) tell us very little. The greater uncertainty in the outcome of litigation in the United States as a consequence of jury trials and the nearly complete autonomy of individual judges in contrast to Japan makes settlement in the United States more difficult and thus lawsuits more likely.[6]

Empirical studies of American businesses confirm, moreover, a strong aversion to litigation. The costs in time and money of a lawsuit, as well as the likelihood of a rupture in the relationship if an aggrieved party were to resort to court rather than negotiate a settlement and compromise the claim, are two of the most frequently encountered responses. All of those interviewed in Seattle expressed similar views. The legal counsel for one large manufacturer stated that despite on-going disputes with all of their major suppliers, "there was no litigation; no outside attorneys were consulted." Even disputes with suppliers over warranty claims and disclaimers are "never resolved by litigation." (Interview 1, August, 24 1994.) All of those interviewed expressed similar sentiments. Except in cases involving unpaid bills and dishonesty, lawsuits are extraordinarily rare. The reasons for not using the courts in resolving disputes were also notably similar. Business considerations - especially concern that the relationship continue on amicable terms - as well as commitment to the terms of the bargain were the most common. The senior vice-president of a Seattle-based public relations firm, for example, in reply to the question of how problems with long- term clients are resolved, replied, "We've eaten bills." He explained: "If, in fact, we think both sides are at fault, we say, 'Hey, let's share the loss on this.' And we talk about it. We do eat parts of the bills. We ask the client to pay extra sometimes. Sometimes that endangers the relationship, but generally speaking people are pretty reasonable." However, the contract governs. Legal rules count. Asked whether the firm would cover the cost where its managers thought they were clearly in the right, the response was: "No, no. We wouldn't let them do that . . . we would hold them to the letter" (Interview 9, August 25 1994.)

Judicial enforcement may also become less available or desirable as a result of various factors extraneous to the judicial process itself or other institutional features of the legal system. Two basic patterns emerge. First, judicial enforce-

---

5 *See* J.M. RAMSEYER & M. NAKAZATO, The Rational Litigant: Settlement Amounts and Verdicts Rates in Japan, 18 J. LEG. STUD. 262 *et seq.* (1989).

6 *See* HALEY, *supra*, note 4, at 364.

ment may not be available because of social or community barriers to litigation. Second, potential litigants may for various reasons prefer an alternative system of rules and enforcement. I should hasten to add that these are not necessarily distinct or separate. In most instances, community and party preferences probably coincide. Tightly knit or cohesive groups tend, for instance, to ostracize those who invite outside intervention against other members. However, members of a community will by definition share its values and thus often freely choose to refrain from seeking outside help. Moreover, maintaining an alternative system of rules and enforcement may be in the long-term economic interest of both the community and most potential litigants. A party in such instances may face community hostility were he or she to seek judicial enforcement, but, irrespective of any potential community pressures, resort to court may not be viewed as an acceptable option by that party in any event.

B. Legal Rules and Contract Disputes

Relations break down under as many different circumstances and for as many particular causes as there are relationships. Some more general patterns, however, can be observed. They begin with a change. The original bargain, the initial understandings and expectations will nearly always have changed. Whether motivated by simple greed or envy, want, or just a change of mind or heart, one of the parties will have ceased to perform or wish to perform as before. The most frequently litigated disputes in otherwise on-going business relations in the United States as evidenced by appellate decisions involve dealer and franchise terminations. Whether caused by a change in marketing strategy by the manufacturer or franchisor, or by shoddy performance by an individual dealer or franchisee - so indeed some other factors - termination and the resulting litigation, these cases suggest, result from the plaintiff's desire for legal redress. One side or the other seeks legal relief in the form of either the imposition of a coercive sanction or its threat. The process of litigation of course transforms the business dispute. Whatever grievances or concerns actually motivated the parties can only be read between the lines. Readers of appellate decisions can only guess at the reality of the disputes involved. Yet, one factor applies to all: litigation was the result of a decision by the plaintiff to seek state intervention. Behind this decision, we can assume, was the perception that the state through its courts could provide some form of redress that, however imperfect, was better than any the claimant could alternatively obtain without state intervention in the context of the business relationship or the business community. Even in Japan, litigation, as both *Kahei Rokumoto* and

Mark Ramseyer have both so ably argued,[7] is the result of conscious choice and the prospect of a more favorable outcome, whether in the interest of the community or the individual.

The Seattle interviews provided substantial evidence of settling disputes within the shadow of the law. As noted above, the contract tends to govern all disputes. In the case of larger firms, one of the principal activities of legal department attorneys is to advise management with respect to the legal rights of the parties and to evaluate whether the firm would "win" or "lose" in a litigated case. However, smaller firms without the luxury of a legal department or in-house counsel use attorneys as sparingly as possible because of the costs involved. Thus, unless the dispute involves a considerable sum, both sides are likely to negotiate with little if any information about their legal rights and duties. In these cases, the legal rules become largely irrelevant except perhaps as a sort of "folk law" assumed by the parties to be valid. In any event, even in the United States, unless the parties have decided to terminate their business relationship, they ordinarily do not sue.

Applied to business disputes in on-going relationships, two possible explanations for relatively less frequent resort to court under similar circumstances in Japan can be posited: the first, as mentioned previously, is the threat or fear of community hostility were the aggrieved party to resort to court; and, second, Japanese society provides more effective means of redress outside the legal system for those involved in long-term business relationships. The second proposition can be amplified and restated as follows: to say that significantly fewer business disputes are litigated in Japan than in America or Europe means, in other words, that such disputes are resolved more to the satisfaction of the aggrieved party without resort to litigation. In deciding whether or not to litigate (or threaten to litigate), the aggrieved party confronts a choice between state intervention and other means of dealing with the grievance (including not taking any action). Assuming that the parties will select the option thought to be best, decisions not to litigate reflect the availability of a perceived-to-be better alternative. The choice need not be positive. The legal rules themselves also matter. Unless they offer some protection to parties with weak negotiating leverage, a lawsuit is unlikely. Those with leverage rarely need the law. Often we face a choice of evils. Still we select the "better" alternative.

Both explanations rest, it should be noted, on similar conditions. Effective mechanisms of community control and enforcement will either constrain resort to court or offer a more appealing enforcement alternative to potential litigants.

---

7 K. ROKUMOTO, *Nihon-jin no hô-ishiki saiho* [Japanese Legal Consciousness Reconsidered], *in: Hô to hô-katei* [Law and the Legal Process] (Mochizuki *et al*, eds. 1986); RAMSEYER & NAKAZATO, *supra* note 5.

In either case, ineffective community controls would fail to discourage litigation.

Expressed in this way, the principal quest for those who wish to ascertain essential differences in contracting between Japan and the Western industrial democracies includes comparative evaluation of the enforcement mechanisms within and without the formal legal system. Redress of grievances is not, it should be emphasized, merely a problem of dispute resolution or "management" that can be understood in terms of mediation and the facilitation of negotiated compromises. However important mediation and dispute management may be in relation to the broader question of the processes of dispute resolution and alternatives to litigation, such focus leaves out the more telling question of choice. As those who explain litigation in Japan in terms of rational behavior are quick to point out, ultimately the aggrieved party who is contemplating the rupture of the relationship and a lawsuit will choose the option that best serves self-interest. What counts and should be at the center of discussion are differences in the remedial options available to the parties. Neither mechanisms to facilitate communication nor negotiation of grievances nor even the legal rules are very meaningful if no effective means exist to constrain those with superior bargaining leverage. Effective means of persuasion and sanctions have overriding importance.

One aspect of the answer is, as noted above, the relative weakness of formal law enforcement. The argument need not repeated here, but the conclusion is pertinent. A dearth of judges and trial lawyers, filing fees, bond-posting requirements, judicially imposed constraints on proof, and other disincentives together increase the costs of litigation and effectively restrict access. While these or similar problems are not unique to Japan, they are relatively more severe in the Japanese legal system. As a result, the aggrieved party receives less state protection and therefore has less to gain from state intervention.

C. Extralegal Means of Redress

The weakness of law enforcement is, however, only one facet of the answer. The potential contract litigant seldom faces a "sue or suffer" choice. Other means of redress from self-help to community support are available options in most conflicts in all systems. Although such options are also present in the United States and, I suspect, other Western industrial societies, extralegal mechanisms for redress of business grievances are considerably less developed and weaker in these systems than in Japan. The published profiles of typical business disputes in Japan reveal a significantly greater emphasis on community-based measures for relief and redress. Boycotts, refusals to deal, and other variants of commercial ostracism not only seem more commonly used in Japan than elsewhere, but are also more socially acceptable. In other words, in comparison to America and Europe, in contrast to the relative weakness and inaccessibility of the formal mechanisms for law enforcement, self-help and community sanctions tend to be more easily and effectively applied.

Why this is so deserves closer attention. We can speculate that the "social density" of Japanese society, especially within its business communities, contributes substantially to the capacity of the community to enforce effectively accepted community norms. Repeated transactions over long periods of time among the same persons not only facilitate communication and enhance the flow of information, they also foster trust, cooperation, and interdependence, which combine to strengthen even further the bonds and cohesion among the participants. The literature on business transactions and contracting in Japan suggests a predominant emphasis on repeated deals based on relationships established over time and avoidance of spot transactions with strangers. Putting aside the question of why this may be so - its causes - the effects of such a prevailing pattern of doing business seem clear - a community of traders who share significant gains by continued cooperation, with significant barriers to withdrawal as well as new entry. And whatever the drawbacks of such communitarian orientation, the cohesion of the participants tends to endure as the well-being and prosperity of each becomes increasingly dependent upon cooperation and reciprocal dealing with the others.

Community should not be confused with association. In the United States, at least, the term community is often used to label voluntary groups of people who join together for a variety of aims, but who remain independent actors, as free to leave the group as they were to join it. Any significant degree of interdependence is rare and the relationships established tend to be superficial. The aims achieved, the group disbands. Community means much more. It has members, not participants, whose entry and exit are constrained by the broad interdependencies and shared interests that develop and are sustained by the group. Community also stimulates reinforcing behavior. Acceptance of communitarian constraints inexorably fosters expectations of future relationships and a willingness or necessity to pursue options that increase mutual dependency rather than those designed to promote greater independence.

D. Repeated Deals and Communitarian Concerns

As stated at the outset, what we know of contracting and business practices from the data collected by *Takeshi Uchida* and his colleagues, as well as previous studies, confirms the proposition that repeated deals are the most common form of long-term business relations. Negotiated and documented agreements are relatively rare in both Japan and the United States. Nevertheless, the data also suggest important differences with respect to the nature of repeated deals in the two countries that may be far more revealing.

The fact that parties tend to transact business together over a continuous period of time is less significant than their actual or perceived freedom to stop. As long as the parties believe that each is free to cease doing business with the other at any time, that neither is obligated legally or otherwise to continue the relationship, they are unlikely to tolerate the same degree of vulnerability that dependence on future dealing might produce, and thus they are less apt to invest the same level of resources to these more uncertain relationships than they would were the assurance of future dealings more secure. Greater employee immobility in large-scale enterprises in Japan as contrasted to the United States, for example, enables Japanese firms to invest more in education and training of mid-career managers. Although firms can create such assurance by contract, the flexibility and other benefits of repeated deals in most instances seem to outweigh any need or desire for contractual security. However, to the extent that the distinction between repeated deals and long-term contractual commitments begin to blur, the need expands to offset the disadvantages of fixed contractual commitments by maximizing their benefits. Thus investments made in reliance upon the continuation of the relationship make greater sense. In the process, as noted previously, both sides are more likely to pursue strategies that promote great interdependency. Constructing a transaction to impose costs in the event of any breach or rupture - for example, by "hostage-taking" - is a common approach in the United States.

The available evidence supports this hypothesis - that is, that (1) the distinction between repeated deals and long-term contracts are more blurred in Japan, and (2) that Japanese firms indeed do tend to act as if the relationship is likely to continue in a greater variety of transactions than the United States.

The most stable business relationships in the United States, it appears from the Seattle interviews, are between insurance agents, accountants, and law firms and their customers. This can be explained by the advantages of their institutional memory of their clients' business and needs as well as the personal relationships that are inevitably formed. Although both sides recognize that they are not bound to continue their relationship in the future, the economic and social incentives reinforcing such continuation are sufficiently strong and apparent to both sides that it makes sense for both to presume that the relationship will endure and thus to make present allocations of resources in reliance on future dealings. Thus a law firm may expand and develop capabilities that a single large client may need.

Similar considerations may also apply in Japan, but it appears that the list of stable partners must be expanded to include suppliers and dealers. Vertical keiretsu in Japan thus differ from American patterns in the sense that they are based on repeated deals but also share many of the attributes and interdependencies of long-term contractual commitments - for example, technology sharing, employee exchanges, financing. Here too the result is greater interdependency.

A communitarian orientation not only reinforces the use of repeated deals, as discussed above, it also tends to obscure any distinction between repeated deals and contracts. Not surprisingly, therefore, the legal rules developed by judges in Japan similarly blur this difference between the two. Courts in Japan, for instance, have repeatedly refused to allow unilateral refusal to renew long-term contracts without just cause.[8] As early as 1942, Japan's highest court implicitly suggested that without some justification a seller might not be allowed to discontinue selling to a buyer when they had been dealing over a long period of time.[9] Many of these cases involve long-term contracts that were simply not received after expiration of the state term. Others, however, appear to involve repeated deals. In either case, the economic interdependency will be the same.[10]

The Seattle interviews evidence a pattern of contracting that depends largely upon a bipolar tension between *independence* and *dependency*. If neither party relies on the other as a supplier or customer - that is, if both are mutually *independent* - long-term relationships tend to take the form of repeated deals without any commitment on either side. Long-term contracts appear to be used only in two situations. One is where one side of the arrangement is significantly more dependent than the other and therefore lacks the leverage to avoid a legally binding agreement, but the other is sufficiently dependent to need a long-term commitment. Such contracts tend to be quite one-sided in favor of the dominant party and thus only a very dependent firm would agree. As the legal counsel for a large Seattle-based manufacturer explained:

> Now with our very biggest suppliers, we would love to have contracts with them so that we can set a price or set all those legal things. But they're big enough to say, "We don't want a contract with you. We prefer doing business this way," because it is advantageous for them to do so. (Interview 1, August 24, 1994.)

Long-term contractual commitments are also made when the parties share at least a sufficient degree of dependency on the other to make such commitments beneficial to both sides. These tend to be carefully negotiated deals. At least in some industries the mutual advantages of long-term commitments seem to be providing the necessary incentives. As one manager described this trend:

---

8 *See*, e.g., *Hannam Kaiun K.K.* v. *K.K. Shimada*, 12 KAKYÛ MINSHÛ 2434 (Osaka District Ct., October 12, 1961); *Hokkaido Ford Tractor K.K.* v. *Minoru Sangyô K.K.*, 1258 HANREI JIHÔ 76 (Sapporo High Ct., September 30, 1987).

9 *See*, e.g., 11 HÔGAKU 1183 (Great Ct. of Cassation, February 1942).

10 *See*, e.g., *Fujikura Gomu Kôgyô K.K.* v. *K.K. Wada Shôten*, 286 HANREI JIHÔ 25 (Tokyo District Ct., December 13, 1961), which involved repeated purchases by the defendant for over three years of over 90% of the golf shoes the plaintiff manufactured.

> [O]ne of the net effects of 20 years ago's practices was that we had quite a proliferation in the number of sources that [our company] had access to or had done business with. I think from then to now a dramatic reduction in the number of sources that we [had has been taking place]. We are going to longer-term contracts. We're developing relationships that [are] above and beyond just that contractual relationship, developing relationships with those sources which are in the [company] family, if you want to call it that, because in order to build the product that we want to build, we want to have suppliers who have more than just [suppliers]. . . . The price in and of itself doesn't necessarily get you the quality. (Interview 11, August 23, 1996.)

The company, we learned, has over 8000 suppliers.

Dependency depends largely on the product. In the case of goods and services bought and sold in a highly competitive market, there may be repeated deals as noted, but seldom a significant degree of mutual dependency with any resulting need or desire for long-term commitments. As the good or service becomes more complex, expensive, and difficult to obtain from other suppliers, the user's dependency increases. Similarly, however, the supplier's dependency will increase to the extent that it relies upon a single or small number of purchasers and thus wishes to assure a stable demand.

None of the Seattle respondents indicated any concern to develop greater interdependency. The goal of each was to create dependency on the part of their customers, but to assure their own independence from those who supplied them with goods and services. Nor did any ever suggest that "community" pressure had any bearing or even existed. Only the attitudes of the parties themselves and their commercial relationship seemed to matter. This is not to say that "community" values are irrelevant. Nearly all of those interviewed expressly or tacitly referred to community standards for commercially honest and fair behavior. For example, a merchandising manager for a large retail grocery chain based in Seattle, explaining why in his experience the company had never stopped buying for suppliers with whom the chain had an established relationship, remarked:

> See in our business it's not like buying a car that you might buy once every five years, or buying a house you might buy twice in a lifetime. You're doing business with these people everyday. We're open seven days a week, and they're shipping us seven days a week and doing business with us. It would be shortsighted to jeopardize that by taking advantage of the situation. You might be able to get away with it if you're a little bit of a negotiator. You might get away with something one or two times, but after that they're going to say, "We don't like doing business with them because they're not fair." (Interview 5, August 23, 1994.)

Shared understandings of what fairness means and the limits of hard bargaining and honest but tough business practices provide important parameters for most on-going relationships. Maintaining a good business reputation is a similarly effective behavioral constraint. Nevertheless, potential "community" or collective action to enforce such understandings or to limit the freedom of the parties to resort to court was simply beyond contemplation.

E. Community Enforcement

Like Japan's traditional mura, its business "communities" in effect have become semi-autonomous social units. To the extent the state allows them freedom from - or for whatever reason does not impose - direct managerial or regulatory controls, they are able to develop and to enforce their own autonomous rules of the game. In other words, except in cases where the state chooses to intervene with coercive commands, these business "villages" function effectively without resort to law.

As law rules, contracts enable the parties to seek state intervention. And with state intervention, the parties no longer control their relationship. The parameters of their autonomy are subjected to state definition. This is not to say that nonlaw rules established by agreement - i.e., legally unenforceable contracts and promises - ensure greater party autonomy. To the extent that the parties are able to enforce rules through some alternative nonstate mechanism, the parameters of their autonomy are similarly determined by those who exercise the powers of enforcement. In either case, the enforcer controls. To the extent therefore that business communities in Japan provide an effective alternative or substitute for judicial enforcement of contracts, these communities define the limits of party autonomy and the applicable rules of the transactions within their ambit.

Community enforcement establishes a system of private ordering as an alternative to the state - a system of private ordering that in the abstract is as much beyond the control of the parties as the system of legal ordering by the state. However, insofar as the efficacy of community enforcement depends upon collective undertakings by the members of the community themselves, each participant has a voice in the process that cannot be duplicated in the legal process. By the same token, those outside the community have little or no say.

Community ordering rarely if ever operates in isolation from state ordering through the legal system. The two systems function concurrently and in competition. The modern state always, of course, has the capacity to intervene. Because the state defines its own competence, it retains the ultimate authority to control the limits of community autonomy. By policing transactions through "public law", the state can intervene directly. Enforcing rules through criminal law or administrative processes empowers prosecutors, regulatory officials, and always judges by enabling them to determine which rules govern. Although the extent of such empowerment of each office depends upon the scope of its "prosecutorial" or enforcement discretion, the state acting through the legislature or the judiciary has the last word.

In the enforcement of contracts as "private law," the state in effect, however, has chosen to restrict its own competence and discretion. By allowing the parties the freedom to choose whether or not to seek to enforce the rules by resort to court, the state permits competition from other systems of ordering. In theory, therefore, the parties have the choice and presumably select the enforcement system that best serves their interests.

Potential litigants can be expected, it is argued, to forecast the outcome of state enforcement and to settle any dispute in conformity with such prediction. As a result, law rules govern without the need (or costs) of actual litigation. Arguments along these lines regarding negotiated settlements with predicted outcomes in conformity to legal rules rest on the pivotal but seldom stated premise that the parties have an unhindered choice to litigate. Moreover, rarely taken into account are the effects of alternative systems of enforcement. If access to court is either precluded or not the preferred system of enforcement, the parties will not bargain in the "shadow of the law" as presupposed. Instead, they will negotiate within the shadow of community norms and the predicted outcomes of community enforcement.

One of the best examples of Japan's private ordering system is the clearing house rule prohibiting all Japanese banks from dealing in any manner for a six-month period with a customer that twice dishonors a check or note. As a result of this rule, few businesses can remain solvent that fail to honor a check or note; consequently, promissory notes in Japan are used as a form of collateral. Although the clearing house rule can be viewed as a contractual obligation, no one considers that it will ever be enforced in court. It remains viable solely because of the consensus that exists among Japanese financial institutions that it serves all participants well. To my knowledge, no bank has ever challenged it. Nor is any likely to do so. Both the rule and its enforcement are part of a system of rules and sanctions that operate quite apart from the state. Although its legality has been unsuccessfully challenged by outsiders (defaulting debtors) as a violation of Japanese regulatory law (antitrust), it remains tolerated by the state.

The clearing house rule on dishonored notes is only one example of the more pervasive pattern of community controls that govern both personal and economic relationships in Japan. The "private" community system of ordering is effective and efficient. Few in Japan seek the alternative of state intervention. In case after case, the courts defer to the community and the legislative process demonstrates public preference. This is not to say that Japanese have no complaints. Many Japanese who have lived abroad marvel at the freedom from social control enjoyed in the United States and other countries, but they seem quite reluctant to trade state coercion for community control.

Many would concede the relative importance of community controls and private ordering in Japan but still question the role of the state. Surely, it can be said, law rules do apply to contracts in Japan and the state does enforce contracts. Litigation rates may be low in Japan relative to other industrial countries, but Japan does have lawyers and judges, lawsuits and enforcement actions. Therefore, do not the parties negotiate in the shadow of the legal rules, except in the presumably rare instances when they can be certain that the community controls will indeed work?

In response to questions like these, I would also concede: the state and the law do have significance. Neither the formal mechanism for law enforcement nor legal rules become irrelevant in Japan simply because of the relative strength of community controls. Rather, I would argue, because of the potential of state intervention they gain a special relevance. In a sense, the community competes with the state as a source of protection and benefit to its members. The community remains cohesive and thus controlling only so long as it also remains a better source of well-being than the state. Thus community norms and controls do have to serve its members better overall than state controls. If the community norms work against the interests of any member for very long, that member will leave and thus cease to be subject to its controls. An isolated defection may not have too significant an effect, but multiplied over time, defections will destroy the community. Thus the community norms will over time reflect the interests of its members in general and not reflect preferential treatment to one group or another. Thus community norms can be expected over time to approximate any legal norms that tend to maximize the interests of its members.

By the same token, however, the state also competes. At least in democracies, administrative officials, including law enforcement authorities as well as legislators, will seek public loyalty and support. They, too, can thus be expected to create and enforce legal rules that serve the broad interests of the public in general and those groups whose loyalty and support is the most crucial. In the process, legal rules as enforced will similarly over time move toward community norms. Differences will of course remain, but the differences will for the most part reflect differences in the interests of separate communities of constituencies. As this process continues, the state will inexorably reinforce rather than erode community cohesion.

In conclusion, the questions to be asked by those seeking empirical data on contracting in Japan should not focus on how the parties bargain or negotiate their disputes but rather on the nature and constraints of their communities. Can business communities be identified? What patterns of dependency and mutual support pertain? How clear is the distinction between repeated deals and long-term contracts? What expectations develop in the course of continuing relationship without contract. Do parties avoid bargains with strangers and those outside known communities? When relations break down, how do the parties respond? What extralegal sanctions are available and applied? How effective is reputation and community censure in ensuring compliance with community norms? And do community norms differ from legal rules? Answers to these questions will tell us more about whether contracts and society in Japan truly differ.

Equally important, those who make the law are themselves subject to the same habits, expectations, and values that are shared broadly throughout the society. To the extent that Japan does indeed have a communitarian orientation, its lawmakers will also tend to construct or redefine legal rules and apply them in ways that conform to this broad cultural orientation.

Chapter Six

Law, Contract, and Society in Japan: A Personal View

*Guntram Rahn**

Contents

A. Introduction

Western law, introduced into Japan from Europe and the United States, has in the course of one century become distinctly Japanese.

Such, of course, has been the fate of all products of foreign culture imported by Japan. Chinese noodles, for example, which were probably introduced into Japan together with Chinese characters and Confucianism in the 5th century, are still called "Chinese noodles" (*chûka soba*) today, but taste quite different and much better, I would say, than noodles served in China. *Tempura* is said to be a Japanese dish of Western fried fish introduced by the Portuguese, the word "*tempura*" being derived from "*tempero*", meaning "cooking" in Portuguese. In the 19th century, the first American envoy to Japan, Townsend Harris, craved for a steak. At that time the Japanese did not eat beef, but a friendly farmer offered his cow. Later a monument was erected with a prayer inscribed for the peaceful repose of the cow which had offered its life to satisfy a human desire.[1] Today, steak from Kobe or Matsuzaka beef is considered superior to the American original, not only by the Japanese. We are presently witnessing a similar cultural assimilation of McDonald's hamburgers in Japan, but it remains to be seen whether the result of this process will also be something superior.

In any case, law has become much more palatable to the Japanese since its introduction from the West, which began more than a century ago.

---

* The following is the text of the oral presentation, extended to include footnotes.

1 A. SAKAI, Japan in a Nutshell, Vol. I, 221 (1949).

The gap between the law in the imported statutes and the rules by which society functioned is said to have been the outstanding characteristic of Japanese legal culture during the past one hundred years.[2] According to *Nobuyuki Toshitani*[3], the isolation (*yûri*) of law from the life of the people was one of the basic problems of the modernization of Japan.[4]

Nevertheless, the one hundred years after the introduction of Western law signify a period of cultural assimilation of law in Japan. But this is only a natural process that has happened at other times and in other places, and it has been aptly described by *A. Warnava* in respect to the development of American law from English common law:

> It was then that, by a process of adaptation and assimilation at one point, and change and compromise at another, we made the common law received from England uniquely our own, shaping it to this nation's indigenous needs.[5]

Looking back on the past century, Japanese jurists may make the same claim.

The historical process of cultural assimilation of law in Japan which changed not only the law as a product of Western culture, but also the recipient Japanese culture itself, has already been described in detail.[6] Although, of course, law and society are in constant evolution, I would pinpoint the end of this process of transformation of Western law into inherently Japanese law and its recognition as such in Japan at the beginning of the 1980s.[7]

This was the time when Japan realized that having surpassed the Western nations economically, it could no longer follow in their footsteps. Economic success lent a new self-assurance to the Japanese which carried over into the field of law. It was in 1983 that *Eiichi Hoshino*[8] declared in an introductory lecture on the study of civil law:

---

2 T. HASEGAWA, *Kokusai hômu no jôshiki* [Common Knowledge in International Legal Affairs] 130 (1990).

3 Professor at the Institute of Social Sciences, University of Tokyo.

4 N. TOSHITANI, *Nihon no hô wo kangaeru* [Thoughts on Japanese Law] 166 (1985).

5 A. WARNAVA, book review of: *Haar, The Golden Age of American Law*, 66 COLUM.L. REV. 996 (1966). The Japanese are sometimes criticized for laying claim to uniqueness, but as the quote from Warnava corroborates, there is really nothing unique about being unique.

6 *Inter alia* Z. KITAGAWA, Rezeption und Fortbildung des europäischen Zivilrechts in Japan [The Adaption and Development of European Civil Law in Japan] (1970); G. RAHN, Rechtsdenken und Rechtsauffassung in Japan [Legal Thought and Conceptions of Law in Japan] (1990).

7 For details, *see* RAHN, *supra* note 6, at 400 *et seq.*

8 Professor of civil law at Tokyo University.

> Now at least Japan has become a first-class country in the world. In newer times one no longer has the opinion that Japanese attitudes are backward or pre-modern, but has come to think that they are excellent as a way of life.[9]

And in regard to the state of Japanese law, Toshitani reported affirmatively in 1985:

> There is even the view that the specifically Japanese interrelationship between law and the concept of law grew and multiplied during the high economic growth. It is therefore understood that the backward Japanese situation did not come closer to the situation in Europe and the United States as modernization progressed, but that the law and concept of law in Japan and the combination of both show a form which is different from those in Europe and the U.S.[10]

On this background, I would like to present to you some personal views on law, contract, and society in Japan today. My view is based on my years of study of Japanese law at Tokyo University and at the Max Planck Institutes in Hamburg and Munich, as well as on my present experience as a business lawyer working on Japan-related cases.

My paper will adress three topics: First, the place of law in Japanese society (B); second, Japanese attitudes in regard to contracts (C), and third, Japanese attitudes in regard to litigation (D).

B. Law in Japanese Society

Although many Japanese may still feel that legal matters and courts of law are something they respect but would like to keep at a distance (*kei shite tôzaketai*)[11], there has evidently been a tendency in Japanese society over the past decades to make law popular and familiarize the Japanese people with legal topics.[12]

Compare Japanese legal journals, such as *Jurisuto* and *Hanrei Times*, with their counterparts in Germany or the United States. In the Japanese journals you will find printed colloqiums (*zadankai*) which are embellished with photographs of the participants, you will find essays (*zuihitsu*) and other personal reminiscences which make for entertaining reading while being related to law. German legal journals appear drab in comparison. Not only legal professionals, but also laymen participate in topics of general interest in the *zadankai*, and one can easily imagine that even the general public may profit

9 E. Hoshino, *Minpô gakushû no tame no sho zentei* [Preconditions of the Study of Civil Law] (1983), *in*: Minpo ronshû V [Collected Essays on Civil Law, Vol. V] 370 (Hoshino, ed. 1986).

10 Toshitani, *supra* note 4, at 201.

11 *See* Hasegawa, *supra* note 2, at 157.

12 *See* also Rahn, *supra* note 6, at 333 *et seq*.

from reading such publications. In Germany, legal journals address themselves to highly specialized professionals only.

Today, there are countless popular books on legal topics available in Japan. Many of these books are authored by university professors or lawyers, written in simple language and often containing illustrations or cartoons in order to attract the general public to matters of law.

Furthermore, there are even comic books on fields of law, for example intellectual property law. The heroine, a beautiful Japanese intellectual property law attorney, falls in love with the in-house lawyer of her client's American competitor, and in between they discuss basic questions of patents, licenses, and intellectual property protection. A glossary explains the relevant legal terminology popping up here and there in this thrilling *manga* adventure. In Germany no literary *manga* culture exists and therefore no such vehicle for the popularization of law.

More on the serious side, Japanese media report extensively, and I would say in greater detail than German media, on enactments of law and court cases of general interest. The discussion on the recent new Product Liability Law[13] was widely covered. The gist of the law was printed and explained in such depth in Japanese daily newspapers that today there is probably nobody in Japan who does not know what the letters "PL" stand for. The main reasoning of important court judgments are often reprinted in full in Japanese newspapers, accompanied by reports, analysis and commentaries. In the present HIV litigation in Tokyo and Osaka, papers carried the text of the settlement proposal and accompanying opinions of the courts. Of course such news is given the full journalistic treatment to attract readers.

Specific areas of law considered to be particularly important to the Japanese nation, such as intellectual property law, receive keen attention by the media. Patent matters, even the increase or decrease of staff in patent departments of major Japanese companies, are reported in the framework of the topic patent strategy, and of course the general public is minutely informed on all litigation in the "patent war" between Japan and the United States. With the support of the Japan Patent Attorneys Association, a "television drama" depicting the life and work of a Japanese patent attorney was presented to the Japanese public a few years ago.

In short, law today has become a part of everyday life in Japanese society, and it is visibly reflected in the mirror of society held up by the Japanese media.

Law on the level of personal interest is, according to *Toshitani*, seen mainly as "something which may be applied flexibly and skillfully" to the benefit of

13 *Seizô-butsu sekinin-hô*, Law No. 85 of 1994.

one's own purposes (*yûzû wo kikasete umaku unyô subeki mono*).[14] A study on Japanese legal conciousness published in 1982 summarizes this attitude as follows:

> Law is considered to be a tool or lubricant for the conduct of daily life. If it obstructs a convenient conduct of life, it is the law which is not adequate. From this results the thinking that the law should be applied flexibly and with a certain magnanimity, and that it does not matter if from time to time one does not observe it at all. If there exist other effective means beside the law (even if they may at times be more severe or troublesome), these means will be used and sometimes a more tolerant, sometimes on the contrary a more rigorous position will be taken (which however will not take recourse to the law).[15]

C. Japanese Attitude Toward Contracts

The flexible approach described here seems to be apparent in an attitude toward contracts which is, to my experience, not uncommon among the Japanese.

According to a study published in 1987, 71% of the commercial contracts made by Japanese companies were conluded only orally. In Japan, Western societies are sometimes called *keiyaku no shakai* (societies of contracts), while Japanese society in contrast has been termed *mokuyaku no shakai* (society of tacit agreements).[16] In many business relationships there may exist voluminous written communication on the specification of products, price, delivery etc., but no document on the conclusion of contract and contractual rights and obligations.

Quite often contracts are not formally concluded in Japan, they evolve. In these cases the party interested in entering into a business relationship will not formally negotiate and then produce a draft written contract. He will present what he has to offer and then try to involve the other party by frequent contacts and personal communication, impressive hospitality, free ancillary services, and a flow of constant information. In this manner a personal relationship is built until sooner or later a point of no return is reached and business orders just have to follow.

It is my impression that Japanese companies sometimes are hesitant to conclude detailed written contracts because they want to retain their flexibility and not be explicitly and extensively bound.[17]

---

14 *See* TOSHITANI, *supra* note 10, at 179.

15 NIHON BUNKA KAIGI (ed.), *Nihon-jin no hô-ishiki* [The Legal Conciousness of the Japanese] (1982), quoted from TOSHITANI, *supra* note 10, at 178 *et seq*.

16 "*Keiyaku no shakai - mokuyaku no shakai*" is the title of a book by K. HISAGI published by *Nikkei Bunko*; *see* HASEGAWA, *supra* note 2, at 236.

17 *See* HASEGAWA, *supra* note 2, at 242.

If a written contract is made, the fact of its formal conclusion may be considered to be more important than detailed contract stipulations. Such a document is regarded primarily as "proof of the relationship of trust" between the parties (*shinrai kankei no akashi*), and as a first step in a contractual cooperation. It is not meant to be a comprehensive body of provisions for the performance of the contract and conflict procedure and a means of evidence in case of dispute, as is common in the "severe" (*kibishii*) contract societies in Europe and America.[18] For all practical purposes, if a more detailed written contract is used, its stipulations may be utilized to put pressure on the other party also by a Japanese company. But generally there is an inclination to believe that a contractual relationship is not fixed once and for all, but may flexibly be adapted to the changing circumstances. In this sense a typical Japanese contract clause which can also be found in many standard lease contracts reads:

> If doubts arise as to matters not provided for in the present contract or as to the interpretation of this contract, the parties shall hold special consultations in good faith. (*betto kyôgi jôkô*).[19]

While the Western type of contract and the attitude underlying it are well-suited to determine what is legally right or wrong in the relationship between the parties, the Japanese attitude towards contracts seems better suited to uphold and continue this relationship - which of course is first of all a business relationship.

A case I have been handling may serve as an example. A Japanese original equipment manufacturer had for several years been supplying fashionable consumer products to his German customer, which the German company had sold under its brand name in the European market. These products were designed and then manufactured by the Japanese company, taking into account additional specifications made by the German customer in the course of the manufacturing process. No formal written contracts were concluded; even order forms were not used regularly and issued only for confirmation's sake shortly before the agreed delivery date. Sales invoices were payable in yen, and when the value of the yen rose against the deutsche mark, the German company found that one specific OEM-product the parties had negotiated on had become too expensive for the European market. When a price reduction offered by the Japanese manufacturer did not seem satisfactory, the German company notified the Japanese company that it would not accept delivery of this product which was in in the final stage of manufacture. In a Western legalistic manner, the

---

18 *Id.* at 247.

19 The Japanese wording is, "*Hon keiyaku ni sadame no nai jikô matawa kono keiyaku no kaishaku ni gigi wo shôjita toki wa, betto seii wo motte kyôgi suru mono to suru.*" *Cf.*, HASEGAWA, *supra* note 2, at 228.

German company gave two reasons for this refusal: first, they said, a contract had not been concluded in regard to the product in question; second, the person handling the matter on the German side, who had been negotiating the details of the order, was not legally authorized to act for the company, which the Japanese side knew or could have known. When the representative of the Japanese company requested to meet the head of the German company in order to discuss the matter, the latter repeatedly refused, ostensibly because of other engagements.

When my Japanese client requested me to institute legal proceedings, he told me that to him it was not primarily a question of money. If the customer had discussed the matter with him, admitting his legal obligation but asking for understanding and apologizing for not being able to pay the agreed-upon price because of the foreign exchange developments, he would have accepted an extension of the term of payment or further price reduction to keep the customer. But the false reasons and insisting on formal legal arguments could not be accepted.

The German company had only looked at the legal dimension of its relationship with the Japanese company for a solution. Had it known that asking for understanding and an apology would have solved its problem, it might have acted accordingly. The business relation would have been saved, and there would have been one lawsuit less in the statistics.

D. Japanese Attitude Toward Litigation

There is no doubt that emotions are a more dominant factor in litigation in Japan than in Western societies such as Germany, and this holds true also in business-related cases. But it is also my impression that the Japanese attitude toward litigation has been changing, which does not necessarily mean that it has become more Westernized.

Previously in Japanese society, the perception seemed to be dominant that the courts of law were part of an authoritarian government system, somber and unfriendly in atmosphere, reminiscent of the *o-shirasu* courtyards and the principle of *kenka ryô-seibai* in feudal times, according to which two parties engaged in a private dispute would both be punished.

There have been efforts to change this negative image of the courts, and popular expectations have changed as well. According to a public opinion poll carried out in 1980, Japanese want the courts to be a place "where a familiar atmosphere reigns, where people ar close to each other and feel that they have friendly relationships."[20]

---

20 N. TANAKA, *Nihon-jin no saibansho imêji* [The Image of the Courts Held by the Japanese], 412 HANREI TIMES 8 (1980).

In January 1990 a "Committee for the Improvement of Written Civil Judgments" (*Minji Hanketsu-sho Kaizen Iinkai*), composed of a group of 19 judges from the Tokyo and Osaka district and high courts, published a proposal which included ten model texts of judgments under the motto, "Judgments which the parties can read and understand".[21] All judges of the nation and legal trainees at the Judicial Training Institute (*Shihô Kenshû-jo*) were to be educated accordingly.

On this background, bringing a matter before the courts seems to be accepted in the Japanese business world today as one option in business strategy, the merits and demerits of which have to be weighed against each other case by case. Among the merits of "*kokubyaku wo tsukeru*", i.e., having a state organ make clear who is right and who is wrong - could be to enforce a right which otherwise would not be enforceable, to obtain emotional satisfaction, or to get the right kind of publicity in a competitive marketplace. Among the demerits are the loss of a business relationship, possible negative publicity in the related business community as a troublemaker who is not able to solve his problems without making waves, and, of course, the cost and time and uncertainty of the outcome of litigation.

In many cases, for example if it is just a question of getting an outstanding debt to be paid, there are other means than civil litigation in Japan to resolve the matter possibly in a more efficient way. First of all, disputes should be resolved by joint negotiation (*hanashiai*). If an agreement is not reached at this stage, an intermediary may be appealed to who will try to reach a solution in the matter. There are many extra-legal and legal possibilities to achieve this end; for example, a private settlement (*jidan*), a mediation (*assen*), an out-of-court or in-court settlement (*wakai*), a formal conciliation (*chôtei*), or arbitration (*chûsai*). Recently, a problem between a European manufacturer and Japanese distributor which might have led to litigation could be solved because the father of the Japanese attorney we were working with had been a member of the same university club as the president of the distributing company, our opponent. Should pressure and a show of force be necessary to realize one's claim, the services of *bôryoku-dan* (gangsters), *toritate-ya* (professional debt-collectors), or *seiri-ya* (professional regulators) can also be enlisted.

In case litigation is resorted to in a business matter, the intention often is to use this "tool" flexibly as a tactical weapon and not to fight to the end. The idea is to strike a heavy blow with the expectation that it will then be easier to come to a settlement.

A look at the Annual Report of Judicial Statistics published by the Supreme Court (*Saikô Saibansho*) shows that the Japanese are gradually making an increased use of the courts and are filing more lawsuits. In 1949, the number of

21 *Tôji-sha ga yonde wakaru hanketsu-bun.*

new lawsuits filed in Japan was about 50,000 (50,255) and the number of conciliation requests 45,000 (44,919). However, in 1990 the number of new lawsuits had risen to 238,000 (237,985), while the number of new conciliation cases amounted to 61,000 (61,007). In only five years from 1990 to 1994, the number of new lawsuits filed rose steadily from 238,000 (237,985) to 424,000 (424,403).[22] In my opinion this is an irreversible tendency.

E. Concluding Remarks

In the past, Japanese and Western legal scholars have put forth numerous theories to explain the phenomena of law and society in Japan. The extreme positions in this debate can be characterized as the theory of cultural individuality on the one side, and the theory of universalism on the other. In the 1950s and 1960s, the theory of the cultural individuality of law and society in Japan was dominant, represented by *Takeyoshi Kawashima, Yoshiyuki Noda, René David* and *Konrad Zweigert*. However, to these scholars, cultural individuality in the role and use of law in Japanese society had a distinctly negative connotation. To Kawashima the attitude toward law in Japan was "pre-modern and feudalistic" and would change to the better only if the Japanese changed their ways to become more "modern", a term which at that time was synonymous to "Western".

The theory of universalism itself is of Western origin and is embodied, for example, in the doctrine that Christian beliefs and values (which are Western values) are universally valid to all mankind. Applied to law, this theory postulates that the values embodied in Western law are and have in fact been the same as in Japan, and that existing practical differences are either negligible or institutional. This was the quite original proposition made by *Masao Ôki*, who argued that the Japanese peasants in the uprisings of feudal Japan had been "fighting for their rights".[23] The theory of the universalism of law was intended to oppose the theory of cultural individuality by focusing on law and the legal process in Japan which exist similarly in Western countries. It was welcomed by those who thought that the theory of cultural individuality had overemphasized Japanese peculiarities and the alleged pre-modern, backward state of law and society in Japan.

---

22 SAIKÔ SAIBANSHO JIMU SÔKYOKU (ed.), *Heisei 6 nen shihô tôkei nenpô, 1 Minji gyôsei hen* [1995 Annual Report of Judical Statistics, Civil and Administrative Law Cases Volume]; for an extensive discussion of this aspect see *Wollschläger*'s contribution in Chapter Three in this volume.

23 M. ÔKI, Schlichtung als Institution des Rechts [Mediation as a Legal Institution], 16 RECHTSTHEORIE 151 (1985); also, M. ÔKI. *Nihon-jin no hô-kannen* [The Concept of Law of the Japanese] (1983).

In my view, both of these theories became obsolete in the early 1980s, and rightly so. Having gained self-assurance through their country's economic success, Japanese legal scholars began to accept the characteristically Japanese elements in their legal culture, realizing that these were different from Western legal culture, but not backward. And obviously these elements did not impair, but rather seemed conducive to the Japanese success. *Kahei Rokumoto* concisely formulated this new perception of law and society in Japan in his book on sociology of law published in 1986, proclaiming "It is natural and probably desirable that each society should have its own legal system which conforms to its cultural tradition."[24]

It is this theory of cultural individuality with a positive connotation which seems more or less undisputed in Japan today.

Today, Japan is a pluralistic society in which traditional and new values, of Japanese and Western origin, co-exist in mutual contradiction, indifference, harmony, or combinations with varying relative weight. Thoughts and actions are rarely determined exclusively by either traditionally Japanese or Western concepts. However, in their search for explanations of cause and effect in society, scientists and scholars tend to offer clear-cut, monocausal theories. Monocausal theories are easily developed, understood, discussed, supported, or disputed. The only problem is that they do not reflect the complex reality of society.

The pluralism of attitudes which are either peculiar to the Japanese or common also in Western societies, as well as their manifold combinations apparent in modern-day Japan, offer a wealth of operational possibilities in business relationships. This variety of operational possibilities is in my opinion greater than in the West and it has contributed to Japan's economic success.

Law and contract are certainly used in Japanese business today to safeguard or enforce business interests. But there are also other instruments for this purpose and all are used alternatively or in combination, as the situation requires.[25] Law and contract are just "one of them", as the Japanese say.

Kenzô Takayanagi, in his preface to *John Henry Wigmore's* "Law and Justice in Tokugawa Japan", relates that Wigmore liked to refer to *Musashi*

---

24 K. ROKUMOTO, *Hô-shakai-gaku* [Sociology of Law] 229 (1986).

25 *Cf.* Z. KITAGAWA, Tradition and Modernity in Dispute Settlement, paper presented for the International Symposium on Theory in the Sociology of Law, Tokyo, September 1975 (unpublished manuscript), p. 19:

> "In many cases it is unrealistic to try to treat a dispute settlement as either a solely traditional or solely modern matter or to consider the settlement of disputes by litigation as superior to that by negotiation. Instead a more pragmatic observation of the problem should lead us to the conclusion that in certain cases the application of the traditional approach is more appropriate while in others the converse is true and finally in some cases the joint application of both would be called for."

Miyamoto in his informal after-dinner speeches. Miyamoto Musashi, as is well known, was a famous fencing master at the beginning of the *Tokugawa* era who won all bouts with the foremost fencing masters in the land because of his double sword style, in which he combined the use of the short sword and the long sword of the samurai. Wigmore likened the traditional spiritual and moral heritage of Japan to the short sword style, and Western learning to the long sword style. "It was his idea," Takayanagi writes, "that Japan, in order to become really great, must master *Miyamoto's* double sword style."[26]

I think, in business, Japan has done just that.

26 J.H. WIGMORE, Law and Justice in Tokugawa Japan, Part I: Introduction, xxiii (1969).

Chapter Seven

Contract Law and Practice in Japan: An Antipodean Perspective

*Luke R. Nottage**

Contents

A. An Antipodean Perspective?

In 1996, a book entitled "Asian Laws Through Australian Eyes" was published in Sydney. Although I can be fiercely proud to be a New Zealander during a rugby test match or an America's Cup yacht race against an Australian team, I was delighted to become an "honorary Australian" and contribute a chapter on Japanese contract law.[1] The book, and a colloquium of contributors and Asian law specialists in Australia held at the Australian National University in early 1995, reflect a sense that many studies of Asian legal systems, including the Japanese legal system, have been largely framed by European, and particularly U.S. perspectives. Of course there are historical reasons for this. But history does not stand still. Australia and New Zealand have become closely linked

---

* I thank the participants at the Berlin Conference for raising points which have stimulated some further thoughts for this paper and my most recent work. Likewise, I thank Professor *Takeshi Kojima* (Chuo University) and participants at a seminar on December 23, 1995, at the Comparative Law Institute in Japan, where I presented a version of the conference paper more tailored to a Japanese audience. This paper is dedicated to Mr *Paul Walker*, Senior Lecturer in Law and Director of the New Zealand Institute of Public Law, Victoria University of Wellington; and Barrister at Law, Gray's Inn. Without his support, it would have been extremely difficult for me to have attended the Berlin Conference. I also thank others who are mentioned in the relevant footnotes. Naturally, I take sole responsibility for any errors and for the perspective presented.

1 L. NOTTAGE, Contract Law, Theory and Practice in Japan: Plus ça change, plus c'est la même chose?, *in*: Asian Laws Through Australian Eyes (V. Taylor, ed. 1996).

since the creation of a free trade zone in 1982, and both are now facing the realities of close and growing links with the wider Asian region, including Japan. Australian and New Zealand scholars - and now lawyers - have reevaluated their traditional focus on England and the U.S. Wider interest in and more thoughtful studies of Asia have emerged. We realize that we now live in a "tri-polar" world, both connected to - yet separate from - Europe, North America, and Asia.[2] An emerging common perspective from "down under", what might be called an "underview", gives me some confidence in proposing here an antipodean perspective on Japanese law, particularly contract law.[3]

First, however, I must apologize to my colleagues from other island nations in the South Pacific for my ignorance of what may be quite unique perceptions of Japanese law. Nevertheless, one example that I have uncovered may have provided an opportunity for certain Fijians, at least, to consider how their own closer economic links with Japan can give rise to legal issues, and hence may have led to distinct perceptions of how Japanese interact with contract law norms.

In *Raniga* v. *Sony (South Pacific) Ltd.*, the respondent, presumably the Fijian subsidiary of Sony Corporation established to distribute its products in Fiji ("the distributor"), successfully sued the appellant, presumably a local purchaser ("the purchaser").[4] The purchaser had bought products from the distributor since at least 1973. On July 1, 1974 the distributor changed its trade discount system, no doubt to one less favourable to purchasers. In September and October 1974 the purchaser bought more products from the distributor. On July 16, 1975, the purchaser tendered a cheque to the distributor, deducting certain amounts from the total invoiced by the distributor, and writing that if the distributor disagreed with the deductions they were to return the cheque. Instead, the distributor banked the cheque, but still sued the purchaser for the deductions made. The Supreme Court upheld the judgment of the Magistrate's Court in Suva, applying the "pre-existing duty rule". The purchaser had argued that its tender of the cheque and accompanying letter constituted an offer to settle the account invoiced as owing to the distributor, and that the distributor accepted this offer (by banking the cheque), creating a renegotiated contract that "effectively rescinded the former contract as recognised under business

2 B. HARLAND, Small Countries in a Tripolar World (1991).

3 Apologies to Emeritus Professor *Coote* and Professor *Rickett*, both of Auckland University, for "stealing a line". *Cf.* B. COOTE, Contract: An Underview, *in:* Contract: An Underview-Souvenir of a Valedictory Lecture (B. Brown, ed. 1995); and C. RICKETT, Different Views on the Scope of the *Quistclose* Analysis: English and Antipodean Insights, 107 L.Q.R. 608 (1991).

4 Fiji Supreme Court, Civil Appeal No. 20 of 1979, reprinted *in* D. ROEBUCK, D. SRIVASTAVA & J. NONGGORR, Pacific Contract Law: A Source Book for the South Pacific 216-7 (1987). I am grateful to Professor *Anthony Angelo*, Victoria University of Wellington, for bringing this essential reference text to my attention.

customs". Put shortly, it was arguing that there had been valid "accord and satisfaction". However the Supreme Court decided that "the alleged contract [the purchaser relies] on is unenforceable since there is no consideration for the alleged contract". In other words, the purchaser's tender of the cheque and accompanying letter could not provide valid "consideration" for the distributor's alleged promise not to enforce payment of the full amount owed under the original contract, because the purchaser was under a pre-existing contractual duty to pay that total.

In this case, the Japanese distributor seems to have taken a particularly hard line towards the Fijian purchaser's suggestion that the contract had been renegotiated, despite a quite lengthy business relationship. Of course, the distributor was presumably just the local subsidiary of a Japanese company, and there is some empirical evidence from other jurisdictions that such subsidiaries generally adapt their attitude to the law to the norms prevailing in their new environment.[5] Norms in purely domestic transactions in both Japan and Fiji should therefore be compared. But what is important for my present purpose is perceptions. It seems quite likely that Fijians involved in this case or who came to hear of it would have disagreed with the following stereotype of the "Japanese Attitude Towards Contracts":[6]

> The fundamental Japanese approach to contracts is to emphasize the relationship being created, instead of the document being drawn up. . . . Most Japanese assume that rights and duties under the contract, even when written down, are provisional and tentative rather than absolute.

Furthermore, it is ironic that the Japanese distributor relied on English law's traditionally strict view of the pre-existing duty rule and the doctrine of consideration, as neither has any obvious equivalent in Japanese law. Rather than applying that blunt rule, the approach of Japanese law seems preferable: allow even unilateral contractual variations (*menjo*), as well as bilateral contracts to resolve disputes (*wakai*), but regulate unacceptable unfairness in the renegotiation process through general standards such as good faith (*shingi seijutsu*) or public order and good morals (*kôjo ryôzoku*).[7] From the reported judgment, there is no evidence of such unfairness in this case, so it seems

5 Y. MATSUMURA, Attitudes of Canadian Subsidiaries of Japanese Firms Towards the Law and the Legal System in Canada, 21 U.B.C. L.REV. 209 (1987).

6 R. MARSH, The Japanese Negotiator: Subtlety and Strategy Beyond Western Logic 112-3 (1988).

7 See respectively Articles 519, 695, 1(2), and 90 of the Civil Code (*Minpô,* Law No. 89 of 1897 as amended by Law No. 79 of 1991; for an English translation *see* EHS, Vol. II, FA, No. 7100); and W. SHATTUCK & Z. KITAGAWA, U.S./Japanese Contract and Sales Problems 205-14, 222-32 (revised ed. 1973). Even those who support the comparative utility of a doctrine of consideration criticize this particular rule as a conceptual refinement which has now gone too far. See J. DAWSON, Gifts and Promises: Continental and American Law Compared 207-211 (1980).

unlikely that any Japanese court would have interfered with the renegotiation. Yet the Japanese plaintiff apparently had no compunction in pursuing this case in Fiji under the strict English law approach, despite the latter's ever more apparent shortcomings.[8] Fijians who were aware of this case may well have

---

8 In fact, the Fiji Supreme Court may have missed a good opportunity to depart from rigorous application of the pre-existing duty rule. In support, it relied on *D&C Builders* v. *Rees* [1966] 2 Q.B. 617. However, in that case, the defendant purchaser knew of the plaintiff supplier's financial difficulties, and an important justification for the English Court of Appeal's finding against the defendant was that the latter was consequently exercising undue pressure or indeed intimidating the plaintiff into renegotiating the original content. There was no evidence that this occurred in the Fiji Supreme Court case. Furthermore, if such unfair advantage-taking is the real concern of the courts, it is arguably better addressed by the more general doctrine of economic duress, rather than the pre-existing duty rule. Indeed, that rule has recently been significantly eroded even in English law. In a first category of cases, as in *Williams* v. *Roffey* [1991] 1 Q.B. 1, one party to a contract was held bound by its further promise to pay more for performance of the duty already agreed to by the other party. In a second category of cases, similar to *D&C Builders (supra)*, the approach in *Williams* v. *Roffey (supra)* has now been extended to the situation where one party suggests paying less than the amount already agreed to be owing and this is accepted by the other party. This happened in *Anangel Atlas Compania Naveira SA* v. *Ishikawajima-Harima Heavy Industries Co. Ltd. (No 2)* [1990] 2 Lloyd's Rep. 526, where the seller (again, coincidentally, the overseas subsidiary of a major Japanese company) had agreed to the lower price renegotiated by the purchaser, and the English High Court held the seller to its promise. However, in that case, there were changes to the initial agreement other than the reduced price (*see* G. TOLHURST, Renegotiation: Offer and Acceptance and Consideration 4 J.C.L. 257 (1991)). When the reduced price is the only change, the English Court of Appeal still refuses to enforce the renegotiated agreement. In other words, notwithstanding *Williams* v. *Roffey (supra)*, the Court of Appeal still applies the pre-existing duty rule in this second category of cases (see *Re C (A Debtor)*, unreported LEXIS transcript of the judgment of 11 May 1994: simply following the result in *D&C Builders, supra*), in deference to *Foakes* v. *Beer* (1889) 9 App. Cas. 605, which although old is still binding precedent (see *Re Selectmove* [1995] 2 All E.R. 531: the Court arguing that any change should come from the Law Commission or Parliament).

Similarly, New Zealand courts have made some inroads into strict application of the pre-existing duty rule. The Fiji Supreme Court unfortunately did not refer to *Cook Islands Shipping Co Ltd* v. *Colson Builders Ltd.* [1975] 1 N.Z.L.R. 422. Admittedly, that case fell within the first category mentioned above, and in the result the first instance Court refused to enforce one party's further promise to pay more for performance of the duty already agreed to by the other party. However, Mahon J. did clarify and focus on the more general policy question: whether that other party was extorting or taking unfair advantage of the first party (*Cook Islands Shipping Co Ltd; supra* at 434-5). Furthermore, *Homeguard Products (NZ) Ltd* v. *Kiwi Packaging* [1981] 2 N.Z.L.R. 322 fell squarely within the second category, and Mahon J. did enforce the supplier's agreement to the lower price renegotiated by the purchaser. Again, the reasoning in this later case was unfortunately not anticipated by the Fiji Supreme Court. In this case, Mahon J.'s primary rationale was that the version of the pre-existing duty rule in *Foakes* v. *Beer (supra)* applied only where there was an undisputed debt in a liquidated amount (*Homeguard,*

thought that this willingness in fact indicated some affinities between English and Japanese law.

Admittedly, much of this remains speculation. At present, I lack the resources to determine how representative this one case is. Nor do I know how (if at all) it may have coloured Fijians' perceptions of Japanese attitudes to contracts, let alone their perceptions of Japanese contract law rules. Furthermore, I am as yet unaware of any other cases, reported or otherwise, that might suggest an overall pattern to those perceptions, or perceptions from other South Pacific island nations. This clearly merits closer examination.

However, the rest of this paper will limit itself largely to a New Zealand perspective - tentative because it too has been rarely (if ever) explicitly formulated - and to generalizations about the Australian perspective, as to which my Australian colleagues may well differ.[9]

Even then, I remain aware of some significant differences between New Zealand and Australia. On the one hand, Australia has always been more affected than New Zealand by encounters with Asia and Japan - whether in terms of immigration, trade, or investment - and the legal problems that those necessarily entail.[10] New Zealand, a much smaller country with comparatively fewer links, has been slower to develop cohesive programmes of Asian studies

---

supra at 327), not where there was genuine dispute over the debt owed. But after reviewing *D&C Builders (supra)*, his Honour again implied that an underlying rationale might be seen as simply whether there has been intimidation, or indeed economic duress (*Homeguard, supra,* at 330). The former rationale is less radical because it is phrased as an exception to the pre-existing duty rule, which itself is still retained. But the more readily the courts find sufficient "genuine dispute", the more that rule is undermined and the more readily the suspicion grows that the real rationale is simply control of unfair advantage taking, which might be better achieved by further expansion of the doctrine of economic duress. *Moyes & Groves Ltd* v. *Radiation New Zealand Ltd.* [1982] 1 N.Z.L.R. 368 is seen as further evidence of such a trend (J. LAND, The Enforceability of Contractual Variations 15 V.U.W.L.R. 287 (1985)), reinforced by the decision in *Williams* v. *Roffey (supra)*; *see* J. BURROWS, J. FINN & S. TODD, Cheshire & Fifoot's Law of Contract 109 (8th N.Z. ed. 1992)). However, *in United Food & Chemical Workers Union of N.Z.* v. *Talley* [1993] E.R.N.Z. 360, 376, the New Zealand Court of Appeal remarked that *Moyes & Groves* (*supra*) should still simply be seen in terms of the doctrine of consideration and the pre-existing duty rule. Furthermore, since *Williams* v. *Roffey (supra)*, New Zealand courts have not been faced by a case involving a renegotiated promise to pay a lesser amount that is clearly not in dispute, as was the case in *D&C Builders (supra)*.

9 *Cf.* M. SMITH, Australian Perspectives on Asian Law: Directions for the Next Decade, *in*: Asian Laws Through Australian Eyes (V. Taylor, ed. 1996); and V. TAYLOR, Beyond Legal Orientalism, *in*: Asian Laws Through Australian Eyes (V. Taylor, ed. 1996).

10 *See*, e.g., N. BENNETT, Bitter Fruit: Japanese Migration and Anglo-Saxon Obstacles, 1890-1924, Paper Presented at the 11th New Zealand International Conference on Asian Studies (Auckland, July 1-4, 1995).

in general, and Asian law studies in particular.[11] On the other hand, Australia is sometimes described as a final bastion of the "true" common law, now that England itself is increasingly subject to "Euro-law", and given New Zealand's various private law reforms in the 1970s and 1980s (notably the contracts statutes, and the well-known Accident Compensation system).[12] But more noticeable, at least from a New Zealand perspective, is how Australian contract law seems to be moving away much more rapidly than New Zealand law from what I later describe as the "formal" orientation of the English legal tradition.[13]

B. Changing U.S. and European Perspectives

Despite these differences, a broadly antipodean perspective does appear significantly distinct from that of European and the U.S. observers, particularly as regards Japanese law. *Zentarô Kitagawa* talks of an initial period through to around 1960, when there was a "one-way" stream of Japanese lawyers learning from Europe and the U.S. (*ô-bei*). Over this period, lawyers there were keen to teach their Japanese counterparts the virtues of a "modern" legal system, rather than to seriously investigate the existing Japanese law on its own terms.[14] To be

11 *See*, e.g., T. BEAL (ed.), Educating for Asia (1994).

12 My thanks to Professor *Francis Reynolds* (Oxford University) for this observation, at an informal talk to the New Zealand Association for Comparative Law on September 20, 1995, at the Wellington District Law Society. Professor Reynolds gave as an example the growing awareness of the different conceptual frameworks apparent or implicit in recent European Community Directives, such as that on commercial agents, brought into force in English law on January 1, 1994 by the Commercial Agents (Council Directive) Regulations 1993 (Statutory Instrument 1993 No. 3053, as amended by Statutory Amendment 1993 No. 3173). To this can be added the EC Directive on Unfair Contract Terms in Consumer Contracts, brought into force in English law on July 1, 1995, by the Unfair Contract Terms in Consumer Contracts Regulations 1994 (Statutory Instrument 1994 No. 3159). *See*, e.g., H. COLLINS, Good Faith in European Contract Law, 14 O.J.L.S. 229 (1994); S. BRIGHT & C. BRIGHT, Unfair Terms in Land Contracts: Copy Out or Cop Out?, 111 L.Q.R. 655 (1995).

On New Zealand's legislative reform in contract law, *see* N.Z. LAW COMMISSION (ed.), Contract Statutes Review (1993) and F. REYNOLDS, Contract: Codification, Legislation and Judicial Development, 9 J.C.L. 11, 19-25 (1995). New Zealand's unique Accident Compensation scheme, substituting blanket state compensation for almost all tort claims for personal injury by accident, seems to have weathered some criticism, and statutory amendment in 1992 that significantly reduced its cover. As to the latter, *see* R. MAHONEY, New Zealand's Accident Compensation Scheme: A Reassessment, 40 Am. J. Comp. L. 159 (1992), and T. ISON, Changes to the Accident Compensation System: An International Perspective 23 V.U.W.L.R. 25 (1993).

13 J. CARTER & A. STEWART, Commerce and Conscience: The High Court's Developing View of Contract, 23 WEST. AUST. L.REV. 49 (1993). *Infra* text at notes 46 and 47.

14 Z. KITAGAWA, *Kokusai masatsu no naka no nihon-hô* [Japanese Law in the Midst of International Friction] 500 N.B.L. 27 (1993).

sure, there were many in Japan who criticized their law as "pre-modern" and were therefore all too willing to receive this teaching.[15] On the other hand, the willingness of European and U.S. lawyers to deliver this message does suggest that they too were influenced by a more general historical tendency - what might be called an "urge to proselytize".[16]

By contrast, at that time, there was little contact whatsoever between the legal systems of Japan and New Zealand, or even Australia. New Zealand did not resume significant trading relationships with Japan until the late 1950s, and the real development began only in the 1970s.[17] Of course, Australian suppliers had developed substantial long-term contractual relationships with Japan since the 1950s. But such relatively simple, long-term arrangements between or through large organizations are generally less likely to give rise to legal disputes, let alone to require much detailed investigation of another legal system.[18]

Occasionally, business relationships did give rise to legal questions. An example is a remarkable case in the Kobe District Court, where a New Zealand beef exporter successfully claimed that the Kobe-based importer had breached a contract formed by an exchange of telexes and correspondence in June 1957.[19] Yet this case is remarkable precisely because it is factually so unique. 1957 was the year in which New Zealand beef exports to Japan began.[20] But any opening of the Japanese market was sporadic, while the main priority of New Zealand

---

15 T. KAWASHIMA (C. Stevens, trans.), The Legal Consciousness of Contract in Japan 7 LAW IN JAPAN 1 (1974); and T. TANASE, *Kindai no rinen to yuragi (1) - kawashima hôshakai-gaku no riron to jissen* [The Ideals and Tensions of the Modern (1): Theory and Practice in Kawashima's Legal Sociology] 65 HÔRITSU JIHÔ 26 (1993).

16 This is better substantiated by historians and ethnographers. *Cf.* D. MASSARELLA, A World Elsewhere: Europe's Encounter with Japan in the Sixteenth and Seventeenth Centuries (1990), with G. SANSOM (ed.), The Western World and Japan: A Study in the Interaction of European and Asiatic Cultures 115-133 (1977), and T. YOKOYAMA, Japan in the Victorian Mind: A Study of Stereotyped Images of a Nation (1987). *See* also S. JOHNSON, The Japanese Through American Eyes 60-65 (1988), and E. SEIDENSTICKER, How They Have Looked to Us, *in*: Showa: The Japan of Hirohito 289-290 (C. Gluck & S. Graubard, eds. 1992).

17 *See* A. TROTTER,From Suspicion to Growing Partnership: New Zealand and Japan, *in*: New Zealand in World Affairs 1957-1972, 195, 203-204 and 208-209 (M. McKinnon, ed. 1991).

18 *See*, e.g., S. MACAULAY, J. KIDWELL, W. WHITFORD & M. GALANTER, Contracts: Law in Action Vol. 1, 511-519 (1995).

19 *Fawlty & Co. Ltd.* v. *Matsui Shôten K.K.*, 13/11 KAKYÛ MINSHÛ 2293 (Kobe District Court, November 10, 1962). I thank Mr. *Rod Miller*, former New Zealand Ambassador to Japan, for some suggestions as to the possible background of this case. However, I reiterate that I take sole responsibility for the points made, which must remain largely conjecture at this stage.

20 TROTTER, *supra* note 17, at 204.

exporters remained to supply the traditional British market.[21] Thus there was unlikely to be much incentive or expectation on either side to develop a longer-term relationship. Indeed, on its face, the contract under dispute took the form of a one-off export sale. Furthermore, the Japanese defendant does not appear to have been a particularly large or reputable company.[22] I suspect that, over this period, other New Zealand exporters tended to deal with more substantial Japanese companies, more likely to be able to absorb losses on a particular deal rather than having to fight it out in court. I also suspect that arrangements usually settled down more smoothly into longer-term relationships, less likely to result in legal disputes.[23] To my knowledge, no other supply contracts involving New Zealand and Japanese parties were litigated, whether in Japan or in New Zealand. Nor have I been able to find out anyone with direct knowledge of this particular case, although I am continuing with various inquiries. Thus, the general point holds: there remained little contact between the respective legal systems.

Furthermore, even if there was some contact, it was likely to have been superficial. For instance, in the Kobe District Court case, it may well have been in the defendant's favour to have argued that New Zealand law applied.[24] But it

---

21 As late as 1967, New Zealand was berated for a lack of commitment to diversification of exports away from the traditional British market and into Japan: "a jibe at those meat exporters who diverted product from Japan when prices were higher at Smithfield" (TROTTER, *supra* note 17, at 217). There may well have been some truth in this criticism; at the time, most of the New Zealand meat exporters were still British owned.

22 Although it was a *kabushiki kaisha* (joint stock corporation), the case report records that the representative director was a woman. I suspect that it would have been even more unusual than it is at present for a woman to be running a large company at that time. *See* M. SASO, Women in the Japanese Workplace 57-59 (1990) and A. LAM, Equal Employment Opportunities for Japanese Women: Changing Company Practice, *in*: Japanese Working Women 197, 198 (J. Hunter, ed. 1993). Also, around that time, meat companies in the Kansai area were generally thought to be rather dubious because of supposed links with *burakumin* (hereditary outcastes) and *yakuza* (gangsters).

23 Furthermore, one suspects that the New Zealand Embassy would have become more cautious in recommending suitable Japanese business partners to New Zealand suppliers. The Kobe District Court judgment records that the New Zealand Legation (as it was until 1956) was responsible for introducing the Kobe importer in that case.

24 The defendant's first main argument was that the contract was not formed until it had signed and returned the plaintiff's confirmation slip. Particularly at that time, it is likely that Japanese law was more likely to hold that the contract was formed at an earlier stage, by some lesser writing. In *Marubeni Iida* v. *Aji no Moto*, 8 KAKYÛ MINSHÛ 1366 (July 31, 1957), the Tokyo District Court had just held against a defendant who had repudiated a supply agreement on a similar argument. *See* generally S. MICHIDA (V. Taylor, trans.), Contract Societies: Japan and the United States Contrasted 1 PACIFIC BASIN L. & POLICY J. 199 (1992). *Cf.* G. CHESHIRE & C. FIFOOT, The Law of Contract 24-25 (2nd N.Z. ed. by J. Northey, 1965).

seems that the defendant did not. The court simply applied Japanese law. This has been questioned.[25] However, at that time, a serious investigation into New Zealand law would probably have overly tasked the research capability of the defendant's lawyer, or even the court. Thus, the path of least resistance seems to have been readily followed: arguing and deciding the case under Japanese law. More generally, even if Japanese lawyers had subjected New Zealand (or Australian) law to more detailed inquiry, either in a court case or out of some broader academic interest, on many points this would have largely led back to the original source of "enlightenment" at that time, namely English law.[26]

Conversely, New Zealand or Australian lawyers would have had few profound encounters with the Japanese legal system over this period. And, in the light of their own rather precarious legal tradition, they would also have felt less secure about their suitability to expound generally on the benefits and means of achieving a "modern" legal system.[27]

Thus, Kitagawa's reference to Europe and the U.S. is apposite: there was really no antipodean perspective on Japanese law until well into the 1960s.

More interest, and hence more of a perspective, began to emerge in the second and third phases identified by Kitagawa. In the second phase, the 1960s and 1970s, Japan emerged again as a "developed" economy. Kitagawa highlights an increased interest in Japanese law, particularly from the U.S.[28] He

---

25 See the reporter's note to the report of the case *in* 320 HANREI JIHÔ 4, and T. KAWAKAMI, *Hôshiki* [Formalities], *in*: *Shôgai hanrei hyakusen* [Anthology of Cases Involving Foreign Elements] BESSATSU JURISUTO 52, 53-4 (1967). (I am grateful to Professor *Akira Takakuwa*, Kyoto University, for sending me the case report and alerting me to this latter commentary.) *See* also K. IWASAKI, *Kokusai keiyaku no seiritsu to keiyaku shomen no sakusei* [The Formation of International Contracts and the Drafting of Contract Documents] 18 KOKUSAI SHÔJI HÔMU 527, 529-531 (1990).

26 Hence, for instance, a second major issue in the Kobe District Court case (*supra* note 19) was whether or not the buyer's promise to open a letter of credit prior to shipment date was an obligation owed prior to the buyer's obligation to ship the goods, so that the buyer's failure to do so would amount to termination attributable as the buyer's breach of contract. On the assumption that New Zealand not Japanese law should have been applied in this case, Professor Kawakami (*supra* note 25, at 55) promptly proceeds to refer to the then leading English authorities.

Interestingly, through a correspondent law firm in Osaka, I happen to be aware of another transnational case involving a very similar question which, over 30 years later, is pending in the same Kobe District Court.

27 Pathbreaking at the time, for considering developments outside English law, was D. MATHIESON, Australian Precedents in New Zealand Courts, 1 N.Z.U.L.R. 77 (1963).

28 He quotes as representative the careful study by D. HENDERSON, Conciliation and Japanese Law, Tokugawa and Modern (1965). To the work of the "Washington School" can be added considerable interest at Harvard Law School: *see*, e.g., A. VON MEHREN (ed.), Law in Japan: The Legal Order in a Changing Society (1963).

also characterizes the overall approach as more pluralist, prepared to acknowledge the possibility of different means of economic, social, and legal ordering.[29] By the third phase, when Japan emerged as an "economic superpower" in the 1980s, Kitagawa suggests that the perspective could even be characterized as "Japanese universalist", with foreign observers more prone to emphasize positive aspects of the Japanese experience.[30]

Rather similarly, in my part of the antipodes, we have witnessed an increasing awareness of the importance of Japan as a partner in trade and investment; but also sometimes as a model in designing institutions and solving problems - including those touching on legal institutions and legal problems. On the whole, this interest did emerge a decade later than in the U.S., namely in the 1970s.[31] Correspondingly, the overall perspective seems to have been positive, rather than some more neutral pluralism. Thus, in the context of iron ore contract disputes, a leading Australian weekly magazine noted in the early 1970s:[32]

> The Japanese concept of contract has always been something less rigid than a strictly enforceable legal right. . . . Rather than approaching the issue so legalistically, the Australian coal and iron ore companies would do better to protect their interests if they were to press for some system of financial stockpiling.

Similarly, some Australian commentators were quite sympathetic to Japanese importers' refusal to honour a five-year supply contract for Australian sugar, concluded in December 1974 at a fixed price initially then about half the world price, when the world price subsequently dropped well below that fixed price.[33] Overall, interest in Japan had become firmly rooted in Australia and New Zealand, and the perspective was rather similar to that of the European and

---

29 *Kitagawa* implies that at this stage, the U.S. and European view of Japanese law became more neutral (*supra*, note 14, at 10). By contrast, *Smith* argues that until the 1980s the view remained essentially negative. *See* M. SMITH, *Soto kara mita nihon-hô kenkyû* [An Outsider's View of Japanese Law Studies], *in*: *Soto kara mita nihon-hô* [An Outsider's View of Japanese Law] 371, 377 (S. Ishii & N. Higuchi, eds. 1995).

30 KITAGAWA, *supra* note 14, at 10. SMITH (*supra* note 29, at 378-379) detects a similar shift in foreign observers' observations.

31 *See*, generally, M. SMITH, Japanese Law in Australia and Canada: 1965-1985, *in*: *Ôbei-hô ronshû* (Collection of Essays on European and American Law], 511 (K. Fujikura, ed. 1987), and note the publication of Y. NODA (A. Angelo, trans. and ed.), Introduction to Japanese Law (1976).

32 P. SAMUEL, From Sweet to Sour Relations, THE BULLETIN 53 (19 February 1972).

33 MARSH, *supra* note 6, at 97-107. Ironically, the response of many Japanese commentators was more critical, blaming the Japanese importers for having speculated on a fixed price in this way, knowing that sugar prices fluctuate on the commodity markets, and for then having refused to honour their commitment. *See* S. SAITO & M. UENO, *Keiyaku ishiki to bunsho hyôgen* [Contract Consciousness and Written Expression] 167-179 (1980).

U.S. observers: Japan may be different, but that was at least acceptable and often even praiseworthy. If I may coin a new phrase, at this stage we might well talk of an *ô-bei-taiyô* perspective: one including not only Europe and the U.S. (*ô-bei*), but also Oceania (*taiyôshu*).

The question, though, is whether the contemporary perception from New Zealand and Australia, at least, differs significantly from that from Europe and the U.S. In many ways, I think it does. Kitagawa identifies a fourth and final phase in European and U.S. views of Japan and Japanese law, overlapping with the third but representing a noticeable change. This change arose when the perceived difference of Japanese institutions came to be seen as deliberately hidden by a surface similarity and thus a problem, a negative influence exacerbating international friction. In the case of Europe and the U.S., of course, such "revisionism" is related to ongoing trade deficits with Japan.[34] It leads to criticism of attempts in the Japanese literature to analyse - or often just to assert - Japanese difference or "uniqueness".[35] It also leads to a reemphasis on the need to bring Japan up to "universal" standards: the tenets of the modern *Rechtsstaat*, and of the neo-classical economic system in particular.[36] As Kitagawa observes, this development harks back to what I earlier termed an "urge to proselytize" stemming from Europe and the U.S. in the first stage, the immediate post-war period.

In contrast, both Australia and New Zealand have maintained trade surpluses or largely balanced trade with Japan. New Zealand has undertaken enormous liberalization (or at least "reshaping") of the state and the economy since the 1980s.[37] But, at least to this observer, its trade negotiators and its general attitude towards Japan have not become significantly more critical or insistent that Japan also adopt such policies.[38] That might well have been different if trade deficits with Japan had emerged, of the magnitude recorded by Europe

---

34 *See*, e.g., J. FALLOWS, Containing Japan, THE ATLANTIC MONTHLY 40 (May 1989).

35 *See*, e.g., R. DALE, The Myth of Japanese Uniqueness (1986).

36 Respectively, K. VAN WOLFEREN, The Enigma of Japanese Power: People and Politics in a Stateless Nation (1989); and J.M. RAMSEYER, *Hô to keizai-gaku: Nihon-hô no keizai bunseki* [Law and Economics: An Economic Analysis of Japanese Law] 143-170 (1990).

37 *See* J. BOSTON, The Theoretical Underpinnings of Public Sector Restructuring in New Zealand, *in*: Reshaping the State: New Zealand's Bureaucratic Revolution 1 (J. Boston *et al* eds., 1991); and E. OMIYA & I. OURA, *Nyûjirando no zaisei kinyû* [Public Finances in New Zealand] (1992).

38 Thus, for instance, New Zealand's response to beef market liberalization in Japan has been low-key and pragmatic, with various joint ventures having quietly got underway despite my call at the time, based largely on an Australian perspective, for more visible long-term strategies to maintain this as a "live" issue. *Cf.* L. NOTTAGE, Japanese Agricultural Policies: The ABARE Study and Beef and Dairy Policies: East Asia ProjectWorking Paper No. 2 (1989); and I. KENNEDY, Japan and New Zealand: Adding Value 91-99 (1992).

and the U.S.[39] But even then, the use of "New Right" argument and rhetoric, and overall attitudes, are likely to have been more pragmatic, less driven by the ideological aspects that Kitagawa mentions. One reason is the comparative lack of history of "proselytization". Another is that small countries like New Zealand, and even Australia, are generally more conscious of practical limits, first as to the extent to which friction can emerge given the size of their economies, and then as to which problems can be resolved by forcing their view of the world on major players like Japan.[40]

Reviewing these changes in U.S. and European perspectives on Japanese law, I am reminded of the well-known "trick picture" in which an old woman or old man (the initial negative perspective) can suddenly come to be seen as a beautiful young woman or handsome young man (the ensuing increasingly positive perspective), and vice versa (the recent reaction to the latter).[41] By contrast, the perspective from New Zealand and Australia has remained more constant. Nonetheless, we have benefited enormously from the increasing theoretical sophistication in the U.S. and European studies of Japanese law. In time, that may also underpin valuable "gestalt shifts" in our perceptions of Japanese law, particularly contract law.

---

39 One should also not overlook the effect of the overall backlash in Australia to intense direct investment from Japan, particularly in the late 1980s. In New Zealand, this has not been an issue; the main problem has instead been perceived as a comparative lack of Japanese investment, a situation which has changed rather rapidly since a task force recommended more active promotion by the government. *See* KENNEDY, *supra* note 38 at 85-90; and T. BOLLINGER (T. Beal, ed.), Investing in a Common Future: Three Case Studies of Asian Investment in New Zealand (1994).

40 A good example is the differing views on the perennial question of liberalization of practice by foreign lawyers in Japan. *Cf.* the strong critique by J.M. RAMSEYER, Lawyers, Foreign Lawyers, and Lawyer Substitutes: The Market for Regulation in Japan 27 HARV. INT'L L.J. 500 (1986), with the pragmatic comment from an Australian perspective by M. SMITH, The Foreign Lawyers of Japan: Application to Australia, 21 LAW IN JAPAN 168 (1988). See also the reformulation of the whole debate called for by L. NOTTAGE, Keeping Lawyers in Comparative and Social Science Perspective: The Issue of Foreign Lawyers in Japan, paper presented at the Kobe International Seminar on The Role of Lawyers in Contemporary Societies (Kobe, August 9-11, 1993).

41 *See*, e.g., S. COVEY, The Seven Habits of Highly Effective People 25, 26, 45 (1989). I am grateful to one of my Honours students for introducing me to these psychological tests: B. PASSL, The Operation of Law within the Japanese Cultural Paradigm, paper presented in fulfillment of the requirements of the LLB (Hons) degree, April 13, 1995.

C. Theory Development

Kitagawa believes that in these times of "international friction", at least between Japan and Europe or the U.S., Japanese lawyers must work harder to present a fuller picture of the Japanese legal system. In today's climate, an excessive focus on the "law in books" will too often lead to the criticism that this hides the quite different reality of the "law in action".[42] Original theories and reconceptualizations must be developed linking the two, demanding renewed emphasis on legal sociology and legal theory, after a period since the 1970s when civil law and contract law scholarship focused more on refining the black letter law to deal with urgent new social and technological problems. Kitagawa believes that this will help uncover some new universals and, indeed, a new paradigm of law.[43]

I largely agree. Elsewhere, I have criticized the two main "outsider's" perspectives on Japanese law: the first, stressing difference and the importance of cultural determination; and the second more recent perspective stressing universal standards, such as those of "law and economics". Both models are excessively abstract, in their view of human agency as well as breadth of analysis, which is particularly problematic as we turn to practical problems and try to assess the question of change in the Japanese system. Looking at a number of "hot topics" touching on contemporary contract law issues, I have advocated more attention to the history of institutions in Japan and their contemporary development, as well to the black letter law and the various "sites" in which "law" is produced: the universities, the bureaucracy, company legal sections, and law offices.[44]

Likewise, writing on Japanese contract law development in "Asian Laws Through Australian Eyes", I have warned New Zealanders and Australians not to overgeneralize about "the Japanese" and their legal system, based on occasional encounters mostly with the practical aspects of contracting with

42 KITAGAWA, *supra* note 14, at 27. Similarly, see the criticism of *Horishi Oda's* recent textbook *in* H. BAUM, Rechtsdenken, Rechtssystem und Rechtswirklichkeit in Japan: Rechtsvergleichung mit Japan [Legal Thought, Legal System, and Legal Reality in Japan: Comparative Law and Japan], 59 RABELSZ 258, 265, 283-286 (1995).

43 KITAGAWA, *supra* note 14. Similarly, SMITH (*supra* note 29, at 377-378) sees the emergence of new methodological approaches to law in society as one of the most important developments in Japanese law scholarship.

44 These included a discussion of the Office of the Trade and Investment Ombudsman, the new Administrative Procedure Law, the Fair Trade Commission of Japan and the *Shiseido* case, recent developments in product liability law, and new dispute resolution mechanisms. These all formed an important backdrop to the more obvious "contractual" issues addressed in that presentation and at an earlier workshop session focused on termination of long-term contractual relationships. *See* L. NOTTAGE, Law in Japan Today: A Changing Interface with Business and Government (1995).

Japanese parties. I suggested that the time has come when we can and must consider the black letter law, and particularly civil law methodology and general theories of contract in Japan, both in resolving a range of practical Japan-New Zealand contract problems and in developing sounder theoretical constructs.[45]

Over the next few decades, New Zealanders and Australians may be more open to this message than European or U.S. scholars. For one thing, the emergence of our perspective is still comparatively recent and less determined by historical preconceptions. For another, New Zealanders and no doubt Australians are now exposed to a comparatively wide range of encounters with the Japanese legal system, including Japanese contract law and practice, as can be seen by a quick computer search of court case databases or a review of some of the practical examples I cite below.

On the other hand, I am less sanguine than Kitagawa about whether such a broader and more balanced approach can be described as uncovering new universals. Partly, this is due to that very same variety of encounters between the legal systems of Japan and New Zealand or Australia, which works against ready generalization. More fundamentally, my doubts stem from the greater complexity in theory-building that is required, and thus more frequent indeterminacy or qualifications in one's conclusions. Related to that is again the difficulty of having to deal with multiple perspectives.

D. Form and Substance

One theoretical framework that I have initially found useful is the set of distinctions developed by *Atiyah* and *Summers* to analyse differences between the legal systems of England and the U.S. respectively.[46] They compared the degree of "substantive" reasoning (involving moral, economic, political, institutional, or other social considerations) from "formal" reasoning on four levels:

- "authoritative formality" (combining "validity formality" and "rank formality");
- "content formality"; and
- "interpretative formality", often related to "mandatory formality".

Further, they argued that more formal reasoning is generally consistent with formality in the legal system on two other levels: "enforcement formality" and

45 NOTTAGE, *supra* note 1.

46 P. ATIYAH & R. SUMMERS, Form and Substance in Anglo-American Law: A Comparative Study of Legal Reasoning, Legal Theory, and Legal Institutions (1987).

"truth formality". To the latter, I have added "didactic formality", and generally considered where New Zealand and Japan would fit into this picture, focusing on contract law and practice.[47]

The first major advantage of this exercise is that it allows us to reevaluate our perspectives in a structured manner. First, we can see how the Japanese legal system lies somewhat closer to the U.S. at the substantive end of the spectrum, while retaining a more formal orientation on certain levels (*see* Figure 1). This result is intriguing, of course, because the Japanese legal system, and particularly its contract law and practice, is often seen by U.S. observers as radically different. Secondly, however, we can also see affinities between Japan and New Zealand (and, all the more so, Australia).[48] Thirdly, this framework emphasizes that it is English and U.S. law which are rather extreme in orientation, not Japanese law.[49]

Lastly, it might help to systematically identify differences within "the civil law tradition" as well as the common law, forcing a reassessment of that overall conceptual distinction.[50] For instance, *B. Nicholas* has suggested that French law remains formal in orientation compared to English law.[51] Adding this to a

---

47 L. NOTTAGE, Form and Substance in New Zealand, U.S. and Japanese Law: What Role for Grand Theory in the World of International Contracting?, in Proceedings of the 1995 Annual Meeting of the Research Committee on Sociology of Law (International Sociological Association), "Legal Culture: Encounters and Transformations" (Tokyo, August 1-4, 1995), Papers of Section Meetings Supplement 1 203 (Japan Committee for the RCSL95, ed. 1995). *See* also L. NOTTAGE, Form and Substance in U.S., English, New Zealand and Japanese Law: A Framework for Better Comparisons of Developments in the Law of Unfair Contracts, 26/2 V.U.W.L.R. 247 (1996).

48 *See*, e.g., CARTER & STEWART, *supra* note 13, and NOTTAGE, *supra* note 47. Consistently with my conclusion, SMITH (*supra* note 29, at 374-375) argues that there are often more affinities between Japan and Australia than between the U.S. and Australia.

49 J.O. HALEY, Authority Without Power: Law and the Japanese Paradox 14, 114-115 (1990) also admits to the extremeness of U.S. law, a point picked up (no doubt with some relish) by T. UCHIDA, *Gendai keiyaku-hô no aratana tenkai to ippan jôkô* [General Clauses and New Developments in Contemporary Contract Law], 514 N.B.L. 1, 15 and fn. 17 (1993).

However, *Haley* makes these observations in drawing a sharp distinction between the extent and coerciveness of legal norms in the U.S. as opposed to those in Japan. In that sense, Haley is mainly stressing greater "enforcement formality" in U.S. law. I agree that along this particular dimension, U.S. law is more formal, not more substantive. However, adding English and New Zealand law demonstrates that these have even greater enforcement formality. Thus, the U.S. in fact appears more substantive along this dimension than might be suggested by a comparison solely with Japan (*see* Figure 1, at 5.). Furthermore, along all other dimensions of my framework, the U.S. is consistently more substantive than Japan.

50 *See*, generally, J. MERRYMAN, The Civil Law Tradition (2nd ed. 1985).

51 B. NICHOLAS, The French Law of Contract 20-22 (2nd ed. 1992). *Nicholas* describes French law as more "conceptual" or "formalist" in two senses. First, it tends to follow logical inference rather than practical considerations. Under *Atiyah*

spectrum including Japanese law immediately identifies a large gap between these two systems (*see* 2. in Figure 2), even though Japanese law is undeniably influenced by the civil law tradition. Adding German law further complicates the picture. *Guntram Rahn* has effectively demonstrated that Japanese law is significantly more substantive in its civil law reasoning.[52] But we still face the problem in deciding where precisely German law sits on this spectrum. *M. Damaska* has argued that civil law jurisdictions such as German law tend to be characterized by an organization of authority along "hierarchical" ideals, compared to the "coordinate" ideals characteristic of common law jurisdictions.[53] As the former ideals are recognizably more formal than the latter, this implies that German law should be added to the spectrum to the left of English law, as with French law (*see* 3. in Figure 3). This result would therefore stress the overall similarity in orientation of French and German law; but it would also heighten the gap between Japanese law, despite the latter's civil law pedigree. Alternatively, we might add German law to the right of English (and New Zealand law), albeit still to the left - relatively more formal - compared to Japanese law (*see* 4. in Figure 2.). Yet this tends to heighten the gaps between French, German, and Japanese law: all supposedly members of the same civil law tradition. I must leave to my European colleagues the task of

---

and *Summers*' framework, this certainly means that the system is characterized by formal rather than substantive reasoning. Secondly, however, *Nicholas* argues that French law is more conceptual in viewing its civil law as part of a systematic and interrelated whole. Again, this may indeed represent greater formal orientation, if this means deference to logical exegesis. On the other hand, it has been noted that French lawyers are more willing to borrow creatively from other parts of their civil law, including individual statutes; and to extract overall principles with closer affinities to moral judgements (Contract Law Today: Anglo-French Comparisons, D. Harris & D. Tallon, eds. 1989). Respectively, this would suggest less "rank formality" and "content formality"; and more "validity formality" and "interpretative" or "mandatory formality". Nonetheless, on the whole, French law seems likely to be more formal than English law. In the area of unfair contracts, for instance, even English law seems to allow for more "content-oriented standards of validity" than French law. *See*, generally, A. ANGELO & E. ELLINGER, Unconscionable Contracts: A Comparative Study of theApproaches in England, France, Germany, and the United States, 14 LOY. L.A. INT'L. & COMP.L.J. 455, 460-482 (1992), and NOTTAGE (1996), *supra* note 47.

52 G. RAHN, Rechtsdenken und Rechtsauffassung in Japan [Legal Thought and Conceptions of Law in Japan] 369-399 (1990). See also *Rahn's* contribution to this volume (*supra* Chapter Six). Although I detect a significantly more formal streak to contemporary Japanese civil law methodology (*see* NOTTAGE, *supra* note 1), I do agree with Rahn's general point.

53 M. DAMASKA, The Faces of Justice and State Authority: A Comparative Approach to the Legal Process 16-18 (1986). Further, consistently with the framework I propose here, *Damaska* notes that the U.S. legal system is much more extreme in promoting coordinate ideals, relative to the English legal system. I am grateful to Professor *Frank Bennett* (University of London) for reminding me of this valuable study.

expanding on the framework proposed here, initially proposed by Atiyah and Summers, to more closely compare these legal systems. However, the exercise also promises to be useful in revising preconceptions, opening up new avenues of inquiry.[54]

Furthermore, analysis under this framework has a second major advantage. It allows direct comparison of some specific points of contract law, such as doctrines regulating unfairness in contractual relations, without underestimating or oversimplifying the many other aspects of the legal system, which interact as the backdrop to the operation of those doctrines.[55]

Lastly, the framework is more than just an analytic structure, to more systematically organize comparisons of each legal system, or even just a catalyst to rethink fundamental conceptions. Important although those two aspects are, the third and perhaps most important advantage of this framework is the way it prompts us to reconceptualize what we mean - or should mean - by "law". Originally, Atiyah and Summers were interested in developing implications gained from their analysis precisely out of this more general jurisprudential interest. My thinking is still evolving on this point, as indeed is

---

54 I use the word "preconceptions" neutrally, not at all pejoratively. To varying degrees, the eminent comparativists who have developed and explored the distinction between the common law and civil law traditions have been careful to stress some important differences within, as well as between, the traditions. *See*, e.g., MERRYMAN, *supra* note 50, at ix, and H. KÖTZ, Taking Civil Codes Less Seriously 50 M.L.R. 1, 7-8 (1987). However, there is now increasing dissatisfaction about the distinction itself. *See*, e.g., A. MARFORDING, An Interdisciplinary Approach to the Study of Foreign Legal Systems, *in*: Proceedings of the 1995 Annual Meeting of the Research Committee on Sociology of Law (International Sociological Association), "Legal Culture: Encounters and Transformations" (Tokyo, August 1-4, 1995), Papers of Section Meetings Supplement 4, 1, 5-11 (Japan Committee for the RCSL95, ed. 1995). I agree with *Marfording* that the traditional analytic distinction is too abstract. I also agree that comparative "law" studies encompassing Japan will need to become more ambitious in exploring cultural, political, and economic realities. Both frameworks suggested in this paper aim to highlight those very two points. Nonetheless, perhaps because I come from a particularly rigid tradition with even less general exposure to Continental European notions than my colleagues in Australia (*see*, e.g., M. VRANKEN, The Relevance of European Community Law in Australian Courts, 19 M.U.L.R. 431 (1993)), I find still find it extremely valuable to see aspects of the Japanese legal system in terms of civil law origins or parallels. Furthermore, I believe that it is still valuable to try to develop some alternative overview - or underview - of a range of legal systems, first to give some guidance into approaching specific transnational problems, but ultimately also to remain open to revising initial preconceptions that are at least kept fairly explicit. Lastly, my development of the *Atiyah* and *Summers* framework raises grave doubts against any suggestion that we are currently witnessing some more extensive "convergence" in private law, going beyond shifting perceptions of civil law orders or even some real change within such orders.

55 *See*, e.g., NOTTAGE (1996), *supra* note 47.

that of Summers.[56] But the framework seems particularly promising in developing new theoretical insights into the nature of law, and certain normative implications - matters which comparativists tend to ignore or oversimplify.[57]

E. Coping with Difference: Improving Legal Comparisons

To similar effect, *Volkmar Gessner* has recently warned against the tendency - even in "functionalist" comparative law - to overly reduce complexity, first in defining the legal "needs" that are supposed to serve as the basis for effective comparisons, and then in failing to sufficiently investigate what are often quite different practical results.[58] He also recognizes that comparative law, as a branch of legal science, is inherently normative, and thus criticizes the way value choices are not made explicit and wider aspects of legal life insufficiently treated. Quoting others who have recently expressed similar concerns, he asks:

> Is it perhaps rather that underlying this universalizing approach lies a dissembled hegemonic project, that the avowed search for global legal concepts conceals a colonizing impulse?

Turning from critique to a search for sounder comparisons, Gessner then proposes an analytical framework involving four levels of increasing complexity. This aims at legal comparison for differing purposes, using differing techniques (*see* Figure 3.). I have also found this framework useful, as a starting point for keeping in view a variety of contemporary New Zealand-Japan contract issues,

---

56 I thank Professor *Masahiko Omura* (Chuo University) for challenging me to consider the links between this analysis and prescriptive legal theory. At present, I am attracted by the views of C. JOERGES, Politische Rechtstheorie, and Critical Legal Studies: Points of Contact and Divergence, *in*: Critical Legal Thought: An American-German Debate 597 (C. Joerges & D. Trubek, eds. 1989). *Cf.* now R. SUMMERS, The Formal Character of Law: Criteria for Validity for Contracts, 9 J.C.L. 29 (1995).

57 Hence, for instance, I am attracted by one aspect of the critique of J.O. HALEY, *supra* note 49, advanced by D. JOHNSON, Authority Without Power: Haley on Japan's Law and Politics, 27 L.S.R. 619 (1993). *Haley* offers an alternative framework for a comprehensive review and comparison of Japanese law and legal history, which is also extremely useful. (See also his contribution to this volume, *supra* Chapter Five.) However, his positivist view of law as justiciable or state enforced rules - ironically formal, for a U.S. legal theorist - risks stifling more far-reachingjurisprudential inquiry.

58 V. GESSNER, Presumptio Similitudinis? A Critique of Comparative Law, *in*: Proceedings of the 1995 Annual Meeting of the Research Committee on Sociology of Law (International Sociological Association), "Legal Culture: Encounters and Transformations" (Tokyo, August 1-4, 1995), Papers of Section Meetings Supplement 2, 41 (Japan Committee for the RCSL95, ed. 1995).

and particularly in suggesting a cohesive and comprehensive strategy for ongoing research.

The first level Gessner identifies is that of the statute book. There may be some doctrinal discussion, but it remains largely "semantic". The second level he distinguishes includes more wide-ranging doctrinal discussions and caselaw development. A third, more ambitious level considers legal practice in the courts of first instance, in the bureaucracy, and within private associations. Most law is "made" at this level, or at least negotiated, often deviating from that developed at the first and second levels. Finally, the fourth and most complex level of comparison focuses on the legal behaviour of private individuals, business actors, and legal professionals, who can decide whether they want to mobilize the law at all, and how to apply it in a world presumably increasingly removed from that of conventional "legal" institutions.

Generally, I would suggest that many contemporary New Zealand-Japan contract issues call for a similar multi-level analysis. However, in my view, the levels may be defined slightly differently, and tend to overlap anyway.[59]

First, I would combine Gessner's first and second levels, and call them collectively "black letter law". He suggests that the "modest" comparative effort involved at his first level of comparison can be useful, for instance, in the preparation of model laws and international conventions. This sort of enterprise is increasingly important for New Zealand and Australia, as they develop institutions and momentum to contribute to the process harmonization, in the Asia-Pacific region and more generally.[60] However, even when considering how to agree on the best possible rule for termination of contract in the Vienna Sales Convention, for instance, the role of caselaw development and academic commentary, Gessner's second level, cannot be overlooked.[61] This becomes all the more important when one has to consider the legal position under the domestic law as the backdrop for any subsequent implementation or amendment of such a convention. Furthermore, consideration of that backdrop requires an analysis of each legal system's overall orientation to civil law methodology and general theories of contract.[62]

Gessner correctly points out that the second level of complexity must be attained when a legal solution for a particular problem or case is called for, as when a court applying domestic rules of private international law must apply

59 For another reformulation, N. MACCORMICK, Four Quadrants of Jurisprudence, *in*: Prescriptive Formality and Normative Rationality in Modern Legal Systems 53 (W. Krawietz, N. MacCormick & G. von Wright, eds. 1994).

60 *See* L. NOTTAGE, Trade Law Harmonisation in the Asia-Pacific Region: A Realist's View from New Zealand - and a Way Forward?, [1995] N.Z.L.J. 295 (September 1995).

61 *See*, e.g., S. MICHIDA, Cancellation of Contract, 27 Am. J. Comp. L. 279 (1979).

62 *See* NOTTAGE, *supra* note 60, at 298.

foreign law. To take a practical example, my law firm was recently involved in advising on the *Multiply Ltd.* case.[63] The High Court in Auckland heard evidence on the effect of an "entire agreement" clause in a contract governed by Japanese law, pursuant to a golf course joint venture in New Zealand. However, once again, it quickly became clear that one's overall perspective will be coloured by a general theory of contract - indeed, to a large extent (but not necessarily completely), by competing general theories, given that opposing expert witnesses in New Zealand courts will be called to give evidence in an adversarial procedure.[64] Furthermore, when we progress to such analysis of underlying general theories of contract, we can move - depending on the nature of those general theories - to express or implicit consideration of Gessner's third level: legal practice in foreign courts.

Gessner suggests that this third level of complexity, the practice of "legal" institutions, is particularly useful in more macro-oriented policy analyses, to identify implementation problems and autonomous processes that can interfere with attempts to "regulate" involving law. The *Multiply Ltd.* case shows the importance of analysis at this level even in resolving particular disputes. Another example reinforcing this point is one that my firm was involved in recently. It settled out of court, so unfortunately I must be even more careful in what I can say now in public. Generally, however, the Japanese plaintiff sued the New Zealand defendant for breach of contract (amongst other things). The questions of what law governs and which country's court should hear the case were at least debatable, so lawyers on both sides would have considered the ramifications under the substantive and procedural law of both New Zealand and Japan. For various reasons, the matter was litigated in a New Zealand court, applying New Zealand law. Even then, however, at the stage of interlocutory procedures (especially discovery), major questions arose as to Japanese "law" at Gessner's third level - the practical approach to legal matters within the bureaucracy, and within voluntary associations (and peripheral institutions).

Further, this latter case also suggests that part of what Gessner considers at his fourth level of analysis, the legal behaviour of legal professionals, may in fact be better analysed at his third level. The role of legal professionals in structuring and advising on transactions, and in resolving disputes, is not

63 *Cf.* 7 N.Z.C.L.C. 260, 746 (1995).

64 *See*, in more detail, NOTTAGE, *supra* note 1. This case was further complicated by major company law disputes being of course governed by New Zealand law, as was the case in the dispute reported by M. GERLACH, Trust is Not Enough: Cooperation and Conflict in Kikkoman's American Development, 16 J. JAP. STUD. 385 (1990).

always purely instrumental.[65] Instead, it can bear more similarity to the peculiar ways in which "law" is created or negotiated as a type of normative order, within what are generally seen as third-party legal institutions: the courts (particularly at first instance), government organizations, and voluntary associations.

Lastly, Gessner describes as the most complex his fourth level of analysis: the legal behaviour of private individuals or business actors, which can be related to overall legal consciousness and legal culture. He describes this as the "action" level, although I would also attach that epithet to his third level and group the two levels together. Certainly, it has been seen more as the province of legal sociologists. However, Japanese civil law scholars have the quite unusual tradition - albeit another legacy in common with the U.S. - of being keenly aware of the practical and theoretical importance of incorporating this "law in action" into their work. At this level, the focus is on the mundane world of people's everyday encounters with and perceptions of the law.

This can often have immediate practical relevance. An obvious example is where systematic evidence or experience, at least with regard to a particular class of Japanese clients in particular types of transaction, provides guidance to a New Zealand or Australian lawyer in advising on the use of a short versus a long form of contract, or indeed an oral as opposed to a written contract, in structuring a transaction or (less frequently) in resolving a wider dispute. Other examples come from an appreciation of the internal workings of Japanese corporations: this can be fleshed out by an analysis of their contracting processes, shedding new light either on the background to contract disputes that are otherwise matters solely of New Zealand law, or on other legal disputes under New Zealand law.[66] However, the challenge remains of coordinating analysis at this level with the analysis at the other levels, and building up a body of knowledge to apply creatively to a range of contemporary problems.

F. An Ongoing Project

In sum, the frameworks proposed by *Atiyah* and *Summers*, and by *Gessner*, require sound comparative analysis to proceed in parallel on multiple levels. At

65 *See* T. TANASE, *Katari to shite no hô-enyô* [The Application of Law as Discourse], 111 MINSHÔHÔ ZASSHI 677 (1995). *Cf.* N. KASHIWAGI, *Hôgaku kenkyû to hôjitsumu no aida* [Between the Study of Law and Legal Practice], AMERICA HÔ35 (1995).

66 Here I particularly have in mind, respectively two other major court cases my law firm has been involved in, on behalf of a well-known Japanese general trading company. The former is also still pending, and the latter involved a sensitive matter of New Zealand tax law. At present, it would be indiscreet to go into more detail; I simply cite them as practical examples that can be usefully fitted into this broader comparative law framework.

present, my research continues to flesh out the various dimensions of formal as opposed to substantive orientation in U.S., English, New Zealand, and Japanese law. At the same time, a particular focus is on termination and adjustment of contractual relations in the wake of extreme changes of circumstances. At one level, I continue to analyse the main statutory rules, legal doctrines, and caselaw development in the New Zealand law of frustration, and in the Japanese law of non-imputable impossibility and the doctrine of changed circumstances, bearing in mind a number of neighbouring areas of law.[67] On the whole, this is more conventional, "black letter law" comparative study. I am also trying to see if, and to what extent, academic theory development is affected by underlying general theories of contract. This is not so commonly done, but my practical and theoretical perspective suggests that it is worthwhile.

Further, in time, I aim to systematically determine the number and types of cases brought before courts and (as far as is feasible) before arbitrators, and the wider process by which they are then resolved. This goes beyond the normal field of study for a contract lawyer, and verges on that traditionally assigned to the legal sociologist. It involves some appreciation of the volume and type of contract cases coming before the courts, for instance.[68] It also involves more qualitative research, such as how legal professionals and bureaucratic mechanisms structure the process. We already suspect that this level of analysis is too lofty: potential legal problems in long-term supply contracts between New Zealand and Japanese parties are simply not registering as "legal" problems. Thus the question is the process by which these may be (re)formulated in "business" terms, in differently structured and sometimes variable markets.[69] As indicated by Gessner, survey research is one basic technique at this level of analysis, and respondents in New Zealand (and Australia) have recently been subjected to *M. Kato*'s multinational survey in

---

67 *See* L. NOTTAGE, The Day After the Kobe Quake: Renegotiating Contracts with Japanese Suppliers 'In the Shadow of the Law', 432 LAWTALK 6 (1995).

68 I look forward to assisting Professor *Wollschläger* (University of Bielefeld) in adding an assessment of New Zealand to his comparative time series (*cf.* his contribution in this volume *supra* Chapter Three). A useful next step will be to break down the types of contract cases reported and filed. *See*, e.g., M. ELLINGHAUS, An Australian Contract Law?, 2 J.C.L. 13 (1989).

69 In the case of iron ore contracts, for instance, *see* T. DAINTITH, The Design and Performance of Long-Term Contracts, *in*: Contract and Organisation 164 (T. Daintith & G. Teubner, eds. 1986). This appears to be another good example of what have been termed "third cultures". *See* V. GESSNER, Legal Certainty in Cross-Border Interactions, *in*: Proceedings of the 1995 Annual Meeting of the Research Committee on Sociology of Law (International Sociological Association), "Legal Culture: Encounters and Transformations" (Tokyo, August 1-4, 1995), Papers of Section Meetings Supplement 2, 79 (Japan Committee for the RCSL95, ed. 1995).

this field. Preliminary results from other countries have been useful in once again "locating" different legal systems along a spectrum, and forcing us to reevaluate stereotypical perspectives.[70] However, in association with colleagues from Japan, this data will be supplemented by more qualitative research in this area.[71]

Comparative research of this nature, sensitive to different and sometimes varying perspectives, and proceeding on multiple levels, poses theoretical and practical difficulties. Above all, as I find these days to my great dismay, it takes time. But, by dint of dedication and focus, some contract lawyers have managed it in the context of their own legal system.[72] The ongoing vigour of Japanese law scholarship gives me some confidence that it can also be managed in a comparative context.[73]

G. Comparative Law and Comparative Economic Success

The theme of the conference in Berlin was "Japan: Economic Success and Legal System". Participants were invited to explore the links between Japan's legal system and its economic system. In this paper, I have focused primarily on the Japanese legal system, and ways we can look at it. However I have considered how foreign perspectives on Japanese law, including an emerging antipodean

---

70 M. KATO & A. FUJIMOTO, An International Comparison of Contract Consciousness: Which is More Unique, Japan or the U.S.?, Paper Presented at the 1995 Annual Meeting of the Research Committee on Sociology of Law (International Sociological Association), "Legal Culture: Encounters and Transformations" (Tokyo, August 1-4, 1995). A difficulty I anticipate is that, particularly in Australia, the "Sugar Case" dispute apparently seems to retain its fascination in the Australian mind. *See* V. TAYLOR, Australian Perceptions of Contract in Asia, *in*: Australia-Asia Perceptions (A. Milner, ed. 1996). This risks biasing their response, even given thevariations used in the survey.

71 Some Interviews were carried out from March to July 1996 in New Zealand, with Professor *Yoshitaka Wada* (Kyushu University). Further interviews will be carried out in New Zealand and Japan. I am grateful to Professor *Wada* and other members of the *Keiyaku Riron Kenkyû-kai* [Study Group on Contract Law Theory] for the opportunity to collaborate in their three-year research programme, and to the New Zealand Asia 2000 Foundation for grants to follow and join in some of that research, as well as to help finance the visit of Professor *Wada* to Victoria University.

72 The work of *Stewart Macaulay* is a major inspiration in this field. *See*, on impracticability, S. MACAULAY, J. KIDWELL, W. WHITFORD & M. GALANTER, Contracts: Law in Action Vol. 2, 621-770 (1995).

73 A pioneer in this area was T. SAWADA, Subsequent Conduct and Supervening Events (1968). Tucked away here and there, particularly in the copious Japanese literature, wealso occasionally uncover some attempts at more broadly based comparative research: *see*, e.g., H. KUBO, *Keizai hendô to keiyaku riron* [Economic Change and Contract Theory] 204-208 (1992).

perspective, may be related to changing economic ties with Japan. I also suggested that new perspectives call for more complex theoretical frameworks. It may prove possible to relate *Atiyah* and *Summers'* multiple distinctions between form and substance, in a legal system's contract law and related legal institutions, to economically efficient design and use of certain contract types or to resolution of disputes arising from those contracts.[74] *Gessner*'s multi-level analysis, by also allowing scope to explore contract law "in action", also promises to readily yield more insight into economic factors affecting this area of Japanese law. Comparative lawyers looking to Japanese law still have much work to do in fleshing out such basic frameworks, and in collating the expanding range and volume of data required by this more ambitious view of comparative law research. But already there should be more scope for some of those theoretical insights, or some of that data, to be usefully drawn upon by those more interested in economic development.

74 *Cf.* T. DAINTITH (*supra* note 69), considering the tension between spot and relational contracting.

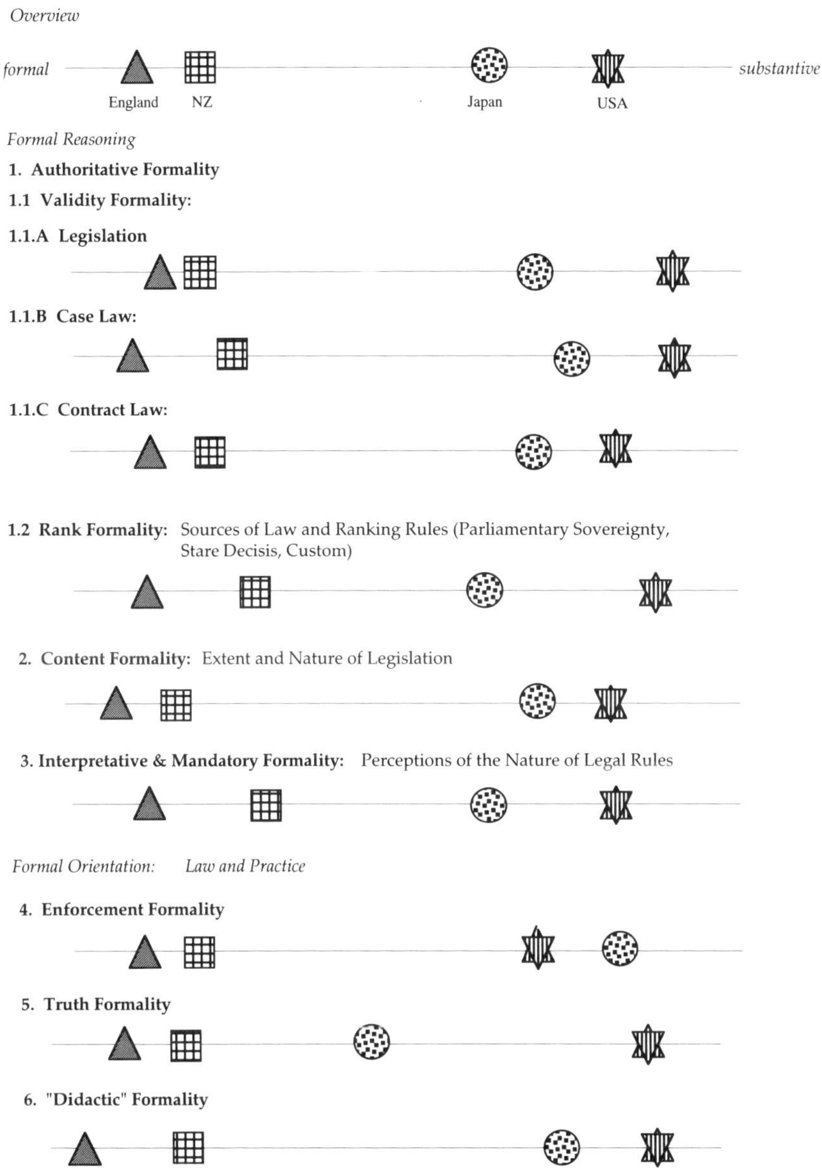
Overview
formal
substantive
England
NZ
Japan
USA
Formal Reasoning
1. Authoritative Formality
1.1 Validity Formality:
1.1.A Legislation
1.1.B Case Law:
1.1.C Contract Law:
1.2 Rank Formality: Sources of Law and Ranking Rules (Parliamentary Sovereignty, Stare Decisis, Custom)
2. Content Formality: Extent and Nature of Legislation
3. Interpretative & Mandatory Formality: Perceptions of the Nature of Legal Rules
Formal Orientation: Law and Practice
4. Enforcement Formality
5. Truth Formality
6. "Didactic" Formality

Figure 1

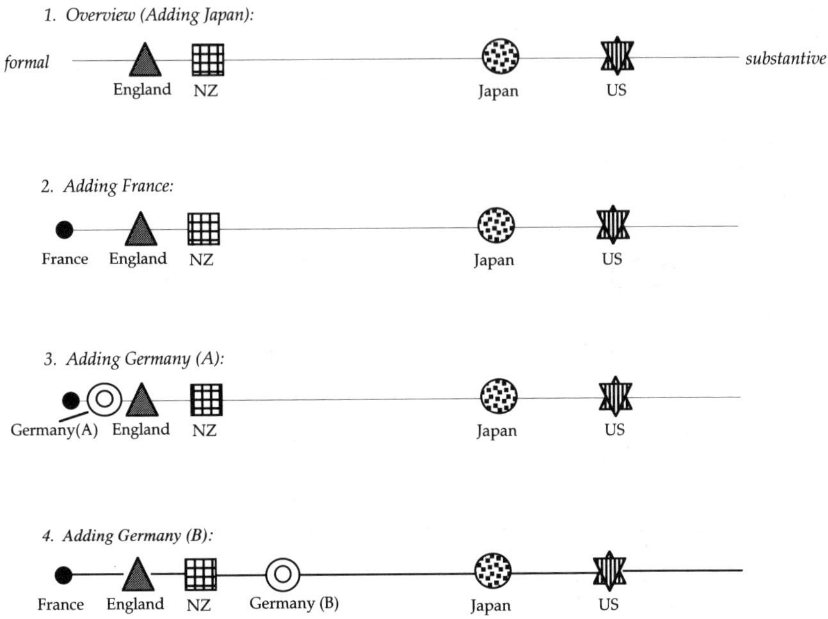

Source for Figures 1 and 2: L. NOTTAGE, Form and Substance in U.S., English, New Zealand and Japanese Law: A Frameworfor Better Comparisons of Developments in the Law of Unfair Contracts, 21/3 VICTORIA UNIVERSITY OF WELLINGTON LAW REVIEW 247 (1996).

Figure 2

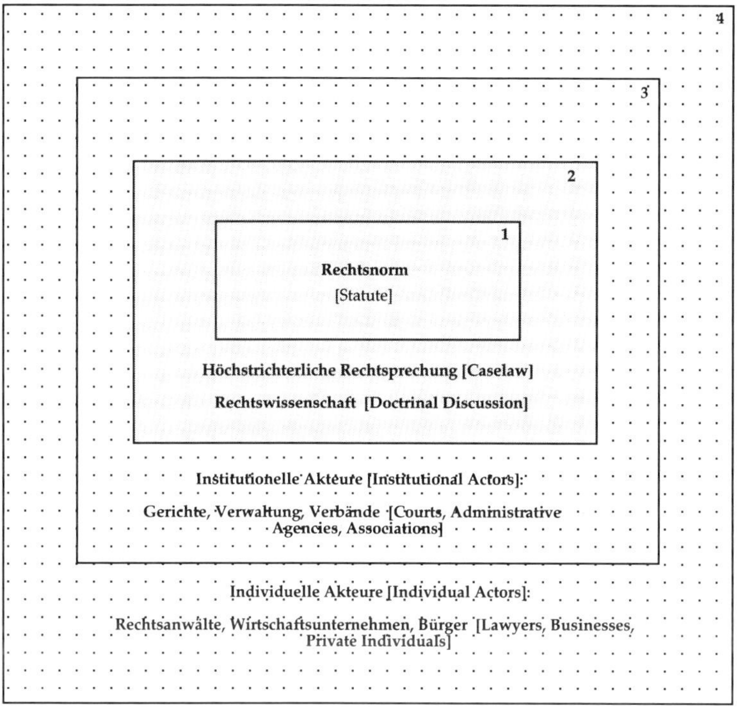

Field 1: Legal-theoretical and legal-dogmatic comparisons
Field 2: Legal comparison
Field 3: Comparative implementation research
Field 4: Comparison of legal systems / legal cultures

"Black Letter Law"

"Law in Action"

Adapted from: V. GESSNER, Presumptio Similitudinis? A Critique of Comparative Law, *in* Proceedings of the 1995 Annual Meeting of the Research Committee on Sociology of Law (International Sociological Association), Legal Culture: Encounters and Transformations (Tokyo 1-4 August 1995), Papers of Section Meetings Supplement 2, 41, 50 (Japan Committee for the RCSL95, ed. 1995). We thank the author for his kind permission to reprint this figure.

Figure 3

Part Three:
Aspects of the Japanese Enterprise

Chapter Eight

Changes in the Japanese Enterprise Groups?

Eiji Takahashi

Contents

A. Introduction: *Zaibatsu* Conglomerates

The emergence of conglomerates and complex groups of companies is not a recent phenomenon in Japan. It has as deep historical roots in Japan as it does in Western countries. From the beginning of this century, the Japanese economy was dominated by the well-known *zaibatsu*, huge and powerful conglomerates under the control of old merchant dynasties. These families, such as *Mitsui*, *Mitsubishi* or *Sumitomo*, contributed much to the economic restructuring during the *Meiji* restoration. They also maintained very close ties to politics.[1]

The *zaibatsu* groups favored a tight, hierarchical organization with a holding company at its head. That holding's capital was entirely in the hands of the controlling family. On the second level were a number of so-called core companies which controlled strategically important areas of activity. Subsidiary companies made up the third level. They were closely controlled in all personal and financial matters, but enjoyed considerable liberty in the operation of their business.[2]

World War II brought a dramatic increase in the power of the *zaibatsu*, providing them with a quasi-monopoly in leading branches of industry. In

---

1 *See* J. HIRSCHMEIER, The Origin of Entrepreneurship in Meiji Japan 216 *et seq.* (1964); T. ABE, *Seishô kara zaibatsu e* [From *seishô* to *zaibatsu*] *in*: *Nihon keizai no hatten to kigyô shûdan* [Development of Japanese Economy and Enterprise Groups] 135-136 (Hashimoto & Takeda, eds. 1992); R. CLARK, The Japanese Company 21-22 (1979).

2 H. TAKEDA, *Takakuteki jigyô bumon no teichaku to kontserun soshiki no seibi* [Establishment of Multiple Operations and Development of Conglomerate Structure], *in*: *Nihon keizai no hatten to kigyô shûdan* (*supra* note 1).

1945, 22.9% of the total assets of Japanese corporations belonged to three big *zaibatsu*: *Mitsui*, *Mitsubishi*, and *Sumitomo*.[3]

After World War II, the Allied powers saw the *zaibatsu* as an obstacle to the democratization of the Japanese economy. They ordered the dissolution of large Japanese industrial and banking conglomerates. The *zaibatsu* groups organized their own liquidation. The holding company and core companies were dissolved by the end of September 1946, thus liberating the subsidiary companies.[4] A number of additional measures were intended to extinguish the personal influence of the old *zaibatsu* families. These included the forced retirement of the management of the holding and core companies.[5]

Nevertheless, the economic reality of today's Japan is different from the ideas of the postwar reformers. The Japanese economy is still dominated by large groups of companies with worldwide activities. Names like *Sumitomo*, *Mitsui* or *Toyota* - often the same as old *zaibatsu* names - are widely regarded as synonymous with Japanese economic power. These conglomerates such as Toyota are often called "families" by the Japanese. The company on the top takes on the role of parent, and the subsidiaries that of their children. The members of these families collaborate very closely and are interconnected in many ways. The inner workings of these networks often appear to outsiders as mysterious and inscrutable. At best, they have been seen as a Japanese cultural phenomenon.[6] The more critical commentators have characterized them as a classical tool used by the Japanese industry to keep foreign competitors out of the market.[7] The degree of concentration in the Japanese economy is illustrated by the fact that about 70% of the shares of Japanese corporations is in the hands of other companies, which rarely sell their shares.[8] Only 25-30% of the

---

3 H. MIYAJIMA, *Zaibatsu kaitai* [*Zaibatsu* Dissolution], *in*: *Nihon keizai no hatten to kigyô shûdan*, *supra* note 1, at 203.

4 *See id.* at 206; E. HADLEY, Antitrust in Japan 68 (1970); T.A. BISSON, Zaibatsu Dissolution in Japan 61 *et seq*. (1954).

5 *See* MIYAJIMA, *supra* note 3, at 211; HADLEY, *supra* note 4, at 88 *et seq*.; BISSON, *supra* note 4, at 161 *et seq*.

6 C. NAKANE, Die Struktur der japanischen Gesellschaft [The Structure of Japanese Society] 132 (1985); J. HIRSCHMEIER, Japans Belegschaftskapitalismus. Eine zukunftsweisende Entwicklung? [Japan's "Employee Capitalism": A Future-Oriented Development?], *in* Die japanische Unternehmung. Schriften aus dem Nachlaß [The Japanese Enterprise: Collection of Unpublished Works] 158 (W. Kraus & E. Louven, eds. 1986); J. SYDOW, Strategische Netzwerke in Japan [Strategic Networks in Japan], ZFBF 248 (1991).

7 Opinion of the U.S. side on the issue of the *Structural Impediments Initiative* (SII) in Japan since 1990.

8 H. BAUM, Aktienbesitz und Publizität [Shareholding and Disclosure], *in* Festschrift für Zentarô Kitagawa [Festschrift for Zentarô Kitagawa] 626 (H.G. Leser & T. Isomura, eds. 1992).

market-quoted shares are actively traded.[9] This situation has provoked the Western comment: "Japan Inc. owns 70% of itself".[10]

B. Vertically Structured Corporate Groups

There are two basic forms of group structures in Japan: the vertical and the horizontal. Groups of the vertical type seem to be relatively close to the conglomerates in the West. They have a hierarchical structure with a central unit on the top. The companies are interconnected by capital participation.

However, inside this seemingly familiar structure, there are important particularities, especially in the area of decision making. It is a traditional and relatively well-known feature of Japanese groups that the decision-making process is not so centralized as in Western groups.[11] We call this decentralized decision making: a company on the top leaves much room for subsidiaries to determine their own business policy. The parent company will not intervene in details of the subsidiary's management, for example, in areas such as product range, price policy, research, and other technical points. This system intends to utilize the special knowledge of the "men on the spot"[12] who can more easily adjust to market developments than men at the top.

The subsidiaries are treated much like a dog on the lead. Their liberty is limited to certain areas, and it is further restricted by tight control in essential areas. The parent company will, of course, control the more basic decisions like capital accumulation, amendments of statutes, and mergers. In order to ensure a continuous influence, the parent company exercises a determining role in the personnel policy of its subsidiaries.[13] Normally, the parent company reserves the right to determine the members of the management. These are often employees of the parent company. It is evident that the parent company can exercise considerable indirect influence on its subsidiaries through the loyalty the management holds towards it.

In this system of liberty limited by checks and balances, ideally, the decision-making process will have a circular structure. The parent company

---

9 *Id.*

10 R. ZIELINSKI & N. HOLLOWAY, Unequal Equities, Power and Risk in Japan's Stockmarket 24 (1991).

11 CLARK, *supra* note 1, at 61 *et seq.*; K. SAKAMOTO, *Seisan ko-gaisha no teinkai* [Development of Subsidiaries as Productive Operations], *in*: *Gendai nihon no kigyô gurupu* [Today's Japanese Enterprise Groups] 47 (Sakamoto & Shimotani, eds. 1987).

12 F.A. HAYEK, The Use of Knowledge in Society, 35 AM. ECON. REV. 524 (1945).

13 *See* M. AOKI, Information, Incentives, and Bargaining in the Japanese Economy 51 (1988).

determines a framework for the subsidiaries' economic performance. The filling out of that framework is left largely to the management of the subsidiary, which will in turn inform the parent company of important facts and developments. That information is then used by the parent company to adjust the framework and so forth.

The *Toyota* group is a good example of such a vertically structured group with a decentralized decision-making structure. The conglomerates are organized in a hierarchy; for example, the holding company, *Toyota Auto, Inc.*, controls subsidiaries by capital participation. The function of the subsidiary companies is mainly the supply of parts. In 1991, the parent company held a 20% or higher share in 193 companies.[14] In spite of the rigid pyramidal structure, the decision-making process is characterized by the circular, collaborative model outlined above.

The multitude of model variants produced made it impossible for parent companies to establish a central production plan. As early as the 1960s, the *Toyota* group created a system of direct communication between production units and supplier subsidiary companies.[15] In that system, vendor companies make daily summaries about the number and types of cars ordered. This information goes directly to supplier companies, who produce parts accordingly. These parts are taken by former production units together with detailed reports about demand.

It is difficult to determine the degree of dependence of subsidiaries in such a structure. On the surface, it is quite evident that the subsidiary depends in many ways upon the parent company. The parent company can exercise the influence it has as a major shareholder. But the parent company is also dependent on its subsidiaries. The Japanese system of lean production makes it essential that the production units dispose of a continuous supply of parts which have to be adjusted exactly to the needs of the production line. If the supplier of vital parts gets into difficulty or leaves the system, the whole production system may be jeopardized.[16] For that reason, Japanese parent companies tend to emphasize the "value" of the subsidiaries as a counterbalance to dependence. It is well known in practice that subsidiaries do not hesitate to exercise their influence

---

14 TÔYÔ KEIZAI SHINPÔ-SHA (ed.), *Kigyô keiretsu sôran* [The Table of the Enterprise Groups] 54 (1992).

15 *See* AOKI, *supra* note 13, at 22 *et seq.*; H. ITAMI, T. KAGONO, T. KOBAYASHI, K. SAKAKIBARA & M. ITÔ, *Kyôsô to kakushin: Jidôsha sangyô no kigyô seichô* [Competition and Innovation: Growth of the Enterprise in the Automobile Industry] 84 (1988); J.C. ABEGGLEN & G. STALK, Kaisha. The Japanese Corporation 93 *et seq.* (1985).

16 *See* Y. MIWA, *Shitauke kankei. Jidôsha sangyô* [Subcontract Relationships. Automobile Industry], *in*: *Nihon no kigyô* [The Japanese Company] 177 (Imai & Komiya, eds. 1989).

against the parent company. There are cases reported in which the subsidiaries have successfully claimed compensation payments for losses caused by a sudden change of the models of cars produced by the parent company.[17]

C. Horizontally Structured Corporate Groups

The real mystery for non-Japanese observers seems to be the structure of horizontally interconnected companies. The mechanism in the vertically organized groups may be in some aspects different from the Western model. Nevertheless, the basic functioning of the group is quite understandable because it works with tools similar to those of the West, such as capital participation and collaboration contracts. Horizontally structured corporate groups are quite different, and may be more unfamiliar to Western observers.

Horizontal corporate groups are large networks that include up to 50 companies, which seem to be only loosely interconnected by minor asset stakes. Typically, in such a network, about 28% of the capital of one participating company is held by about 20 other network companies with an average individual share of approximately only 1.6%.[18] There is no group center, and the relatively small capital participation makes it technically impossible for network companies to exercise a formal influence. It is not easy to make out where the reasons for this share-holding structure lie. There is no command line from the parent to the children, and there is no leading company that could determine a framework of collaboration.

It is obvious that a Western-style legal analysis of formal influences and power will not help. The only thing which could remotely resemble a command unit is the famous "presidents' club", where the presidents of network companies hold regular informal meetings. No outsider really knows what goes on at these meetings. The companies themselves describe the meetings as a purely friendly exchange of views and information comparable to a meeting of old classmates. To put it in the words of an organizer of the presidents' meeting of the *Mitsubishi* group:[19] "The aim of our meeting is only the protection of the name *Mitsubishi* and its trademarks. Besides that there is nothing. We don't talk on subjects concerning concrete business relations, such as intra-group trade." But it is doubtful whether that statement reflects the whole truth. There

---

17 *Id.* at 175; B. ASANUMA, *Nihon ni okeru buhin torihiki no kôzô* [Organization of Parts Purchases in Japan], 133 KEIZAI RONSÔ 156 (1987).

18 Sumitomo Group in 1989. *See* KÔSEI TORIHIKI I'INKAI (ed.), *Saishin nihon no rokudai kigyô shûdan no jittai* [The Reality of the Big Six Enterprise Groups in Present Japan] 121-123 (1994).

19 NIHON KEIZAI SHINBUN-SHA, *Terasu de yomu nihon no kigyô gurupû* [The Japanese Enterprise Groups] 95 (1991).

are no protocols of these meetings available to outsiders. The secretive character of that body has given raise to all kinds of theories about their function and influence. The position of Japanese economists is mainly influenced by their political bias: while neo-classicists[20] deny any influence of the presidents' meeting, Marxists[21] tend to denounce it as a kind of secret power arsenal.

In a realistic approach to decision-making structures in these horizontal networks, one must consider the basic structures of the groups. The network reduces the influence of shareholders, and, in particular, prevents hostile takeovers because the shares held by other network companies are not under the influence of the capital market. Viewed this way, the network appears to be mutual cooperation by company managements to escape the control of shareholders and of the capital market and increase independence.[22] Here lies also the reason for the scattering of participants. The system is just intended to minimize the influence of a single shareholder. The network companies simply do not want to fall under the formal influence of other participating companies. In other words, this type of horizontal group structure is a mutual accord among participating managements to assure each other a degree of independence by eluding the control mechanisms provided by company law. It is based on the general assumption that the management of the other network companies will use their minor stakes to prevent a hostile takeover.

The power of the presidents' club is dependent on the basic consensus of participating managements. But it seems that the presidents' club has no power to compel member companies to carry out or abandon certain projects. This lack of power of the presidents' club may be illustrated by the conflict in the *Sumitomo* group in the early 1970s.[23] In December 1970, *Sumitomo Light Metal Corporation* decided to enter the aluminum smelting industry. However, since aluminum belongs to the domain of *Sumitomo Chemical, Inc.*, a conflict between the two companies arose. Members of the presidents' club of the Sumitomo group tried to persuade the Sumitomo Light Metal to renounce the project. But the attempt failed. The president of the Sumitomo Light Metal announced on January 6, 1972, its plan to establish the aluminum smelting plant which would start operations in late 1975. Fearing excess capacity in aluminum production, the Minister of International Trade and Industry

20 AOKI, *supra* note 13, at 120.

21 T. ÔUCHI, *Nihon Keizai Ron. (Ge)* [The Japanese Economy. Book II] 404 (1963); T. SAKAMOTO, *Kigyô shûdan zaimu ron* [The Finance of the Enterprise Group] 171 (1990).

22 T. KIKKAWA, *Senzen nihon no sangyô hatten to zaibatsu* [Development of Japanese Industry in the Prewar Period and *Zaibatsu*], 47 SHAKAI KAGAKU KENKYÛ 180 *et seq* (1995).

23 A. GOTÔ, Business Groups in a Market Economy, 19 EUROPEAN ECON. REV. 55 (1982).

mediated between the two companies. The following agreement was reached on June 16, 1972. Sumitomo Light Metal established a new smelting plant as a subsidiary, and Sumitomo Chemical agreed to cooperate with Sumitomo Light Metal and own a certain number of shares in the new firm. This case shows that when a member company begins a project which jeopardizes the harmony of a corporate group, member companies of the presidents' club try to persuade this company to abandon the project. What is interesting about this case is that Sumitomo Light Metal, regardless of pressure from the the presidents' club, persisted in its original plan and realized it. The presidents' club had no power to force the member company to renounce its project when the member company considered it against its interests.[24]

D. Changes in the Japanese Corporate Groups?

One of the more intensely discussed questions with respect to the Japanese industrial structure is the question of how the horizontal corporate groups will develop in the future. I think that the horizontal corporate group will continue to exist in the future as a distinctive phenomenon, but that the relationships among the member companies within the group will become looser.

As I have previously mentioned, the predecessor of the corporate group was the *zaibatsu*, a conglomerate of companies which was in most cases under the control of old merchant dynasties. The member companies of the corporate group were led by presidents who had been hired by the old *zaibatsu* companies before World War II. These people continued to maintain strong ties of identity and friendship toward each other, even after the dissolution of the *zaibatsu*, because they had once worked together for the same *zaibatsu*. The basis for strong personal ties among the presidents of member companies lies in this experience. But now this type of president is retiring from member companies. Most member companies are now managed by a new generation which has no experience of working at the old *zaibatsu*. This generational change makes the personal ties among the managers of the member companies weaker.[25]

Another sign of change in the corporate groups lies in their stock-holding structure. The golden age for the Japanese economy has now passed. Japanese companies have ceased to grow at spectacular rates. The price of shares of Japanese corporations does not appreciate automatically, as it did before the sweeping stock market crash in the year 1991. Now the group companies must

24 E. TAKAHASHI, Konzern und Unternehmensgruppe in Japan-Regelung nach dem deutschen Modell? [Combines and Enterprise Groups in Japan: Regulation According to the German Model?] 31 (1994).

25 H. ODAGIRI, Growth Through Competition, Competition Through Growth: Strategic Management and the Economy in Japan 195 (1992).

take the risk of depreciation in the stocks which they hold in other member companies. Thus, holding their stock does not always mean gain. It may, in fact, result in losses, if the stock price depreciates. It is now reported that companies of the corporate groups are starting to sell off the stocks of their member companies.[26] The stock-holding structure of the corporate group is said to be losing its identity.

It is now being discussed in Japan whether the Antimonopoly Law[27] should be reformed.[28] Article 9 of the Antimonopoly Law prohibits corporate groups from establishing a pure holding company whose aim lies only in the control of other companies. Discussions are being held as to whether this article should be abolished. The Ministry of International Trade and Industry (*Tsûsan-shô*) is strongly for abolition, while the Fair Trade Commission (*Kôsei Torihiki I'inkai*) is reluctant to see abolition go through. The Fair Trade Commission argues that one possible result of the abolition might be the reappearance of the former *zaibatsu* conglomerates. If Article 9 of the law were abolished, it would be possible for corporate groups to build a holding company as their controlling organ. The corporate groups could then change their structure from horizontal to hierarchical and reappear as monopolies in the domestic market.

I think, however, that there is no need to establish a pure holding company for the corporate groups. As I have already explained, the central aim of building corporate groups lies not in group policy decision making, but in reducing the influence of shareholders and creating increased independence for management to reach this goal; the present stock-holding structure of the corporate group is enough. It is therefore unlikely that the corporate group would build a pure holding company as the central decision-making organ of the group, even if it were possible by law. On the contrary, the relationships between the member companies of the corporate groups will become weaker. In the future, not only will the strong personal ties among the presidents of the member companies be lost, but the stock-holding structure of the corporate group will also become less rigid. This corresponds in some ways with another trend, the subject of the final section of this paper.

E. Corporate Networks and the Economic Success of Japan

In conclusion, I would like to talk about the link between the economic success of Japan and the corporate networks. In my view, a crucial factor for the

26 NIHON KEIZAI SHINBUN, Apr. 7, 1995.

27 *Shiteki dokusen no kinshi oyobi kôsei torihiki no kakuho ni kansuru hôritsu* [Antimonopoly Law], Law No. 54 of 1947 as amended by Law No. 89 of 1993. For an English translation, *see* EHS, Vol. II, KA, No. 2270.

28 NIHON KEIZAI SHINBUN, Mar. 25, 1995.

economic success of Japanese corporations was the application of the policies typical for the corporate group in a wider context. This policy is called "stock stabilization policy".[29] As a result, most Japanese corporate stocks are not owned by the public but by a corporation's business partners or its "main bank(s)", as mentioned previously. There is an unwritten agreement among them that they will not sell off the shares of their business partners, so long as their business relationship continues. In this sense, most Japanese companies are bound to each other through reciprocal stock holdings, thus building a network of companies. According to recent statistical research for the year 1993, 21.2% of market-quoted shares were reciprocally held by two companies, and 23.7% of market-quoted shares were held by banks and other financial institutions.[30] This stock stabilization policy is directed toward making it difficult to take over Japanese corporations, and toward reducing the influence of shareholders, giving management a wide range of discretion.[31] Thanks to this policy, the managers of Japanese corporations can follow a growth-oriented policy and make long-term investments, regardless of the short-term interests of shareholders.

At the same time, Japanese corporations have adopted policies which have had a profound impact on employee loyalty. These policies include permanent employment, salaries dependent upon age, and a strong promotion system.[32] Under these policies, the employee has a lifetime guarantee of a job. In addition, during his or her employment period, the worker receives pay in accordance with the length of service years. And corporate managers are selected from employees of the same company through heavy competition. All of these factors have contributed to the success of the Japanese company in the postwar period.

Under this management system, the virtual owners of the company are managers and workers, not shareholders. However, shareholders are not dissatisfied: although shareholders may not get a high rate of dividend, they have enjoyed capital gain by the appreciation of their shares - at least in the past. The postwar economic success of Japan was realized through this change in the concept of the corporation, whose owners must be the shareholders by the law, into the community of employees, who are loyal to their corporations.

But this style of management now faces difficulties. As already mentioned, since the stock market crash in 1991, the price of shares of Japanese

---

29 R. DORE, Taking Japan Seriously: A Confucian Perspective on Leading Economic Issues 114 (1987).

30 H. KAWAKITA, *Nihon gata kabushiki shijô no kôzô henka* [Change in the Japanese Stockmarket Structure] 125 (1995).

31 R.J. GILSON & M.J. ROE, Understanding the Japanese Keiretsu: Overlaps Between Corporate Governance and Industrial Organization, 102 YALE L.J. 897 (1993).

32 *See* CLARK, *supra* note 1, at 221-223.

corporations no longer appreciates automatically. Now Japanese companies must take the risk of depreciation in the stocks they hold in their business partners. In the mid-1990s, reports surfaced that companies were starting to sell off the stock of their business partners, a situation which would cause the network of the reciprocal stockholding of Japanese corporations to shrink as a whole.[33] If this trend continues, the influence of the shareholder will become strong again, and it will be difficult for the corporate manager to make long-term policies without considering to the short-term interests of shareholders. If the network created by reciprocal stockholding dissolves in the future and stockholders pressure the company to increase dividends, Japanese companies will have to be managed based upon short-term interests.

An additional concern is employee loyalty. Under the stagnating structural recession since 1991, Japanese companies are looking for ways to cut back expenses. One typical place to cut back is to trim the payroll. It will also be difficult for Japanese companies to sustain their pay-by-age policy, life-long employment, and promotion systems at the same time as the "baby-boom" generation reaches the age of management in the next few years.[34] The overflow of management age employees will result in lost jobs for the older workers in these firms. This situation is likely to result in decreased morale among the employees as they become concerned about job security. It is reported that the electronic industry workers' union has decided to fight for the coming five years to sustain the life-long employment system;[35] sustaining the pay-by-age policy is no longer a goal of the union's activity. Many Japanese companies are now beginning to introduce the merit system, in which the worker receives pay in accordance with her or his performance or ability.[36]

How will Japanese management change? It is difficult to give a clear answer. But taking the new trends into account, it appears that the Japanese corporation may lose some of its traditional character as a workers' community.

33 KAWAKITA, *supra* note 30, at 127.

34 I. NAKATANI, *Tenkan suru nihon kigyô* [Change in the Japanese Enterprise] 133 (1987).

35 YOMIURI SHINBUM, Jun. 6, 1995.

36 NIHON KEIZAI SHINBUN, Oct. 31, 1995.

Chapter Nine

Shareholders in Japan: Attitudes, Conduct, Legal Rights, and their Enforcement

*Masaru Hayakawa**

Contents

A. Introduction

It has previously been pointed out that the Japanese concept of contract and consciousness of individual rights is (arguably) weak, or at least less strict in a formal sense than, for example, in the United States or Germany.[1] Furthermore, it is widely known that, due to the small number of judges, Japanese courts take too long to resolve disputes, making it undesirable for

---

* I would like to thank *Jeremy Kloise-Jones*, a graduate student in law at Kyoto University, for translating this paper.

1 *Cf.*, e.g., the contribution of *G. Rahn*, chapter six.
This can be seen not only in the behavior of individuals, but also in that of industry. *Cf.* T. Ishii, *Kigyô to saiban* [Enterprise and Judicial Trial], *in*: *Shôhô no kihon mondai* [Fundamental Problems of Commercial Law] 555 et seq. (S. Wagatsuma & T. Suzuki, eds. 1952).

people to approach the courts for a legal solution to their problems. This restrictiveness of the current judicial system cannot be ignored when considering the exercise of shareholders' rights. Consequently, the enforcement of shareholder rights under the current system can be said to be compromised because of this factor alone. Does, however, the weak consciousness of shareholders' rights have any additional real effect on shareholder behavior? By distinguishing shareholder activity accompanying each stage of the development of company law, from its enactment in 1899 to the present, we can start to see an answer to this question.

B. Shareholders' Rights Under Japanese Law

The legal rights of shareholders have expanded with each successive amendment of the Commercial Code,[2] so that under current law shareholders possess a large number of rights in relation to the company.[3] Shareholders in Japan have much the same rights as those recognized in the company laws of most other countries, giving a favorable impression of progress in this area. However, in Japan, there are still shareholding conditions for the exercise of certain shareholder rights that require amendments to make them less restrictive.

The Japanese Commercial Code initially borrowed heavily from German law. Following World War II, however, under the strong influence of American company law, there were many amendments concerning, among other things, organs of a company, the distribution of rights among these organs, and the strengthening of shareholders' individual rights, thereby following the U.S. model. Specifically, in respect to shareholder rights, the former position of the general meeting of shareholders as the pivotal organ of the company changed, with the authority of the shareholders in general meeting shifting to the directors and board of directors. In response to this development, the law has since attempted to balance the broad authority which directors have come to possess by strengthening shareholders' rights. Though this process of legislative change, the character of shareholder rights has come to be seen as embodying the rights to supervise management decisions and to make correctional demands regarding directors' conduct.

---

2 *Shôhô*, Law No. 48 of 1899 as amended by Law No. 66 of 1994. For an English translation, *see* EHS Vol. II, JA, No. 2200.

3 For a more detailed explanation of the particulars of each revision, *see* I. KAWAMOTO, M. KISHIDA, A. MORITA, Y. KAWAGUCHI & Y. IGA, Corporations and Partnerships, 54 (1994).

C. The Standards for Shareholder Behavior: The Majority Shareholder

While it may be impossible to distinguish with any certainty a general trend in the behavior of all shareholders, we can at least isolate a trend or behavioral standard for one group by considering how majority shareholders preserve their economic interests. To do this we must analyze how the legal framework has changed, trace how the company law system has developed since the introduction of company law, and distinguish the trends of these various periods.

1. The Introduction of the Company System

After the commencement of the *Meiji* Restoration in 1868, the Japanese government, believing that a company system would contribute to the economic development of the country, introduced and promoted it with vigor. The Commercial Code was enacted in 1899 and the joint-stock company became increasingly used and accepted. In the beginning, investors' knowledge about the joint-stock company was scant, resulting in a dearth of awareness about shareholders' rights. From this latter half of the *Meiji* period, however, until the plunge into the Sino-Japanese War in 1937, shareholders increasingly demanded their own economic rewards. More specifically, the payment of extremely high dividends was demanded of the company through the general meeting of shareholders.[4] Furthermore, in this period, shareholders as a class grew from being confined to the wealthy to include the small-scale investor. Behind the majority shareholders' demands for high dividends lay their reliance on bank borrowing to finance their stock investments. High dividends were required to satisfy the interest payments on such borrowing and to maintain the value of shares offered as security for loans. It was not unusual for management to pay a bogus dividend (a dividend out of fictitious profits) in response to such demands for high, and, occasionally, exorbitant percentage distributions from shareholders. In addition to such improper accounting practice, improper conduct of corporate managers and numerous company failures, especially during the 1920s, brought companies as a whole into disrepute, and there was a fear that the joint-stock company system would destroy the country.[5] However, this distrust of companies was not universal. Starting in the first decade of the

---

4 A comparison of the net profit distributions of Japanese and U.S. companies in 1928 shows that Japanese companies (taking the average of 1,860 companies) paid out 65% of the net profit figure in dividends and directors' bonuses, whereas the corresponding figure for U.S. companies was in the range of 20-40%, *cf.* K. TAKAHASHI, *Kabushiki kaisha bôkoku ron* [Essay on the Destruction of the Country by the Joint-Stock Company] 14 (1930).

5 As representative of this opinion, *see* TAKAHASHI, *supra* note 4.

century, wealthy merchant families increasingly reorganized their growing business empires using the stock corporation as a legal vehicle. They formed family-owned holding companies, which in turn held the shares of the various stock corporations belonging to one specific enterprise group, a so-called *zaibatsu*. Being more directly concerned with the perpetuation of their powerful positions, the *zaibatsu* families demanded little in the way of dividends. Instead, company profits were invested in the expansion of the company, and also, because the rate of dividends of directly controlled subsidiary companies was not high, stable company managememt was continued. For the *zaibatsu* company, the main motivation for the majority shareholder was not direct economic gain, but the preservation and continuation of the company-controlling rights of the *zaibatsu* family.[6]

2. *The War Period*

The period up to the end of World War II was a dark era for sharcholders, in contrast to the stable position of both employees and management. This was the period when share ownership began to shift from individual shareholders to corporate shareholders. During the militarization process of the country in the 1930s - and especially during the Second World War - the Japanese economy had increasingly become a command economy. The pursuit of profit by industry was gradually restricted, and the distributions of dividends to shareholders was kept low under a special law.[7] Although concrete data are lacking, under such conditions it seems that even for corporate shareholders the exercise of their rights for the purpose of their own economic gain was extremely difficult. It is not hard to imagine such an exercise of rights being met with various types of unfavorable governmental treatment.

3. *The Post-War Period*

In the period following Japan's defeat in World War II until the present, Japan has increasingly come under the influence of the American legal system, resulting in a shift from the former German company model adopted earlier. It has been a time of ever-increasing separation of ownership and control, and a

---

6 T. Yui & E. Daitô, *Dai-kigyô jidai no tôrai* [The Advent of the Age of Big Business] 85 (1995).

7 T. Okazaki, *Kigyô shisutemu* [The Industrial System], *in: Gendai nihon keizai no genryô* [The Origins of the Modern Japanese Economic System] 116 *et seq.* (Okazaki & Okuno, eds. 1993); H. Kobayashi & T. Okazaki, *Nihon kabushiki kaisha no shôwa-shi* [The History of the Japanese Joint-Stock Company in the Showa Period] 115 (1995).

period in which the system of share ownership by corporate shareholders has become firmly established. Since the latter half of the 1960s, industry, which had relied on borrowing from banks for the greater part of its capital needs, has turned slowly from indirect financing to direct financing through capital markets. The number of individual shareholders has decreased, and a cross-shareholding system has taken hold. In such a system, if a company in its role as a corporate shareholder were to demand a high rate of dividends, it would be counterproductive to its own economic interests. Under the cross-shareholding system, such a demand would result in the other party - the company conversely holding shares in the corporate shareholder - claiming dividends in a similar way. Cross-shareholding thus eventually works as a device to usurp the rights of shareholders.[8]

Following the burst of the so-called "bubble economy" in the early 1990s, share prices entered a long slump from which they have yet to recover. Consequently, an increasing number of corporations and banks that had increased their shareholdings during the years of the equity boom have begun selling. On account of this, some forecast that in the future there will be an increasing decline in cross-shareholding among major listed companies.[9] An opposing view, however, denies that current practice represents a structural change signalling the end of cross-shareholding, suggesting rather that it is a temporary response to deal with the current recession in the aftermath of the bubble economy.[10]

4. *Summary*

In light of the above discussion concerning the general trends of large shareholder activity - with the exception of the war period until the close of World War II - we can say that throughout each period the most important factor underlying majority shareholder behavior was the shareholder's economic interests. This was so whether the majority shareholder was an individual or a corporation. Low dividends have been criticized as disregarding the interests of the average shareholder. However, for the majority shareholder (which here includes companies with interlocking share ownership relationships such that their interests sufficiently converge to make them act as a majority shareholder), low dividends do not conflict with their own economic interests.

8 NIHON KEIZAI SHINBUN-SHA (ed.), *Zeminaru gendai nihon kigyô* [Seminar in Modern Japanese Enterprise] 276 (1990).

9 NIHON KEIZAI SHINBUN, April 4, 1995.

10 N. KONYA, *Kabushiki kaisha wa hi-kôritsu demo fu-kôhei demo nai* [Joint-Stock Companies Are Neither Inefficient Nor Unfair], EKONOMISUTO, May 30, 1995, 62 *et seq*.

Consequently, they have little incentive to actively exercise their rights and sue. But this restrained practice does not necessarily answer the question of consciousness of their rights.

D. Some Types of Shareholders and Features of Their Behavior

The shareholder behavioral trends in the previous section focused on the power of a majority shareholder to influence a company's management. Under a legal system like Japan's which separates ownership and control, owners have come to comprise a diverse range of shareholders. However, it is difficult to generally distinguish all the various types of shareholders and their corresponding behaviors. Consequently, the following brief explanation will be limited to four characteristic types of shareholders which have recently become topics of discussion.

1. Institutional Investors: The Liberalization and Internationalization of the Stock Market

The institutional investors referred to here include banks (long-term credit banks, "city banks", and regional banks), trust banks, investment trusts, pension funds, and insurance companies. These institutional investors, a class of shareholders in a position to exert the most influence upon a company's management, are prohibited from holding more than 5% of a company's shares under Article 11 of the Anti-Monopoly Law (the limit is 10% in the case of an insurance company).[11] However, prior to the burst of the bubble economy, these institutional investors rarely expressed dissatisfaction with a company's management concerning the low level of dividends. This was because, with rising share prices, the asset value of their shareholdings rose, and these capital gains represented substantial hidden assets.

Since the burst of the bubble economy and the subsequent drastic fall of the stock prices, with the exception of trust banks and pension funds, the shareholding ratio of these institutional investors has fallen slightly.[12] One result of the long period of depressed share prices is the difficulty which institutional investors have in selling their shareholdings. Consequently, in order for them to alleviate the cost burden of holding shares over a long period,

---

11 *Shiteki dokusen no kinshi oyobi kôsei torihiki no kakuho ni kansuru hôritsu*, Law No. 54 of 1947 as amended by Law No. 89 of 1993. For an English translation *see* EHS, Vol. II, KA, No. 2270.

12 T. KAGA, *1994 nendo kabushiki bunpu jôkyo chôsa kekka no gaiyô* [An Outline of the 1994 Survey of the State of Share Distribution], 1399 SHÔJI HÔMU 28 *et seq.* (1995).

sufficient motivation has now arisen for the previously "silent shareholder" to evolve into one who "speaks up" to the management of industry to demand better performance and higher returns.[13]

Among institutional investors, of particular note are the recent activities of some U.S. institutional investors who hold shares in Japanese companies. For example, the large-scale public pension fund California Public Employees Retirement System (CALPERS) exercised its voting rights in 1992 at the general meeting of shareholders to make demands against Nomura Securities and Daiwa Securities to accept outside directors. Other public pension funds have also demanded increases in dividends.[14] Such a phenomenon is an inevitable consequence of the internationalization of the stock market. The activities of such foreign institutional investors are also having an effect on domestic institutional investors. Given the current business climate, it would not be surprising if these domestic institutional investors also began to exercise their shareholder rights in a similar way.

2. *Employee Shareholders: Employee Stock-Ownership Plans*

Since around 1969, employee stock-ownership plans have spread quickly among listed companies. As of 1992, the number of listed companies which had an employee stock-ownership plan stood at 1,980 companies (this represented 94% of the total 2,106 listed companies), and the related employee shareholders numbered 2,380,000 (44.6% of the employees of these companies).[15] The number of shares held by these employee stock-ownership plans represented 0.91% of the total number of listed company shares. According to a 1988 survey, the reasons given for the setting up of employee stock-ownership plans were the creation of assets for employees, the creation of stable shareholders, and the advancement of employees' feelings of participation in management. Few companies mentioned the importance of profit distributions to employee shareholders.

So how do these employee shareholder groups go about exercising their voting rights? Since each particular employee shareholder scheme differs, it is difficult to trace a general pattern. However, one common factor is that those

13 H. Mizuguchi, *Keiei konturoru ga kuwawaru kabushiki shijô to kikan tôshika no yakuwari* [The Stock Market, Management Control, and Role of Institutional Investors], 1050 Jurisuto 104 *et seq.* (1994).

14 T. Aihara, *Beikoku kikan tôshika no nihon ni okeru kabunushi katsudô ni tsuite* [On the Shareholder Activities of U.S. Institutional Investors in Japan], 112 Daikô Ripôto 1 *et seq.* (1995).

15 Nihon Keizai Kenkyûsho, *Jûgyô-in mochikabu seido no jittai chôsa-1985 nendo no jitsujô* [1985 Research into the State of Affairs Concerning Employee Stock-Ownership Plans], 94 Shôken Shiryô.

responsible for the administration of the scheme are usually middle- or upper-level company managers, i.e., those in a senior position to the majority of the members. Given the hierarchical structure of the Japanese company and the problems which could come from disagreeing with one's superiors, therefore, it is not practical for employees to have their say, regardless of the actual rights conferred upon them by the employee stock-ownership plan rules. It has been pointed out that the exercise of such voting rights in fact serves to shore up the controlling position of management.[16]

3. *Rogue Shareholders: The Sôkaiya*

A shareholder who receives compensation for cooperating to ensure that the general meeting of shareholders runs smoothly according to the chairman's agenda is referred to by the special name of *sôkaiya*. These *sôkaiya*, who are paid by the company, deprive other shareholders of the opportunity to ask questions by various means - often by bullying, occasionally by the use of force - and cooperate to have management's proposals approved in the shortest possible time. There seems little reason to doubt the assertion that the large role played by the *sôkaiya* is the reason why the average duration of the general meeting for the majority of Japanese companies is only 28 minutes.[17]

A phenomenon similar to this had already appeared in general meetings by the early *Shôwa* era, and at this time they were referred to as *goyô-kabunushi* (a shareholder in the service of the company). In an attempt to control the increasing tendency of gangsters to act as *sôkaiya* as a source of funds, and to restore the general meeting to its rightful status, the Commercial Code was amended in 1981 to prohibit the provision by the company of any benefit for the exercise of shareholders' rights.[18] Since this amendment of the Commercial Code there has been a decrease in the number of *sôkaiya*, but according to the public papers of the National Police Agency, as of the end of 1994 there were still about 1,000 *sôkaiya* active throughout the country. Some 300 of these were organized into 40 *sôkaiya* groups.[19] To date there have been only 24 arrests in connection with the passing of a benefit under the new provision. The passing of benefits from company to *sôkaiya* occurs in the majority of listed companies.

---

16 K. ICHIKAWA, *Jûgyô-in mochikabu seido to giketsu-ken* [Employee Stock-Ownership Plans and Voting Rights], 7-2 KAGAWA HÔGAKU 30 *et seq.* (1987); Y. USHIMARU, *Jûgyô-in mochikabu seido* [The System of Employee Stock-Ownership Plans], 121 HÔGAKU KYÔSHITSU 148 *et seq.* (1990).

17 *Kabunushi sôkai hakusho 1994 nenban* [1994 Whitepaper on the General Meeting of Shareholders], 1373 SHÔJI HÔMU 72 (1994).

18 *Cf.* Article 294-2, Article 497 of the Commercial Code.

19 E. TAKANO, *Kigyô taishô no bôryoku ni taisuru taisaku* [In Consideration of a Strategy Towards Violence Against Industry], 1385 SHÔJI HÔMU 22 *et seq.* (1995).

It has been pointed out that one reason for this is the fact that, for a company employee, to commit a crime for the company is not accompanied by a consciousness or awareness of wrongdoing. This contrasts with the relatively high level of law-observing consciousness held by individuals.[20] As long as this situation continues, it will not be possible for the legislature to realize its intention of attempting to revitalize the general meeting of shareholders.

Through disbursing company money and by using *sôkaiya*,[21] a company's management can easily evade criticisms of its own management performance from shareholders at the general meeting. It cannot be said that no companies are making an effort to sever relations with the *sôkaiya*, but those companies which do refuse to provide pay-offs receive harassment from gangs. Before the meeting, these companies spend time rehearsing in preparation for harassing questions and other obstructive actions of the *sôkaiya*. Paradoxically, the actions of the *sôkaiya* cause the company to place great importance on the general meeting. Thus, in a strange way, the *sôkaiya* have a meaningful existence.

4. Activist Shareholders: The Citizens' Movement

Commencing around the beginning of the 1970s with cases involving pollution, a type of citizens' movement developed in which the average citizen acquired shares of a company, not for the purpose of direct economic gain, but to air citizens' demands at the company's general meeting.[22] The rights of shareholders to make proposals and to present questions at the general meeting were recognized in the 1981 company law amendments. Prior to this there were no laws giving the explicit right to raise questions at a general meeting, and conditions for presenting a proposal to the meeting were extremely onerous. Since the 1981 amendments there has been an increase in the activities of these citizens' movement shareholders. Taking the anti-nuclear movement as one example, the shareholders of power utilities have increasingly used shareholder rights to propose changes in the articles of association concerning environmental protection and the abolition of nuclear power stations. So long as the exercise of these rights follows the rules applicable to the general meeting, it

---

20 K. KAWAKAMI, *Keiei-sha shihai no heigai to keiji seisai* [The Abuse of Management Control and Criminal Sanction], 1364 SHÔJI HÔMU 25 *et seq.* (1994).

21 The way in which *sôkaiya* are paid is a secret of each particular company. From the details revealed in judicial precedents we can see companies paying inflated prices to buy back a *sôkaiya's* shares, paying agency fees for real estate transactions, and also companies being threatened into accepting the debts or otherwise guaranteeing the obligations of *sôkaiya*.

22 *See* T. GOTÔ, *Hitokabu undô no susume* [The Progress of the One-Share Movement] (1971).

does not present a problem. However, if such exercise of rights impedes the proper exercise of rights by other shareholders, then such conduct becomes an abuse of shareholders' rights.[23]

E. The Enforcement of Shareholders' Rights

Finally, let us look at the way in which the courts are being used to enforce shareholders' rights. A good explanatory example may be the rights of minority shareholders to demand dismissal of a director, and the right of a sole shareholder to bring an action on behalf of the corporation (a derivative suit). The former functions as the most effective way for a minority shareholder to demand redress from company management for improper conduct, and the latter is an important legal measure to hold directors responsible for wrongs inflicted on the company. The derivative suit has seen a sharp increase in use in recent years.

1. The Enforcement of the Rights of Minority Shareholders: The Right to Demand the Dismissal of Directors

A shareholder who acquires and continues to possess for six months at least 3% of the issued shares of a company can ask the court to dismiss a director who has breached his duties towards the corporation or has violated the law, even if the general meeting of shareholders had refused to dismiss that director in spite of his inappropriate behavior.[24]

How many shareholders who are eligible to exercise this right are there? Although these are old figures, of the 363 companies that were listed on the Tokyo Stock Exchange in 1955, the number of shareholders who met this 3% ownership requirement was 1,157, on average three per company.[25] If we additionally consider that in most cases these shareholders were companies, and that share ownership in recent years has become even more dispersed than at the time of these figures, we can see that the possibility of a minority shareholder being able to ask the court to dismiss a director is in fact very limited. Naturally, the shareholding requirement does not require a single shareholder to satisify it alone, and hence there is always the option of acting together with other shareholders to fulfill it. But such a course requires the

23 M. YANAGA, *Hitokabu undô to kaisha-hô* [The One-Share Movement and Company Law], 1050 Jurisuto *et seq.* 109 (1994).

24 Article 257 III of the Commercial Code.

25 HÔSEI SHINGI-KAI SHÔHÔ BUKAI [Legislative Committee, Commercial Law Section], *Shiryô 1, Shôsu kabunushi-ken to tôkei* [Materials 1: Statistics Concerning Rights of Minority Shareholders, etc.], 35 SHOJI HÔMU 2 *et seq.* (1955).

difficult task of searching the register of shareholders and finding other members willing to exercise their rights jointly.

Since the 1950 amendments, which eased the shareholding requirement for applying to the courts for help from 10% of a company's paid-up capital to 3% of the issued shares, there have only been 11 court cases reported. Of these, nine cases involved small closely-held companies, of which there were two cases[26] where the demand for dismissal of a director was approved by the court. The right to dismiss directors is a basic device for shareholders to control management. Particularly in the case of the closely-held corporation, it serves an important role in protecting the company's interests from improper or illegal conduct of business by directors or majority shareholders. However, judging only from an analysis of the circumstances of the decisions to date, it seems that it is used instead primarily as a tool for winning internal struggles between directors over management authority.

To promote the use of the right to request the dismissal of a director in large companies, the shareholding requirement must be reduced so that it becomes the right of every shareholder. Although this may sound like an invitation for abuse of shareholder rights, the requirement that there must be decisive wrongdoing on the part of the director would act as a restraint on such potential abuse by individual shareholders.[27]

2. *Enforcement of the Individual Shareholder's Rights: The Derivative Action*

If a shareholder acquires and continues to possess for a minimum period of six months at least one share of a company, he or she has the right to file a liability suit on behalf of and for the benefit of the company against directors engaged in activities which were illegal or against the interests of the company and have caused damages, provided the board refuses to pursue such a claim.[28]

Since 1950, when the right of the individual shareholder to file a derivative suit was first recognized, until the 1993 amendments of the pertinent statutes of the Commercial Code, no more than 31 cases had reached the courts. In comparison with the United States this is an incredibly low number. The main reason why this system was so rarely used was the lack of economic incentives to commence litigation, due to the difficulty in obtaining the necessary information to pursue an action, and, even in the event of success, the absence of any direct benefit to the plaintiff shareholder. Accordingly, in the 1993

26 Tokyo District Court, December 28, 1953, 37 HANREI TAIMUZU 80 (1954); Tokyo High Court, May 16, 1979, 946 HANREI JIHÔ 107 (1980).

27 M. HAYAKAWA, *Torishimari-yaku no kainin* [Dismissal of Directors] 672 HANREI TAIMUZU 67 *et seq.* (1995).

28 *Cf.* Article 267 of the Commercial Code.

Commercial Code amendments, the court fee to file a derivative action was lowered from an expensive fee structure based on potential recovery to just ¥ 8,200 (about US$ 80), making the launching of an action substantially cheaper. In addition to this, the right of a successful plaintiff to claim necessary expenses for an action against the company was recognized, thereby reducing the individual burden of the shareholder bringing an action, as his expenses are shared indirectly among all the beneficiaries of such an action, the shareholders as a whole. At the time these amendments came into force, commentators predicted that derivative actions would not increase greatly, and that therefore the possibility of shareholders bringing vexatious suits would not be a serious problem. This assumption was based on a perceived lack of direct economic benefit for successful plaintiff shareholders even after the amendments.

However, in contrast to these expectations, by 1994 there were 145 cases in the courts; among these was one case involving Japan Airlines in which the astronomical figure of ¥ 1,150,000,000,000 was demanded in compensation.[29] The presence of such a large number of cases involving liability claims against the directors of publicly listed companies, and the large amounts of compensation demanded in these suits, drew particular attention. The type of shareholders who are bringing these derivative actions include company insiders, the general citizenry (including lawyers), and *sôkaiya*. In response to the application of a director in the event of a seemingly vexatious suit, the court may order that the plaintiff shareholder post security with the court. There have already been three incidents of suits being dropped because of such an order having being made.[30] Also, recently there have been an increasing number of directors of Japanese companies purchasing insurance to provide for potential liability arising from derivative actions.[31]

It can certainly be said that the recent increase in derivative actions is a result of shareholders, via the courts, properly exercising their supervisory authority over management for the deplorable affairs of the bubble economy period. However, we can also surmise that there are a number of vexatious suits among these. Furthermore, the fact that quite a number of suits have been filed in connection with internal power struggles in small closely-held companies must also be kept in mind.

---

29 This suit has since been dropped with no explanation as to why.

30 *Cf.* Tokyo High Court, December 26, 1994, 131 SHIRYÔBAN SHÔJI HÔMU 81 (*Sanai* case); Tokyo District Court, July 8, 1995, 136 SHIRYÔBAN SHÔJI HÔMU 72 (*Mitsui Bussan* case) and Nagoya District Court, June 17, 1995, 136 SHIRYÔBAN SHÔJI HÔMU 85 (*Tôkai Ginkô* case).

31 As of April 1994, there were some 400 insurance policies in force concerning directors' and senior officers' liability. *See* K. KITAGAWA, *Kabunushi daihyô soshô - torishimari-yaku no sekinin seido no genjô to kadai (ge)* [The Derivative Action and Liability Directors: The Present State and Issues (2)], 1397 SHÔJI HÔMU 32 (1995).

In Japan today we are witnessing an extraordinary phenomenon, described most appropriately by the expression "shareholder revolt". Will this phenomenon, like the bubble economy, be just a passing phantom and disappear again, or will it become the starting point for a new direction in the enforcement of shareholders' rights? It seems as if we will have to wait a little longer for the answer to this question.

Chapter Ten

Law as an Agent of Change? Governmental Efforts to Reduce Working Hours in Japan

*Daniel H. Foote**

Contents

---

* I am grateful to the Japan-U.S. Educational Commission for support of a Fulbright Research Fellowship and to the Council on Foreign Relations for the support of an International Affairs Fellowship; to the University of Tokyo Faculty of Law and the Japan Institute of Labour, for inviting me for positions as visiting professor and visiting researcher, respectively, during research on this article; and to Professor *Yasuo Suwa* and, above all, Professor *Kazuo Sugeno*. All views reflected herein are mine.

From the perspective of 1996, reduction of working hours may not seem to be an important concern for Japan. In the midst of the current prolonged recession, unemployment in Japan, while modest by international standards, is at its highest level in the postwar era,[1] and working hours are at some of their lowest levels ever.[2] Yet in the late 1980s and early 1990s, when Japan's economy was still booming, reducing working hours was the single most widely discussed topic in Japanese labor law circles. The debate spawned a new word - *jitan* (short for *rôdô jikan tanshuku*). More significantly, it produced three new pieces of legislation between 1987 and 1993: a major set of amendments to the Labor Standards Law (hereinafter LSL)[3] in 1987; the Temporary Measures Law to Promote Reduction in Working Hours[4] in 1992; and then a broad set of amendments to both those laws in 1993.[5]

As discussed below, each of the pieces of legislation reflects a somewhat different set of concerns. Yet all are linked by a single overarching theme: the conscious attempt by the government of Japan to use legislation to change business practices and social standards. Thus, it is appropriate to consider the three pieces of legislation as a linked series, aimed at the ultimate goal of reducing working hours to some appropriate level, and then to ask what success the laws have had in achieving that goal. The three laws are linked by another common element: the central role that an advisory council (*shingi-kai*), the Central Labor Standards Council (*Chûô Rôdô Kijun Shingi-kai*, hereinafter CLSC), played in their formulation and enactment.

This article begins by examining the background to the legislation and the key features of each law, together with some of the individual themes specific to each piece of legislation. The article then considers the role played by the CLSC, before closing with an overall evaluation of the success the laws have had in achieving social change.

---

1 *See:* JAPAN DIGEST, March 1, 1996, 5 (unemployment rate stood at postwar record 3.4% for third consecutive month in January 1996). The unemployment rate was 2.0% five years earlier, *see* JAPAN LAB. BULL., Vol. 30, No. 6, at 2 (June 1991) (statistics for Jan. 1991).

2 *See:* text accompanying notes and notes 178-179 *infra*.

3 *Rôdô kijun-hô*, Law No. 49 of 1947, as amended by Law No. 99 of 1987, *translated in* MINISTRY OF LABOUR, Japan, Labour Laws of Japan 1990, at 59.

4 *Rôdô jikan no tanshuku no sokushin ni kansuru rinji sochi-hô* [the full title is: Temporary Measures Law Concerning Promotion of Reduction in Working Hours], Law No. 90 of 1992 [hereinafter Temporary Measures Law].

5 Law No. 79 of 1993.

PART I: BACKGROUND AND IMPETUS FOR CHANGE

A. The Legal Framework Prior to 1987

Japan's first hours legislation was contained in the Factory Law of 1911.[6] For children[7] and women, that law established a maximum work day of 12 hours,[8] prohibited work at night, and required at least two rest days per month.[9] There were limits even to these protections. Employers were given a grace period of five years before they had to comply with any of the provisions, and 15 years before the prohibition on night work, which they regarded as the most onerous, took effect.[10] Even after the law was extended from factories with 15 or more to those with ten or more workers, it still did not cover an estimated 20% of women and minors working in private business.[11] Finally, the law contained no restrictions on working hours for adult male workers.

During the occupation following World War II, legal provisions governing labor were thoroughly revised. One of the most fundamental reforms was the enactment in 1947 of the Labor Standards Law. That law established a wide range of minimum working conditions generally consistent with international labor standards recognized by the International Labor Organization (ILO). With regard to working hours, it adopted the principle of an eight-hour work day and 48-hour work week[12] - a principle that the ILO had announced in 1919 in its very first treaty[13] - and required employers to provide workers with at least one rest day per week.[14] The law also provided six days of paid annual leave for workers who had been employed for a year or more.[15]

These provisions did not represent absolutes. In addition to exceptions for certain types of enterprises and certain positions,[16] the LSL provided a broad

6 *Kôjô-hô*, Law No. 46 of 1911.
7 The law initially applied to minors under the age of 15; it was subsequently amended to cover those under the age of 16.
8 This was later reduced to 11 hours, but with exceptions.
9 *See,* e.g., I.F. AYUSAWA, A History of Labor in Modern Japan 106-11, 182-93 (1966); S. GARON, The State and Labor in Modern Japan 18-38 (1987).
10 *See* GARON, *supra* note 9, at 29.
11 *See id.* at 202.
12 Article 32 of the LSL (revised in 1987).
13 *See* Constitution of the International Labor Organization, Article 427, 2 TIAS 241, 253-54 (1919).
14 Article 35(1) of the LSL.
15 *Id.* Article 39(1) (1947) (amended to a minimum of ten days in 1987). This provision applies to workers who have reported for work on at least 80% of the total working days. Under Article 39(2), employees who have worked for longer periods are entitled to one additional day of paid leave for each additional year of continuous service, up to a maximum of 20 days.
16 *Id.* Article 40 (exceptions to working hours provisions permitted for certain types of enterprises, in accordance with standards to be set by ordinance), Article 41

exception permitting employers to utilize overtime and work on rest days.[17] For adult men, apart from those working in mines and other dangerous jobs,[18] there were no limits on the amount of overtime that could be assigned.

The law did establish certain additional requirements for overtime: pursuant to Article 36, before assigning overtime, the employer must enter a written agreement authorizing such work, with a representative of a majority of the workers,[19] and must file that "Article 36 agreement" with the Labor Standards Inspection Office.[20] In addition, the LSL required employers to pay an overtime premium equal to at least 25% of normal wages (i.e., time-and-a-quarter pay).[21]

In a separate chapter, the LSL established stricter limits on working hours for minors and women.[22] When the so-called Equal Employment Opportunity Law (EEOL) was enacted in 1985,[23] the women's protective provisions were

---

(exceptions to both working hours and rest day provisions for agriculture, fishing, and similar enterprises and for those in supervisory or managerial positions and certain other types of positions).

17 *Id.* Article 36.

18 For those positions, legally permitted overtime was limited to two hours per day, *see id.*

19 Japan does not follow the principle of exclusive representation, and recognizes minority unions. *See*, generally, K. SUGENO, Japanese Labor Law 24 (L. Kanowitz, trans. 1992). Where a majority union exists, the law requires the employer to enter an Article 36 agreement with that union; where no such union exists, it simply requires the agreement to be entered with "a representative of a majority of the workers."

20 *See* Article 36 of the LSL. For a more detailed description of Article 36 agreements, *see* SUGENO, *supra* note 19, at 234-38.

21 Article 37 of the LSL. The same 25% premium applied both to overtime on regular work days and to work on rest days.

When the LSL was being drafted in 1946, consideration reportedly was given to setting the premium at 50%, on the view that the value represented by overtime should be paid out in wages, rather than increase the company's profits, and that businesses even then could afford to pay a premium of 50%. In view of the economic devastation at that time, however, "it was thought that, giving consideration to business, 25% after all was appropriate as the minimum standard," K. KOBAYASHI, *Jikan-gai rôdô sakugen ni mukete* [Toward Reducing Overtime Work], 1854 RÔDÔ HÔGAKU KENKYÛ KAIHÔ 38, 53-54 (1991) (quoting *Hirosaku Teramoto*, head of Ministry of Labor's Labor Standards Inspection Section at the time of the LSL's enactment).

22 Until 1985, women, regardless of occupation, were strictly limited to a maximum of two hours of overtime per day, six hours per week, and 150 hours per year; no work could be assigned on rest days. LSL ch. VI (subsequently revised pursuant to the Equal Employment Opportunity Law and currently codified as ch. VI and VI-2).

23 That law, Law No. 45 of 1985, was not a separate new law, but rather a set of amendments to existing laws, most notably the LSL and the Law Respecting the Improvement of the Welfare of Women Workers, Law No. 113 of July 1, 1972 (renamed in 1985 as the Law Respecting the Improvement of the Welfare of Women Workers, including the Guarantee of Equal Opportunity and Treatment between Men and Women in Employment [*Koyô no bunya ni okeru danjo no kintô*

revised (but not eliminated).[24] Otherwise, the basic provisions on working hours in the LSL remained unchanged until 1987, forty years after they were first adopted.

This of course does not mean actual working hours went unchanged. Total annual working hours for full-time workers peaked in 1960 at 2,426 hours.[25] During the period of high economic growth that followed, overall working hours declined rather steadily, as industry increased hiring[26] and achieved consistent gains in productivity.[27] Between 1960 and 1973, overall annual working hours fell by nearly 250 hours, to 2,184.[28] During the same period, wages increased steadily.[29]

Then the pattern changed. Following the first Oil Shock in late 1973, Japan entered a period of low growth.[30] Wages continued to increase.[31] When coupled with the rising value of the yen, by the late 1980s these increases placed average Japanese wages at among the highest in the world, at least when measured on the basis of official exchange rates.[32] In sharp contrast, the pattern of slow but steady declines in working hours came to an end. In the first two full years after the Oil Shock, working hours dropped substantially, bottoming out at 2,064 hours in 1975. The following year, they rebounded to nearly 2,100

---

na kikai oyobi taigû no kakuho tô joshi rôdô-sha no fukushi no zôshin ni kansuru hôritsu], *translated in* MINISTRY OF LABOUR, *supra* note 3, at 190).

24 The two-hour-per-day limit was dropped, and the overtime limitations were abolished entirely for women in certain specified managerial and professional positions; but otherwise the limits remained largely unchanged. *See,* e.g., Y. SUWA, The Equal Employment Opportunity Law, JAPAN LAB. BULL., Vol. 24, No. 7 (July 1985); A. WATANABE, Ordinance and Guidelines for Implementing the Equal Employment Opportunity Law, JAPAN LAB. BULL., Vol. 25, No. 4 (April 1986).

25 *See: Rôdô jikan no shiori* [A Guide to Working Hours] 27 (*Rôdô-shô Rôdô Kijun-kyoku* [Ministry of Labor, Labor Standards Bureau], ed. 1994).

26 *See,* e.g., JAPAN INSTITUTE OF LABOUR, Labour-Management Relations in Japan 11 (1991) [hereinafter JIL].

27 *See,* e.g., *id.* at 23-24, and statistics summarized therein.

28 *See* INT'L LAB. ORG., Year Book of Labour Statistics 1978, at 325 (table 11); SUGENO, *supra* note 19, at 207.

29 Wage gains consistently outpaced inflation by substantial amounts, and at times significantly exceeded productivity gains, *see* JIL, *supra* note 26, at 23-24; RÔDÔ-SHÔ [Ministry of Labor (Japan), hereinafter MOL], *Rôdô jikan tanshuku suishin keikaku* [Plan to Promote Reduction in Working Hours] 35 (1988).

30 *See,* e.g., JIL, *supra* note 26, at 5.

31 Wage increases, although steady, were at a rather modest pace, apart from a huge increase of over 30% in 1974, when inflation exceeded 20%, *see id.* at 23-24.

32 Given higher living costs in Japan, however, when measured by buying power average Japanese wages do not look quite so high. *See,* e.g., NIHON KEIEISHA DANTAI RENMEI (NIKKEIREN), RÔDÔ MONDAI KENKYÛ IINKAI [Japan Federation of Employers' Organizations (*Nikkeiren*), Study Committee on Labor Issues], *Rôdô mondai kenkyû iinkai hôkoku: Shin no senshin-koku e no dappi wo mezashite* [Report of the Study Committee on Labor Issues: Seeking a Breakthrough to Becoming a True Advanced Nation] 32-38 (1988) [hereinafter NIKKEIREN].

hours; and for more than a decade thereafter, they continued to hover between 2,094 and 2,116 - well below what they had been until 1973, but still far above average working hours in the United States and Europe.[33]

This, then, was the situation in the early 1980s, when the debate over working hours began to gain steam.

B. Impetus for Change

In considering the impetus for change, one might examine at least three key sets of actors: business, labor, and the government. In addition, it is important to consider the shifting stances of each group over time.

1. Early 1980s

a. Business

As of the early 1980s, business had no desire to change the applicable legal standards. The stabilization of working hours discussed above resulted in part from a deliberate strategy by management to adapt to the tighter economy by "slimming down"[34] their core work force. Business did so largely by deferring new hiring and otherwise reducing the number of regular employees,[35] and then meeting additional labor requirements both by assigning more overtime to those employees[36] and hiring part-time workers.[37] Given these circumstances,

---

33 *See,* e.g., T. MURAKI, *Kaisetsu: Rôdô jikan no tanshuku no sokushin ni kansuru rinji sochi-hô oyobi jikan-gai rôdô kyôtei no meyasu jikan ni tsuite* [Commentary: Regarding the Temporary Measures Law to Promote Reduction in Working Hours and the Hours Guidelines for Agreements on Overtime Work], 1477 RÔDÔ KEIZAI HANREI SOKUHÔ 50, 53 (1992) (as of 1990, manufacturing workers worked 2,124 hours in Japan, 1,953 in England, 1,948 in the U.S., 1,683 in France, and 1,598 in Germany).

34 The term *surimu-ka* in Japanese, taken directly from the English "slim," appears frequently in literature about personnel management. *See,* e.g., PÂTO TAIMU RÔDÔ TAISAKU KENTÔ CHÎMU [Team Considering Ways of Dealing with Part-Time Labor], *Kongo no pâto taimu rôdô taisaku no arikata ni tsuite* [Regarding the Proper Handling of Part-Time Labor in the Future] 5 (1988).

35 *See,* e.g., SUGENO, *supra* note 19, at 33-34.

36 *See,* e.g., N. SUZUKI, *Rôdô jikan no genjô to mondaiten ni tsuite* [Regarding the Current Status of and Issues Concerning Working Hours], 828 CHÛÔ RÔDÔ JIHÔ 10, 11-12 (June 1991).

37 As one study concluded in 1982, "Part-time workers began as a peripheral work force. Yet this [part-time] labor market, which has by now become too large to be labeled 'peripheral,' now surrounds the core workers . . . and has begun to encroach on their work," M. TSUDA, *Pâto taimu rôdô o kangaeru shiten* [Perspectives for Considering Part-Time Labor], 284 NIHON RÔDÔ KYÔKAI ZASSHI [Journal of the Japan Institute of Labour] 1 (1982).

business naturally opposed any change in the minimum legal standards governing working hours.

b. Labor

Business's stance is hardly surprising. Yet what of labor? After all, the LSL established only minimum standards. Unions and individual workers were free to negotiate for stronger protection. Given the legal requirement for an Article 36 agreement before business could assign overtime, unions appear to have been granted a natural tool for insisting on limits on overtime or for a higher overtime premium than 25%. Thus, an outside observer might assume that the primary push for a reduction in working hours came from labor, and especially from the large unions.

That was not the case. As of the early 1980s, reducing working hours was not a major issue for most unions. Indeed, the unions rarely held out for greater benefits as a condition for accepting Article 36 agreements,[38] and labor was not heavily involved in the initial push for lower hours.

Several interrelated factors help explain labor's reluctance to press the hours issue. First, job security has long been a critical issue for unions in Japan. Presumably, reducing working hours and limiting use of part-time employees would have resulted in more jobs for full-time employees. Yet this was not a key concern for the existing union members, since membership in most Japanese unions is reserved for so-called "regular employees,"[39] who already

---

38 According to MOL statistics, even as of 1990, over 82% of workplaces provided only the statutorily required minimum overtime premium of 25%, and another 10% either did not specify the overtime premium or paid *less* than the statutorily required rate, *see* RÔDÔ-SHÔ, RÔDÔ KIJUN-KYOKU, CHINGIN JIKAN-BU, RÔDÔ JIKAN-KA [MOL, Labor Standards Bureau, Wages and Hours Division, Working Hours Section], *Rôdô jikan sôgô jittai chôsa kekka* [Results of Comprehensive Survey of Actual Conditions for Working Hours] 20 (1991) (statistics for 1990).

39 The expression "regular employees" (*sei-shain*) is a term of art in Japan, with implications for union membership, salary structure, work assignments, job security, and many other aspects of the employment relationship. Nonetheless, the expression does not appear in any of the major labor statutes and is not defined precisely. In essence, it includes full-time employees, both white- and blue-collar, hired under contracts without a fixed term, with the expectation that the employee will remain in the enterprise on a long-term basis and advance in accordance with a seniority-based promotion system, *see,* e.g., K. HOBARA, New Forms and Aspects of Atypical Employment Relations in Japan, *in:* National Report (Japan), IX World Congress of The International Society for Labor Law and Social Science 1 (Sept. 1985).

Recently some unions have begun including part-time employees, but traditionally part-timers have been excluded from union membership. *See,* e.g., Y. SUWA, Why Are Part-Time Workers Not Well Organized?, JAPAN LAB. BULL., Vol. 28, No. 2, at 5 (Feb. 1989).

had full-time jobs. In fact, in some respects the retrenchment served the interests of union members by enhancing their job security. In the event of a future turndown in economic activity, cutting back overtime and reducing the part-time work force would serve as buffers protecting them from layoffs.

Overtime work also represented a bread-and-butter issue for workers. Even with an overtime premium of only 25%, overtime wages constituted an important part of the family budget for many workers. A 1990 Ministry of Labor survey found that over 80% of workers were using overtime pay for "everyday living expenses,"[40] and studies historically have found that a substantial percentage of workers prefer overtime pay to reduced hours.[41] Even as of late 1991, a knowledgeable observer commented that union leaders did not feel they could press for limits on overtime; they were convinced that, if they did so, they would be voted out of office at the next union elections.[42] Indeed, until recently, while labor may have perfunctorily listed reducing working hours as one of its goals, "there was a sense among union leaders that it was taboo for them to refer to the working hours issue, out of a view that placing reduction in working hours at the forefront might risk slighting their struggle for higher wages."[43]

On top of all of these factors, Japanese unions have faced a fundamental structural weakness that limits their ability to press effectively for shorter

40 *See: Rôdô jikan no shiori*, *supra* note 25, at 130.

41 Every two years, *Rengô*, the Japanese Trade Union Confederation, conducts a survey of union members that includes this issue. In 1993, for the first time ever, more workers expressed a preference for more free time, even if it meant a drop in pay, *see* 1303 Rôdô Hôritsu Junpô 109 (1993) (news summary). Given this circumstance, it is not surprising that a 1990 MOL study found 60% of unions surveyed regarded loss of income as a significant barrier to reducing overtime hours, *see: Rôdô jikan no shiori*, *supra* note 25, at 130. *See also,* e.g., Reduced working hours: the long and short of it, Japan Times Weekly Overseas Edition, May 27, 1989, at 8 (describing surveys of workers - both union and non-union - conducted by Prime Minister's Office: 1985 survey found that over 40% of workers in their 40s preferred working more to taking more holidays; by 1988, this figure had fallen to 30.5%, and only 23.3% of workers in their 30s expressed this view); 1277 Rôdô Hôritsu Junpô 69 (1991) (news summary: in a similar survey conducted by the Prime Minister's Office in 1991, 41.3% of all workers expressed a preference for shorter hours over more pay; only 26.3% expressed the opposite preference).

42 Comments of Professor *Yasuo Suwa*, at *Rôdô Hanrei Kenkyû-kai* [Study Group on Labor Precedents], University of Tokyo, Nov. 21, 1991.

43 K. Ashimura, *Saikin no rôdô jôsei* [Recent Labor Conditions], 782 Chûô Rôdô Jihô 2, 6 (1988). Even though hours began to take on more prominence by the late 1980s, *see,* e.g., H. Shimada, Shorter Working Hours, Japan Lab. Bull., Vol. 28, No. 3, at 5 (March 1989), wages continued to remain the paramount concern for most unions.

working hours. This lies in the well-known phenomenon of "enterprise unions" - unions organized at individual enterprises and typically embracing the full range of non-managerial full-time regular employees at that enterprise, as opposed to trade unions linking workers in similar fields across enterprises.[44] The prevalence of enterprise unions in Japan has left unions weak when it comes to bargaining for benefits that might affect an enterprise's competitive position.[45] For enterprise unions, unilaterally taking a hard-line stance on benefits or working conditions might result in short-term gains for its members; but, by weakening the enterprise vis-à-vis its competitors, it could leave those gains - and even job security itself - vulnerable in the long run.

In the area of wages, this structural weakness of the enterprise union system has been ameliorated through the so-called *Shuntô* - the Spring Labor Offensive - in which enterprise unions have collaborated in order to present a relatively united front.[46] In the early 1980s, however, discussions of working hours and other working conditions were deliberately segregated from the spring bargaining over wages.[47] Such non-wage issues were reserved for discussion in the fall of each year, when no unified front existed.[48]

One labor group that has been active in the struggle for shorter hours summed up the dilemmas facing enterprise unions in the following way:

> Some view [the failure to win reduced working hours] as the responsibility of the moderate unions that have followed the philosophy of labor-management cooperation. Yet even [the more progressive] unions that . . . style themselves as democratic unions engaged in the class struggle face difficulties. The reality is that even those unions hesitate to undertake a true fight for reduced working hours. As reasons, those unions say, "If we insist on refusing overtime, other companies will take the work and our company will slip," and "Overtime wages would fall, so our union members wouldn't go along with the effort."[49]

Despite this pessimistic appraisal, the group, the Tokyo Joint Struggle Council for Saturday Leave and Reduced Working Hours, which was formed in 1981,

---

44 *See*, generally, e.g., T. SHIRAI, A Theory of Enterprise Unionism, *in:* Contemporary Industrial Relations in Japan 117 (T. Shirai, ed. 1983).

45 The system has been credited, however, with facilitating cooperation between management and labor, including consultation on major structural issues and future plans, *see id.* at 120-21.

46 *See,* e.g., M. NITTA, Where Will Shunto Go?, JAPAN LAB. BULL., Vol. 29, No. 12, at 4 (Dec. 1990), and sources cited therein.

47 This tendency has even been reflected in one of the popular translations for the term *shuntô*. Although that term literally means simply "spring struggle" or "spring offensive," it has widely been referred to as the "Spring Wage Offensive" - which until very recently was an accurate characterization.

48 *See: Rôdô jikan no shiori*, *supra* note 25, at 141.

49 TÔKYÔ DOKYÛ - JITAN KYÔTÔ KAIGI [Tokyo Joint Struggle Council for Saturday Leave and Reduced Working Hours], *Yôroppa chôsadan hôkoku, Doyôbi wa kazoku sorotte sora no shita* [Report of the Europe Study Mission, Saturdays with the Family Together Under the Sky] 9 (1987) [hereinafter JOINT STRUGGLE COUNCIL].

insisted that organized labor should campaign for reduced hours. As this reflects, some elements of labor had begun to push for shorter hours by the early 1980s.[50] Many individual workers undoubtedly shared the concerns over working hours. Yet, up through the mid-1980s, this issue was not high on the agenda for labor as a whole.[51]

Thus, at least as of the early 1980s, neither business nor labor was truly pushing the working hours issue. Later, in looking back over developments in the working hours field, one knowledgeable observer commented:

> To date, there has been a feeling of emptiness to the debate over working hours. Both management and labor extemporized long and hard over the necessity for reducing hours, yet employers did not try in any way to reduce work, and in the bottom of their hearts workers were relying on overtime work. . . . One is even left with the feeling that, in truth, nobody really was pushing for a reduction in working hours.[52]

c. Government

A third key actor in the process was the government. In considering the government's stance, it is useful to examine the courts, the legislature, and the administrative branch (especially the Ministry of Labor) separately.

---

50 Notably, the moderate unions that raised the hours issue faced criticism from the more progressive unions for selling out the labor cause by providing management with a potential excuse for rejecting wage demands. *See id.* at 18. In a report published in 1987, after the working hours issue had come into vogue in Japan, one such moderate labor group observed:

> In Japan rightist labor unions have placed emphasis on employment and the movement to reduce working hours. On the other hand, most of the leftist unions in Japan, which stress the struggle over social issues, have continued to place emphasis on wage policy and have criticized the rightist unions as not fighting for wage increases.

Id. at 18-19. That report took rather obvious pleasure in recounting that in Germany the situation had been just the opposite, with the leftist unions, "which stress the struggle for social issues," pushing for a reduction in working hours in order to reduce unemployment, *id.* at 17-19.

51 Notably, even the Joint Struggle Council held little hope that labor alone could achieve much success. As alternatives, it noted two other possible approaches: (1) formal governmental policies, including amendment of relevant legislation and effective utilization of administrative guidance, *id.* at 76, and (2) bringing "international pressure" to bear, through the medium of "determinations by an advisory council," *id.* at 77. As discussed below, these two elements proved especially important in the push for shorter hours.

52 K. YAMAGUCHI, *Rôdô kijun-hô minaoshi no ronten* [The Debate over Reexamination of the Labor Standards Law], 998 JURISUTO 43, 48 (1992).

aa. The Courts

The stance of the courts can be summed up very briefly, for the courts played virtually no role in the push for shorter hours. As discussed below,[53] one of the first judicial decisions of note in this context came in 1991, when the debate over working hours was at its peak. Even then, the Supreme Court upheld Hitachi Manufacturing Company's discharge of a worker for refusing overtime.

bb. The Legislature

As of the early 1980s, reduction of working hours was not a major issue for the Diet and politicians. This is not surprising. The then-ruling Liberal Democratic Party (LDP) historically has derived much of its support from business, which opposed any change in the legal standards. Even assuming that the LDP had begun to regard labor as another important constituency,[54] there would have been little reason for it to push this issue, given labor's passivity toward it. The same factor helps explain why the Japan Socialist Party, which historically has been closely linked with labor, did not strongly press this concern.

cc. The Administrative Branch

This leaves the administrative branch. In fact, the bureaucracy, and in particular the Ministry of Labor (*Rôdô-shô*, hereinafter MOL), was the most important initial player in the drive for lower working hours. One important reason for this support appears to have been concern over Japan's international standing. A second factor was the desire to maintain and expand employment levels. A third was genuine concern over the lives and welfare of workers.

As early as 1978, MOL recognized that the long downward trend in working hours had come to an end and identified working hours as an area of concern. In 1979, the Cabinet (with input from MOL) adopted, as resolutions, a seven-year economic plan and an employment measures plan, both of which called for reducing working hours as a means for maintaining and expanding employment opportunities and achieving, in what was to become a common phrase in later years, full and meaningful (*jûjitsu shita*) working lives with *yutori* (a broad term conveying the notions of both free time and extra space, akin to the phrase "quality of life"). Following up on these resolutions, in late 1980, MOL, with the approval of the CLSC, issued its first plan for reducing working hours, a

---

53 *See* text accompanying note and note 189 *infra*.

54 *See,* e.g., I. KUME, Changing relations among the government, labor, and business in Japan after the oil crisis, Int'l Org., Vol. 42, No. 4, at 659 (1988).

five-year plan which set the goal of reducing average annual hours to 2,000 by 1985.[55]

MOL sought to achieve that target through administrative guidance (*gyôsei shidô*). The main objectives were a shift to a five-day work week, rather than the six-day work week expressly permitted by the LSL (and, as of 1980, still followed by nearly 90% of Japanese enterprises[56]), and reductions in overtime. MOL had one major tool at its disposal: the requirement that businesses register Article 36 agreements with the Labor Standards Inspection Office before assigning overtime. By refusing to register improperly prepared Article 36 agreements and by urging, through a 1982 notification issued by the Minister of Labor,[57] the parties to specify goals for the maximum number of overtime hours in those agreements, MOL sought to reduce overtime and, consequently, total working hours.

None of MOL's steps was mandatory, however; and the efforts did not bear much fruit.[58] In 1985, MOL tried again. It announced a second five-year plan. As with its predecessor, this plan set a goal of 2,000 hours, again to be achieved through administrative guidance, this time just pushing the target date back to 1990.[59]

At least as early as 1982, however, MOL had become convinced of the need for legislative action, in addition to administrative guidance, in order to reduce working hours. That year it asked the Labor Standards Law Study Group (a group composed of labor law scholars and other experts on labor matters,

---

55 *See: Rôdô jikan no shiori*, *supra* note 25, at 17; N. HATAKENAKA, *Rôdô-shô no jitan suishin keikaku no naiyô* [The Contents of the Ministry of Labor's Plan to Promote Reduction in Working Hours], 1706 RÔDÔ HÔGAKU KENKYÛ KAIHÔ 1, 2 (1988).

56 *See: Rôdô jikan no shiori*, *supra* note 25, at 36, tables II-2 and II-3 (as of 1980, 88.3% of Japanese businesses, employing 71.4% of workers, granted only one rest day per week).

57 MOL Notification No. 69 of 1982, cited at SUGENO, *supra* note 19, at 236.

58 The percentage of companies granting two-day weekends at least once or twice a month gradually rose, but even at the end of the five-year plan, only 3% of Japanese companies (albeit primarily large companies, which together accounted for over one-quarter of all workers) had totally moved to a five-day work week, and well over half the companies still granted only one day off per week. *See: Rôdô jikan no shiori*, *supra* note 25, at 36. Moreover, it is debatable how much of the increase should be attributed to MOL activities. The greatest increase came among major companies, for which competition to attract promising new recruits has long been intense, and the five-day work week had become an important factor for many potential recruits. *See,* e.g., *id.* at 35-37.

As to MOL's second target, overtime, employers appear to have begun exercising greater care in preparing Article 36 agreements. Yet that did not translate into an actual reduction in overtime hours. In fact, during the five-year plan, average annual overtime hours rose, from 161 hours in 1980 to 179 in 1985. Even total annual hours increased, albeit only slightly, from 2,104 to 2,112, but still a far cry from the target of 2,000. *See id.* at 28.

59 *See* HATAKENAKA, *supra* note 55, at 2.

which was originally established in 1969 as a body for personal consultation by the Minister of Labor[60]) to consider the need for revisions to the LSL.[61] Ultimately, that study group's final report, which it submitted to the Minister of Labor in December 1985,[62] laid the groundwork for the first package of legislation.

Through these and related efforts, MOL bureaucrats provided the primary impetus for reform in the early 1980s.

2. *Mid-1980s*

Before the Diet acted in 1987, various developments influenced the stances of many of the key players. One set of developments related to Japan's international image. In 1985, Japan's trade surplus set a new record,[63] resulting in widespread international criticism of Japan. In addition to the by-then standard charges of unfair formal and invisible trade barriers, this criticism included a rather new theme: arguments, later formalized in the so-called Structural Impediments Initiative talks, focusing on fundamental differences in the structures of the economy and society in the United States and Japan. One of these contentions focused on the heavy export orientation of Japanese manufacturers and argued that, as a key step to reducing the trade imbalance, the Japanese government should take the lead in fostering a shift to a domestic demand-led economy.[64]

In the face of this type of criticism, and with Japan scheduled to host the so-called Tokyo Summit of the leaders of the seven major industrialized nations in 1986, Prime Minister *Yasuhiro Nakasone* established the Study Commission on Economic Structure for International Cooperation (*Kokusai Kyôchô No Tame No Keizai Kôzô Kenkyû-kai*), a special study group chaired by former Bank of Japan Governor *Haruo Maekawa*. In April 1986 that commission issued a report (the so-called Maekawa Report), in which it called for a reorientation of the Japanese economy from exports to domestic demand.[65] Early the following month, the government, in a Cabinet resolution, adopted the Maekawa Report's

60 *See: Rôdô jikan no shiori*, *supra* note 25, at 58.
61 *See,* e.g., K. SUGENO, Final Step Toward Revision of the Law Regulating Hours of Work, JAPAN LAB. BULL., Vol. 26, No. 4, at 5 (April 1987).
62 *See* K. SUGENO, Another Step Toward Revision of the Law Regulating Hours of Work, JAPAN LAB. BULL., Vol. 25, No. 3, at 5 (March 1986).
63 *See,* e.g., INT'L MONETARY FUND, Int'l Fin. Stat's, Vol. 40, No. 11, at 296 (Nov. 1987).
64 *See,* e.g., H. SHIMADA, Structural Distortions of the Japanese Economy and SII: Labor's Perspective, JAPAN LAB. BULL., Vol. 29, No. 5, at 4 (May 1990).
65 *See,* e.g., SUGENO, *supra* note 19, at 210-13.

proposals as official policy.[66] As one step toward attaining this reorientation, the resolution expressly included "the realization at an early stage of a five-day work week and annual overall working hours similar to those in the advanced industrial nations of Europe and America."[67] (A second Maekawa Commission Report, in 1987, first formally announced the goal of 1,800 hours.[68]) In this way, reducing working hours was suddenly elevated to a topic with significance for Japan's international relations. It also became a topic of considerable concern to politicians - because of both the international implications and the growing desire to foster a domestic-demand driven economy.

A second major development came on the economic front, as the value of the yen began to soar. The exchange rate against the dollar rose from ¥250 per dollar in May 1985 to ¥185 in July 1986.[69] In retrospect, Japanese industries successfully adapted to this rise, which also helped fuel a wave of investment in the United States and other foreign countries. On the domestic front in 1986, however, there were widespread fears, particularly in the export-oriented manufacturing sector, that the soaring yen would undermine international competitiveness, thereby forcing declines in production and, concomitantly, in employment levels. These concerns strengthened management support for measures to increase domestic demand.[70] Presumably, they also made business more receptive to the calls for reducing working hours.

For these reasons, as of the mid-1980s, both business and the politicians had become more willing to consider calls for reducing working hours, and moderate labor unions increasingly had begun to join in the push.

3. *Late 1980s*

In the late 1980s, a further set of developments produced nearly contemporaneous pressures for change from both labor and business. Both related to the booming economy.

On the labor side, perceptions were growing that, while businesses had overtaken the West, the workers themselves were not seeing enough of the fruits of that success. One major complaint focused on the heavy workload and lack of leisure time. This complaint was symbolized, and to a large extent crystallized, by the concept of *karôshi* - death from overwork. Beginning in 1988, the National Defense Counsel for Victims of Karôshi, an advocacy group

---

66 *See id.* at 211-13.

67 *See id.*

68 *See,* e.g., *Rôdô jikan no shiori*, *supra* note 25, at 18.

69 *See* INT'L MONETARY FUND, Int'l Fin. Stat's, Vol. 38, No. 12, at 277 (Dec. 1985) (exchange rate of ¥250.07 = $ 1 in May 1985); *id.*, Vol. 39, No. 9, at 291 (Sept. 1986) (¥185.73 = $ 1 in July 1986).

70 *See* SUGENO, *supra* note 19, at 211.

spearheaded by lawyers,[71] had undertaken an attack on *karôshi*. The National Defense Counsel was soon joined by leagues named "The Families of Karôshi Victims" in Tokyo and other locations.[72] These groups fought on both the legal and political fronts; and, in an attempt to bring public pressure to bear, they undertook extensive activities, both within Japan and abroad, aimed at publicizing the circumstances of *karôshi* and overwork in Japan.[73] Those efforts resonated with Japanese workers; and they helped to strengthen the view that not only was it neither unfair nor selfish for workers to insist on more reasonable hours, but it was instead unfair - and even potentially life-threatening - for employers to keep demanding such long hours.[74] Organized labor began to pick up the call, and by the late 1980s and early 1990s, labor increasingly began to include working hours as a bargaining topic during the spring offensive.

A second and perhaps even more important factor related to the businesses' own competitive situation during the boom years. Faced with increased demand, many businesses sought to expand. Yet employment was running at virtually full capacity, and the number of job openings still vastly exceeded the number of job seekers.[75] On first blush, those conditions might have seemed ready-made to increase the load on existing employees. Yet, given the intense labor shortage, workers were in a strong position to resist any such demands. In fact, so many workers refused to work in less desirable positions that a widely repeated refrain of business was that it was virtually impossible to find workers for the so-called Three K industries (standing for *kiken*, *kitanai*, and *kitsui*, which translate rather closely into English as the Three D's of "dangerous, dirty, or demanding").[76] One business response was to expand the

---

71 *See,* e.g., C. OKAMURA & H. KAWAHITO, *Preface*, *in*: NATIONAL DEFENSE COUNSEL FOR VICTIMS OF KARÔSHI, Karôshi: When the "Corporate Warrior" Dies [hereinafter "CORPORATE WARRIOR"] iii, iv (1990).

72 *See* H. KAWAHITO, Karôshi and Its Background: From the "Karôshi Hotline" Program, *in*: "Corporate Warrior", *supra* note 71, at 4, 13.

73 *See,* e.g., "Corporate Warrior," *supra* note 71; ÔSAKA KARÔSHI MONDAI RENRAKU-KAI, *Karôshi 110-ban* [Dial 911 for Karôshi] (1989). Notably, many of the examples cited by the league involved staggering amounts of overtime, much of it unpaid and unreported.

74 *See,* e.g., K. HOBARA, *Rôdô jikan-sei no arikata* [The Proper System for Working Hours], 1000 JURISUTO 260, 261 (1992) (citing survey finding that 48% of Japanese workers were concerned about the possibility of *karoshi*).

75 *See* text accompanying notes 77-78 *infra*.

76 *See,* e.g., D. FOOTE, Japan's "Foreign Workers" Policy: A View from the United States, 7 GEORGETOWN IMMIG. L.J. 707, 726 (1993). In a similar vein, a survey conducted in 1992 found that the longer the working time, the more difficulty employers had in attracting new workers, *see* 1293 RÔDÔ HÔRITSU JUNPÔ 77 (1992) (news summary); and another survey conducted in late 1992, of college students in the Tokyo area, found that over 91% regarded good vacation benefits as an

pool of workers to include those who were in less position to be picky, including foreign workers. Another was to make the positions more attractive to the existing pool of workers. And one way of doing this was to reduce working hours.

Thus, by the late 1980s, virtually all of the key players agreed on the importance of reducing working hours (although not on the specifics of how to achieve reductions).

4. *The 1990s*

Japan's employment boom peaked in early 1991, when there were 147 job openings for every 100 job seekers, and continued into 1992.[77] Then the employment situation shifted dramatically. In October 1992, the number of people seeking jobs exceeded the number of openings for the first time in nearly five years. Just one year later, in October 1993, there were only 67 openings for every 100 job seekers,[78] and the employment market continued to erode thereafter.

Not surprisingly, these developments yet again altered views. In the early 1990s, the major players continued to regard reducing working hours as a major concern. As late as early 1992, *Nikkeiren* (the Japan Federation of Employers' Associations) commented: "In this age when people are seeking leisure and prosperity, reducing working hours is the most important matter for labor and management."[79] By later that very same year, though, business had begun to urge a go-slow approach on the hours issue; in November 1992, a *Nikkeiren* subcommittee counseled caution, because "reducing hours would lead to an increase in costs, which would have a major impact on finances and management during this period when further worsening of the economic and management circumstances is foreseen."[80] Since then, that sentiment has intensified, and not just in business circles. In the period since enactment of the 1993 amendments discussed below, the hours issue has ceased to be a major concern for the legislature or even for labor - although MOL has continued to promote a broad range of activities aimed at reducing hours.

---

important factor in their job decisions - making this the most often cited factor, even exceeding pay levels, *see* 1306 RÔDÔ HÔRITSU JUNPÔ 69 (news summary).

77 *See* FOOTE, *supra* note 76, at 726, and sources cited therein.

78 *See* JAPAN LAB. BULL., Vol. 33, No. 2, at 2 (Feb. 1994).

79 *See* S. NISHITANI, *Rôdô jikan rippô no rinen to seisaku* [The Ideals and Policies of Legislation on Working Hours], 1305 RÔDÔ HÔRITSU JUNPÔ 6, 14 (1993).

80 NIKKEIREN RÔDÔ KIJUN-HÔ KENTÔ SHÔIIN-KAI [Nikkeiren Subcommittee for Consideration of the Labor Standards Law], *Rôdô kijun-hô no rôdô jikan kankei kitei no minaoshi ni kansuru iken* [Opinion Concerning Reevaluation of the Provisions Related to Working Hours of the Labor Standards Law] 1 (Nov. 9, 1992) [hereinafter NIKKEIREN SUBCOMMITTEE].

PART II: NEW LEGISLATION

With the above background, we can turn to the three key pieces of legislation enacted in the drive to reduce hours.

A. 1987 Amendments to the Labor Standards Law

1. *Amendment Process*

As noted above, in 1982 MOL asked the Labor Standards Law Study Group to consider revising the LSL. The study group collected extensive information and held a series of hearings with representatives of labor and management. It considered various approaches, including modifying the standard 48-hour work week, the number of days of paid annual leave, and the amount of the overtime premium, as well as possible adoption of provisions authorizing flextime and other flexible scheduling alternatives.[81]

At those hearings, labor insisted that it was absolutely essential to amend the LSL to specify a five-day, 40-hour work week.[82] Labor also argued for increases in the number of days of annual leave and in the overtime premium (to 50% for overtime on regular working days and to 100% - double-time - for work on rest days), but opposed the flexible scheduling provisions on the ground that they would simply provide management with another means of exploiting the work force.[83]

Not surprisingly, management took precisely the opposite positions. Management supported the flexibility measures, arguing that employers needed greater flexibility in scheduling work.[84] Management strongly opposed the other revisions, though, asserting that they would impose excessive costs on employers and that small and medium-sized enterprises, in particular, could not survive.

81 *See* SUGENO, *supra* note 62.

82 At the time, organized labor was split among four national centers. The divisions between the centers frequently were characterized by rather deep ideological (and personal) opposition, but all four agreed on the need for a five-day, 40-hour standard. *See id.* The four national centers subsequently unified, in a series of steps culminating in November 1989 with the formation of *Rengô*, the Japanese Trade Union Confederation, which covers approximately 80 affiliated labor organizations and eight million workers, *see* JIL, *supra* note 26, at 17-20.

83 *See* SUGENO, *supra* note 61.

84 *See id.* The existing LSL provisions spoke solely in terms of a six-day 48-hour week and did not permit hours averaging over longer periods.

An interim report recommending a shift to a 44-hour standard week[85] met with strong opposition from both management and labor, and the study group went back to work. In December 1985, it presented the Minister with its final report. The report recommended reducing the maximum standard work week from 48 to 45 hours, raising from six to ten the number of days of annual paid leave for an employee with one year of service, raising the overtime premium to 50% for work on rest days (but not increasing the 25% premium for overtime work on normal working days), and authorizing flexible scheduling.[86]

The final report did little to ease the controversy. Despite continued divisions between business and labor, in March 1986 the Minister sent the final report to the CLSC and requested it to prepare a set of proposals based on that report.[87] As discussed in more detail below,[88] the CLSC is composed of equal numbers of representatives of employers, labor, and the public interest. Naturally, given the divergence in interests, the views of the labor and management representatives frequently are diametrically opposed. Initially, that was the case here, as well.

But the CLSC came up with a masterful compromise. To satisfy labor's insistence on a 40-hour week and adamant opposition to any lesser standard, Article 32 of the LSL would be amended to establish the 40-hour principle explicitly. At the same time, to meet management's concerns over the difficulty of adjusting to the shorter hours, the new standard would not take effect immediately. Rather, the 40-hour week would represent a "goal," to be achieved in stages in order to permit business sufficient time to adapt (and giving special consideration to the circumstances of smaller establishments). To provide for this phased implementation, a new provision in the law would authorize the Cabinet and MOL to promulgate ordinances establishing exceptions to the 40-hour standard - with the unwritten understanding that the first such ordinance would set forth a 46-hour standard, to be reduced to 40 hours in stages as circumstances permitted.[89]

This compromise proposal offered a way out of the deadlock. For labor, the explicit legislative recognition of the 40-hour principle represented a significant victory, for which the phased implementation approach was an acceptable (and likely unavoidable) price. For management, the phased implementation (ultimately to be determined, it bears note, through ordinances promulgated by the Cabinet, which business might have assumed would continue to be

85 *See* K. SUGENO, The Movement Toward Revision of the Law Regulating Hours of Work, JAPAN LAB. BULL., Vol. 23, No. 12, at 5 (Dec. 1984) (part 1); Vol. 24, No. 1, at 5 (Jan. 1985) (part 2).

86 *See* SUGENO, *supra* note 62.

87 *See* SUGENO, *supra* note 61.

88 *See* text accompanying notes 156-161 *infra*.

89 *See* SUGENO, *supra* note 61.

controlled by the normally pro-business LDP, and MOL), together with the deletion of any mention of an increase in the overtime premium, proved sufficient conditions for acceptance. Once consensus of labor and management had thus been attained, the amendments moved through the Diet with the support of all major parties and were enacted in September 1987.[90]

2. *Substance of the Amendments*

On its face, the amended LSL seemed clear and absolute. As revised, Article 32 provided simply:

> 1. An employer shall not have a worker work more than 40 hours per week, excluding rest periods.
> 2. An employer shall not have a worker work more than eight hours per day for each day of the week, excluding rest periods.[91]

Articles 32-2 through 32-5 were newly added, these being the flexibility provisions supported by management.[92] In addition, Article 39 was revised to increase, from six to ten, the number of annual days of paid leave for an employee with one year of service. Apart from existing exceptions for certain types of positions and occupations,[93] however, Chapter IV of the LSL, which governs working hours and leave, contained no other qualifications to the 40-hour principle set forth in Article 32.

In fact, one would search in vain through the entire main text of the LSL without finding any mention of the phased implementation scheme. It was relegated to Articles 131 and 132, which appear in the Supplementary Provisions following the main text. Of course, that placement was purely symbolic. Given the crucial nature of the phased approach in obtaining consensus on the amendments, all involved parties were acutely aware of it, regardless of where it appeared.

Article 131 set out the basic framework of the compromise. Paragraph 1 replaced the phrase "40 hours" in Article 32 with the following language: "the number of hours, greater than 40 but not to exceed 48, specified by order." Paragraph 2 in turn stipulated that the relevant order "shall be promulgated, and revised, so that the number of hours may be reduced in stages, taking into account workers' welfare, trends in working hours, and other circumstances, in

---

90 Law No. 99 of Sept. 26, 1987.

91 Article 32 of the LSL (as amended pursuant to Law No. 99 of 1987).

92 In essence, these newly added articles permitted employers to exceed the 40-hour weekly limit and eight-hour daily limit, provided the worker's average hours, over settlement periods ranging from one week to three months, did not exceed those limits.

93 *See* Article 40 and Article 41 of the LSL.

order to move to a 40-hour work week as expeditiously as possible."[94] The implementing ordinances set forth a rather complex scheme, under which the basic standard would be 46 hours for the first three years after the amendments took effect on April 1, 1988, and many businesses would remain exempt even from that modest step. No timetable was announced for further reductions in the standard work week.[95]

3. *Characteristics of the 1987 Amendment Process*

Two characteristics of the amendment process and resulting revisions bear especial note: the role of international opinion and the adoption of a gradualist approach.

a. International Opinion

The primary impetus for the 1987 amendments did not lie in international pressure. Despite some references to Japan's long working hours in trade negotiations, the drive to reduce working hours represented a domestic policy choice, not compelled by international criticism. Still, international standards and views played significant roles in two respects.

First, statistics on annual working hours in other major industrialized nations provided the basic rationale and target for the hours debate. In this sense, one basic rationale offered for the drive was neither concern over the health and well-being of the workers nor foreign criticism, but rather the deep-rooted desire to overtake the West - the *oitsuke oikose* ("catch up and then exceed") spirit, now transformed from the purely business realm to the field of working conditions.[96]

---

94 The remainder of Article 131 permitted temporary exceptions, again to be designated by order, for enterprises under a certain size and for enterprises in certain industries, *id.* Article 131(3), and required MOL to obtain the views of the CLSC when formulating or revising relevant orders, *id.* Article 131(4).

95 For a rather detailed summary of the applicable standards, *see* Y. SUWA, Cabinet Order and Ministry Ordinance Regarding Working Hours and Paid Holidays, JAPAN LAB. BULL., Vol. 27, No. 4, at 4 (April 1988). As described therein, the applicable Enforcement Regulations continued to apply the existing 48-hour standard to enterprises deemed likely to have difficulty meeting the 46-hour standard. The size of enterprises entitled to that treatment varied depending on the industry. Under the Regulations, moreover, the 48-hour standard would remain in effect even beyond the three-year period for very small firms (those with no more than ten employees) in certain industries. The Regulations even recognized a 54-hour work week for firms with no more than four employees in certain industries, for the three-year transitional period.

96 *See,* e.g., MOL, *supra* note 29, at 1:

The mere fact that achieving international parity on working conditions could become a rallying point not just for workers, but for MOL, is significant. Yet it is questionable whether that objective alone would have done much to sway the government as a whole, which throughout this period was controlled by the LDP, or the business establishment, on whose support the LDP was heavily dependent.[97] For the government and business, a more pragmatic reason for supporting reductions in working hours lay in another rationale: shifting Japan from an export-led to a domestic demand-driven economy.

As of 1986 and 1987, the possibility of direct retaliation against Japanese goods by foreign nations on the basis of Japan's longer working hours would have seemed distant indeed; and it is highly unlikely that scattered references to Japan's working hours by major trading partners alone would have led to reform. Given the attention to this issue already existing within Japan, however, international comments linking working hours to trade, coupled with the appeal of increased domestic consumption in an era of some uncertainty regarding future exports, helped propel the issue to the forefront.

b. Gradualism

A second noteworthy characteristic of the 1987 legislation was its reliance on gradualism, through the phased implementation approach. Here, the legislation bears striking parallels to two other major laws that have received wide attention in the West,[98] the Factory Law of 1911 and the Equal Employment Opportunity Law of 1985 (EEOL).[99]

Today, Japan has achieved a place as a leading economic power. Japan accounts for about 10% of the world GNP, and per capita GNP is at the highest level in the world. In terms of the lives of citizens, wages have almost caught up to the level of the major nations in Europe and America. Yet working hours are 200-500 hours longer than in those countries. This is one factor underlying the gap between Japan's economic power and the feelings of well-being of the Japanese people.

97 *See*, generally, e.g., J.M. RAMSEYER & F. MCCALL ROSENBLUTH, Japan's Political Marketplace 27-28, 90-93 (1993).

98 With respect to the Factory Law *see*, e.g., AYUSAWA, *supra* note 9; GARON, *supra* note 9; and J.M. RAMSEYER & F. MCCALL ROSENBLUTH, The Politics of Oligarchy: Institutional Choice in Imperial Japan 149-157 (1995). With respect to the EEOL (*supra* note 23), *see*, e.g., F.K. UPHAM, Law and Social Change in Postwar Japan 144-165 (1987); M. KAMIYA, A Decade of the Equal Employment Opportunity Act in Japan: Has It Changed Society?, 25 LAW IN JAPAN 40 (1995); NOTE [L. PARKINSON], Japan's Equal Employment Opportunity Act: An Alternative Approach to Social Change, 89 COLUM. L.REV. 604 (1989); and K. KAMIO KNAPP, Still Office Flowers: Japanese Women Betrayed by the Equal Employment Opportunity Law, 18 HARV. WOMEN'S L.J. 83 (1995).

99 Indeed, those two laws also offer close parallels with respect to the role of international opinion. Protective legislation adopted in other nations affected the nature of the proposals for and debate over the Factory Law, and strident criticism

The similarities to the Factory Law are obvious. In the face of strong business opposition and repeated claims that the new limits would threaten the survival of weak and small companies, both that law and the 1987 amendments established grace periods and provided for implementation of the new standards in stages, in order to give businesses time to adapt. Both laws also provided special treatment for small companies and companies in certain weak industries.

The parallel to the EEOL's gradualism is less immediately apparent, but reflects a more fundamental issue: the perceived necessity of changing deep-rooted aspects of corporate culture in order to bring about real reform. Given the pervasive use of gender-based classifications (or, to use a blunter term, discrimination) at Japanese companies, achieving equal opportunity for women would require not only changing long-standing corporate practices, but altering fundamental attitudes widely shared by employers. The EEOL explicitly recognized the need to bring about such attitudinal change and sought to do so in a gradual manner. Rather than impose a sweeping set of mandatory standards enforceable through penal sanctions, the EEOL consisted in large part of broad provisions calling for employers to "strive" to eliminate discrimination. These hortatory standards were to be accompanied by MOL administrative guidance - through issuance of guidelines, jawboning, and other similar activities - designed to modify employers' attitudes.[100] The effectiveness[101] and even the sincerity[102] of this approach have been subject to question, but the rhetorical stance of the legislation is clear: to bring about meaningful reform, proponents argued, one must change fundamental attitudes, and this can only be accomplished gradually, not by fiat.

---

of Japan at the ILO reportedly directly influenced amendments strengthening that Law in 1919, *see* AYUSAWA, *supra* note 9, at 182-91. Similarly, ample evidence from the legislative record and debate surrounding the EEOL reveals that a key reason that law was enacted in 1985 was to enable the government of Japan to claim to have fulfilled its pledge to reform domestic laws to meet the standards of the U.N. Declaration on Elimination of All Forms of Discrimination Against Women by the end of the U.N.-declared Decade of Women - which ended that year, *see,* e.g., KAMIYA, *supra* note 98, at 47-48. Nevertheless, the initial impetus for those pieces of legislation did not come from international pressure, but from domestic conditions. In the case of the Factory Law, a principal motivation lay in concern over the health of Japanese workers, spurred on by widespread domestic publicity over the horrifying working conditions of girls working in factories at the turn of the century, *see,* e.g., GARON, *supra* note 9, at 28. For the EEOL, the impetus lay in a growing movement for employment equality, accompanied by a series of judicial decisions recognizing rights to equal treatment in numerous aspects of the employment relationship, that began as early as the late 1960s, *see,* e.g., J. BROWN, Japanese Approaches to Equal Rights for Women: The Legal Framework, 12 LAW IN JAPAN 29 (1979); UPHAM, *supra* note 98, at 144-65.

100 *See,* e.g., NOTE, *supra* note 98.

101 *See,* e.g., KAMIYA, *supra* note 98, at 63-69; KNAPP, *supra* note 98.

102 *See,* e.g., KAMIYA, *supra* note 98, at 52-53.

The same theme applied to the effort to reduce working hours. In the eyes of many, this was not simply an economic issue. Rather, given the importance in Japan's corporate culture placed on devotion to one's company, as demonstrated in part by long working hours and short vacations,[103] achieving significant reductions in working hours would require changing the basic mindset that long hours are a key measure of merit and that work should take precedence over all else. The view that such changes in attitude could only be achieved gradually, with the phased implementation of the 40-hour week to be accompanied by jawboning and administrative guidance aimed at modifying existing views, thus provided an additional rationale for the gradualist approach adopted by the 1987 amendments.

B. The 1992 Temporary Measures Law Concerning Promotion of Reduction of Working Hours

1. Background and Substance

Working hours began to decline gradually after 1988 (whether as a result of the 1987 amendments or other factors is a question to which we will return below). But many observers, including MOL, feared that there were limits to the progress that could be made and that without further steps it would be impossible to reach the goal of 1,800 hours. Large companies - many of which were in a position to attract additional employees, to invest in labor-saving machinery, and to take other steps to reduce hours - were achieving considerable success in lowering hours. The real problem lay with small and medium-sized companies. By the late 1980s and early 1990s those companies complained bitterly of their difficulty in attracting new workers and freely admitted that reducing working hours might help them do so, but claimed that competition limited their options. Their customers, they asserted, had come to expect rapid turnarounds and unstinting service. If the businesses unilaterally lowered their hours and were no longer able to meet the customers' requests, their competitors would step into the breach.

Apparently to deal with such concerns, in October 1991 MOL floated a proposal for new legislation - tentatively entitled "Promotion of the Achievement of Appropriate (*tekisei-ka*) Working Hours." As first suggested, that legislation would have contained language along the following lines: "When a substantial number of workers or employers within a given region and industry have filed an application seeking establishment of standards for reducing working hours, the local Labor Standards Office may establish such

103 *See,* e.g., KAWAHITO, *supra* note 72, at 10-12.

standards, after obtaining the views of the local Labor Standards Council."[104] Initially, businesses would only have been required to exert efforts (*doryoku*) to meet the standards; but once the standards covered three quarters of the relevant workers, the labor authorities could declare void any specifications, rules of employment, or collective bargaining agreements that did not meet the standards. In addition, the proposal encouraged the establishment of special labor-management consultation committees at the enterprise level to discuss steps for reducing hours, and authorized MOL to designate the maximum amount of overtime that could be set forth in Article 36 agreements.

MOL officials presented this proposal to a subcommittee of the CLSC's Committee on Working Hours in mid-October 1991 as a fast-track item to be prepared for submission to the Diet by the start of 1992. At the start, that timetable appeared completely unrealistic. Questions about the proposal abounded. They began with its very title: What exactly was meant by "achieving *appropriate* hours"? And if there was an "appropriate" level, shouldn't the legislation have a sunset provision, whereby it would terminate once that level was reached?[105]

The most important debate focused on the provision to permit establishment of regional standards. Labor naturally welcomed it. Businesses did not. To the extent that the proposal reflected the aim (admitted to by MOL authorities, but not directly reflected in the proposal) of permitting businesses to consult with each other over working hours without fear of challenge under the Antimonopoly Law,[106] management found some merit in it. But management strongly opposed giving labor any power to initiate a process by which government officials could then set new standards. Management observed that, if labor wished to consult and bargain over working hours, it already had ample authority to do so; there was no need to give labor any special additional tools.[107]

---

104 *Rôdô jikan no tekisei-ka no sokushin tô ni kansuru hôritsu no kentô naiyô ni tsuite* [Respecting Matters for Consideration with Respect to the Law Concerning the Promotion, etc., of Normalization of Working Hours] (submitted to a subcommittee of the CLSC's Committee on Working Hours in mid-October 1991).

105 Another issue was why the authority to set official standards for Article 36 agreements (as opposed to the informal guidelines that already existed) was being proposed through this separate legislation, rather than by amending the LSL itself: Was this a subterfuge that would give the government authority to set limits, rather than leaving them to negotiations between management and labor?

106 *Shiteki dokusen no kinshi oyobi kôsei torihiki no kakuho ni kansuru hôritsu* [Law Concerning Prohibition of Private Monopoly and Maintenance of Fair Trade], Law No. 54 of 1947 as amended by Law No. 89 of 1993. For an English translation *see* EHS Vol. II, KA, No. 2270.

107 Comments by Professor *Kazuo Sugeno*, at *Rôdô Jikan Kenkyû-kai* (Study Group on Working Hours), Japan Institute of Labour, Tokyo, Jan. 30, 1992.

Over the next few months, the proposal underwent a series of revisions, each of which took it progressively closer to business's position. Most significantly, labor went from having a central role to virtually no role at all. At the start, either management or labor could have initiated the hour reduction plans. Under a later revision, authority to initiate plans was reserved to employer organizations in a given industry or region, but a statement added that it was "important" that labor's views be considered.[108] A subsequent revision went even further by permitting any "two or more employers" in the same industry to prepare plans and submit them to MOL for approval, with no mention of a duty or even the desirability of considering labor's views.[109]

Numerous other changes also reflected business concerns. Thus, for example, MOL's authority to issue new binding standards for Article 36 agreements was first reduced to authority to issue new *non*-binding guidelines,[110] and then to merely a pledge to exert efforts to effectuate the guidelines that already existed.[111] Similarly, the initial proposal for potentially binding region-wide standards was relaxed to a proposal for non-binding guidelines.[112] Antitrust protections were made explicit in the first set of revisions and later were strengthened further.[113] A five-year sunset provision was added.[114] In addition, the proposal was revised, first, to call for various types of governmental aid - notably, almost exclusively of the advice and

---

108 *See: Rôdô jikan no tanshuku no sokushin ni kansuru shisaku no jûjitsu ni tsuite* [Regarding the Enrichment of Measures Concerning Promotion of Reduction in Working Hours] (submitted to subcommittee of CLSC's Committee on Working Hours on Jan. 30, 1992) [hereinafter Jan. 30 Proposal].

109 *Rôdô jikan no tanshuku no sokushin ni kansuru rinji sochi hôan* [Bill for a Temporary Measures Law Concerning Promotion of Reduction in Working Hours] Article 8(1) (March 24, 1992) [hereinafter Bill]. The bill did require the labor authorities to determine that hours reduction plans "will not unduly impair the interests of consumers and related employers" before granting their approval, *id.* Article 8(3)(item 3), but contained no mention of the interests of labor.

110 *See: Rôdô jikan no tanshuku oyobi tekisei na kanri no sokushin ni kansuru hôteki seibi ni tsuite* [Regarding Legal Preparations Concerning the Promotion of Reduction in and Appropriate Management of Working Hours], *Shiryô* [Materials] No. 1 (date not specified) [hereinafter Regarding Legal Preparations].

111 *See* Jan. 30 Proposal, *supra* note 108.

112 *See* Regarding Legal Preparations, *supra* note 110.

113 Under the revised proposal, labor authorities, upon approving an hours reduction plan, would consult with the Fair Trade Commission [*Kôsei Torihiki Iinkai*] to be sure that the plan would not violate the Antimonopoly Law (not a full exemption from that law, to be sure, but an important protection), *see* Regarding Legal Preparations, *supra* note 110. In the form ultimately submitted to the Diet, the bill expressly required the Commission to respond to any inquiries it received from MOL (or other ministries with jurisdiction over the industry concerned) and to notify MOL (and such other ministries) if it perceived any violation of the Antimonopoly Law. Bill, *supra* note 109, Article 10(2), (3).

114 *See* Bill, *supra* note 109, Supp. Provisions Article 2.

informational variety, rather than actual subsidies[115] - and, then, to require the government to prepare a comprehensive plan for reducing working hours[116] and to undertake efforts to educate and "enlighten" (*keihatsu*) businesses, workers, and the general public on the importance of reducing hours.[117] Even the title was revised twice before the bill for the "Temporary Measures Law Concerning Promotion of Reduction in Working Hours" - popularly known as the *Jitan Sokushin-Hô* [hereinafter the Temporary Measures Law] - was submitted to the Diet on March 24, 1992.

That bill received final approval less than three months later, on June 19.[118] On first glance, the final statute looks virtually identical to the bill; the only change was the addition of a three-line sub-Article. That change was significant, however, for the newly added language states that, when considering whether to approve an hour reduction plan, MOL "shall strive [*tsutomeru*] to consider the views of the workers."[119] Notwithstanding labor's grudging acquiescence to the bill at the CLSC level, labor had continued to push for explicit inclusion of this language and had taken its concerns to the Diet. While labor had lost the ability to initiate hour reduction plans on its own, it ultimately succeeded in obtaining official recognition that it would have at least some voice in the process.

2. *Evaluating the Temporary Measures Law: Neocorporatist Roots, Business-Oriented Blossoms*

In contrast to the gradualism of the 1987 amendments, the Temporary Measures Law reflects another common pattern in Japanese legislation: governmental encouragement of unofficial associations, and even sponsorship of official associations, in which key interest groups are represented, with the views of those associations then accorded great deference in the legislative and regulatory process.

Prime examples of this pattern at the national level lie in the *shingi-kai*, which are discussed at greater length below.[120] Such mechanisms are widespread and are officially encouraged at lower levels, as well. The LSL provides for establishment of tripartite (labor, management, and "public

115 *See* Jan. 30 Proposal, *supra* note 108.
116 Bill, *supra* note 109, Article 4.
117 *Id.* Article 3.
118 *See*, e.g., *Rôdô jikan no shiori*, *supra* note 25, at 144. The Temporary Measures Law was officially promulgated on July 2, 1992, and took effect on September 1 of that year.
119 Article 8(5) of the Temporary Measures Law.
120 *See* text accompanying notes 153-177 *infra*.

interest") *shingi-kai* for labor standards issues at the prefectural level;[121] and parallel provisions call for establishment of *shingi-kai* in each prefecture on such issues as minimum wages,[122] employment security,[123] and vocational training.[124] The Temporary Measures Law in its initial formulation, and the Minimum Wages Law on which the initial proposal was partially based,[125] provide examples of a similar approach: the encouragement of labor-management consultation on a region-wide basis, aimed at agreement on minimum standards that will apply to all similar employers in the region.[126]

---

121 Article 98 of the LSL. Under the Industrial Safety and Health Law [*Rôdô anzen eisei-hô*], Law No. 57 of 1972, Article 6, those same bodies are given responsibility for advising on matters of industrial safety and health.

122 Minimum Wages Law [*Saitei chingin-hô*], Law No. 137 of 1959, Article 26.

123 Employment Security Law [*Shokugyô antei-hô*], Law No. 141 of 1947, Article 12.

124 Human Resources Development Promotion Law [*Shokugyô nôryoku kaihatsu sokushin-hô*], Law No. 64 of 1969, Articles 5 to 7.

125 Article 11 of the Minimum Wages Law stipulates that, when a majority of workers in a given line of work in a given region have entered into one or more collective bargaining agreements with a majority of the region's employers conducting that type of work, providing for the same or a substantially equivalent minimum wage, the relevant labor authorities may treat that wage as the applicable minimum wage for *all* workers engaged in that type of work in the region. In other words, if a majority of workers and employers in the same line of work in a given region agree, they can increase the otherwise applicable minimum wage without fear of being undercut by low-wage competitors.

When labor's Joint Struggle Council issued its report on working hours in 1987, it explicitly referred to this provision of the Minimum Wages Law as a model, under which representatives of a substantial portion of either management or labor in a particular region or industry could petition to establish stiffer standards on working hours than those contained in the LSL, *see* JOINT STRUGGLE COUNCIL, *supra* note 49, at 83-84; and MOL's original proposal for the Temporary Measures Law appears to have adopted that approach.

Although the system under Article 11 was introduced in 1968 through a major revision of the Minimum Wages Law, it has rarely been used outside the mining industry. Moreover, the parallels to the Minimum Wages Law only heightened management's concerns over the initial proposal for the Temporary Measures Law, since many business leaders felt that they had been co-opted in the minimum wage arena. Comments by Professor *Kazuo Sugeno*, at *Rôdô Jikan Kenkyû-kai* [Study Group on Working Hours], Japan Institute of Labour, Tokyo, Jan. 30, 1992.

For a thorough discussion of Japan's minimum wage system, *see* K. SUGENO, Minimum Wages in Japan: A System for Social Equity In Decentralised Industrial Relations, *in*: The Changing Face of Labour Law and Industrial Relations: Liber Amicum for Clyde W. Summers 216-27 (R. Blanplain & M. Weiss, eds. 1993).

126 For a fine example of such structured deference to local determinations outside the labor context, *see* F. UPHAM, Privatizing Regulation: The Implementation of the Large-Scale Retail Stores Law, *in*: Political Dynamics in Contemporary Japan 264 (G.D. Allinson & Y. Sone, eds. 1993) (examining the functions of Commercial Activities Adjustment Boards and advisory councils in the context of the Large-Scale Retail Stores Law). *See also* the contribution of *Toshiyuki Kôno* in this volume (*supra* Chapter Two).

This pattern has been described by some experts as "loose neo-corporatism."[127] This differs from the strict neocorporatism more common in Germany, which has been defined as a system in which "governmental[ly] recogni[zed] or permit[ted]" "compulsory associations" "are explicitly allowed a monopoly of representation."[128] In the more typical Japanese pattern, in contrast, private associations may be officially encouraged, but are not compulsory, and their decisions are not accorded binding power. To the contrary, as with the Temporary Measures Law, their decisions normally constitute "recommendations" to the bureaucracy, with the final standards ultimately subject to bureaucratic control.[129]

Despite this ultimate potential for bureaucratic control, the approach remains significant. First, it reflects a conscious attempt to involve key members of the affected community in the decision-making process, coupled, in a pattern with roots deep in Japanese history,[130] with a deference to such locally generated decisions. Perhaps even more importantly, *failure* to reach agreement by consensus typically ends the matter, thereby effectively according a veto power to each of the various affected parties - or, at least, to those parties who have been officially recognized as having a voice in the matter (thus making membership on advisory councils and similar bodies all the more crucial). In turn, this frequently results in the necessity of "consensual governance" that *John Haley* has identified as a key theme in Japanese law.[131]

Viewed in this context, MOL's initial proposal for the Temporary Measures Law was exceptional in that it would have permitted labor acting alone to initiate the process for establishing binding standards. By the same token, the legislation as introduced to the Diet went to the other extreme, by allowing any two or more businesses to petition MOL, without regard to labor's views. As finally enacted, the law adopted an intermediate position: while businesses can

127 *See,* e.g., K. SUGENO, Japan: The State's Guiding Role in Socioeconomic Development, 14 COMP. LAB. L. 302, 320 (1993), and sources cited therein.

128 G. TEUBNER, The "State" of Private Networks: The Emerging Legal Regime of Polycorporatism in Germany, 1993 B.Y.U. L.REV. 553, 563 (quoting P.C. SCHMITTER, Still the Century of Corporatism?, *in*: The New Corporatism: Social-Political Structures in the Iberian World 85, 94-95 (F.B. Pike & T. Stritch, eds. 1974)).

129 This is true in the minimum wages context, as well. Even where a substantial majority of the workers in a given industry in a prefecture are covered by collective bargaining agreements providing for the same minimum wage, that wage becomes binding on other companies in the same industry only if and when adopted as the prefecture-wide standard by MOL officials.

130 *See,* e.g., D.F. HENDERSON, Village "Contracts" in Tokugawa Japan 1-32 (1975); D.F. HENDERSON, Conciliation and Japanese Law, Tokugawa and Modern 127-31, 171-81 (1965); J.O. HALEY, Authority without Power: Law and the Japanese Paradox 58-65 (1993).

131 *See* HALEY, *supra* note 130, at 139-168.

initiate the process, MOL is expected to consider labor's opinion. And while the law speaks only of an obligation to "endeavor" to consider the labor position, it seems likely that, in practice, MOL will treat this as an important step in the process.

Another way of looking at the Temporary Measures Law is as an example of bureaucratic paternalism. By this view, labor, unable to secure shorter working hours through its own efforts, turned to MOL for help in achieving that aim, and MOL complied by pushing for legislation that authorizes it to give such help. Significantly, however, jawboning is about the only thing that MOL can do on its own under the Temporary Measures Law. While the law establishes an enabling environment for businesses that wish to reduce hours, nearly all of the new tools lie in the hands of management.

In view of this circumstance, some observers worried that business, in insisting on all of the revisions to the original draft, was secretly seeking to co-opt labor further. Under one such cynical view, the Temporary Measures Law, despite its stated goal of reducing hours, might become a device for maintaining them. Pursuant to guidelines under the law, MOL requires at least a 5% reduction in working hours before it will approve an hour reduction plan.[132] Yet, if the Temporary Measures Law had not permitted - indeed, even encouraged - businesses to consult and agree on a united front, largely free from antitrust concerns, competition for labor might have led to even greater reductions.

A second, more widely voiced fear was that the Temporary Measures Law was a subterfuge, designed to stall further mandatory steps under the LSL. In the phased implementation of the shift to a 40-hour week described earlier, the standard work week was reduced from 48 to 46 hours in 1987, and then from 46 to 44 in 1991. At the time the 44-hour standard was adopted, the CLSC had reached an unwritten understanding that the next revision, scheduled for 1993, would complete the move to a 40-hour standard week in one step, without an additional intermediate reduction to 42 hours. Particularly given that background, some observers worried that business, and even MOL, may have promoted the Temporary Measures Law in order to deflect attention from the LSL and justify a further delay in implementing the 40-hour week.

---

132 *Rôdô jikan no tanshuku no sokushin ni kansuru rinji sochi-hô no sekô ni tsuite* [Regarding the Implementation of the Temporary Measures Law Concerning Promotion of Reduction in Working Hours], Labor Standards Division, MOL, Circular No. 494 of 1992, Article 5(3), reprinted in *Rôdô jikan no shiori*, *supra* note 25, at 223, 232.

C. The 1993 Amendments

1. Background and Substance

As it turned out, attention was not deflected away from the 40-hour standard, but its adoption was delayed nonetheless. In point of fact, MOL had undertaken steps for further revision of the hours provisions in the LSL even before the Temporary Measures Law was introduced. Those efforts reached fruition in a broad set of amendments to both the LSL and the Temporary Measures Law, enacted in 1993. Those amendments provided for implementation of the 40-hour standard from 1994, rather than 1993; and, after a highly controversial debate to be discussed below,[133] the amendments were conditioned on a one-year extension of the 46-hour "exception" for nearly half of all businesses (with many of those businesses then to enjoy the 44-hour standard until 1997).[134]

In April 1991, MOL asked the CLSC, through its Working Hours Subcommittee, to consider further revisions to the LSL.[135] In addition, in July 1991, MOL asked the Labor Standards Law Study Group - the "experts group" composed of labor law and labor economics scholars - to undertake a comprehensive review of needed revisions to the LSL.[136] In September 1992, the study group issued a report calling for: (1) a reduction in the standard work week to 40 hours by April 1994, (2) an expansion of the flexibility provisions, (3) increases in the overtime premium for both overtime hours and work on rest days, (4) implementation of measures to permit leeway in the calculation of hours for work by certain white collar employees,[137] and (5) vesting of the right to annual paid leave after six months, rather than one year.[138]

Both business and labor promptly issued formal statements criticizing these proposals. For business, a subcommittee of *Nikkeiren* released an "opinion" in early November 1992 that approved the recommendations related to hour averaging and white collar employees.[139] Otherwise, business found little good

---

133 *See* text accompanying notes 166-177 *infra*.

134 *See,* e.g., JAPAN LAB. BULL., Vol. 32, No. 8, at 4 (Aug. 1993) (describing the new standards).

135 *See: Rôdô jikan no shiori*, *supra* note 25, at 59.

136 *See id.* at 58.

137 Article 41 of the LSL contains exemptions from the hours provisions for supervisory and managerial employees, but does not contain an exclusion for professional employees.

138 Report of the Labor Standards Law Study Group, summarized in *Rôdô jikan no shiori*, *supra* note 25, at 58-59, and MURAKI, *supra* note 33, at 58, and reproduced in full in *id.*, at 60-64. The study group also considered the possibility of establishing fixed limits on the number of overtime hours permitted, but chose not to make any recommendations on that point.

139 NIKKEIREN SUBCOMMITTEE, *supra* note 80. *Nikkeiren* argued, though, that the revisions should go further and should include a completely new system for white collar workers.

in the proposals. Noting the rough state of the Japanese economy, it argued for an intermediate move to a 42-hour week, and claimed that the very survival of many small and middle-sized companies depended on granting continued exceptions to the new standards. In addition, business bitterly opposed any increase in the overtime premium.[140]

Not surprisingly, labor's position, as reflected in a statement released in late September 1992 by *Rengô* (the Japanese Trade Union Confederation), was diametrically opposed to that of business.[141]

Despite these sharp differences, on December 18, 1992, less than three months after the study group had issued its report, the CLSC submitted a very similar set of recommendations to the Minister of Labor. Those recommendations included: (1) reducing the standard work week to 40 hours, effective from April 1994 (but with certain categories of business to be granted exceptions, at either 44 or 42 hours, until 1996); (2) permitting averaging of hours over periods of up to one year, subject to certain conditions; and (3) reducing the period for vesting of the right to annual leave to six months. In addition, despite a continued split between the business and labor representatives, the public representatives on the CLSC recommended an increase in the overtime premium, at least for work on rest days, to some figure in the range between 25% and 50%. Finally, the CLSC called for further consideration of the issue of calculating hours for employees whose work involves broad discretion.[142]

MOL promptly prepared a proposal for a new bill on working hours. For the most part, the proposal tracked the CLSC's recommendations, including the

---

140 In this regard, *Nikkeiren*'s subcommittee stated:

> There is no consensus as to whether an increase in the premium has any effect in reducing overtime. In fact, many people have observed that, given the marked preference of Japanese workers for income [over reduced hours], such a step, rather than contributing to a decrease in overtime, might well lead to a rise in overtime hours. . . . Moreover, an increase in the premium, coupled with the reductions in the standard work week, would have a serious impact on the management of businesses, especially small and medium-sized businesses.

Id. at 4.

141 *See* RÔDÔ KUMIAI SÔ-RENGÔ-KAI [Confederation of Trade Unions], *Rôdô kijun-hô kenkyû-kai hôkoku ni taisuru rengô no kenkai* [The Views of *Rengô* concerning the Report of the Labor Standards Law Study Group], Sept. 28, 1992, *reprinted in* 1297 RÔDÔ HÔRITSU JUNPÔ 51 (1992). Labor supported the proposals for implementing the 40-hour week, for increasing the overtime premium, and for earlier vesting of the rights to annual leave - albeit arguing that the 40-hour week did not come soon enough (it should be implemented a year earlier, in 1993, *Rengô* said) and the overtime premium proposal did not go far enough (*Rengô* insisted that it should be increased to at least 50%, with bonuses and housing allowances included in the calculation base). Labor strongly opposed the recommendations for allowing hour averaging over a one-year period and for granting leeway in calculating hours of white collar workers.

142 *See: Rôdô jikan no shiori*, *supra* note 25, at 59-60.

public members' recommendation for an increase in the overtime premium.[143] In addition, it contained amendments to the Temporary Measures Law, designed to encourage "even faster" progress in reducing hours (including establishment of a system of subsidies).[144]

The CLSC accepted this proposal on January 21, 1993.[145] After it was placed in final legislative form, the Cabinet submitted the resulting bill to the Diet on February 19, 1993. It was passed, without changes, by the Lower House on May 11 and by the Upper House on June 2, and became law on July 1, 1993.[146]

2. *Evaluating the 1993 Amendments*

The package of measures passed by the Diet in 1993 represented the broadest and strongest set of steps to date. In view of its symbolic value, the move to the 40-hour norm may rate as the centerpiece of the legislation, even though that move was to take effect in 1994, not 1993 (and was still subject to broad exceptions).

In practical terms, however, the most significant development in the 1993 amendments may rest in a change in what had long been the great untouchable: the overtime premium. This might appear to have been the most natural target all along. After all, while workers may have been unwilling to fight hard to reduce overtime because of concerns over lost income, they presumably would have been much more supportive if the reduction in hours were tied to an increase in the overtime premium. And, despite the comment by one academic in a study group I attended that an increase in the premium would not reduce hours because the higher pay would simply induce workers to work even more hours, there clearly is some economic level at which the size of the premium would induce companies to hire additional workers rather than resort to overtime.[147]

---

143 Although the proposal avoided the broad issue of white collar workers in general, it included provisions permitting the use of fixed standards for hours for certain specified types of work that depend heavily on workers' discretion.

144 *See: Rôdô jikan no shiori*, *supra* note 25, at 60-61.

145 The proposal for an increase in the overtime premium still represented the views of the public members; labor and business remained deadlocked on that issue.

146 *See: Rôdô jikan no shiori*, *supra* note 25, at 61-62. The law, Law No. 79 of 1993, bore the official title: *Rôdô kijun-hô oyobi rôdô jikan no tanshuku no sokushin ni kansuru rinji sochi-hô no ichibu o kaisei suru hôritsu* [Law Amending the Labor Standards Law and One Portion of the Temporary Measures Law Concerning Promotion of the Reduction in Working Hours].

147 *See* NISHITANI, *supra* note 79, at 11-12 (describing similar assertions by management, and dismissing them as based on misguided assumptions). According to MOL estimates the premium would have to be raised to 62.9% before it would become more economical for businesses to hire new workers than to assign overtime to existing workers, *see* HOBARA, *supra* note 74, at 264.

In fact, in arguing against any increase in the premium, business had emphasized its vulnerability, stating that "the use of overtime and work on rest days is widespread in Japan, and the overwhelming majority of businesses pay only the statutorily prescribed premium for such work, so an increase in the premium would have a serious effect on the management of businesses, especially small and medium-sized companies."[148] The fear that a rise in the premium might lead to the failure of many businesses appears to have been a major reason why the overtime premium had been almost a taboo topic prior to the 1993 amendments. This fear also appears to have influenced the extent to which the government was willing to increase the premium in 1993. On their face, the amendments authorized the MOL to order an increase in the premium to 50%, both for overtime hours on normal working days and for work on holidays and rest days. Yet this amendment was subject to another *sub rosa* agreement by the CLSC: an undertaking that the premium for overtime hours on normal working days would remain at 25% "for the time being," and that the premium for work on rest days would be increased, but initially only to 35%.[149] As of this writing in early 1996, there has been no further increase. Moreover, since bonuses are not taken into account in calculating the premium, the effective overtime rate is much lower than even those figures would suggest.[150] Thus, while the 1993 amendments are noteworthy for having adopted the "stick" of higher overtime premiums, rather than simply the "carrot" of encouragement, to date the stick is far from a heavy one.

In fact, the 1993 amendments may be even more notable for the broad range of "carrots" they offered. They contained a package of incentives, including subsidies, low-interest loans, and tax breaks for small and medium-sized companies that invest in labor-saving machinery or take certain other measures to reduce working hours.[151] In addition, the 1993 amendments endorsed a

---

148 NIKKEIREN SUBCOMMITTEE, *supra* note 80, at 4.

149 *See: Chûkishin ga tôshin - shû 40 jikan e yûyo sochi* [CLSC to Consider Exception to 40-Hour Week], NIKKEIREN TAIMUZU, Feb. 4, 1993, at 1.

150 At most Japanese businesses, substantial bonuses are paid twice a year (in the summer and at year-end). Together, these bonuses typically amount to between two and six months' worth of wages, and thus represent approximately one fourth of the overall compensation package. *See,* e.g., K. SUGENO & Y. SUWA, The Changing Japanese Labour Market and Legal Adjustments: Wages and Working Time, JILL Forum Paper No. 2, at 11-12 (1994). These bonuses are not taken into account in calculating the overtime rate, nor are housing and other allowances. As a result, the effective overtime premium is considerably lower than it might first appear. *See,* e.g., S. MORI, *Jikan-gai rôdô no sakugen to hôteki kisei* [Reducing Overtime Work and Legal Restrictions], 998 JURISUTO 58, 60 (1992).

151 The incentives were relatively modest, however. For companies with up to 30 employees, for example, the maximum subsidy available was ¥500,000, *see: Rôdô jikan no shiori*, *supra* note 25, at 153-54; and the loans bore an interest rate of 4.8% and were subject to various other conditions, *see id.* at 164-65.

broad range of "enlightenment" activities by national and local governmental bodies, and to that end established a Center to Aid in Reducing Working Homes (*Rôdô Jikan Tanshuku Shien Sentâ*).[152]

Yet the 1993 amendments are perhaps most noteworthy for the fact that they occurred at all. By the time they were enacted, Japan was well into a recession accompanied by a major downturn in employment. Nonetheless, the debate over working hours had generated sufficient momentum to carry this package of legislation to completion.

PART III: THE *SHINGI-KAI* PROCESS

As the preceding discussion reflects, in each of the three packages of legislation one can find themes that at times have been labeled as characteristically Japanese: gradualism and the impact of international pressure in the case of the 1987 amendments, quasi-neocorporatism and paternalism in the Temporary Measures Law, and heavy reliance on governmental encouragement in the 1993 amendments. Yet a strong argument can be made that each package reflected the most that could have been achieved politically, in light of the existing power balance, at each stage. Before turning to that issue and an overall evaluation of the laws, however, it is worthwhile to reexamine the process that led to their enactment, with particular attention to an element common to each: the role of the CLSC.

The CLSC was established pursuant to Article 98 of the LSL. By law, its functions include investigating matters related to the enforcement and revisions of the LSL, the Industrial Safety and Health Law, and several other employment-related statutes, and making recommendations on standards for working conditions.[153] In this connection, the CLSC, normally through committees and subcommittees, undertakes studies of pertinent issues, typically in response to requests from MOL but at times on its own initiative, and issues reports and recommendations. As with other *shingi-kai*, the CLSC's most important functions include serving as a sounding board for proposals from the ministry and building consensus for those proposals among the most affected constituencies before they are put into legislative form for submission to the Diet.

While that role is similar to that played by other *shingi-kai*, the CLSC's makeup is somewhat special. Many *shingi-kai* attached to such economic-oriented ministries as the Ministry of Finance and the Ministry of International Trade and Industry are heavily weighted toward representatives of business -

152 *See* Articles 14 to 17 of the Temporary Measures Law (added in 1993).
153 Article 98 of the LSL.

especially big business.[154] In contrast, the CLSC is explicitly tripartite in nature: the LSL requires equal numbers of members representing employers, labor, and the public interest.[155]

Of course, this does not mean that the Minister of Labor has complete discretion in choosing members, nor that the group is all-inclusive. Selection of the employer and labor representatives typically is based upon recommendations from trade organizations and unions.[156] The employer representatives normally include officials from employer organizations for both large and small businesses, as well as executives from major businesses.[157] The labor representatives, however, are routinely chosen from major unions, even though unorganized workers now account for over three quarters of all Japanese workers and organization rates are especially low for part-time and temporary workers and for women.[158] Furthermore, despite a strong Communist influence in the labor movement, the unions do not recommend Communists for membership on the CLSC; reportedly, the unions recognize that recommending a radical unionist would be "inconvenient" for the government, so they exercise

---

154 To take one example, on the Financial System Research Council attached to the Ministry of Finance, as of mid-1991, the chair and nine of the 14 main members came from major businesses and such business-related organizations as *Keidanren* and the Japan Securities Dealers Association, five came from academics, and only one - the president of the Housewives' Association - came from a consumers' group. The numbers are even more striking when one considers the list of supplementary members to that Council; 13 of the 14 were from business, the other was a professor.

For further discussion of the *shingi-kai* process, *see*, e.g., F. SCHWARTZ, Of Fairy Cloaks and Familiar Tales: The Politics of Consultation, *in*: Political Dynamics in Contemporary Japan, *supra* note 126, at 217; F. SCHWARTZ, Advice and Consent: The Politics of Consultation in Japan (forthcoming).

155 Article 98(4) of the LSL. There are currently seven members from each group.

156 *See* SCHWARTZ, Advice and Consent, *supra* note 154, ch. 5 (draft on file with author).

157 As of 1994, the business members included representatives from the Japan Chamber of Commerce and Industry [*Nihon Shôkô Kaigi-sho*], the Japan Federation of Employers' Organizations [*Nikkeiren*], and the National Association of Medium-Sized and Small Businesses, along with representatives from four major companies: Kobe Steel, Toray, Mitsui Tôatsu Chemicals, and Toda Construction. *Shingi-kai sôran, Heisei 6-nen ban* [Comprehensive Survey of Advisory Councils, 1994 ed.] 459-60 (*Sômu-chô* [Management and Coordination Agency], ed. 1994).

158 *See id.* As of 1994, labor members included one representative from *Rengô* itself; one each from the Japanese Federation of Textile, Garment, Chemical, Mercantile, and Food, and Allied Industries Workers' Unions; the General Federation of Private Railway Workers' Unions of Japan; the Japanese Federation of Metal Industry Unions; the Japan Federation of Food and Tobacco Workers' Unions; the National Union of General Workers; and the All Japan Municipal Transport Workers' Union. All of these unions are members of *Rengô*, *see: Directory of Major Trade Unions, Employer's Associations and Labour Administration in Japan '94*, JAPAN LAB. BULL. (March 1994).

a voluntary screening process themselves.[159] There are no specific limitations on the public interest members, but historically most have been selected from among retired MOL bureaucrats and academics. As with the labor representatives, despite a large Marxist school among academics in the labor law and labor economics fields, it is unheard of for a Marxist scholar to be appointed as one of the public interest members of the Council; those members are expected to be politically "neutral," and are typically chosen from among moderates without pronounced ideological views.[160] As with other *shingi-kai*, the CLSC membership is notable in another respect: it is almost exclusively male.[161]

As noted above, the CLSC's specified roles include investigating and providing its views on revisions to the LSL and related laws. A common view is that the ability to achieve consensus within a *shingi-kai* ordinarily assures clear sailing for legislation once it reaches the Diet. Conversely, it is sometimes said, failure to achieve consensus often will block a proposal, thereby providing *shingi-kai* representatives with something approaching a veto power. To a large extent, the history of the three laws on working hours reduction bears out this picture. Yet that history shows that neither aspect of the picture is entirely accurate, and also reflects the broader role that *shingi-kai* sometimes play.

If one believes the rhetoric surrounding the laws, the CLSC actually initiated some of the legislation. Thus, for example, an MOL publication on the Temporary Measures Law characterizes it as having been suggested by the CLSC.[162] That is an overstatement. In reality, in each of the three cases MOL officials passed along proposals for the CLSC to review.[163] Yet the CLSC's role was by no means limited to a passive, reactive stance. As reflected most

159 *See* SCHWARTZ, Advice and Consent, *supra* note 154 (quoting *Tatsuya Ôtani*).

160 *See id.*

As of 1994, the public interest members included one attorney, one representative from the Smaller Enterprise Retirement Allowance Mutual Aid Association (a retired MOL bureaucrat), one member from the Japan Boiler Association (a retired MOL bureaucrat), one from Asahi Newspaper's research division, and three professors - an emeritus professor from the medical faculty of Kitasato University, and labor law professors from the University of Tokyo and Sophia University (the latter, *Tadashi Hanami*, was chair of the CLSC). *See: Shingi-kai sôran*, *supra* note 157, at 459-60.

161 As of 1994, its 21 members included only one woman - an attorney who was one of the public interest members. *See id.* All of the employer and labor representatives were men.

162 *See: Rôdô jikan no shiori*, *supra* note 25, at 143-44.

163 As discussed previously, the road to the 1987 amendments began with an MOL request to the Labor Standards Law Study Group, which led to a report that MOL then passed on to the CLSC for its review; the original proposal for the Temporary Measures Law in fact came from MOL officials, who first floated it before a CLSC subcommittee; and the 1993 amendments grew out of MOL requests addressed to both the CLSC and the Labor Standards Law Study Group.

clearly by the gradualist approach to the 40-hour limit contained in the 1987 amendments, the CLSC frequently helped to develop compromise proposals that would satisfy both business and labor. Moreover, the individual members' role was not limited to expressing their own views. Members frequently disseminated information on matters under consideration to their own and other businesses and organizations, and solicited opinions on the proposals.[164] Thus, the CLSC served as a device for gathering views and achieving prior consensus on the proposals.

Indeed, one might view the CLSC itself as a loose neo-corporatist mechanism, designed to delegate important matters of decision making to self-determination by the relevant parties. To the extent that the CLSC functions in this fashion, the gaps in representation on that body - in particular, the virtual absence of representation for unorganized workers and women - present a substantial concern.

Without meaning in any way to understate the significance of that concern, it is clear that the CLSC does not exercise full decision-making authority. Consensus at the CLSC is important to the ultimate success of legislation. Yet simply reaching "agreement" at the CLSC does not necessarily mean that the process is at an end. In the case of the Temporary Measures Law, for example, labor was able to obtain at least some recognition for its role in considering hours reduction plans, through an amendment after the legislation had reached the Diet.[165]

Nor do CLSC members automatically exercise veto power over legislation. As reflected most clearly by an incident that occurred during the 1993 amendment process, politicians remain in ultimate control, and CLSC members cannot necessarily thwart the legislative process simply by refusing to participate.

Given the attention that incident received, it is worth describing in some detail. The key issue related to the exception pursuant to which small and medium-sized businesses continued to operate under a 46-hour work week.[166] By the terms of the ordinance that created it, that exception was due to expire on March 31, 1993. Labor had argued for a complete abolition of all excep-

---

164 Thus, for example, members appointed from companies often would canvass other companies within the same industry, and union representatives often would consult with other related unions. Indeed, this collecting of views was not limited to the employer and labor representatives; public interest representatives also often sought the views of others, with academics, for example, seeking input from other scholars at study group sessions.

165 *See* text accompanying note 119 *supra*.

166 In fact, this "exception" applied to 49.6% of all workers, whereas the 44-hour "norm" then in effect covered only 36.3%. *See: Shû 46 jikan no yûyo - '1 nenkan enchô' hobo kakujitsu ni* [46-Hour Exception: 1-Year Extension a Virtual Certainty], Rôdô Shinbun (Feb. 22, 1993) [hereinafter *Shû 46 jikan no yûyo*].

tions;[167] business had pressed for a continuation for at least two more years; and, as mentioned earlier,[168] the CLSC appeared to have reached agreement in December on a compromise in which the exception would be maintained, but at either the 44- or 42-hour level.

Business had far from given up, though, and could count on the support of a very important ally - the then-ruling LDP. As a condition for obtaining the LDP's support for the 1993 legislation, MOL officials reportedly promised LDP leaders that the ministry would issue an ordinance extending the 46-hour exception for most businesses up to 100 employees.[169] In fact, on February 22, 1993, a newspaper covering labor issues reported a "virtual certainty" that the 46-hour exception would be extended until at least 1994.[170]

This report - and MOL's "promise" to the LDP - ignored one important matter, however: a statutory requirement that MOL refer the proposal to extend the exception to the CLSC for its consideration. When Minister of Labor *Murakami* finally requested the CLSC to consider the extension on March 8, the labor representatives expressed outrage at what they deemed a perversion of the *shingi-kai* process. All seven labor members took the apparently unprecedented step of walking out of the meeting in protest, stating their refusal "to participate in an unprincipled *(ri-fujin)* hearing in which the conclusion has been predetermined, without any prior consultation with the CLSC."[171] Despite efforts at persuasion by the CLSC's chair, Professor *Tadashi Hanami*, labor refused to return to either that meeting or a meeting on March 17 at which MOL's request was to be formally considered. Labor apparently had despaired of getting MOL to change its mind, but hoped that the CLSC would refuse to take up the matter and would send back MOL's request blank, thereby perhaps forcing its withdrawal.

If that was the aim, the strategy did not succeed. At the March 17 meeting, the public interest members accepted MOL's (and business's) explanation that a one-year extension in the 46-hour exception was essential as an "emergency measure" to protect small business. In doing so, however, the public interest members issued a public statement sharply critical of MOL. That statement read in part:

---

167 *See: Yûyo sochi no haishi mo* [Possible Abolition of the Exception], SHÛKAN RÔDÔ NYÛSU 1 (Dec. 7, 1992).

168 *See* text accompanying note 142 *supra*.

169 *See: Rôdô-gawa, kesseki no mama - 46 jikan yûyo sochi ichinen enchô o tôshin* [Request for Consideration of One-Year Extension of 46-Hour Measure: Pushing It Through Without Labor Present], SHÛKAN RÔDÔ NYÛSU 2 (March 23, 1993).

170 *See: Shû 46 jikan no yûyo, supra* note 166.

171 *See: Rôdô-gawa iin chûkishin o taiseki* [Labor-Side Members Walk Out on CLSC], SHÛKAN RÔDÔ NYÛSU 1 (March 15, 1993).

> While we highly evaluate the strong efforts of MOL in coordinating the various interests and achieving the introduction in the Diet of legislation reflecting the CLSC's recommendations . . . , it is truly regrettable that in that process MOL took actions with respect to the extension of the exception . . . without sufficient communication with this Council, and we urge MOL to give sincere reflection to [these shortcomings] and to act in an appropriate manner in the future.[172]

The public interest members also implicitly criticized both labor, for walking out and refusing to engage in deliberations, and business, emphasizing that the one-year extension was an *emergency* measure and that the parties should not "blithely feel self-satisfied at getting an extension, but should sincerely strive for rapid implementation of the 44-hour standard."[173] As that statement reflects, a further condition of the agreement concerning passage of the 1993 amendments was that, even after the one-year extension of the 46-hour standard, most small businesses would continue to operate under a 44-hour standard until 1997.[174]

The labor members were far harsher in their comments. "This *shingi-kai*," they stated, "has ignored the rules, was convened in order to endorse a conclusion already issued by MOL, and represents an impermissible perversion of the process that destroys the role of the *shingi-kai*. . . . We harshly criticize MOL . . . and the business members, who sought a political solution in violation of the rules."[175]

Given that Article 41 of the Constitution expressly provides that "[t]he Diet shall be the sole law-making organ of the State,"[176] this statement reflects an interesting conception of "the rules." CLSC Chair *Hanami*'s appraisal of the situation seems much more realistic. With respect to MOL's reported promise to the LDP, he commented, "While not a desirable thing, the *shingi-kai* is not completely separate from politics."[177]

As this episode reflects, even substantial representation on a *shingi-kai* does not always guarantee a veto power, nor does failure at the *shingi-kai* level preclude taking one's case to the higher authority of the Diet. Still, the very fact that this incident attracted such widespread attention and stirred such strong sentiments stands as a testament to the importance accorded to achieving consensus at the *shingi-kai* level. That, in turn, renders especially important the question of the representativeness of the CLSC.

---

172 *See: 46 jikan yûyo sochi ichinen enchô - shiryô* [Materials on the One-Year Extension to the 46-Hour Exception], SHÛKAN RÔDÔ NYÛSU 4 (March 23, 1993).

173 *Id.*

174 *See,* e.g., JAPAN LAB. BULL., Vol. 32, No. 8, at 4 (Aug. 1993).

175 *46 jikan yûyo sochi ichinen enchô - shiryô, supra* note 172.

176 Article 41 of the Constitution of Japan [*Kenpô*].

177 *Rôdô-gawa, kesseki no mama, supra* note 169. *Hanami* then added: "Still, I wish MOL had consulted us first."

PART IV: EVALUATION OF THE LAWS

This final section returns to the question posed at the outset: Have the three packages of legislation, taken as a whole, been a success? This question could be rephrased as: Has the Government's stated goal of 1,800 working hours per year been achieved? Formulated in this manner, there would be a simple answer: No, but considerable progress was made. As recently as 1988, Japanese employees on average worked over 2,110 hours per year.[178] By 1993, average annual working hours had declined nearly 10%, to just over 1,910 hours.[179]

Yet evaluating success is plainly much more complicated than simply looking at official statistics on working hours. First, the timing makes evaluation problematic. In this connection, one finds yet another parallel to the Equal Employment Opportunity Law. When that law went into effect, Japan's economy was booming. That boom made the EEOL look like an immediate success, with women gaining more jobs, and more responsible jobs. But the recent downturn in the economy revealed most of that apparent success to have been a mere illusion.[180]

Similarly, the current recession clearly is affecting the statistics on working hours. Still, even before the recession, hours were on a downward trend. Between 1988 and 1991, average annual working hours fell by almost one hundred hours, so nearly half of the reduction was achieved when the economy was still strong.[181]

The figures remain hard to evaluate, however. Among various concerns over the accuracy of the official statistics,[182] one aspect provides perhaps the most telling example of the difficulty Japan faces in the efforts to reduce hours. That is the phenomenon of so-called "service overtime" (*sâbisu zangyô*), or "voluntary" unpaid and unreported overtime. Of course, Japan is not unique in having workers who are willing to put in unpaid time.[183] Yet the extent of the

---

178 JAPAN INSTITUTE OF LABOUR, Japanese Working Life Profile: Labor Statistics 1989, at 41-42.

179 *See* JAPAN INSTITUTE OF LABOUR, Japanese Working Life Profile: Labor Statistics 1994-95, at 41 (average of 1,912.8 hours for 1993). Working hours dropped slightly in 1994, to 1,904 hours, *see: White Paper on Labour 1995: Outline of the Analysis*, JAPAN LAB. BULL., Vol. 34, No. 10, at 11 (Oct. 1995).

180 *See,* e.g., KAMIYA, *supra* note 98, at 63-69.

181 *See* JAPAN INSTITUTE OF LABOUR, Japanese Working Life Profile: Labor Statistics 1993-94, at 41 (decline from 2,111 hours in 1988 to 1,972 in 1991).

182 Many of the official statistics, for example, are based upon firms with 30 or more employees. Working hours historically have been much higher at smaller firms.

183 In the United States, many workers - even among those paid on an hourly basis - put in unpaid overtime. Sometimes this reflects a desire to impress superiors and perhaps gain a promotion; at other times it is regarded as the price for keeping a job. Still, in the United States this practice is generally viewed as an aberration to

phenomenon is striking. By all accounts, the practice is pervasive.[184] While it cannot legally be demanded, it is clear that in many cases it is at least expected as the contribution of a loyal employee. Moreover, there have been relatively few attempts to curtail the practice of *sâbisu zangyô*, and those that have occurred have for the most part been unavailing.[185] Consequently, the official overtime figures miss many of the hours actually worked.

---

the normal work pattern. In Japan, in contrast, *sâbisu zangyô* is widely regarded as nothing out of the ordinary. *See,* e.g., MORI, *supra* note 150, at 59 (existence of *sâbisu zangyô* is a "widely known fact").

184 Precisely because *sâbisu zangyô* involves unreported hours, it is impossible to get a truly accurate handle on how many workers and hours are involved. A 1990 MOL survey found that 29% of workers were receiving less overtime pay than they were entitled to, *see* K. HAMAGUCHI, *Sôjitsu rôdô jikan 1,800 jikan ni mukete* [Moving Toward 1,800 Total Actual Working Hours], 162 KIKAN RÔDÔHÔ 65, 77-78 (1992). Many observers place the numbers much higher than MOL figures. For example, a 1991 survey by a private company, Recruit Research, found that only slightly over half of all workers were receiving all the overtime pay to which they were entitled, *See* MORI, *supra* note 150, at 63 note 3. The amount of *sâbisu zangyô* was far higher in some industries, with some three quarters of those in the financial and insurance industries putting in unpaid overtime hours, *see* HAMAGUCHI, *supra*. *See*, generally, K. MORIOKA, *1,800 rôdô jikan keikaku no kenshô* [Evaluation of the Plan to Achieve 1800 Working Hours], *in*: 87 *Kansai daigaku keizai-seiji kenkyû-sho, Kenkyû sôsho, Gendai nihon no chiiki to keizai* [Kansai University Economics and Politics Research Institute, Research Series, Regions of Current Japan and the Economy], at 88-92 (1994).

The experiences of a friend are instructive in this regard. In the early 1990s, a major U.S. law firm (which itself has a reputation for hard work, and where he had a personal reputation as one of the firm's hardest-working associates) seconded him to the head office in Tokyo of a major Japanese financial institution. When he began work there, he asked how he should fill out his weekly time sheet, and was told just to do what he would normally do at his law firm. Following those instructions, he kept track of all his hours and filed a time sheet accurately showing that he had worked over eighty hours. He was promptly informed that that was too high - that it made it look as though the company was working him too hard. So the following week he submitted a time sheet in the 40-50 hour range. This time he was promptly informed that it fluctuated too much from the prior time sheet and made it look as though the department did not know how to allocate its work load properly. Thereafter, he let prudence be his guide. He asked someone else to fill out his time sheets for him, putting down whatever would be typical for Japanese employees in that department (who, he observed, frequently worked even longer than he did). He never had any more problems.

Yet *sâbisu zangyô* is by no means limited to white collar workers in the service sector. Reports abound of the practice even among blue collar manufacturing workers. Moreover, it is not an isolated occurrence limited to special emergencies.

185 In theory, directly affected workers could demand the pay to which they are entitled, ultimately backed by the threat of litigation. (The LSL provides for full payment of wages, Article 24(1), and workers may file claims for deficiencies.) Unions also could insist that workers be fully paid for overtime. In a few cases reported recently, unions have protested *sâbisu zangyô* and ultimately have won agreements by the employers to pay workers previously unpaid overtime premia for a two-year period (that being the statute of limitations under the LSL), *see* 1317

To the extent that the reductions during the boom years were real, one is still left with the question of how much of the decline reflected the impact of the laws and how much the impact of the economy, in the form of labor market pressures to improve working conditions in order to attract workers. Thus, the real test will come when the recession ends and business picks up to moderate levels.

Even after the latest round of amendments, the coercive impact of the legal provisions remains limited. Despite the government's stated commitment to the goal of 1,800 hours, it has been reluctant to take concrete steps that are adverse to business interests or might threaten competitiveness. Moreover, the laws provide few new tools for labor.

If not the stick, how about the carrot? The 1993 amendments contained a package of incentives, including subsidies, low-interest loans, and tax breaks for small and medium-sized companies that invest in labor-saving machinery or take certain other measures to reduce working hours. The incentives are modest, however, and do not appear likely to have a major impact.[186]

Given the modest nature of the legal steps, the government is aware that the key to avoiding a jump in hours as soon as the recession ends lies in changing

---

RÔDÔ HÔRITSU JUNPÔ 65 (1993) (news summary of Hokuriku Bank case); 1303 RÔDÔ HÔRITSU JUNPÔ 104 (1993) (news summary, describing similar resolutions of cases involving banks in Akita and Niigata Prefectures). These remain rare cases, however; historically, neither workers nor unions have been aggressive in opposing *sâbisu zangyô*. This has left the task of curbing *sâbisu zangyô* to the government, in particular the Labor Standards Inspection Offices. Apart from jawboning, those offices have undertaken some highly-publicized efforts to deal with the unpaid overtime problem. The efforts have included a series of carefully coordinated late-night raids on the Tokyo headquarters of several of Japan's largest banks - raids that disclosed pervasive *sâbisu zangyô* and widespread violations of the banks' Article 36 agreements. *See* 1282 RÔDÔ HÔRITSU JUNPÔ 81 (1992) (news summary). Although the failure to pay wages in full constitutes a violation of the penal provisions of the LSL (subject to a fine of up to ¥100,000, which presumably could be assessed on a per violation basis), Article 120 of the LSL, MOL authorities have been reluctant to refer *sâbisu zangyô* cases to prosecutors for institution of penal actions, and instead have relied primarily on publicizing violations and taking other informal actions. The Hokuriku Bank case mentioned above is apparently the first case in which MOL sought prosecution, *see* 1305 RÔDÔ HÔRITSU JUNPÔ 65 (1993) (news summary). Even if enforcement were to be stepped up significantly, it is doubtful how much could be accomplished through such official efforts, since about 350 Labor Standards Inspection Offices, 4 KODANSHA ENCYCLOPEDIA OF JAPAN 358 (1983), have responsibility for policing more than six million businesses, *see* JAPAN LAB. BULL., Vol. 34, No. 6, at 1 (June 1995) (as of April 1994, there were 6.55 million private-sector businesses).

186 For companies with up to 30 employees, for example, the maximum subsidy originally available was ¥500,000, *see* note 151 *supra*. In 1995, MOL increased the maximum subsidy to ¥750,000, reportedly in recognition of the need for greater subsidies to encourage small companies to achieve the 40-hour week, *see* 1358 RÔDÔ HÔRITSU JUNPÔ 72 (1995) (news summary).

the underlying attitudes of employers, workers, and even society itself. Thus, the real measure of success may be: Have basic attitudes been changed?

Achieving such attitudinal change is not an easy task, for the attitudes involved are deep-rooted. In business circles, long hours have widely been regarded as almost a virtue in themselves, as a sign of commitment and devotion to the company.[187] The view of hard work as a virtue is not necessarily limited to business executives, either. For years, Japanese workers have seemed willing to sacrifice, both as part of the price for Japanese industry to advance and, for reasons discussed earlier, to ensure their own job security. Indeed, phrasing this as a "sacrifice" may constitute a loaded formulation. Despite gradual increases in the desire for leisure time, many Japanese workers continue to view long working hours as a natural part of their commitment to the company.[188]

Furthermore, in seeking to alter these attitudes, MOL could not count on assistance from the courts. In 1991, when concerns over long working hours and *karôshi* were at a peak, the Supreme Court upheld Hitachi Manufacturing Company's disciplinary discharge of an employee for refusing overtime on a single occasion.[189] The Court stated that, since the company's overtime order

---

187 *See,* e.g., R. WHYMANT, Have the Japanese Got Tired of Work?, THE DAILY TELEGRAPH, May 27, 1992, at 21; *Zadankai, Jitan sokushin-hô no kôzô* [Panel Discussion, The Structure of the Temporary Measures Law], 998 JURISUTO 10, 24 (1992) (comments of *Kôichi Satô*). In 1992, *Akio Morita*, then chairman of the Sony Corporation, raised eyebrows among Japanese businesses when he published an article advocating cuts in hours (and increases in wages) for Japanese workers, in part to avoid trade friction, A. MORITA, *"Nihon-gata keiei" ga ayaui* ["Japanese-Style Management" Is in Danger], BUNGEI SHUNJÛ 94 (Feb. 1992), published in English as: A Turning Point for Japan Inc., DIRECTORS & BOARDS, Vol. 7, No. 1, at 1 (Sept. 22, 1992). His were views that few Japanese business leaders shared (and to which even fewer would admit). In fact, in a 1992 survey of over 2,000 top executives, some 40% expressed concern that prosperity was eroding the work ethic, *see* WHYMANT, *supra*. It bears note, moreover, that there was more than a trace of self-interest involved in Morita's statement: Sony would be one of the big winners if Japanese workers had increased leisure time and spending power.

188 This view is not nearly so unanimous as commonly held stereotypes would suggest, however. The very fact that businesses felt the need to reduce working hours in order to attract good workers during the boom years leads to the unsurprising conclusion that Japanese workers are not totally wedded to the workplace. Moreover, surveys have shown considerable increases since 1985 in the value that workers place on leisure time, although that trend seems to have reversed in the midst of the recession. *See* note 41 *supra*, text accompanying note and note 206 *infra*, note 211 *infra*.

189 *Tanaka* v. *Hitachi Manufacturing Co.*, Supreme Court [*Saikô Saibansho*] 1st P.B., Judgment of Nov. 28, 1991, 594 RÔDÔ HANREI 7. The employee had been asked to stay on the occasion in question to correct improper work; he reportedly had been disciplined on three prior occasions - apparently for politically related (presumably leftist) activities; and on this occasion he had compounded his "fault" by insisting on his right to refuse overtime and failing to show any remorse even after a two-

had satisfied the terms of the Article 36 agreement with the union, the employee bore the duty to comply with the order.

Given the fact that unions have shown little ability, or even inclination, to pursue strict Article 36 agreements,[190] this decision in effect left only the bureaucracy - and, of course, independent economic pressures from the labor market - to regulate overtime. Yet even for the bureaucrats, jawboning is about the only real tool available. At least in this context,[191] however, they have not been at all shy about using that power.

---

week suspension. *See* K. SUGENO, The Supreme Court's Hitachi Decision on the Duty to Work Overtime, JAPAN LAB. BULL., Vol. 31, No. 5, at 5 (May 1992). Yet as the grounds justifying the disciplinary discharge, the Supreme Court simply referred to "the fact that the overtime was ordered for the purpose of completing and correcting slipshod work performed by appellant and other facts as found by the court below," 594 RÔDÔ HANREI at 10.

In a similar vein, in mid-1992, the Supreme Court reversed a lower court decision and held that a news service, *Jiji Tsûshin*, acted within its discretion in refusing to permit a reporter to utilize accumulated vacation time to take an extended (month-long) vacation, and instead demanding the reporter break up the vacation time into smaller units. *K.K. Jiji Tsûshinsha* v. *Yamaguchi*, Supreme Court, 3d P.B., Judgment of June 23, 1992, 1296 RÔDÔ HÔRITSU JUNPÔ 44.

190 In 1992, *Rengô* pledged that it and all of the labor organizations belonging to it would "struggle with all of the organization's power in discussions with business organizations . . . toward the realization of a 40-hour work week and 1,800-hour year. . . ," *see* RÔDÔ KUMIAI SÔRENGÔKAI, *supra* note 141, at 52. Yet a leader of the General Federation of Private Railway Workers' Unions seems to have more accurately described the current situation: "Although *Rengô* has followed the policy of self-determination of *wages* on an industry-by-industry basis, when it comes to *working hours*, unless they're determined by law, we'll never be able to achieve reductions in hours [through our own efforts]," quoted in *Yûyo sochi no haishi mo*, *supra* note 167 (emphasis added).

191 Viewed as a whole, the legislative efforts on working hours follow the classic pattern of seeking to achieve change not through the coercive force of law, but by using law, and governmental persuasion, to change attitudes. To a large extent, this is the same pattern one finds in the equal employment opportunity area. Yet one cannot escape a sense that the "enlightenment" activities and the extent of governmental pressure have been greater with respect to working hours than in connection with the EEOL. *See,* e.g., KAMIYA, *supra* note 98, at 58-62, 76-80; SÔMUCHO [Management and Coordination Agency], *Fujin shûgyô taisaku tô ni kansuru gyôsei kansatsu kekka ni motozuku kankoku* [Recommendations Based on Results of Administrative Inspection of Measures Relating to Employment of Women] (June 1991), *in* 1260 RÔDÔ HÔRITSU JUNPÔ 51 (1991). Furthermore, in the working hours field, the original legislation was not simply billed as gradualism, with the labor market then left to take its own course, as appears to have been largely the case with the EEOL. Rather, here the government followed up the 1987 amendments with two additional sets of legislation and a wide range of other activities. This contrast between efforts on working hours, on the one hand, and equal employment opportunity, on the other, may simply mean the former is regarded as less controversial and more amenable to change. Yet it may suggest a more sobering conclusion: that in the Japanese context reducing working hours is treated as a more serious goal than achieving gender equality.

At both the national and local levels, MOL and other governmental bodies have undertaken extensive campaigns bearing catchy slogans such as "Enjoy Life" (*enjoi raifu*),[192] designed to teach workers how to do just that: how to use and enjoy leisure time. The bureaucrats have also engaged in extensive activities aimed at business. These activities have included campaigns aimed at educating employers on the benefits of reducing hours and on ways to achieve that goal, with suggestions as to both process and substance.[193] MOL and many municipal governments have also sponsored forums to aid businesses in meeting concerns over competition and customer reaction.

MOL recognizes that the issue of working hours goes well beyond the workplace and extends to "all aspects of national life, including family life, leisure activities, and consumption patterns."[194] Accordingly, in addition to efforts directed at workers and business, MOL has undertaken broad activities aimed at developing societal consensus on the importance of reducing working hours. Through its prefectural offices, MOL has convened numerous local discussion groups. MOL also has pursued major publicity campaigns, using everything from television and newspapers to posters and leaflets, seeking to foster a public appetite for taking "long" vacations (which, by Japanese standards, means anything longer than a few days). Every year since 1986, moreover, MOL has designated one month as "Leisure Creation Month" (*yutori sôzô gekkan*). During that month, it sponsors symposia at both the national and local levels and conducts many other activities to publicize hours reduction, including, since 1989, awards ceremonies to honor those who have made especially great contributions to reducing hours. With the assistance of local communities, MOL has even instituted a type of "Model Cities" program for hours reduction, providing special guidance and assistance to cities that have pledged to take aggressive efforts to promote the cause.[195]

Notably, the substantive focus of these efforts has had a rather Japanese flavor. MOL has identified three major obstacles to lower working hours: overtime, the number of days off (including two-day weekends) granted by

---

192 *See*, e.g., TÔKYÔ-TO RÔDÔ KEIZAI KYOKU [Tokyo Municipal Labor and Economy Division], *Motto yutori o - enjoi raifu* [For Greater Leisure - Enjoy Life] (1991).

193 As to process, one handbook prepared by MOL contained the following suggestions, along with many others: establish a top-down approach, or an official responsible for reducing hours, or a project-team, or a labor-management committee; establish a concrete plan, based on a careful evaluation of existing work patterns, business needs, and worker attitudes; and consult with customers and suppliers to resolve problems that might arise, *see: Rôdô jikan no shiori*, *supra* note 25, at 89-105. For a description of some of the substantive steps MOL has advocated, see text accompanying notes 196-202 *infra*.

194 *Id.* at 167.

195 *See id.* at 167-171. As of 1993, 75 "Cities Pledged to Leisure Creation" [*Yutori sôzô sengen toshi*] had been named, *see id.* at 171.

employers, and the so-called vacation utilization rate - the amount of paid vacation that workers actually take (which historically has hovered at only about 50%[196]). As means for reducing overtime, MOL has promoted various steps aimed at changing the business environment to make it more acceptable for a worker *not* to work overtime.[197] One such step is for businesses in essence to compel workers to leave promptly at closing time by adopting company-wide practices applicable to all employees - through "No Overtime Days" or "No Overtime Weeks," for example. Another MOL recommendation is for businesses to discourage managers from working overtime or on rest days, in order to create an environment in which their subordinates will not feel compelled to do so. Both stand as reflections of the extent to which workers still feel that failure to work late, or that leaving before one's superior, might be taken as a lack of commitment to the company[198] - and as reflections of MOL's recognition of the need for creative approaches to overcome that mindset.

Onc of the most interesting, and successful, sets of creative MOL tactics are those aimed at increasing the vacation utilization rate by encouraging workers to take longer vacations. Yet again, MOL actively promoted an approach designed to take individual employee choice out of the picture,[199] so that workers would not face fears of being branded as disloyal. Through use of jawboning, together with modest subsidies, the government has encouraged businesses simply to adopt company-wide "vacations," during which operations are completely shut down for a week or longer during the Bon festival period in the summer. On a parallel front, governmental authorities have sought to foster

196 *See id.* at 43, table II-9.

197 *See id.* at 124-135.

198 When I worked at Nissan Motor Co. in the mid-1980s, I observed a similar phenomenon. At the time, the normal workday ended at 5:30 p.m. Overtime was calculated in one-hour increments, so workers who stayed until 6:30 were entitled to an hour of overtime pay, but those who left earlier were not. Virtually no one left promptly at 5:30. Workers gradually trickled out between about 5:45 and 6. Yet I was struck that some workers left at 6:20 or even 6:25. As long as they'd stayed that long, I thought, they might as well remain a few minutes longer and receive an extra hour's pay. When I mentioned this to a Japanese co-worker, he explained that if those workers left promptly at 6:30, it would look as though they'd timed their departure just so they could collect overtime. Since this might be seen as a lack of sufficient commitment, they'd have to stay till at least 6:45 before they'd feel comfortable in claiming the overtime pay. Naturally, these extra quarter, half, and even nearly full hours do not appear in the official working hour statistics.

199 In the words of one MOL official, "If it were left up to voluntary choice by the workers themselves, the rate of vacation utilization wouldn't increase very much, so the discussion turned to creating a system in which there was a degree of compulsion, so workers could take time off without feeling ill at ease." SUZUKI, *supra* note 36, at 15.

the "tradition" of long vacations by actively promoting long breaks and travel during so-called "Golden Week" (the seven-day period between April 29 and May 5, which contains three national holidays and one national "rest day" - the last of which was newly created as part of the push to increase use of leisure time[200]) and in the summer (under the catch phrase "Hot Week"[201]).

Perhaps the most crucial measure of attitudinal change may lie in the five-day work week, however. By the 1980s, the two-day weekend already had become a selling point for large companies seeking to attract new recruits. The government sought to help spread the five-day work week by gradually adopting its use at government offices and encouraging its adoption by banks.[202] Those efforts initially seemed to be working: as of 1988, under 30% of Japanese workers enjoyed a five-day work week; by 1992, over half did.[203] Then progress stalled. As of the end of 1993, the figure had only inched up to 52.9%.[204]

In a reflection of just how interrelated the topic of working hours is with other aspects of society, what may well prove to be the most important single step toward changing attitudes toward weekend work involves the Ministry of Education even more than MOL. That lies in a move to reduce the school week from six to five days. An educational advisory council first proposed this step in 1986; the Cabinet recommended it in a 1988 economic plan; and it was adopted on an experimental basis in 1990, with 68 schools nationwide taking

---

200 As of the early 1980s, this period included three holidays: the Showa Emperor's Birthday on April 29, Constitution Memorial Day on May 3, and Children's Day (formerly Boys' Day) on May 5. To ensure at least three consecutive days off, the National Holidays Law [*Kokumin no shukujitsu ni kansuru hôritsu*], Law No. 178 of 1948, was amended in 1985 to provide that "a day that is both preceded by and followed by a national holiday . . . shall become a rest day," *id.* Article 3(3) (added by Law No. 103 of 1985). Currently, the only day that is affected by that change is May 4. As a further step aimed both at maintaining Golden Week and at expanding the list of official holidays, following the death of the Showa Emperor (Emperor *Hirohito*), April 29 was maintained as a holiday by redesignating the Showa Emperor's Birthday as "Greenery Day" (*Midori no hi*), and the Heisei Emperor's Birthday, December 23, was added as a new national holiday, *id.* Article 2 (as revised by Law No. 5 of 1989).

201 "Hot Week" reflects a play on words. *Hotto* in Japanese serves as both the transliteration of the English "hot" and an onomatopoeic word used to indicate relief (as in *hotto shita*). Notably, MOL relaxed the push for Hot Week in 1988, as the economy began to expand, *see: Manatsu no yume? Hotto uîku* [A Midsummer's Dream? Hot Week], RÔDÔ SHINBUN, Aug. 8, 1988, at 7.

202 *Rôdô jikan no shiori*, *supra* note 25, at 35 (in 1989, government offices began closing two Saturdays per week and financial institutions moved to a true five-day work week; from 1992, all national governmental offices moved to a five-day week; and as of late 1993, over 90% of local governmental offices had also adopted the five-day week).

203 *See id.* at 36.

204 *See* JAPAN LAB. BULL., Vol. 34, No. 1, at 1 (Jan. 1995).

Saturdays off once or twice a month. Since the fall of 1992, all schools from kindergarten through high school have taken off one Saturday per month.[205]

If that trend were to continue and expand to a true five-day school week, it might have more of an impact on working hours than any of the steps taken by MOL. Despite the widespread stereotype that Japanese workers value their companies over their families, a survey conducted in 1993 by the Japan Federation of Business Organizations (*Keidanren*) cast some doubt on that image. According to the survey, most workers feel that, when company outings and other functions conflict with family matters, under current circumstances they have no choice but to place the company first. As for the future, though, the vast majority either expressed no preference or stated that they would like to place priority on their families, and the trend toward valuing the family over the company was especially pronounced among younger workers.[206] Nonetheless, past attempts to appeal to that sentiment as a way to reduce working hours, utilizing a catch phrase that reportedly had proven successful in Germany, "On Saturday Papa belongs to me,"[207] had rung false in Japan for obvious reasons. Even if "Papa" got Saturdays off, his children didn't. Yet if the shift to a five-day school week were to become a reality, this generation of fathers might choose to spend more time at home, and less at the company. And for the next generation, a five-day work week might come to be seen as a given, rather than a special privilege.

Of course, all this assumes that a true five-day school week might become a reality. It also assumes that the Saturdays in official schools would not simply be replaced by Saturdays in private cram schools (*juku*). In the spring of 1996, the push to an official five-day school week was extended, but still to only two Saturdays per month. In Japan's highly competitive exam-oriented society, moreover, many observers believe that even if regular school is reduced to five days every week, cram schools will simply fill any void left by the official education system (and in the process heighten the advantage of wealth).

This entire debate might well strike American observers as ironic. After all, in recent years the United States has witnessed occasional proposals to *extend* the school week or the school year, and on those occasions Japan is typically referred to as the model with which the United States is (or should be) competing. Moreover, despite the chorus of outrage that met comments by then-Japanese Speaker of the House *Yoshio Sakurauchi* in early 1992 characterizing U.S. workers as "lazy" and by then-Prime Minister *Kiichi*

---

205 *Rôdô jikan no shiori*, *supra* note 25, at 173-174.

206 *See* 1309 RÔDÔ HÔRITSU JUNPÔ 64 (1993) (news summary). *But see* note 211 *infra*.

207 *See* JOINT STRUGGLE COUNCIL, *supra* note 49, at 17. As the title for one of its major reports, the Joint Struggle Council adopted a slightly different version of that catch phrase: "Saturdays with the family together under the sky."

Miyazawa shortly thereafter questioning the "work ethic" in the U.S.,[208] some Americans publicly stated (and many more undoubtedly thought to themselves) that there was considerable truth to their comments and that the United States should treat those comments as a wake-up call for a rededication to the work ethic. Regardless of whether those Americans would think that the government should be promoting *longer* working hours, the notion that the government should be taking the lead in urging workers to slow down - to stop and smell the flowers, as it were - would undoubtedly strike many Americans as odd. To have this campaign orchestrated by the very government that Miyazawa himself headed lends an additional air of unreality.

In the end, that leads us back to the central question: Why *has* the Japanese government placed such great efforts into the campaign to reduce hours? One possible answer is that, given the absence of legislation with any substantial coercive impact, MOL has had no choice but to resort to such jawboning. Yet that begs the question of why the government and MOL have felt the need to do anything at all. After all, the LSL requires labor's agreement to overtime and to the conditions governing it. If the workers themselves have not pushed for shorter hours, despite having such a seemingly powerful weapon at their disposal, why should the authorities take that task on themselves?

Notwithstanding the *karôshi* movement, the primary reason does not appear to be a broad concern over workers' health or over the economic impact of workers' compensation claims. Nor, notably, is it part of a full employment policy. Even with the long working hours, Japan has consistently achieved close to full employment rates. Rather, for politicians and the Cabinet as a whole, the answer appears to lie in certain factors mentioned earlier: Japan's perceived international reputation (along with some international pressure) and, more importantly, the view that reducing hours is an important step in moving Japan to a domestic consumption-led economy that will be less dependent on exports for growth.

In this context, many MOL officials appear to stand in a somewhat different position from the politicians and the Cabinet.[209] For those MOL officials, an

---

208 *See,* e.g., S. BRULL, A Tale of Two Work Ethics: By Many Yardsticks, the U.S. Tops Japan, INTERNATIONAL HERALD TRIBUNE, Feb. 7, 1992, available in Nexis, ASIAPCS File.

209 A striking example of the difference in attitudes is afforded by news reports that appeared on subsequent days late in 1995. On December 25, *Nihon Keizai Shinbun* reported that the LDP had decided to push for new legislation that would extend the date by which small businesses must meet the 40-hour week from 1997, as currently required by law, to some unspecified future date, *see* 1375 RÔDÔ HÔRITSU JUNPÔ 117 (1996) (news summary). Apparently in response, on the same day that that report appeared, MOL Vice Minister *Kunihiko Saitô* stated: "We are fully aware of the difficulties that small and medium-sized businesses face, but we wish them to endeavor to meet the course that has already been decided. We must not have another situation similar to that which occurred last time (in 1993)," *see id.* at

important concern appears to relate to workers' welfare, based on the implicit view that MOL understands the true importance of shorter hours and also recognizes that, given the realities of Japan's enterprise union system, the workers will not be able to achieve shorter hours on their own, despite the existence of Article 36. In short, MOL's stance is fundamentally paternalistic.

In pursuing this paternalism, however, MOL cannot - nor does it wish to - ignore the interests of business. Rather, it finds itself engaged in a rather delicate balancing act. It hopes to achieve a modest change in the ethos of business, in which workers will get weekends off and take somewhat longer annual vacations, without altering the strong work ethic or in any way undermining the competitiveness of Japanese business. As one Labor Ministry official put it: "We . . . have absolutely no intention of turning the Japanese people into a lazy people. Rather, we are seeking a society in which people work hard, but also enjoy leisure . . . ."[210] The three packages of legislation, with their near lack of new coercive measures, their only modest increase in the overtime premium, and their heavy reliance on consultative measures, jawboning, and voluntariness, all reflect this cautious approach.

How successful the government's efforts ultimately will be is another question. During the boom years of the late 1980s and early 1990s, when labor was in very short supply, business agreed that one of the most crucial issues in the labor field was reducing working hours - which not so coincidentally had become an important concern of prospective employees. With the advent of a labor surplus in the current recession, business has changed its tune and has begun to urge a go-slow approach on the hours front. That shift in business's attitude, more than anything else, may encapsulate the dilemma MOL faces. Despite all the posturing and jawboning, trends in working hours - in Japan as in the United States and elsewhere - ultimately depend most heavily on the labor market itself. Yet, upon close examination, the legislative packages have done little to alter the basic incentives in the labor market. Accordingly, unless MOL's publicity and related efforts, or other societal trends, increase the relative value that workers accord to leisure,[211] in the final analysis all the

---

118 (summary of article that appeared in *Asahi Shinbun* on Dec. 26, 1995). For a discussion of the events in 1993 to which *Saitô* presumably was referring, *see* text accompanying notes 166-177 *supra*.

210 Hatakenaka, *supra* note 55, at 3.

211 In the "bubble" years of the late 1980s and early 1990s, survey results seemed to indicate that worker attitudes indeed were shifting, *see,* e.g., text accompanying notes and notes 41 and 206 *supra*. More recent survey results reflect a shift back, thus suggesting just how closely attitudes remain tied to economic circumstances. In a survey of male workers between 30 and 60 years old and their wives, conducted in the Tokyo area in early 1995 (in the heart of the recession), for example, 55% of the men said they placed greater value on the company than the family, with only 20% expressing the opposite view (although the latter figure was somewhat higher for men in their 30s, at 29%). Notably, over half of the wives

legislative efforts of the past decade may turn out to have little practical impact on working hours.

---

said they like it that way - that they want their husbands to value the company more than the family. *See* 1362 RÔDÔ HÔRITSU JUNPÔ 68 (1995) (news summary). A survey conducted each year for incoming company recruits provides another interesting set of data in this regard. Each year, that survey contains the following question: "If you had made a date (with a girlfriend/boyfriend), and then were ordered to work overtime, would you cancel the date?" In 1991, some 40% of the recruits said they'd refuse the overtime and go on the date, 1269 RÔDÔ HÔRITSU JUNPÔ 64 (1991) (news summary); by 1994, that figure had dropped to 30% (and, in response to the question, "If you were assigned work you didn't like, what would you do?", over half said, "No matter what kind of work it is, I'll put up with it and work very hard."), 1340 RÔDÔ HÔRITSU JUNPÔ 79 (1994) (news summary).

Part Four:
The Bureaucracy in Japanese Economic and Legal Affairs

Chapter Eleven

Finance Bureaucracy and the Regulation of Financial Markets in Japan

Hideki Kanda

Contents

A. Introduction

While administration, legislature, and judiciary are given equal weight in advanced countries' institutional framework, how these bodies operate depends very much upon the historical, political, and cultural environment in which they are found.

With regard to the regulation of financial markets in Japan, bureaucrats in administrative branches have long played a predominant role. In Japan, legislative power is exclusively vested in the Diet. But someone must prepare a bill for legislation. With regard to Japanese legislation concerning financial markets, the bureaucrats of the Ministry of Finance (and sometimes those of other ministries) have always prepared proposed legislation. Judicial powers cannot be exercised unless someone brings a dispute before the courts. Until recently, litigation involving the financial markets has almost never been brought before the courts in Japan.[1]

---

1 In Japan, it is popular for investors who suffer trading losses to sue the broker. But litigation challenging legislation or administrative rulemaking is very rare.

The Ministry of Finance (*Ôkura-shô*, hereinafter MOF) and its bureaucrats thus appear to be quite powerful in Japan. Their powerfulness, however, should not be overemphasized. The Diet is not prohibited from drafting a bill on its own. Market participants are not prohibited from bringing lawsuits before the courts. Thus, the role of the finance bureaucracy is a contingent one, and must be carefully examined in the context in which it exists.

This article will examine the role of the Japanese finance bureaucracy as it relates to the capital markets.[2] Part B will describe the "battle" between the banking and securities industries. Under the regulation fragmenting these industries, when a new financial instrument is created, the battle between the banking and securities industries often results in unique regulatory rules. The finance bureaucrats play an important role in the process where the final rules were developed. Part C will take up commodity funds' legislation as an example of an inter-ministry battle. Part D will offer the theory that the behavior of Japanese finance bureaucrats is better understood if it is viewed as a part of the monitoring mechanisms of the capital markets. Part E will discuss the future implications arising out of the analysis advanced in Part D, as well as brief comments on recent trends. Part F will conclude this article.

B. The Battle Between the Banking and Securities Industries: New Financial Instruments

The fundamental statute for the regulation of capital markets in Japan is the Securities and Exchange Law[3] (SEL). This statute was modeled on the U.S. federal securities laws, specifically the Securities Act of 1933[4] and the Securities Exchange Act of 1934[5]. The SEL provides two basic sets of rules for investor protection: mandatory disclosure and anti-fraud rules. There are important differences between the legal framework of Japan and that of the United States. For instance, in Japan, a firm must obtain a license from MOF to serve as a broker-dealer. The entry barrier to this intermediary service is

---

2 This article is based on my past research. *See* H. KANDA, Politics, Formalism, and the Elusive Goal of Investor Protection: Regulation of Structured Investment Funds in Japan, 12 U.PA.J.INT.BUS.L. 569 (1991). For an excellent book about finance bureaucracy in Japan, *see* F.M. ROSENBLUTH, Financial Politics in Contemporary Japan (1989). *See* also M. AOKI, Japanese Bureaucracy in Economic Administration: A Rational Regulator or Pluralist Agent?, *in* Government Policy Toward Industry in the United States and Japan, 265 (J. Shoven, ed. 1988).

3 *Shôken torihiki-hô*, Law No. 25 of 1948 as amended by Law No. 106 of 1995. For an English translation *see* CAPITAL MARKETS RESEARCH INSTITUTE (ed.), Securities and Exchange Law (1994, suppl. 1995).

4 15 USC §§ 77a *et. seq.*

5 15 USC §§ 78a *et. seq.*

higher in Japan than in the U.S., where registration rather than licensing is required to serve as a broker-dealer.

Most important for this article, however, are the following two respects. First, while the notion of "security" is broadly defined in the U.S., it is limited in Japan. Until 1992, the SEL, in its Section 1 of Article 2, defined a security as one of the following items:

(1) government debt security;
(2) municipal debt security;
(3) debt security issued under a special statute by a corporation;
(4) secured or unsecured debt security issued by a business corporation;
(5) stock issued by a corporation organized under a special statute;
(6) stock and warrant issued by a business corporation;
(7) beneficial certificate under a securities investment trust or loan trust;
(8) security or certificate issued by a foreign government or foreign corporation that has the characteristics of the security or certificate listed in the above (1)-(7); and
(9) any other security or certificate designated by cabinet order.

Although MOF was empowered to designate any new instrument as a security under item 9, it never exercised this power after the amendment in 1953. Thus, in Japanese practice, the definition of a security was quite limited.

Second, again until 1992, by employing the notion of a security, the SEL linked its investor protection rules to Article 65 of the SEL (a rule similar to the U.S. Glass-Steagall Act), which essentially prohibits banks (and insurance companies) from engaging in the securities business except for government and public securities. This regulatory structure was known as the "one-set structure" in Japan and was (and still is) the key to understanding past (and current) developments in the regulation of new financial instruments in Japan. If a financial product is a security, as defined by the SEL, investors enjoy the protection of the SEL, while banks are prohibited from handling such a product. Note also that Article 43 of the SEL prohibits securities companies from handling a product other than a security unless they obtain special permission from MOF. If a product is not a security, banks may handle it, while securities companies may not, and investors receive no protection from the SEL.

When a new financial instrument emerges, the banking and securities industries compete over the intermediary service of such an instrument. In response to the battle between the banking and securities industries, MOF placed priority on the issue of which industry handles each new product over the issue of investor protection. For example, MOF adopted a policy of allowing both banks and securities companies to handle commercial paper. The securities companies received special permission to handle commercial paper under Article 43 of the SEL. Meanwhile, the banking industry successfully persuaded MOF to exclude securities companies from intermediary services for residential mortgage trusts and securitized bank loans. Thus, MOF treated these instruments as non-securities, which banks may handle under the SEL.

The above approach resulted in the absence of legal protection for investors. To remedy this situation, MOF took two actions. First, it had special legislation enacted to protect investors. For example, *teito shôken*, or a mortgage deed, is in this category. Second, by rule or administrative guidance, MOF mandated that banks (and securities companies with regard to commercial paper) not sell these products with a unit value of less than one hundred million yen. The purpose of this limitation was to prevent the sale of such products to the general public, which was said to need protection by the securities law. Commercial paper and residential mortgage trusts were in this category.[6] Certificate of deposit issued in Japan was (and still is) also in this category, but the "minimum unit rule" has been liberalized for this instrument.

In short, all new financial instruments that emerged in the past were treated as "non-securities securities", and they were marketed and sold to Japanese investors outside the SEL.

To remedy this situation, the SEL was substantially amended in 1992. First, the definition of "security" was expanded, and Section 1 of Article 2 of the SEL was amended to include the following:

(8) A promissory note issued by a corporation for funding for its business, as designated by MOF regulation;
(9) [same as item 8 of the old SEL];
(10) A security or certificate issued by a foreign corporation, which represents a beneficiary trust interest or similar interest in loans by a bank or any other lending institution, as designated by MOF regulation.

Commercial paper was designated as a security under item 8 above, and securitized credit card receivables organized in the U.S. (known as CARDS) were designated as securities under item 10 above. Either of these could have been designated as securities prior to the amendment, but, as mentioned previously, no such designations were made under item 9 of the old SEL.

In addition, the catch-all provision of the old SEL, item 9, was replaced by the following:

---

6 For a detailed analysis of the introduction of the commercial paper market in Japan and in the United States, *see* D.G. LITT, J.R. MACEY, G.P. MILLER & E.L. RUBIN, Politics, Bureaucracies, and Financial Markets: Bank Entry into Commercial Paper Underwriting in the United States and Japan, 139 U.PA.L.REV. 369 (1990).

(11) Any other security or certificate designated by cabinet order as necessary to ensure the public interest or investor protection, with consideration given to its transferability and other conditions.

While more narrowly defined than the old catch-all provision, this new provision is expected to be relied upon by MOF to designate new securities. The new provision permits MOF to have any other "paperized" (i.e., "certificated") instrument designated as a security under item 11, unless the transferability of the instrument is restricted or, for instance, the instrument is governed by a different statute concerning investor protection (typically administered by a different ministry).

Section 2 of Article 2 of the SEL was amended to expand the definition of a "deemed" security to include, not only a right which, in principle, is expected to be paperized (though it may not actually be certificated), but also a right which is not, in principle, expected to be paperized, if such right falls within one of the following three categories:

(1) A beneficial trust interest in loans by a bank, trust company or any other financial institution or any other lending institution which provides long-term credit for housing (including land or an interest in land for housing), as designated by cabinet order;
(2) A right in a foreign corporation that has the characteristics of a right in (1); and
(3) Any other monetary claim designated by cabinet order as similar in transferability to security listed in Section 1, as necessary to ensure the public interest or investor protection, with consideration given to the similarity in economic characteristics to any security listed in Section 1 and other conditions.

A beneficial interest in a residential mortgage trust was designated as a security by cabinet order. In addition, MOF is empowered to have any right or interest designated as a security by cabinet order if the right is a monetary claim, the designation of the right as a security is necessary to ensure the public interest or investor protection, and consideration is given to the transferability of the right and other conditions.

These amendments to the definition of "security" were shaped by compromises reached between the banking and securities industries. And it must be noted that Article 65 of the SEL was also amended and under the new Article 65, banks are empowered to handle financial instruments that were "non-securities" under the old SEL and became securities under the new SEL.

C. The Inter-Ministry Battle: Commodity Funds Legislation

In May of 1991, new legislation was introduced in Japan to regulate commodity futures funds, which are known as commodity pools in the United States. This law, the Law for Commodity Investment Business[7], has an interesting story. In 1990, when trading companies and leasing companies found off-shore commodity futures funds to be attractive for marketing to Japanese investors, these companies successfully persuaded the Ministry of International Trade and Industry (*Tsûsan-shô*, hereinafter MITI) to launch a project for special legislation. MITI first contemplated legislation with the same statutory structure as the U.S. Commodity Exchange Act[8], which regulates commodity pool operators, the sponsor in this field. However, the draft prepared by MITI encountered strong opposition from MOF.

MOF rejected the statutory approach directly regulating commodity pool operators on the grounds that the business of such operators consists of financial services. Such a business is similar to the function of trust banks. MOF also argued that when financial institutions participate in commodity futures fund business, either as a sponsor or a seller of the units, they should be subject to their home regulator, that is, MOF.

This battle between MITI and MOF resulted in MITI's abandonment of the legislation that would directly regulate the sponsor of commodity futures funds. In its place, a compromise was developed. The compromise legislation was jointly sponsored by the Ministry of Agriculture, Forestry, and Fisheries, MITI, and MOF. Consequently, its regulatory structure is highly complex.

In creating this legislation, an initial practical assumption was made by the drafters. It was that there are two legal types of commodity futures funds: the contract type and the trust type. The former is typically organized in the limited partnership form. The latter is generally structured in the trust form. On this assumption, the new legislation was structured to impose licensing requirements - and other supervisory and "conduct-of-business" regulations - on the seller of the fund and the adviser for the fund. The scope of the seller's permissible activities is broadly defined so as to include fund organizing and sponsoring; however, such activities are permissible only for the contract type fund. For the trust type fund, if a trading company or leasing company, for instance, obtains an adviser-license and employs a trust bank as trustee for the fund, the trading company or leasing company can manage the fund by entering into a management contract that requires the trustee to follow the adviser's investment directions. For both fund types, if a trading company or leasing company obtains a seller-license, it can market the fund under the supervisory and

---

7 *Shôhin tôshi ni kakaru jigyô no kisei ni kansuru hôritsu*, Law No. 66 of 1991.

8 7 USC §§ 1 *et. seq.*

"conduct-of-business" regulations of the law and the rules promulgated by MITI. The units of the fund, however, are not "exempted securities" under the SEL. The SEL is triggered if the units fall within the SEL's definition of "security."

Financial institutions, such as banks, trust banks, securities firms, and sponsoring companies of securities investment trusts, are exempted from the applicable licensing requirements under the law. Thus, these institutions may serve as sellers or advisers without a license. This exemption from the licensing requirements stems from the fact that these institutions are subject to their "home" regulation of MOF. However, MOF promulgated a detailed set of supervisory rules and "conduct-of-business" regulations under the new law, to regulate (by way of providing a level playing field) the activities of these exempted financial institutions.

In 1992, special legislation for the securitization of the financial assets of credit companies and leasing companies was passed.[9] Here again, the battle between MITI and MOF resulted in a unique statutory structure. The scheme of the securitization must be registered with MITI. The special purpose vehicle must be licensed both from MITI and MOF, but if the vehicle is a financial institution, typically a trust bank, such institution is exempted from the licensing requirement. For the marketing of the securitized units to investors, those who sell the units to investors are generally required licensing both from MITI and MOF, and are subject to various conduct-of-business rules. Again, financial institutions are exempted from this licensing requirement. While the detailed description of this legislation is beyond the scope of this article, it is important to note that the compromise "model" adopted at the time of the legislation for commodity futures funds was adopted in this legislation for securitization.

D. The Role of Bureaucrats in the Capital Markets

1. Conventional View

Under the conventional view of a finance bureaucracy, the two primary tasks of a regulator are law enforcement and rulemaking. In Japan, it has often been pointed out that bureaucrats play yet another, distinctive role: market control. Thus, for example, the eligibility standards for bond issuance (which only permit the issuance of low risk bonds in the Japanese capital markets) was said to be established and maintained by MOF rather than by market participants. Also, the issuance of new shares was said to be controlled by MOF in the form

9 *Tokutei saiken to ni kakaru jigyô no kisei ni kansuru hôritsu* [Law for Regulating the Business of Specified Claims], Law No. 77 of 1992.

of agreements reached at the meetings of managers of the underwriting departments of the "Big Four" securities companies. In response to the recent, rather inactive, stock market in Japan, MOF is said to have tried "PKOs" (price keeping operations) by asking institutional investors to buy shares.

While anecdotal evidence can be found to support these phenomena, it is misleading to submit that MOF controls Japan's capital markets. With regard to PKOs, for instance, institutions were free to buy or not to buy shares.

2. *Another View: Monitoring Theory*

It is promising to analyze the role of bureaucrats and related characteristics of the Japanese system within a broader inquiry regarding how capital market activities are monitored in Japan. This inquiry is more meaningful than, for instance, simply asking whether MOF is powerful.

a. The Process of Legislation and Administrative Rulemaking

The discussion in Parts B and C suggests several characteristics in the legislative and administrative rulemaking processes of Japan. While it is universally observed that various special interest groups compete in most legislative and administrative rulemaking processes, the entire Japanese political environment in which private interest groups and regulators interact might be viewed as unique to Japan. As shown earlier, the treatment of "non-security securities" under the SEL might look familiar at first glance; the banking and securities industries competed and MOF served as a mediator. The battle resulted in the classification of new financial instruments as "non-security securities" under the (old) SEL, which enabled banks to enter the market. To insure investor protection, MOF actively intervened either by making special legislation or by promulgating new rules or administrative guidance. MOF's action can be viewed as a function of the battle between the special interest groups. The promulgation of administrative guidelines that create the "minimum unit rule" for certain public offerings of "non-security securities" represents a victory for the securities industry to the extent that the rule is applied and effectively enforced. Public investors suffer to the extent that "non-security securities" with small investment units are not available in the marketplace.

In this connection, an important customary "rule" exists in Japan. That is, the non-existence of an "explicit" legal rule endorsing a certain activity under explicit regulatory conditions is understood to mean that such activity is prohibited in Japan. When no explicit rule exists as to whether a particular new instrument - such as a negotiable certificate representing the beneficial interest of a trust (other than a loan trust or securities investment trust)[10] - is treated as a security under the SEL or if the rules are unclear, institutions do not invent and market such instruments. Put differently, until a consensus is reached and an explicit rule or administrative guideline is established on a financial device, followed by a lengthy process, virtually no one creates or markets such a financial instrument.

In the case of commodity futures funds, it is easy to see why MITI sought to introduce new legislation to "deregulate" the area. One common explanation is that the introduction of new means of investment in commodity futures enhances public investors' welfare. Another explanation for MITI's conduct is found by examining the interests of trading companies and leasing companies. These companies did not want to violate the "no-rule-means-prohibition" rule. Instead, they persuaded their regulator, MITI, to "regulate" them. The real estate industry did not join this chorus, simply because its regulator is the Ministry of Construction and not MITI. MITI's plan encountered strong opposition from MOF, which apparently received support from the securities and banking industries. The result was a compromise.

The originally proposed statutory structure, under which pool operators would be subject to regulation sorely within the jurisdiction of MITI (and not MOF), was abandoned. But as a practical matter, trading companies and leasing companies can operate commodity futures funds by obtaining a seller-license from MITI. Financial institutions can operate such funds without a license from MITI, but they are subject to additional requirements that MOF promulgates. Beyond the area regulated by the new legislation, which is narrower in its scope of application than the originally proposed draft, the "no-rule-means-prohibition" rule controls. Until the Ministry of Construction introduced new legislation (for property funds), the real estate industry was left unregulated and was subject to the "no-rule-means-prohibition" rule during the transitional period.

It is important to mention that there is no litigation in this area in Japan. Relevant parties participate in the administrative rulemaking and legislative processes. Once an accord is reached, it is unlikely that such an accord will be challenged before the courts. When a dispute is resolved by introducing new legislation, it may be difficult and costly to judicially attack such legislation. Likewise, judicial challenges against administrative rulemaking are also rare. The lack of judicial challenges in this area may initially seem puzzling.

The "special interest theory" of legislation is well-established in the United States.[11] For instance, it was pointed out that the U.S. Glass-Steagall Act,

10 The beneficial interests of a loan trust and securities investment trust are securities under items 7 of Section 1, Article 2 of the SEL.

11 *See* generally S. PELTZMAN, Toward a More General Theory of Regulation, 19 J.L. & ECON. 211 (1976); G. STIGLER, The Theory of Economic Regulation, 2 BELL J.

which separates the banking and securities businesses, stems from the special interest of the investment banking industry, rather than from the public interest.[12] However, the exact effect competing private interests have on the final product of legislation has not been studied in depth.[13] It might be difficult to prove that when legislation is the product of a battle among multiple competing private interests, a more beneficial result is attained for the general public. The Japanese legislation on commodity future funds, however, protects investors to the extent that it is coupled with the Japanese "no-rule-means-prohibition" rule under the SEL, though this is not the best situation.

In the United States over the past few decades, federal agencies have shifted the bulk of their activities "from case-by-case adjudication to general rulemaking proceedings in order to develop administrative policy."[14] While it is well-known in the United States that administrative rulemaking is more vulnerable to judicial challenge than administrative adjudication, the reverse is true in Japan.[15] Indeed, in Japan, administrative adjudication has sometimes been litigated,[16] but no one has challenged a rule that was created through a lengthy decision-making process in which relevant parties participated.

The complicated and time-consuming decision-making process that accompanies legislation and administrative rulemaking in Japan may be viewed as a "monitoring" mechanism of the conduct or activities covered by the legislation or administrative rulemaking. Parties with multiple interests who participate in the process serve as *ex ante* monitors, while parties who litigate legislation or administrative rules serve as *ex post* monitors. Since ex ante monitoring exists, it is not surprising that there are virtually no judicial challenges to legislation or administrative rules in Japan.

It is difficult to determine, as a general matter, whether ex post monitoring is more costly than ex ante monitoring. However, ex ante monitoring has certain advantages. First, while competing ministries and private industries seek to further their own interests, a compromise will often be reached, when a norm enhancing public interest is developed. Second, ex ante negotiation may

---

ECON. & MAN. SCIENCE 3 (1971), revised and reprinted *in*: G. STIGLER, The Citizen and the State: Essays on Regulation (1975).

12 *See* J.R. MACEY, Special Interest Groups Legislation and the Judicial Function: The Dilemma of Glass-Steagall, 33 EMORY L.J. 1 (1984).

13 *See,* e.g., E.L. RUBIN, Law and Regulation in the Administrative State, 89 COLUM. L.REV. 369, 369-370 (1989).

14 R.B. STEWART, Vermont Yankee and the Evolution of Administrative Procedure, 91 HARV.L.REV. 1805, 1811 (1978). *See* generally D.L. SHAPIRO, The Choice of Rulemaking or Adjudication in the Development of Administrative Policy, 78 HARV.L.REV. 921 (1965).

15 *See* STEWART, *supra* note 14, at 1810.

16 For instance, administrative adjudication of the *Kôsei Torihiki I'inkai* [Fair Trade Commission] has often been litigated in Japan.

mean that the cost of uncertainty is not borne by investors. Thus, in Japan, investors can choose from stable alternatives. In contrast, a system that does not have ex ante monitoring offers more choice and more innovation, but at a cost.

One might ask whether there is anyone who directly represents public investors in legislation and administrative rulemaking processes. Japanese custom provides that the decision-making process at the ministry level is accompanied by a lengthy discussion at an advisory council (*shingikai*). An advisory council is organized at the ministry and some of its participants are selected as representatives of public investors. Although the primary purpose of the advisory council is to accommodate the competing interests among the relevant private industries, the interests of public investors are considered, at least to some extent, through certain advisory council representatives.

Viewed in this light, the "no-rule-means-prohibition" rule makes sense in Japan. Conduct that is subject to this rule, such as marketing negotiable trust certificates, has not received the scrutiny of the ex ante monitoring process. Thus, if one pursues such conduct, it is likely to be monitored ex post, perhaps by litigation or by some other social sanction. Ex post monitoring may be undesirable in Japan.

The dominance of administrative rulemaking over administrative adjudication also makes sense in Japan. Less ex ante monitoring exists in an administrative adjudication, because the number of participants in the adjudication process is limited. Further, ex post litigation might be costly. Thus, the Japanese may favor general administrative rulemaking, when it is coupled with ex ante monitoring.

b. Formalism in Administrative Rulemaking

MOF's rules and guidelines under the SEL are formal. The legal norm for a particular activity or conduct consists of complex formal rules. Before the amendments in 1992, in the context of differentiating between a public offering and a private placement, the term "many and unspecified number" is interpreted as fifty or more persons, irrespective of whether the offerees can "fend for themselves". As mentioned above, the "minimum unit rule" for certain "non-security securities" is simply a hundred million yen. Under the SEL, the determination of whether units of an investment fund (other than a securities investment trust) are treated as securities depends on the legal form of the fund. If the fund is organized as a corporation, the units are securities; however, if the fund is organized in the trust form, the units are not securities. Emphasizing legal form over economic substance often creates loopholes. The Japanese formalism in administrative rulemaking appears bewildering.

Since an administrative branch of government is often better equipped to gather and evaluate information in the development and implementation of a policy as compared to a judicial branch of government, one might expect that an administrative branch prefers to enforce substantive rules instead of formalistic rules. In Japan, the reverse is true.

In the United States, extensive studies have been conducted that analyze how an administrative branch or administrative agency of the government chooses among multiple means in developing and implementing a policy goal. However, studies have not focused on whether these groups prefer to enforce formalistic rules. Japan's tendency to favor formalistic rules may be better understood by focusing on the rulemaking process in Japan.

First, at the political level, a legal norm for a particular activity or conduct consists of complex formalistic rules. These rules represent the compromise that was reached during the rulemaking process. Each formalistic rule is easy to observe. The participants in the rulemaking process may clearly indicate each "point" in order to specify the concessions made to each participant.

Second, a legal norm with multiple formalistic rules may withstand a subsequent judicial challenge better than a substantive norm would withstand such a challenge. Judges are better equipped to make a substantive inquiry as it pertains to a particular case. Further, judges may not want to involve themselves in the hard task of dealing with a complex mixture of formalistic rules. This in turn might discourage litigation.

Third, at the theoretical level, formalistic rules might better fit ex ante monitoring than substantive rules. If the legal norms or constituent rules are of a substantive nature, future activities or conduct might be difficult to identify ex ante. Consequently, ex ante monitoring may become extremely difficult and ineffective. Formalistic rules help ex ante monitors to identify future activities and conduct during the rulemaking process, which facilitates the development of a final legal norm.

E. Future Implications

The analysis in Part D suggests several important points. First, administrative guidance which is not backed by formal rules may become less effective. The new legislation contained in the Administrative Procedure Law[17] now requires that, with regard to administrative guidance, administrative agencies must provide the party who is given the guidance with their answers in written form. While this new rule applies only when the party initiates an inquiry, it is easy

---

17 *Gyôsei tetsuzuki-hô* [Administrative Procedure Law], Law No. 88 of 1993. For an English translation *see* 25 LAW IN JAPAN 141-159 (M.A. Levin, trans. 1995).

to see that administrative agencies feel more comfortable when the administrative guidance in question is backed by formal rules, and this is supported by the analysis of Part D. As a result, activities such as PKOs (which, in the author's view, are not administrative guidance at all) will not work as administrative guidance.

Second, the rulemaking process as it now exists may be improved without losing its advantages. The government announced in September 1995 that the discussions held at each meeting of various advisory councils (*shingikai*) will be immediately made public in written form. This will allow more input from the general public in the rulemaking process.

Third, and most importantly, as capital markets become more internationalized, the traditional regulatory environment in Japan may gradually change. These changes may arise in response to differences in the regulatory environment of various countries. The increased need for regulatory cooperation in the international financial services area, such as in the enforcement of insider trading regulations, may influence Japanese regulators to use a more universal standard in administrating and enforcing their policies.

The regulatory environment in Japan thus may change in the future as a result of competitive pressure coming from outside Japan. Over time, the time-consuming process of legislation and administrative rulemaking processes may result in unfavorable consequences for Japan, and it may then recognize the need for responding both politically and economically to a rapidly changing global environment in the financial services area. If Japan moves in such a direction, the analysis advanced in Part D suggests that the ex ante monitoring mechanism of legislative and administrative rulemaking processes will gradually disappear. It will be substituted for by an ex post monitoring mechanism. However, if such a shift does not take place rapidly, it might reinforce the argument that the ex ante monitoring mechanism as it presently exists in the Japanese legislative and administrative rulemaking processes is efficient.

Finally, the above discussion focused on the role of MOF in the rulemaking for new financial instruments or new businesses. One may argue, however, that MOF has maintained a more general, macro policy over the past decades in Japan: industry fragmentation and the concept of "no failure." The financial services industry was divided, or fragmented, into many sub-industries, and regulated separately. This led to market fragmentation as well as industry fragmentation. Thus, there emerged a "specialized banking system," where long-term credit banks, "ordinary" banks, and foreign exchange banks were separately regulated. The trust banking business was also regulated separately. The banking and securities industries were kept separate.[18] Under this policy of

18 *See*, e.g., M.J.B. HALL, Banking Regulation and Supervision: A Comparative Study of the U.K., U.S.A., and Japan (1993).

fragmentation, a policy of "no failure" of any financial institution was adopted as the price for MOF's strong regulatory powers. This system worked quite well after World War II. MOF has allowed virtually no new domestic bank entries since World War II, nor have virtually any new domestic securities firms been licensed during the period. There has been no bank "payoff."

Again, however, it is an overstatement that bureaucrats "controlled" the Japanese financial markets.[19] As deregulation became an international trend, the importance of competition in financial services was widely recognized, and the liberalization of market fragmentation began in 1992 when the "new financial system" was adopted in the form of the amendments to the Banking Law, the SEL, and related statutes.[20] For instance, a bank is now permitted to establish a subsidiary that undertakes the securities business, and vice versa. Behind this liberalization was again the battle between the banking and securities industries, and MOF served as a mediator. Various complicated "fire wall" rules and guidelines exist between the parent bank and its securities subsidiary (or between the parent securities firm and its bank subsidiary), and theory aside, MOF played an active role in promulgating these rules and guidelines. A more or less similar analysis can be applied to the role that MOF played in this liberalization of market fragmentation.

It might be noted that the ministry seems to pursue this liberalization of financial market fragmentation without giving up industry fragmentation. But the above discussion simply suggests that industry fragmentation is a somewhat necessary condition for ex ante monitoring to work properly. Thus, the future success (or competitiveness) of the Japanese financial services market seems to depend upon whether fragmented industries can compete in the liberalized marketplace, unless the whole system changes toward an ex post monitoring system.

Also, the no-failure policy is difficult to maintain, once the market becomes highly competitive. Although this is unrelated to the central theme advanced in this article, suffice it to note that the no-failure policy does not stem directly from the power of the Japanese bureaucrats, but was dependent on the organization of the financial industry in Japan.

F. Conclusion

Bureaucrats act within a certain environment. The regulatory environment for Japanese capital markets, like that in other countries, is complex and difficult to understand in isolation. It is historically and politically contingent. The

---

19 *See* ROSENBLUTH, *supra* note 2, at 17-49.
20 *See* HALL, *supra* note 18.

worldwide trend toward deregulation and increased competition among intermediaries has had a great impact on Japanese developments both in regulation and practice during the past few years. The new regime brought about by the amendments in 1992 as well as other recent trends perhaps show an inevitable change in the response to this worldwide trend. Nevertheless, it is difficult to predict how rapidly and when the Japanese regulatory environment will change to a point where Japanese regulation and practice become indistinguishable from other international forms of regulation and practice.

The role and function of the Japanese finance bureaucracy will change accordingly. But probably its importance will not change in a drastic way. The analysis of the financial bureaucracy will become richer if coupled with the analysis of the environment within which bureaucrats act. This article has made a rather straightforward point: the existence of different environments in different countries suggests that whether they are powerful or not, bureaucrats act (probably properly) within a relevant environment.

Chapter Twelve

Virtual Reality In Japan's Regulatory Agencies

E.B. Keehn

Contents

In the summer of 1991, the Ministry of Finance (*Ôkura-shô*, hereinafter MOF), reacting to stories in the press, confirmed that a number of Japan's securities houses and trust banks had been regularly reimbursing favored corporate clients for losses on their market investments since 1989. Interestingly, this did not lead to public calls for the punishment of brokers who were involved. Instead, the loss compensation scandal resulted in an international condemnation of MOF's regulatory style. This dissatisfaction led to attempts to move control of regulation of the securities industry out of MOF's Securities Bureau, culminating a year later in the creation of the Securities and Exchange Surveillance Commission [*Shôken Torihiki Tô Kanshi I'inkai*, hereinafter SESC].

During the debates leading up to the creation of the SESC, *Anthony Rowley* of the Far Eastern Economic Review commented, "The scandals are woven too deeply into the fabric of Japanese society to be dismissed as a legacy of financial excess. They demonstrate, in fact, how far business practices, governance, and accountability are lagging in Japan."[1] There is no question that the loss compensation scandal would have been regarded as a regulatory failure in New York or London. But in Japan this sort of "failure" is by design and is an integral part of the way in which the bureaucracy influences the nation's economy. Universalistic ideas about how markets should be regulated are secondary to the flexible use of bureaucratic power to bring about specific market results. The case of the SESC, and the philosophy behind its creation, highlights how this flexibility helps to shape Japan's system of capitalism. *Nathan Rosenburg* has suggested that "economists who purport to have

1 A. ROWLEY, Ministry of Myopia: Japanese Scandals Lay Bare the Nexus Between Bureaucrats and Brokers, FAR EASTERN ECONOMIC REVIEW, September 12, 1991, p. 48.

something to say that is pertinent to the contemporary operation of capitalism have the obligation to deal with certain distinctive patterns of capitalist behavior and to explain their consequences."[2] The case of the SESC, and the philosophy behind its creation, highlights part of what is distinctive in Japan's system of capitalism.

The SESC began operations in July 1992. It was touted by Japan's financial press as the functional equivalent of the Securities and Exchange Commission (SEC) in the U.S., an independent regulatory agency which relies on the skills of in-house lawyers and financial specialists to oversee the securities business in the U.S.[3] If Japan's SESC were to approximate the operations of the SEC, it would need to demonstrate levels of transparency in regulatory behavior new to Japan.[4]

This makes the creation of the SESC an important test case for claims that Japan's government began a process of fundamental change in its relationship with the economy in the 1990s. If, as a regulatory office with a new philosophy, the SESC succeeded in working around the entrenched power of MOF, it would be an important piece of evidence supporting the idea often heard in the press that Japan is reshaping its marketplace to more closely resemble that of the U.S. But an SESC that failed to gain independence from MOF and its old regulatory approach would mean business as usual, and provide evidence that we are still waiting for fundamental change in the collusive relationship between the bureaucracy and the market that has long characterized Japan's approach to its economy. An SESC without operational independence would mean not only a failure to challenge MOF's authority, it would also mean that Japan's political leadership had failed to meet public demands for regulatory changes. Similarly, it would suggest that Japan's securities industry is still unable to wean itself away from MOF's particular brand of regulatory behavior.

In fact, the creation of the SESC turned out to be a textbook example of how reformist sentiments can be systematically short-circuited by the entrenched power of the bureaucracy. As *Hiroshi Mizuguchi* explains, the SESC turns out

---

2 Though he makes this comment with regard to *Schumpeter's* interest in economic change instead of economic stability, it is a comment that is equally relevant to the study of state-guided capitalism. *See* N. ROSENBERG, The Emergence of Economic Ideas: Essays in the History of Economics, 158 (1994).

3 NIHON KEIZEI SHINBUN-SHA, *Ôkura-shô no yûutsu* [MOF's Melancholy] 61-52 (1992).

4 Studies of the SEC suggest that it is not an organization that is historically above reproach, and that the effectiveness of ist operations has varied with the leadership of its commissioner. Yet, the principles of SEC regulation have remained relatively clear over the years. *See* J. SELIGMAN, The Transformation of Wall Street (1982).

to be only "superficially similar" to the SEC in the U.S., with the Japanese agency "muzzled" because it was designed to remain under MOF's control.[5]

A. Scandal and "Reform"

The circumstances behind the cycle of scandal and "reform" which created the SESC demonstrates the bureaucratic logic that structures the reshaping of the Japanese marketplace. In the early days of the loss compensation scandal it was reported that Japanese brokerage houses and trust banks had paid out as compensation a total of ¥78 billion to corporate clients who had taken market losses. But it soon became clear that Japan's big four securities companies - *Nomura, Nikko, Daiwa*, and *Yamaichi* - as well as 13 second-tier firms, had paid at least ¥171.9 billion in compensation to 608 corporate clients.[6] In all likelihood this is a low estimate. The true extent of loss compensation practices have never been made public by MOF,[7] nor were the companies and individuals involved required to publicly disclose the full dimensions of their involvement. This in itself highlights one of the problems associated with MOF's self-interested approach to regulation, which often falls short of thorough disclosure on information important to markets, and to the making of public policy. In part, this is what an independent SEC-style approach to regulation would have helped to correct.

Loss compensation was one of the ways brokerages and trust banks in Japan competed for deposits by corporate clients throughout the years of the bubble economy. But it was a practice that was increasingly difficult to sustain in the shrinking market that began in 1989. Japan's big four securities companies were all criticized by the Ministry of Finance for this practice, as were a number of trust banks. Yet when MOF went public with its information on loss compensation practices and forced their halt, *Yoshihisa Tabuchi*, the president of Nomura, argued that this practice was not only well known to MOF, but was informally approved as a way to keep the Tokyo market buoyant during the bubble economy and its early aftermath. MOF denied this, and Tabuchi was forced to resign, though it was widely acknowledged by market watchers that loss compensation was indeed informally supported by MOF's Securities Bureau. But if Nomura and others were engaging in a practice with MOF's unwritten approval, why did MOF decide to condemn this practice when it did?

---

5 M. HIROSHI, Political Reform: Much Ado about Nothing, 40 JAPAN QUARTERLY 253 (July-September 1993).

6 *Id.*

7 The same lack of clear governmental reporting on losses has also been apparent in the bad-debt problem in Japanese banks throughout most of the 1990s. *See* R.T. MURPHY, The Weight of the Yen (1996).

The most commonly accepted theory is that by doing so, the "guilty" brokerage houses would no longer be held liable for their clients' losses. By June 1991 the Tokyo stock market had fallen 42% from its high in 1989, but most clients who were promised compensation had only had their losses reimbursed up to March 1990. MOF's "disciplining" of firms for compensating clients for their losses - an action apparently sanctioned by the ministry - MOF bureaucrats potentially saved Japan's brokerage houses billions of yen in further compensation payments.

If correct, this meant that regulators had allowed the nation's equities markets to function as a source of risk-free profit for a small number of privileged Japanese firms. And when the practice became unsustainable - as the Nikkei index continued to search for the bottom of the market - MOF stepped in to end it. This suggested that the Tokyo market was anything but a level playing field, whether or not one accepts the theory that the market was rigged at the highest levels by its regulators. As *Peter Tasker* suggested at the time, "The way in which Japan responds to the securities scandals will be an important indicator of how capitalism Japanese-style develops in the 1990s. . . . Do the authorities attempt to preserve their arbitrary power over the nation's economic life or will the principles of an open economy triumph?"[8]

The damage to public confidence as a result of the loss compensation scandals was enough to lead to demands, at least in some segments of the popular press, for a basic change in the regulatory framework governing the securities industry in Japan. MOF was judged by its critics to be too close to the industry to act as an impartial regulator, and too reliant on unwritten rule to achieve its ends. But in a market where insider trading was not even made illegal until 1987, the selective use of regulations, and informal approval of questionable practices, had long been the norm and used as a flexible tool by Japan's financial authorities. Even in the case of loss compensation, MOF's Securities Bureau never made it clear whether the practice was or was not illegal, only that they wanted it stopped.

The loss compensation episode suggested that MOF's role as both advocate and regulator of the securities industry raised natural questions about conflict of interest, and was inconsistent with principles of transparent and equal protection of small and large investors alike found in markets such as New York and London. It would appear that the disregard for small investors was not unlike that expressed by the president of the American Sugar Refining Company, voiced in 1900 in opposition to the idea of full disclosure and the public's purchase of shares: "Let the buyer beware; that covers the whole business. You cannot wet nurse people from the time they are born until the

8 Y. IDEI, Securities Scandals Expose Holes in Ministry Guidance, THE NIKKEI WEEKLY, September 14, 1991, p. 1.

time they die. They have got to wade in and get stuck, and that is the way men are educated and cultivated."[9]

The fact that less-favored clients of brokers were left to take their losses, combined with Tabuchi's charge that loss compensations were done with MOF's knowledge and at least tacit approval, did little to inspire public confidence in the ministry's regulatory impartiality. This led to debates over the need to place some regulatory distance between MOF and the securities industry.

The debate on changing the regulatory environment boiled down to two options. One option was to create an independent commission with full regulatory and investigatory powers, including the ability to subpoena evidence, similar to the SEC in the U.S. The Provisional Council on Administrative Reform, a quasi-official governmental body, made it clear it preferred this option. But this option was seen as "impractical" by MOF because of the fundamental changes it would introduce in its operations in Japan's marketplace. MOF advised keeping regulation within the ministry but, in a nod to public criticism, removing it from under the direct administrative wing of its Securities Bureau, though regulation would still follow the bureau's cues. MOF favored and fought for this second option. Once the ministry made its position clear, it did not matter what the Provisional Council on Administrative Reform wanted, and it never lost control of the political debates and the planning process, resulting in an SESC which remains tied to MOF regulatory concerns.

The MOF team which led the battle to prevent the creation of an independent SEC in Japan was partially led by *Akira Ogawa*. Ogawa was a powerful figure within his ministry, particularly on tax affairs, where he played an important role in getting Japan's VAT system introduced during *Noboru Takeshita's* prime ministership. He was closely connected to LDP grandees, particularly to Takeshita whom he served twice, first as personal secretary when Takeshita was finance minister, and again as personal secretary while Takeshita was prime minister. For his efforts in limiting the powers of the SESC, Ogawa was awarded the directorship of MOF's Securities Bureau,[10] the same bureau whose regulatory interests he protected by helping to prevent the creation of an independent U.S.-style SEC in Japan.

The SESC began operations in July 1992. Its executives included a chairperson and two commissioners with a tenure of three years, appointed by

---

9 INDUSTRIAL COMMITTEE, Preliminary Report on Trusts and Industrial Combinations, H.R. Doc. No. 476, 56 Cong., 1st Sess. (1900) 123. Quoted in L. LOSS, Fundamentals of Securities Regulation, 25-26 (1983).

10 N. KISHI, *Ôkura-shô o ugokasu otokotachi* [The Men Who Move the Ministry of Finance] 100-101 (1993).

the Ministry of Finance.[11] A staff total of 202 was divided between the Coordination and Inspection Division and the Investigation Division. However, this is a misleading figure since market surveillance was originally designed to be in the hands of only 12 staffers, with another 26 involved in inspections. This small number was responsible for tracking the operations of 265 firms with about 3,000 branches and around 153,000 employees nationwide. This compares with approximately 2,600 staffers in the SEC in the U.S., about 800 of whom are engaged exclusively in surveillance and inspection work.[12] There is no question that staff and resource shortages seriously hampered the SESC's ability to carry out its appointed tasks. When it prepared its first case, against a small group of four speculators charged with driving up the price of *Nihon Unisys* stock between October 1990 and May 1991, its inspection staff were overwhelmed with the preparations. There simply were no resources left over for the investigation and preparation of other cases.

SESC staffing levels are likely to increase over time. Even if staffing were not an issue, the problem remains that the SESC is an organization with limited independent powers of its own. It is responsible for examining the books of securities dealers and financial institutions, but it can only turn its findings over to the Ministry of Finance and the Japan Securities Dealers Association.[13] MOF is then free to use or ignore this information as it sees fit. There are no clear regulations or procedures requiring the ministry or the courts to act on SESC findings in any preordained or predetermined way. Moreover, MOF made sure that the SESC's establishing law would allow the ministry to carry out the same work as the commission if it so desired.[14] In practice this means that the SESC follows MOF's lead on investigations to insure against pointless duplicated effort. As if this were not enough, the watchdog abilities of the SESC are hamstrung in still other ways. The commission has no subpoena power and it cannot assess penalties without prior MOF approval. Even if penalties are assessed they are not particularly severe, with a maximum fine of ¥3 million and jail sentences of up to three years.[15]

---

11 MOF's selection of the chair and two commissioners is in the hands of the finance minister, and requires Diet approval. However, to date, recommendations of MOF's bureaucrats on these matters have been followed.

12 M.L. MAGDICH, The Failure of Financial Market Regulators and Regulations in Japan to Meet the Needs of a More Efficient Securities Market (Contemporary Japan Centre, University of Essex, 1993). I would like to thank *Dr. David Campbell*, Essex University, for directing me to this excellent thesis. This article would not have been possible without it.

13 M. HOTTA, Securities Watchdog Chained by Limited Staff, THE NIKKEI WEEKLY, August 2, 1993, p. 2.

14 MAGDICH, *supra* note 12, at 29.

15 MAGDICH, *supra* note 12, at 35.

B. Virtual Reality

In the Japanese context, an SESC without independence makes sense. The selective enforcement of vague regulations, coupled with bureaucratic discretion, is viewed by MOF and other ministries as a crucial part of its economic management tool kit.[16] *Eamonn Fingleton* points out that "even top Japanese lawyers have difficulty understanding regulatory nuances."[17] This is reinforced by a political culture in which "[m]ost Japanese citizens are not even aware of the [constitutional] principle that interpretation of the law is a matter for the courts, and instinctively turn to the bureaucrats if they need a law interpreted."[18] Under these conditions, an independent SESC without accompanying reforms that would put an end to MOF's discretionary use of vague regulations, would have done little to create a more transparent regulatory regime.

This raises the question of whether deregulation campaigns can hope to deliver fundamental change without clearer and more objective regulatory arrangements. As a reading of the Deregulation Research Group's (*Kisei Kanwa Kenkyû-kai*) 1994 study makes clear, despite the numerous deregulation measures that are likely to pass into law in Japan throughout the rest of this decade, there will be no fundamental changes made in the bureaucratic behaviors which so often leave Japan's marketplace dependent on informal rules and selective enforcement of regulations.[19]

The lack of functional independence in Japan's regulatory agencies contributes to this state of affairs. This does not result from simple bureaucratic intransigence, as is often portrayed by deregulation campaigners.[20] It is brought about by design. In East Asian systems of state-guided capitalism, pioneered by Japan, compromised regulatory agencies are often a basic component in the successful implementation of strategic economic policy. Truer regulatory independence could too easily contradict the plans of the leading economic bureaucracies and frustrate their use of flexible and informal regulatory tools.[21]

---

16 L. HOLLERMAN, Japan Disincorporated (1988).

17 E. FINGLETON, Blindside: Why Japan Is Still on Track to Overtake the U.S. by the Year 2000, 157 (1995).

18 M. UCHIDA, The Iron Triangle: Bureaucrats, Businessmen and Politicians at the Core of Corruption, TOKYO BUSINESS TODAY, November 1993, p. 7.

19 KISEI KANWA KENKYÛ-KAI, *Kisei kanwa de nihon ga kawaru* [Through Deregulation Japan Will Change] (1994).

20 *See*, for example, T. YAYAMA, *Kanryô bôkoku-ron* [Bureaucrats Ruin the Country] (1993).

21 M. TILTON, Informal Industry Governance in Japan's Basic Materials Industries, 48 INTERNATIONAL ORGANIZATION 663-685 (No. 4, Autumn 1994). *See* also M. TILTON, Why the 1991-1992 Anti-Monopoly Law Reforms Have Not Curbed Japan's Cartels, conference paper, Annual Meeting of the Association for Asian Studies, April 8, 1995, Washington, D.C.

From their perspective, independent regulatory agencies would introduce unwanted levels of uncertainty into the already difficult tasks of goal-oriented economic management. Regulation based on universalistic economic principles would complicate the state's ability to influence markets with flexibility, speed, and favoritism. Neutrality in regulation - a simplistic "rules of the game" approach - would too easily permit industries to seek their own market outcomes, separate from the strategic interests of the state.

For these reasons, the SESC's lack of independence from MOF follows a consistent pattern in Japan's governmental system of binding the behavior of regulatory agencies to the interests of the economic ministries. In fact, all postwar regulatory agencies have been made dependent upon the very ministries whose interests they were designed to assault.[22] This can be done, as in the case of the SESC, by keeping the new regulator under the influence of the ministry most effected - the preferred course. Or it can be achieved by sabotaging new agencies from the inside, by using personnel exchanges as an organizational weapon.[23] In this case, ministries reserve the new agency's key executive and research positions for their own elites, who are rotated through these posts on a regular basis.

This is the "reserved seat" (*shitei-seki*) system, and it is used in all of Japan's regulatory agencies, from the Fair Trade Commission to the Environment Agency. These rotated individuals manage the internal life of these agencies to encourage them not to make decisions that could threaten the interests of their ministries. This is the regulatory equivalent of virtual reality. Regulatory agencies appear on government organization charts, but they do not have independence and generally are subservient to the strategies of the economic bureaucracies. Tensions and policy contradictions between regulatory agencies and the manipulatory economic ministries do occur, but these differences are rarely sustainable in the long term.

It is significant that other ministries in Japan have taken MOF's creation of the SESC as a model for their own "virtual" regulation. A year after the SESC was established, the Ministry of Construction announced its intention to set up an "independent body to oversee the bidding process for public works."[24] As the ministry singularly responsible for encouraging and entrenching the practice of bid-rigging (*dangô*) on public works in the first place, any "independent"

---

22 E.B. KEEHN, The Mandarins of Kasumigaseki (London, Macmillan, in press). *See* also E.B. KEEHN, Managing Interests Inside Japanese Bureaucracy: Informality and Discretion, ASIAN SURVEY, 1021-1037 (November 1990).

23 P. SELZNICK, The Organizational Weapon: A Study of Bolshevik Strategy and Tactics (1960).

24 This was a development that rapidly disappeared from sight. *See* Ministry to Set Up Watchdog, THE NIKKEI WEEKLY, November 8, 1993, p. 2.

body it creates it likely to have more public relations value than genuine regulatory effect.

C. Why Change?

If transparency and neutral enforcement of regulations is at fundamental odds with the economic bureaucracy's interactive and strategic role in Japan's marketplace, what are the prospects for fundamental change? The arguments for true liberalization, both by American trade negotiators and Japan's own domestic critics, are well rehearsed in the press and need not be restated here. Instead I would suggest that, despite the ongoing discussion on deregulation in Japan, the prospects for liberalization may actually be weakening, and this includes changes to dependent systems of regulation as represented by the SESC. Japan faces increasing economic competition from the high growth economies of East Asia on the one hand - most of whom have adopted some form of state-led economic development - and a U.S. that is increasingly interested in managing its international trade with Japan (which amounts to an implicit industrial policy, if not particularly well thought out). Under these circumstances, a Japanese economy in which the government exercises less strategic control may not be regarded by Japan's collective leadership as the wisest way forward in an increasingly complex and challenging global marketplace.

Added to this is the weight of Japan's existing economic institutions, which, when all is said and done, have consistently produced good economic results. As *Taichi Sakaiya* explains:

> Japan's system of firm bureaucratic guidance was greatly strengthened in the days leading into World War II, and it has been left largely intact throughout the postwar period. Until recently the Japanese were virtuously unanimous in the view that the features of this system were virtues. . . . Any attempt to discard a bureaucratic system that has been in place for half a century will naturally meet with strong resistance. After all, virtually every existing organization has developed under this system, and almost all the leading figures in society have benefited from it and have had their ethics and aesthetic values shaped by it.[25]

It is worth noting that Japan's economy, despite high levels of regulation, has consistently proven itself to be highly adaptable to new economic challenges. This has included the oil shocks of the 1970s, the bubble economy of the 1980s, and, at least to date, the high yen of the 1990s.

This does not rule out the possibility of unanticipated economic shocks too severe for Japan's marketplace to absorb in its current structural guise. But

25 T. SAKAIYA, *Kanryô no shinwa* [Bureaucratic Myths], BUNGEI SHUNJU, February 1994, p. 157.

short of that, history will continue to set the terms of Japan's internal debates about the reshaping of its marketplace - as it does in every other country - with decision makers at least as influenced by their own experiences as by demands or expectations on the part of its trading partners. Economic structure and regulatory philosophy will not remain static but will evolve within the context of pre-existing institutions, and the changes will likely be consistent with the lessons Japan's decision makers learned over several decades of state-influenced economic development. And as the case of the SESC suggests, this is at least as likely to result in the reorganization of old practices as it is in fundamental change.

Chapter Thirteen

Bureaucracy and the Protection of National Interests in Japan: Exemplified for Intellectual Property and Competition Law

Christopher Heath

Contents

A. Introduction

It is quite a common phenomenon that in shaping their legal system, countries are likely to protect what is close to their own heart, and less likely to protect what from their own point of view could be detrimental to their own country's development.

> *1st précis*
>
> In trying to foster economic development, countries tend to put their own interests first. This extends to the economic and legal structure supporting such development.

Economic development in Japan has been one of the nation's driving forces in recent years. In 1990 alone, US $660 billion, or 25% of the gross national product, was invested in modernizing and rationalizing its industry[1] - an impressive figure. Economic development can be fostered by the state in many ways, both economic and legal. As a lawyer, I will focus on the promotion of economic development by legal means, namely the framework of intellectual property rights, and competition and anti-trust law - areas closely linked to economic development.

---

1 *See* H. BAUM, Marktzugang und Unternehmenserwerb in Japan [Market Access and Acquisition of Companies in Japan] 30 (1995).

The first patent system was introduced in England (the so-called *Statute of Monopolies*) in the 17th century when the Industrial Revolution made the protection of technical achievements desirable. It took Germany more than 250 years to follow suit. This was partly due to a closely related system of business privileges (*Gewerbeprivilegien*), but also due to a widespread opinion that Germany fared better in copying than in protecting inventions.[2] The initiative for enacting a patent law in Germany came mainly from a generation of famous inventors such as *Siemens, Borsig*, and *Daimler*. The German Patent Act of May 1877 (*Patentgesetz*) was enacted when domestic development swung in favor of protection.

Another example is the protection of literary works copyrighted by foreigners and the treatment that used to be meted out to them in the United States. Significantly, at a time when the very popular author *Charles Dickens* vainly tried to obtain protection for his works in the United States, a contemporary commentator wrote: "Complete with the piracy provision it can be viewed as the action of a developing country to protect its burgeoning culture while exploiting the cultural products of more developed nations".[3] It goes without saying that at a time when the United States would like every country to join in the world-wide fight against computer software piracy (to protect U.S. software, *nota bene*), the United States would now prefer to eat its words of only a century ago.

These two examples should make sufficiently clear that the national interest is dictated by the economic development of a country, and that what are nowadays promoted as "fundamental principles" more often than not have been an expression of a wish to protect certain interests that reflect economic development.

---

2 *See* F.K. BEIER, Gewerbefreiheit und Patentschutz. Zur Entwicklung des Patentrechts in Deutschland im 19. Jahrhundert [Trade Liberalisation and Patent Protection: The Development of German Patent Law in the 19th Century], *in*: Wissenschaft und Kodifikation des Privatrechts im 19. Jahrhundert [Science and the Codification of Civil Law in the 19th Century], Vol. IV, 183, 201 *et seq.* (H. Coing & J. Wilhelm, ed. 1979); F.K. BEIER, Grundlagen und Probleme des deutschen Patentschutzes [Basic Problems of German Patent Protection], *in*: Gewerblicher Rechtsschutz in Deutschland und Japan [Industrial Property Protection in Germany and Japan] 42, 44 *et seq.* (G. Rahn & M. Scheer, ed. 1994); W. TREUE, Die Entwicklung des Patentwesens im 19. Jahrhundert in Preußen und im Deutschen Reich [The Development of German Patent Law in the 19th Century in Prussia and the German Reich], *in*: Coing & Wilhelm, *supra* at 163, 175 *et seq.*

3 T.H. HOEREN, Charles Dickens und das internationale Urheberrecht [Charles Dickens and International Copyright Law], GRUR INT. 195 (1993).

B. Intellectual Property and Competition Law as Examples of the Protection of National Interests in Japan

1. After this brief introduction, in which I have outlined what I perceive as a general principle of all nations - that is, that they are very likely to protect their own economic interests against those of other nations - I will turn to a more detailed analysis of this principle in the context of Japan. Because of its close connection with economic developments, I will focus my attention on examples in the field of intellectual property and competition. While in the case of competition, namely anti-trust law, Japan has been subject to scrutiny for a number of years,[4] the same cannot be said for intellectual property rights. This is a little surprising given that a nation's economic success and position in the 21st century will depend less on the organization of its anti-trust laws and their enforcement than on its ability to generate and protect research and invention. When talking about economic interests, therefore a closer look at intellectual property rights should therefore be helpful, if not essential.

While the intellectual property régime, as well as the management of the Unfair Competition Law,[5] is administered by the Ministry of Trade and Industry (*Tsûsan-shô*, hereinafter MITI), the Antimonopoly Law[6] comes under the jurisdiction of the Fair Trade Commission (*Kôsei Torihiki Inkai*, hereinafter FTC). In addition, the courts have increasingly taken the initiative in developing all these fields of law. I will now turn to the examination of certain cases.

2. At the legislative level, the legal framework for competition law has been a product more of foreign pressure (*gai-atsu*) than of domestic initiative. While the Unfair Competition Law was only enacted because of obligations under the *Paris Convention for the Protection of Industrial Property of 1883*,[7] the

---

4 Specifically by the United States, which has voiced concern about how Japan protects its national interests by keeping foreign competition out: *See*, e.g., the following contributions from K. YAMAMURA (ed.), Japan's Economic Structure: Should It Change? (1990): K. YAMAMURA, Will Japan's Economic Structure Change? 13-64; C. JOHNSON, Trade, Revisionism, and the Future of Japanese-American Relations, 105-134.; K. IMAI, Japanese Business Groups and the Structural Impediments Initiative, 167-202; J.O. HALEY, Weak Law, Strong Competition, and Trade Barriers: Competitiveness as a Disincentive to Foreign Entry into Japanese Markets, 203-236.

5 *Fusei kyôsô bôshin-hô*, Law No. 14 of 1934, completely revised by Law No. 47 of 1993.

6 *Shiteki dokusen no kinshi oyobi kôsei torihiki no kakuho ni kansuru hôritsu*, Law No. 54 of 1947 as amended by Law No. 89 of 1993. For an English translation *see* EHS, Vol. II, KA, No. 2270.

7 *See* G. RAHN & C. HEATH, What is Japanese about the Japanese Unfair Competition Act?, 25 IIC 343 (1994).

Antimonopoly Law was enacted as a direct result of American occupation of Japan in 1947.[8] Because the Unfair Competition Law has no special enforcement agency, its fate has been rather different than that of the Antimonopoly Law, which from the very start came under the jurisdiction of a reasonably independent body, the FTC. For this reason, the development of the Unfair Competition Law has been shaped mainly by industrial policy perceptions of MITI. In consequence, the law was particularly ineffectual in its first four decades. This was due to legal obstacles and the underlying perception that the development of Japanese industry would be impeded by the serious application of unfair competition laws.[9] Legislative changes which enhanced protection were either initiated by the occupying forces under foreign pressure or have proved mostly ineffective.[10]

In the case of the antitrust law, differences between MITI's industrial policy and the FTC's handling of the Antimonopoly Law were predictable, but have probably been exaggerated. Though competition within Japanese industry was of vital interest to both, for the FTC this was a goal *per se*, while for MITI it was rather part of an overall industrial policy. Clashes were also due to the fact that the FTC was meant to enforce a law that also had other objectives beyond the protection of competitors (*see* part C below). But even given these differences, the FTC actively sought to protect Japanese industry, especially against foreign licensors and manufacturers, by means of strict notification requirements and a regime of specific provisions protecting licensees against clauses that were viewed as anti-competitive and thus unenforceable.[11]

As to intellectual property rights, the legal framework was in place very early, as Japan viewed the perfection of inventions as essential for its own economic development[12]. At this level, legislation has always given preference

---

8 H. Iyori, A Comparative Analysis on Japanese Competition Law: An Attempt to Identify German and American Influences, *in*: Die Japanisierung des westlichen Rechts [The Japanization of Western Law], 227 (H. Coing *et. al.*, eds. 1990).

9 *See* Rahn & Heath, *supra* note 7, at 344; K. Toyosaki, Unfair Competition in Japan, 2 IIC 372 (1971).

10 One recent example has been the 1990 enactment of provisions for the protection of trade secrets in order to fend off U.S. criticism. The fact thatat no procedural protection by *in-camera* proceedings is available has rarely been mentioned.

11 *See* H. Iyori & A. Uesugi, The Antimonopoly Laws and Policies Japan 301 (1994). One typical case involved a contract with an anti-competition clause (non-competition after the expiration of the agreement). Due to the questionable handling of the case by the FTC, the foreign licensor was even unable to obtain legal redress against the decision: Decision of the Supreme Court, November 28, 1975, 800 Hanrei Jihô 35 (1976) ["Novo Industri"].

12 Reportedly, the first president of the Japanese Patent Office and later prime minister, *Korekiyo Takahashi*, stated while in the U.S., "We have looked about us to see what nations are the greatest, so that we can be like them. We asked ourselves: What it is that makes the United States such a great nation? And we investigated and we found that it was patents. And so we will have patents."

to small-step inventions rather than basic ones, thereby reflecting the needs and preferences of Japanese industry. This can also be said of Japanese court decisions, which have consistently refused to apply the so-called doctrine of equivalents to the interpretation of patent claims, thereby keeping the scope for patent rights very narrow[13]. This trend is also reflected in a recent decision that has effectively denied protection for a basic patent applied for in 1959 (*Kilby-patent*). Despite the fact that the whole of present-day semi-conductor technology has been based on this invention, the court ruled that it is now so far removed from the original claim terminology that infringement could not be found[14]. In another even more extreme decision, the Tokyo High Court overlooked international obligations under the Paris Convention in the case of an invention which claimed priority of a U.S. patent that in the United States fulfilled all national requirements for a full discovery of the invention. A later application of the same invention in another country that enjoys priority rights fulfills the discovery requirements in the second country, if those of the first country are met (Article 4(h) Paris Convention). Nevertheless, the court held that this was insufficient to satisfy Japanese standards of discovery - which may be so, but is beyond the point[15]. Somewhat more subtle is the discrimination in the case of an infringement of trademark rights where the trademark has been licensed out to a non-exclusive licensee, something more likely to occur to foreign than domestic trademark owners. Where there were infringements, the Tokyo High Court took the view that because the use of a trademark by the licensee could not count as use by the trademark owner (which quite evidently contravenes Article 50 of the Trademark Law[16]), the licensor was therefore not in a position to claim the infringer's profit as damages, because the trademark owner could not be considered to have used the trademark[17].

Quoted after US DEPARTMENT OF COMMERCE/PATENT OFFICE (ed.), The Story of the United States Patent Office, 20 (1972). After having set up the legal framework for the protection of intellectual property rights, in the last 30 years the Ministry of Trade and Industry has effectively supported a policy of research and development in order to enhance competition and increase the number of inventions: J. ERRICO, Licensing Law Handbook (Pacific Rim) 127 (1995).

13 *See*, e.g., H. YAMASAKI, Interpretation of Patent Claims and the Application of the Doctrine of Equivalents, 25 PATENTS & LICENSING 7 (April 1995).

14 Decision of the Tokyo District Court, August 31, 1994, 1510 HANREI JIHÔ 35 (1995) ["Kilby Patent"].

15 Decision of the Tokyo High Court, October 20, 1993, AIPPI JOURNAL OF THE JAPANESE GROUP 155 (1994) ["Tetracycline"].

16 *Shôhyô-hô*, Law No. 127 of 1959 as revised by Law No. 65 of 1991. For an English translation *see* EHS, Vol. VI, VA-A, No. 6880 A.

17 Decision of the Tokyo District Court, March 24, 1993, 26 IIC 566 (1995) ["Type Chanel No. 5"].

3. These few examples should be at least enough to prove that, consciously or unconsciously, Japanese interests are well served by the competent national authorities. Despite often-stressed differences in ethos, I find it difficult to assume that this preference for Japanese interests has *only* been pursued unconsciously and never on purpose.

4. The idea that the relevant authorities have used the tool of intellectual property rights as a means of protecting national interests can also be viewed from another perspective. Actual *protection* of inventions in the national interest would make little sense if there was no *encouragement* for inventions in the first place: a government that views the encouragement of inventions as a matter of national interest will be likely to act in an equally protectionist way when it comes to the protection of results. As to the encouragement of inventions in the national interest, two observations may be worth making.

First, there can be little doubt that the Ministry of Trade and Industry has actively supported research and development activities in Japan in order to help Japanese industry become a world leader. This has been done not only by targeting industries of the future and heavily investing in these by tax breaks, etc., but - allegedly - also by buying up foreign technology cheaply and in bulk, mostly from highly innovative but small companies abroad. In addition, there have been allegations that Japan has tried to gain access to foreign research laboratories and institutes by providing them with funding[18].

Second, the Ministry of Finance has helped to create a climate of high growth, with low interest rates and a booming stock market, in order to enable companies to borrow money almost interest-free, thereby enabling them to invest heavily in research and development and buy up small but inventive foreign companies[19].

Given these facts, it would be surprising if the actual protection of inventions would follow a different path from the encouragement for inventions.

C. Making, Unmaking, and Balancing of Interest in the Context of Economic Development

2nd précis:

Pursuing national interests has its limits. In Japan, an increasingly open society has given voice to a number of concerns hitherto unheard of; economic necessities have changed, and bureaucratic in-house quarrels have helped to fuel a

---

18 *See* ERRICO, *supra* note 12, at 148-149.

19 *Cf.* BAUM, *supra* note 1, at 44-45. Efficiency of this system is guaranteed by the fact that very little of this "excess pocket money" has been passed on to consumers or shareholders (*id.* at 31 quoting *K. Courtis*).

certain loss of direction. Finally, Japan's international obligations in some fields have generated new pressure.

1. Clashes about what should be defined as national interest have certainly been most conspicuous in the field of antitrust law when it came to the protection of consumer interests. Part of the dispute has certainly been the quarrel about who should administer antitrust policy. In this respect, MITI has been largely discredited by helping the oil cartels in the beginning of the 1970s[20]. Yet it would be wrong to assume that MITI looks askance at competition as such. This is certainly untrue. To the FTC, however, competition is a goal in itself, while to MITI competition should be part of a wider industrial policy. While consumers have proved good allies of the FTC in times of economic depression, they do not exactly loom large in MITI's industrial policy. After much hesitation, especially about the question of liberalizing the distribution system, MITI has gone onto the defensive over the opening of large superstores[21], while the FTC is counting public support for the liberalization of retail structures and abolition of the retail price maintenance system for even more goods[22]. Also, under a still obscure relationship between civil law, unfair competition, and antitrust law, the courts have assumed an increasingly active role in this field[23]. But the protection of consumer interests has not been limited to antitrust law. This year's hit-list of decisions is certainly topped by the Tokyo High Court's decision to allow parallel imports of patented products exactly because consumer interests should be balanced with those of the patent holder[24]. And, wonder of wonders, foreign countries that have been most reassuring when it came to cracking up the Japanese distribution system have voiced considerable indignation about this decision, while the FTC (which has always encouraged parallel imports) fell remarkably silent, probably in order not to stir up angry reactions from its best ally, the United States. Thus, not only have different decisions by different authorities finally led to something close to active competition regarding whose interests

---

20 *See* J.M. RAMSEYER, The Costs of Consensual Myth: Antitrust Enforcement and Institutional Barriers to Litigation in Japan, 94 YALE L.J. 654 (1984).

21 Until 1990, MITI had almost always blocked the opening of large superstores, arguing that this would bankrupt small shops. It was only as a result of foreign pressure that this policy was changed in 1990.

22 *See* IYORI & UESUGI, *supra* note 11, at 115.

23 *See* the decisions reprinted in M. MATSUSHITA & T. OKADA, *Dokkin-hô ihan wo meguru minji soshô ni kansuru hanrei bunkatsu* [Analysis of Court Decisions Concerning Civil Actions against Antimonopoly Law Violations], 353 NBL. 6 (1986); 354 NBL. 27 (1986); 356 NBL. 46 (1986); 370 NBL. 32 (1987) and 375 NBL. 32 (1987). Cracks in the distribution system have been spurred by the decision of the Tokyo District Court, July 18, 1994, 855 HANREI TIMES 111 (1994), concerning retail price maintenance of cosmetics.

24 Decision of the Tokyo High Court, March 23, 1995, GRUR INT. 423 (1995).

should be given preference, but they have also fostered academic discussion on a hitherto unprecedented scale[25].

2. Over the years, along with the change in economic necessities, national interests certainly change as well. Here are a few examples. In practice, until the 1930s, foreign (and to a lesser extent national) copyright owners did not get a single penny for the use of their copyrighted works. Change was then spearheaded by a German called *Plage* (which, in fact, translates as "plague", and such he was, at least to the Ministry of Culture)[26]. Nowadays, not only is there a collecting society, but the courts have also widened the scope of those responsible for copyright infringements as technical development has facilitated infringement. Recently, a court has held that not only the owner of a *karaoke* parlour, but also the franchisor of *karaoke* machines should be responsible for ensuring that proper contracts with the collecting societies are concluded[27]. In antitrust law, heavy-industry alliances of old have given way to coordination efforts in the field of research and development[28].

In both cases, without the laws having actually changed much, interests have been redefined and rebalanced.

3. Such development has certainly not taken place without friction between the competent authorities in Japan. In most cases these also represent different interest groups. Defending as well as pursuing national interests has become much more complex than it was. This is one of the reasons why MITI's industrial policy has become much less effective. I will give some examples:

a. In matters of copyright law, MITI has already been rapped twice over the knuckles by the Ministry of Culture. The first issue concerned the protection of computer programs that MITI would not only have liked to have under its competency, but also make dependent upon registration. The Ministry of Culture prevailed mainly because of efforts for international harmonization

---

25 I have counted more than ten recent articles on the distribution system, and probably even more on the permissibility of parallel importation of patented products. In 1990, the *Nihon Keizai-hô Gakkai* held its annual seminar on "The Japanese Distribution System", while the annual seminar of the *Kôgyô Shoyûken-hô Gakkai* in 1995 was dedicated to problems of parallel importation.

26 *See* S. OIE, *Nippon chôsaku-ken monogatari* [Tales of Japanese Copyright] (1981).

27 Decision of the Osaka District Court, March 17, 1994, 438 HANREI HYÔRON 211 (1994) ["Laser Disk Karaoke"].

28 For the industrial policy of the 1960s, *see* E. HADLEY, Antitrust in Japan, 390 *et seq.* (1970); the FTC Guidelines for Research and Development (April 20, 1993) basically permit all forms of cooperation for research and development, but not for joint production and sale.

within the scope of copyright law[29]. In the present debate about multimedia, MITI's first concern was that multimedia producers should be protected at the expense of authors. This lop sided and ill-conceived concept was countered by proposals from the Ministry of Culture in an attempt to balance interests more thoroughly that will presumably prevail[30].

b. In the field of unfair competition law, MITI may be responsible for legislative changes, but it has hitherto been unable to control the courts which are increasingly unwilling to stay within the framework of an unfair competition law that not only falls short of international obligations[31], but has also become inadequate even for the needs of Japanese industry. It is no coincidence that the legislative changes embodied in the Unfair Competition Law in 1994 were brought about by court decisions[32]. Shortly afterwards, in order to make the courts toe the line again, MITI "prophylactically" edited a commentary on the Unfair Competition Law[33]. It is quite evident that the courts favor a broader concept of unfair competition, something MITI has always claimed would run counter to the interests of Japanese industry[34].

D. Conclusion

3rd précis:

One of the best strategies for countering nationalistic policies is to foster the development of an open society. In addition, so-called international harmonization efforts should try to change systems rather than isolated problems.

1. I have stated above that it is a common phenomenon in virtually all countries to build the legal system around economic and thereby national

---

29 Interesting insights in this respect are provided by G. RAHN, Sonderrechtsschutz für Computerprogramme in Japan? [Special Protection for Computer Programs in Japan?], GRUR INT. 217 (1984).

30 *Chôsaku-ken shingi-kai murutsuimejia koiinkai warukingu gurupu kentô keika kôkoku* [Announcement of the Research Progress of the Multimedia Working Group of the Copyright Committee] (1995).

31 As explained above, only the introduction of a general clause would meet the requirements of Article 10*bis* Paris Convention: RAHN & HEATH, *supra* note 7, at 357.

32 Namely a continuous development from the danger of *confusion* to that of *dilution*, exemplified in the decision of the Tokyo District Court, August 30, 1966, 17-7 KAKYU MINSHU 729 (1966) ["Jashica"], and recognition of slavish imitation ("dead copy" in Japanese) as an act of unfair competition: Decision of the Tokyo High Court, December 17, 1991, IIC 805 (1994) ["Decorative Veneer"].

33 TSUSHÔ SANGYO-SHÔ (ed.), *Fusei kyôsô boshi-hô* [Prevention of Unfair Competition Law] (1994).

34 *See* TSUSHÔ SANGYO-SHÔ (ed.), *Fusei kyôsô boshi-hô ni kansuru chôsa kenkyû* [Study on the Prevention of Unfair Competition Law] (1993).

interests. Japan is certainly no exception to this rule. In the field of competition and intellectual property law, there are fairly clear examples of international obligations being flouted and laws being interpreted to serve national interests[35].

2. Such examples can certainly be found in many countries. In the case of Japan, aggravating circumstances such as an economy less accustomed to financial and personal participation by foreigners than those of other industrialized countries, and a postwar period that one-sidedly favored economic development over the protection of consumer interests, *inter alia*, contributed to a legal system tailor-made to the needs of Japanese economy. While these circumstances will certainly not change overnight, recent developments seem to indicate that, at least within a national context, a number of sometimes divergent interests are being looked after and promoted by different and mostly competing authorities. If the assumption is correct that the Japanese legal system is the result of a balancing of different interests rather than of principles[36], this development should not go unnoticed in regard to the protection of foreign interests in Japan.

The thesis that Japan's legal developments are driven by "fuzzy logic" rather than ethical principles may sound less surprising when taking a look at the political system that in the end of the day, has to be held accountable for enacting laws. Here,

> no one is ultimately in charge. . . . We are dealing not with lobbies, but with a structural phenomenon unaccounted for in the categories of accepted political theory. There is, to be sure, a hierarchy or, rather, a complex of overlapping hierarchies. But it has no peak; it is a truncated pyramid. There is no supreme institution with ultimate policy-making jurisdiction. Hence there is no place where. . . the buck stops. The buck keeps circulating.[37]

Thus, if political decision making represents a balancing of different political factions standing for different interest groups, it would in fact be surprising if political decisions on enacting laws were made differently. They are not. We are, in other words, in "fuzzy logic" land.

3. In trying to unravel the above observations and turn them into answers to the question, "How are foreign interests affected by these developments?", I would like to suggest the following conclusions:

---

35 Interestingly enough, this view is also shared by two Japanese economists, *cf.* ITO & KIYONO, Economic Analysis of Industrial Policy 3 (1988).

36 In this respect, *Rahn* has spoken of "fuzzy logic", which in fact is an electronically guided, fairly efficient way to balance different incoming signals for air-conditioners: RAHN & HEATH, *supra* note 7, at 345.

37 K. VAN WOLFEREN, The Enigma of Japanese Power 5 (1989).

a. In the case of antitrust and competition law, the protection of consumer interests has gathered significant momentum. Even if it may once have been necessary to try and open up markets "American-style", this policy will certainly no longer be necessary and could prove rather counterproductive. It would be more useful to participate constructively in the debate that is already going on in Japan. For this reason, putting Japanese antitrust law on the agenda of any trade talks seems to be outdated. Discussion in this field within Japan at the moment is more lively than it has ever been. The same is not yet true of competition law, but Japanese economic development seems to indicate that it soon will be[38]. This is also true for some aspects of copyright law and problems of procedure[39]. Such unprecedented debate on function, scope, and basis of consumer protection has put MITI at a loss. Presently, MITI is pondering over amendments of the Unfair Competition Law that would mean a harmonization with corresponding provisions of the Antimonopoly Law. Even this might be too little, too late: the new "model Unfair Competition Law" for developing countries from the *World Intellectual Property Organization* (WIPO) includes a general clause as the only proper way to comply with the Paris Convention. There is little chance that Japan can do less than to also introduce a general clause for its own Unfair Competition Law.

b. What I am more worried about is the structure of most industrial property laws. Their application very often is disadvantageous to foreign applicants, while little necessity is seen for a change (as only foreign interests are at stake). Foreigners are especially put at a disadvantage by a combination of high costs for applications (particularly translation costs)[40]; a narrow interpretation of claims[41]; a claim interpretation that does not take into account description and drawings of the patent (which in some cases could remedy

---

38 It should be noted here that the latest change in the Unfair Competition Prevention Law mainly was based on internal pressure rather than foreign demands. Recent court decisions seem to indicate that such change is still inadequate. The Tokyo High Court decision of December 24, 1993, TOKKYO KANRI 1105 (1994), ["Yawata"], has broken the chains of that law again by giving protection not only to tangible, but also to intangible goods. On the other hand, consumer interests have not been given a standing, and this probably will not change in the near future.

39 As to copyright, *see* the discussion on multimedia, *supra* note 30. MITI is currently studying the system of damage awards in foreign countries in order to revise the system in Japan.

40 One could certainly argue that translation costs incurred by foreigners in Japan are offset by comparative translation costs for Japanese companies when applying for patents abroad, but this calculation does not completely add up. In order to receive the same protection in Japan, more patents have to be filed than in the United States or in Europe due to very narrow claim interpretation.

41 *See*, e.g., YAMASAKI, *supra* note 13, and T. TAKENAKA, Claim Interpretation in the U.S., the Federal Republic of Germany and Japan, IIC STUDIES No. 17 (1995).

translation errors that, alas, are still fairly frequent)[42]; interpretations that run counter to international obligations, such as the Paris Convention[43]; and finally some aspects of the decisions concerning damages[44].

This comment may come as a surprise, since foreign interests are supposedly best served in a field that has been as harmonized as that of intellectual property rights. Insofar as Japan has been able to pursue its nationalistic policy by flouting its international obligations, some stronger reminders should be addressed to Japan, in addition to pressing for greater harmonization.

E. Outlook

1. To the degree deemed necessary to get things changed, pressure should be directed first of all at the Japanese bureaucracy, as the balancing of interests is basically done by the ministries at the stage of lawmaking rather than in court, as has been pointed out elsewhere in this volume in great detail[45]. Courts are unlikely to upset a balance of interests that supposedly has taken care of all interests involved. The exception - consumer interests - has been highlighted above.

2. A closer look at Japan's handling of foreign industrial property rights might help to put pressure on Japan at the appropriate spots. But still, the easiest way to make the stubborn donkey walk may be its own idea of where the bagfuls of carrots can be found.

In the past, Japan has done extremely well with its policy of putting national interests first. Presently, it rather feels its limits. Japan sees the need to pay a lot of foreign experts in order to get a more clement reporting in the press and wherever relevant, hoping that their "agents of influence"[46] will do the job. Furthermore, it gives a lot of development aid, but in fact seems to be mainly concerned with a development of its own industry in developing countries; developing countries, in turn, feel little inclination toward Japan. All this does not help to spread the "Japanese model", let alone the Japanese language, culture, etc. While Japan tries to promote its intellectual property system in

42 Translation errors can now be remedied by a correction even after the patent has been granted, on condition that the scope of the patent is not broadened and at a cost of ¥19,000.

43 Apart from Article 10*bis* and Article 4(h), one could also mention Article 6*bis* and Article 6*septies*.

44 I can only refer to the "Chanel No. 5" decision, *supra* note 16, which is indeed incomprehensible as a treatment for licensed trademarks.

45 *See* the contribution of *Hideki Kanda* in this volume (*infra* Chapter Eleven).

46 P. CHOATE, Agents of Influence (1989), who in fact rather bemoans that his fellow countrymen are something money can buy.

other Asian countries, the response is lukewarm at best: Europe is considered a model less prone to protecting national interests and thus holds greater attraction.

Such mismanagement of foreign appreciation for Japan is surprising for a country that attaches so much importance to how it is perceived by foreigners and that reacts very sensitively towards any form of criticism.

In 1995, The English newspaper *The Economist* carried an article with the telling title, "The Economic Benefit of Altruism". Quintessentially, it claimed, being nice may not only reap heavenly rewards, but also those measured in hard, cold cash. And this is something the Japanese bureaucracy should think about when assessing Japan's national interests - being fair may simply pay off (*banji wa utagaisama*).

Chapter Fourteen

The "Old Boy" Network and Government-Business Relationships in Japan

*Ulrike Schaede**

Contents

A. Introduction

One of the striking features of Japanese government-business relationships is the existence of an extensive "Old Boy" network consisting of retired government officials who "descend from heaven" (*amakudari*) into the board rooms of private corporations. In the *amakudari* environment, the term "Old Boy" (OB) refers to a former government official who, after retirement from long years of civil service, is reemployed in the private or quasi-private sector and begins a "second life", in which he draws heavily on the expertise and the personal relations that he accumulated in his "first life" as a bureaucrat.[1] The large numbers of these OBs in the Japanese private sector, and the institutionalized mechanism of their reemployment, give rise to some puzzling questions: What do these OBs do? Why are firms interested in hiring an OB?

---

* This article was published in the JOURNAL OF JAPANESE STUDIES, 21:2, p. 293-317 (1995). The editor acknowledges his gratitude to the Journal for its kind permission to reprint the article in these conference proceedings. The form of the references has been changed in accordance with the form of citations used throughout this volume.

The author is indebted to *Harald Baum, Richard Brahm, Peter Gourevitch, John McMillan, Charles O'Reilly, Mark Ramseyer, Frank Upham* and *Kozo Yamamura* for helpful comments and discussions.

1 There are also "corporate OBs", "banking OBs", "politician OBs", etc.; this paper focuses on "bureaucrat OBs".

What are the implications for economic policies, corporate strategies, and government-business relationships in Japan?

The OB phenomenon is mentioned in almost every comprehensive study on current Japan as an indicator of tight government-business relationships.[2] However, its scope, the reasons for, and the implications of this phenomenon have not yet been empirically analyzed in any systematic way. In the first comprehensive scrutiny of the phenomenon, *Johnson* states that the reemployment of government officials leads to hand-in-glove relationships between government and industry.[3] For Johnson, the OBs constitute part of the underlying mechanism of the "bureaucrat-led economic growth" of postwar Japan. The OB phenomenon is, at the same time, the primary tool and the proof for complete economic guidance by the Japanese bureaucracy. In contrast, *Calder* suggests that OBs are hired only by firms that have a definite need for government help.[4] Rather than constituting a tool of bureaucratic regulation, OBs are employed by smaller firms, or firms not located in Tokyo, in order to "equalize" their power positions, i.e., to overcome a size or location disadvantage. In Calder's view, the smaller firms need OBs for access to governmental information and for lobbying with the government for continued protection.

A number of questions remain. First, how large or pervasive is this phenomenon in terms of total number of OB directors on private corporate boards? Second, while the argument that OBs are a critical component of the "developmental state" model is very powerful for the period of 1950-1975, some modifications may be needed to explain why large Japanese multinationals hire OBs in the 1990s. The general assumption seems to be that concurrent with economic growth, large Japanese firms experience an increase in relative power vis-a-vis the regulator, because they could shift their production and headquarters to countries where regulation and control is less stringent.[5] In

2 For example, M. AOKI, Information, Incentives, and Bargaining in the Japanese Economy (1988); C.V. PRESTOWITZ, Trading Places (1988); J.M. RAMSEYER & F. MCCALL ROSENBLUTH, Japan's Political Marketplace (1993); K. VAN WOLFEREN, The Enigma of Japanese Power: Power and People in a Stateless Nation (1989).

3 C. JOHNSON, The Reemployment of Retired Government Bureaucrats in Japanese Big Business, 14 ASIAN SURVEY 953-965 (November 1974); C. JOHNSON, MITI and the Japanese Miracle: The Growth of Industrial Policy 1925-1975 (1982).

4 K. CALDER, Elites in an Equalizing Role: Ex Bureaucrats as Coordinators and Intermediaries in the Japanese Government-Business Relationship, COMPARATIVE POLITICS 379-403 (July 1989).

5 The Japanese refer to this situation as the threat of "hollowing out" (*kûdôka*), which became a catchphrase in the second half of the 1980s, and again after the attempts of political reform and deregulation were halted in 1993/94; *cf.* U. SCHAEDE, Change and Continuity in Japanese Regulation, (University of California, Berkeley, BRIE Working Paper No. 66, 1994); reprinted in 1/1 ZEITSCHRIFT FÜR JAPANISCHES RECHT 21-31 (1996).

other words, Japanese firms should now be less dependent on the regulators than in the 1950 and 1960s, and should therefore hire fewer OBs.[6] Third, if the OB is simply an instrument used by smaller firms to equalize power, then there should be fewer or no OB directors on the boards of large firms; therefore, the phenomenon should be less relevant for tight relationships between the Japanese government and large firms than usually asserted.

This paper analyzes the OB phenomenon based on data of government OBs on the board of directors in the period of 1979 through 1991, using a sample of the largest 100 firms as of 1991. The firms in the sample are, therefore, currently the largest 100 firms, and their employment of government OBs is traced back over twelve years. Interestingly, the data suggests that large firms hired more OBs in the early 1990s than in the late 1970s. I then examine whether there are differences in the tendency to hire OBs across industrial sectors. A pattern emerges showing that certain sectors are more apt to hire OBs than others. The next question is whether these sectors share common characteristics in terms of business or regulatory constraints. A consistent pattern in these characteristics across firms will help to better understand the reasons why private firms hire OBs, and the functions of the OBs once they have joined a private firm.

The paper begins by describing the typical path of a Japanese career bureaucrat, the network of relationships that results from this career path, and the incentive structure for retired bureaucrats. A "management of regulation" model is developed that relates the role of OBs to the process of regulation and administrative guidance. The model suggests certain situations when we would expect firms to hire OBs. The second section introduces the data set and presents summary statistics of OBs by industries. It explores the major business constraints faced by large Japanese firms in the years 1979-1991, especially in the form of extra-legal administrative guidance, a large number of business laws, and trade restrictions. The increase in government OBs on the boards of these firms over time is then related to different sets of business constraints and changes in these constraints. The model suggests that the strongest need for OBs is by those firms that face an external constraint which (a) influences their competitive position within the industry and (b) is controlled by the regulators. The essay concludes with a set of implications for government-business relationships in Japan.

---

6 Examples of this view are K. CALDER, Strategic Capitalism: Private Business and Public Enterprise in Japanese Industrial Finance (1993); D. OKIMOTO, Between MITI and the Market: Japanese Industrial Policy for High Technology (1989).

B. The Old-Boy Network

Japanese bureaucrats are "professional" long-term civil servants who follow a standard career path. They are hired after graduation at around age 22. The large ministries employ about 25 new civil servants every year, who as a group are known as the "class of 19nn". In the first two years, the members of one "vintage" go through a joint training program. Their careers begin to take different paths as they work their way up the ministerial hierarchy by rotating through several departments in two-year terms. However, the vintage stays in close contact.[7]

In the beginning, all members of a class are promoted at about the same pace. As they get older, there are fewer and fewer positions, and winnowing begins. Only a few members of one class can make it to the very top echelons. Realizing that, some leave early to enter politics. Others are consecutively "retired" beginning at around age 50. Because the salary of a bureaucrat is low as compared to private industry and the pension system for civil servants is poorly endowed, bureaucrats are dependent on further employment and income at that point.[8]

To understand the process of early retirement and the incentive structure for OBs, it is important to appreciate how this process unfolds. Two primary regulations pertain to *amakudari*. First, the "National Public Service Law"[9] prohibits retiring bureaucrats from assuming a position in a corporation that

---

7 The effects of this system were described by one bureaucrat as follows: "We do everything together, so eventually we become friends. Later on, we still meet, talk to each other, exchange experiences and ideas. The whole group is very smart to begin with, and then receives very good training, and we add to this the *dôki no ishiki* ("same-class consciousness"). We identify ourselves through this group. Accordingly, the OB form a *dôki no kaigo* ("same-class get-together") (Interview summer 1993).

For a detailed analysis of the promotion process see: T. MUROBUSHI, *Kôkyû kanryô* [High-Ranking Bureaucrats] (1987); M. SAKATA, *Nihon kanryô hakusho* [White Paper on Japan's Bureaucracy] (1989); also in English: M. AOKI, Information, Incentives, and Bargaining 264-265 (1989); R. KOMIYA, Economic Policy Makers in the Japanese Government, *in*: The Japanese Economy: Trade, Industry, and Government 370-374 (Komiya, ed. 1990); B.C. KOH, Japan's Administrative Elite (1989).

8 *Inoki* suggests that the *amakudari* system constitutes deferred compensation which introduces competition into the bureaucracy and thus enhances the bureaucrats' productivity and performance: the harder they work as civil servants, the better their *amakudari* positions and the higher their lifetime income. Inoki shows in case studies that the post-retirement income of the very high-ranking bureaucrats exceeds the income of those who have to retire earlier; *see* T. INOKI, Japanese Bureaucrats at Retirement: The Mobility of Human Resources from Central Government to Public Corporations, (EDI Working Papers [Economic Development Institute of the World Bank] No. 93-32 1993).

9 *Kokka kômuin-hô*, Law No. 120 of 1947 as amended by Law No. 54 of 1995.

they used to regulate for at least two years after retirement. Therefore, the bureaucrat is first sent to a non-profit organization abroad or within Japan for two years before he descends into the domestic private sector. Second, the retiring bureaucrats do not go out and look for positions. Neither are they sought after by headhunters or approached by corporations directly, as would be the case in the U.S. Rather, there is a special government office which is legally responsible for post-retirement personnel administration. This National Personnel Authority (*Jinji-in*) stays in charge of the former bureaucrats for the rest of their professional lives and acts as the ultimate *de facto* employment agent.[10] Since only a few ex-bureaucrats stay with one firm after *amakudari* and changing firms on a two-year basis is common, the retired officials are dependent on the National Personnel Authority for good placement and hence increased lifetime income. The OB also earns a new retirement stipend with each promotion. This mechanism provides a strong incentive to act in the interest of the former employer, the administration.

Bureaucrats can "descend" to different destinations. Next to *amakudari* in the narrow sense into private business, the government official can also become the head of a public corporation such as the electric utilities, Japan Airlines, or the Kansai Airport Corporation. Private non-profit associations for which the government deems regulation essential, such as the Tokyo Stock Exchange, also fall into this category, which is sometimes called *yokosuberi*, "sideslip".[11] The third post-bureaucratic career option is politics. A fourth destination are the trade associations that represent the interests of corporations. Finally, a top bureaucrat can, on retirement from his ministry, be transferred to a further government agency. For example, the presidency of the Japan Development Bank, a government financial institution, is occupied by a former Bank of Japan director. The governor of the Bank of Japan is either a former official of the Ministry of Finance (*ôkura-shô*, hereinafter MOF) or a Bank of Japan director. Therefore, a post-bureaucratic career path can include a combination of various "sideslips" (to public corporations) and a "descent" (to the private sector). In addition to linking government institutions to each other as well as private

---

10 In the actual process of finding firms for a retiring bureaucrat, the secretary of the ministry (*Kanbôchô*) is usually the primary intermediary, since he knows the career, expertise, and interests of the bureaucrats, and also is approached by firms who are trying to hire an OB. Personal relations (*jinmyaku*), trade associations (*gyôkai*), and "related interests" (*nawabari*) all also play into this process.

The *Kanbôchô* then advises the *National Personnel Authority* on retiring paths for the OBs of his ministry. However, in strictly legal terms, the Personnel Authority is ultimately in charge of administering the "National Public Service Law"; it grants permission for an OB to join a specific private firm, and it can also revoke this permission.

11 *See* JOHNSON, "The Reemployment...", *supra* note 3, at 953; KOH, *supra* note 7, at 235-244.

business to the government, this mechanism reinforces the connections between private and public enterprises.

1. Maintenance of the OB Network

There are three major mechanisms in place that support the underlying operation of the network. First, there are personal connections and seniority hierarchies.[12] More than 50% of all bureaucrats hired by the ministries each year are graduates from the law school of Tokyo University.[13] Next to breeding bureaucrats, Tokyo University also has a record of spawning politicians and chief executive officers (CEOs). While one should not generalize and exaggerate the relevance of the university relation, in individual cases it can be very important.

The second mechanism for maintaining the bureaucrat-OB network is "vintage meetings". Each class of bureaucrats in a certain ministry holds regular meetings, typically a monthly lunch. Because of the progressive retirement process, some members of the group may still be in the ministry, while others are politicians, heads of public corporations, or in private business. These meetings are continued even after the whole vintage has retired. When asked what they talk about during these regular lunches, most OBs first denied the relevance ("we do not talk business") and then explained that "we are talking about what each of us is doing right now and what the news is".[14]

Third, the smooth flow of information to and from the ministry is guaranteed even after all members of one year have eventually retired in so-

---

12 The influence of former government officials is based on cross-cutting influences of school ties, marital alliances (the so-called *keibatsu* that align business families with politicians and bureaucrats through strategic "placement" of daughters), clan networks, deliberation councils, senior-junior relations, and ministerial clubs (such as MITI's "Tuesday Club") of retired bureaucrats. For *keibatsu* with ministries, politicians, and industry related to the Ministry of Finance, *see* S. MANABE, *Ôkura-sho: korinai kenryoku* [Ministry of Finance: Power Without Learning by Experience] 61-89 (1992); I. JIN, *Keibatsu* [Business Cliques] (1989), presents maps of the most important personal connections between *Nagatacho*, *Kasumigaseki* and *Marunouchi*.

13 All 37 administrative vice ministers (i.e., the highest bureaucratic position within a ministry) of MOF between 1945 and 1995 graduated from the Tokyo University Law School. Among the 26 postwar MITI administrative vice ministers, only one did not graduate from that same school, and out of the 27 administrative vice ministers of the Ministry of Posts and Telecommunication, six graduated from Law Schools other than Tokyo University. *See* I. MURAKAWA, *Nihon no kanryô* [Japan's Bureaucracy] (1994).

14 Interviews with retired and incumbent Ministry of Finance officials, summer 1993. In some cohorts, there are also separate "vintage wives meetings" who gather, without the husbands, to strengthen ties.

called "OB meetings". These meetings are arranged by the ministry itself and are held on a quarterly basis. During the lunch-box meeting, an incumbent bureaucrat delivers a speech to his retired seniors concerning regulatory or policy issues currently discussed within the ministry. Thus, the former bureaucrats are kept informed of the ministerial stance on current issues, which guarantees their continued value as insiders.

There are major differences between the U.S. and Japan in hiring former government officials. First, in the U.S., ex-Congressmen (i.e., politicians) and fixed-term commissioners are the preferred insiders. Commissioners and political appointees tend to change with each administration and are therefore not "lifelong" bureaucrats.[15] The "revolving door" mechanism also allows them to switch back and forth between the government and the private sector. In contrast, in Japan the process is unidirectional; once a bureaucrat has left civil service, he cannot rejoin. Further, upon joining a firm, Japanese bureaucrats do not shift their interests exclusively to the firm but remain loyal to the interests of their former employer, the government. The government ensures this loyalty by keeping ex-bureaucrats involved and by making them dependent on a "government employment agency" mechanism.[16]

2. *The Role of the OBs: The "Management of Regulation" Model*

Three major theories have been advanced to explain the OB phenomenon in the private sector. The first argument is a "government action" argument that interprets OBs as a direct tool for implementing regulation.[17] One variety of this is the "thank you" argument: firms hire OBs because the government did them a favor earlier on, and the firm hopes that by hiring the OB it may receive preferential treatment in the future. A further variant of this argument is suggested by *Okimoto* who claims that OBs retire primarily into growth sectors, and rather than to unilaterally regulate, the government uses this mechanism to

---

15 R.D. ECKERT, The Life Cycle of Regulatory Commissioners, 24 J. L. & ECON. 113-120 (April 1981); H. HECLO, In Search of a Role: America's Higher Civil Service, *in*: Bureaucrats and Policy Making: A Comparative Overview 8-34 (E.N. Suleiman, ed. 1984).

16 The French system of *pantouflage* is also different in important aspects. A French bureaucrat who becomes the CEO of a public corporation can remain a civil servant, and therefore may return to the government after his term in the firm expires. His incentive structure therefore differs significantly from that of a Japanese civil servant; for a detailed discussion, *see* E.N. SULEIMAN, Elites in French Society: The Politics of Survival (1978).

17 JOHNSON, "The Reemployment..." *supra* note 3; C. JOHNSON, Japan: Who Governs? An Essay on Official Bureaucracy, 2 J. JAP. STUD. 1-28 (Autumn 1975); C. JOHNSON, Japan's Public Policy Companies (1978); JOHNSON, "MITI", *supra* note 3.

consolidate its ties with business.[18] The second argument centers around "motivation". Here, the *amakudari* process is explained as a lifelong employment scheme for bureaucrats, in which the prospect of a high-paying "second life" motivates the bureaucrat to work hard while he is an underpaid servant in the ministerial hierarchy.[19] In both of these arguments, the expertise of the individual bureaucrat is ignored; he serves just as an instrument. However, among the 177 OBs that were directors in the top 100 Japanese firms in 1991, some 40% were in leading positions, such as CEO, chairman, or executive director. If the OB was just an instrument, why would he be appointed to a leading position within the firm? These schools do not adequately explain the incentives of firms to hire OBs in large numbers into high positions.

The third school presents the "power equalization" argument.[20] As discussed above, while this offers a good explanation for OBs in smaller firms, it does not help explain why there should be many OBs in the largest corporations. An extension of this argument is that firms hire OBs exclusively for their expertise (superior education and long-term on-the-job training). While this certainly applies in individual cases, it does not explain patterns of OB employment across industries, or why there should have been an increase in OB employment in some industries in the 1980s.

I suggest that the OB phenomenon can be explained more powerfully by a "management of (non-transparent) regulation" mechanism. This model applies to both government and private firms. From the firm's perspective, regulation can be regarded, in the terminology of resource dependence theory, as an external constraint on its behavior. The larger the constraint (i.e., the more regulation), the more efforts the firm will undertake to manage the regulator (i.e., lobby, or try otherwise to influence the regulatory decision-making process).[21] For the government, on the other hand, regulation requires a system

---

18 OKIMOTO, *supra* note 6. There is, however, no proof for the "growth sector" argument. Okimoto analyzes government data on how many OBs descended into what kind of industries in one year, 1976, thereby not controlling for the fact that some industries (construction, semiconductors, banking) consist of more firms than others (cars, petroleum). We need to look at percentages rather than absolute numbers to properly evaluate the relative impact of OBs on individual industries.

19 *See* T. BLUMENTHAL, The Practice of Amakudari within the Japanese Employment System 310-321, 25 ASIAN SURVEY (No. 3, March 1985); and the "productivity enhancement through deferred payments" argument proposed by INOKI, *supra* note 8.

20 CALDER, *supra* note 4.

21 Resource dependence theory provides an analytical framework for this intuition. Since organizations are not internally self-sufficient, but depend on outside groups that control important inputs or resources, they are interdependent with the outside elements with which they transact. In response, the organization will develop strategies to alter the situation it confronts in order to make compliance with the

to ensure compliance and to curtail circumvention. The more extralegal the regulatory process, the harder it is for the government to police behavior. The OB acts as an intermediary (a) to lobby for changes in, and (b) to monitor existing regulation.

The Japanese regulatory framework has two features that differentiate it from Western economies: (1) its wide range, especially in the form of specific industry laws (e.g., the Banking Law, the Insurance Business Law, The Travel Business Law, etc.); and (2) a large number of ad hoc rules for particular situations based on non-codified administrative guidance (*gyôsei shidô*).[22] Administrative guidance is not based on a law. Rather, an administrative agency acts within its scope of jurisdiction in order to induce specific behavior with the aim of realizing an administrative goal through industry cooperation. Administrative guidance is not transparent and often involves delicate conversations between ministry officials and management representatives. Informal industry estimates claim that this regulatory practice may constitute up to 60-90% of all the regulation of a given industry.[23] Rules can be implemented or revoked at the discretion of the ministry in charge, and without any prior notice; hence, the strong situational character of administrative guidance. The enforcement of decisions is based on a carrot-and-stick principle. Corporations know that by following "advice" they may reap rewards later. On the other hand, if the ministries find a noncompliance with administrative guidance, they have numerous options to obstruct future business of the party concerned.[24]

---

external constraints less burdensome. The smaller the organizations that are controlled, or the more unified their interests, the higher the likelihood that they will form associations to increase bargaining power in their attempt to manage the resource. For organizations that react to an external control individually, one means of mitigating dependencies is through personnel ties. *See* J. PFEFFER & G.R. SALANCIK, The External Control of Organizations: A Resource Dependence Perspective (1978).

Regulation can be considered an external constraint on a firm's activities. It implies dependencies and therefore creates incentives for organizations to manage the dependencies. In their compliance to regulation, firms will try to influence the formulation of demands in order to mitigate the effects of regulation on their strategic choices, or to evoke favorable treatment.

22 The Japanese "regulatory set" consists of four layers: (i) the pertinent statute (*hôritsu*); (ii) supplementary rules to the law formulated in ordinances (*seirei* and *shôrei*) issued by the Cabinet and the competent ministry respectively; (iii) written notifications (*tsûtatsu*) by the ministry concerned; and (iv) informal, typically oral, "invitations" to certain actions, addressed to an individual or a group of market participants. Notifications and "invitations", which are delivered by the ministries without Cabinet approval, are called "administrative guidance".

23 Interview summer 1993.

24 *See*, e.g., M. SHINDO, *Gyôsei shidô: Kanchô to gyôkai no aida* [Administrative Guidance: Between Government and Business Circles] (1992); G.C. EADS & K. YAMAMURA, The Future of Industrial Policy, *in*: The Political Economy of Japan - Vol. 1: The Domestic Transformation423-468 (K. Yamamura & Y. Yasuba, eds.

Effectively, there is no legal recourse to regulation in the form of administrative guidance, because compliance is "voluntary". The discretionary and situational nature of the rules make it hard to forecast changes, and regulation, therefore, creates a high degree of uncertainty. The new rules provided by the Administrative Procedures Law[25] of October 1994 cannot be expected to change this situation significantly, because the law deals with the procedures rather than the underlying power structure of the guidance mechanism.[26]

The extensive use of situational administrative guidance in the Japanese regulatory framework has two implications. First, there is a high need for direct access to government information and for influencing regulatory decision-making. Since OBs provide for direct information channels, this could be the reason for the overall large number of OBs. Second, there should be differences across industries in the need of hiring OBs, depending on the degree and predominant character of regulation (codified or situational), and on the need for individual lobbying by a single firm or for lobbying through a trade association (in which case the association could be headed by an OB). At the same time, the government would see a higher need to dispatch former bureaucrats to firms that are primarily regulated through extralegal administrative guidance in order to increase its access to and leverage over the firm.

According to this "management of regulation" logic, we could expect to find not only an overall large number of OBs, but also an accumulation of OBs in the following cases:

(1) in industries that are heavily regulated by specific industry laws (e.g., pharmaceuticals, banking);

1987); F.K. UPHAM, Law and Social Change in Postwar Japan (1987); T. SEKI, *Gyôsei-shidô* [Administrative Guidance] (1991).

25 *Gyôsei tetsuzuki-hô*, Law No. 88 of 1993. For an English translation *see* 25 LAW IN JAPAN 141-159 (M.A. Levin, trans. 1995).

26 The law aims to make the process of administrative guidance more transparent by requiring identification of the individual bureaucrat in charge and a written statement of justification should the guidance be challenged. The law also introduces three new rules to the process: (1) a ministry cannot reach beyond its regulatory territory in its guidance; (2) implementation should to the largest extent possible be achieved through voluntary cooperation by the regulatee; and (3) the ministry cannot use non-compliance as a reason for unfavorable treatment of the non-complying regulatee. None of these rules seems to be powerful enough to change the system. The law is also watered down by the fact that prefectures, including public corporations, are not subject to the administrative guidance stipulations. For a detailed discussion, *see* interview with Y. SUZUKI, *Yakusho no saji-kagen wo yurusanai tsuyoi mikata* [A Strong Position Against Permitting the Discretion of the Goverment Offices], EKONOMISUTO 80-83 (Nov. 15, 1994).

(2) in industries that, while not subject to a specific industry law, are nevertheless subject to extensive administrative guidance (e.g., steel); and/or

(3) in industries that are subject to particular constraints that impact their competitive position within the industry, especially if these constraints are controlled by the regulators (e.g., public procurement), i.e., where regulators have control over competitive behavior.

These assumptions are tested in the following section.

C. Data Analysis

The data base consists of a sample of the largest 100 stockholding corporations in Japan as of 1991.[27] For these, data on board members and prior affiliations of directors were collected from *Kaisha nenkan* bi-annually for the years 1979 through 1991.[28] Since the typical employment of an OB lasts for two years, bi-annual data capture all important movements.

Table 1: General Data Summary - Government OBs between 1979 and 1991

	Total Number of Board Members (a)	Total Number of Firms with OBs	Bureaucrat OBs: Govt OBs	Bureaucrat OBs: Public Corp. OBs	Bureaucrat OBs: Total (in % of (a))	Former Bankers	Former Corporate Directors	Concurrent Interlocking Directors (in % of (a))
1979	2715	35	35	23	58 (2.13)	41	35	80 (2,94)
1981	2727	40	41	37	78 (2,86)	36	32	85 (3.12)
1983	2965	39	50	37	87 (2.9)	34	31	94 (3.2)
1985	3122	50	71	59	130 (4.2)	43	30	109 (3.5)
1987	3216	62	68	102	170 (5.3)	40	21	112 (3.5)
1989	3423	65	69	103	172 (5.02)	38	12	127 (3.71)
1991	3605	67	85	92	177 (4.91)	44	31	95 (2.64%)

Source: Nikkei, *Kaisha Nenkan*, various issues.

27 As listed in TOYO KEIZAI (May 1992); this list is the equivalent of the Fortune 500 list in the U.S.

28 NIHON KEIZAI SHINBUN-SHA (ed.), *Kaisha nenkan* [Corporations Yearbook] (various issues, 1980 through 1992).

Table 1 summarizes the overall findings. As of 1991, 4.9% (or 177) of all directors of the largest private firms were "Old Boys". As a yardstick to evaluate this number, the table also lists the number of retired bankers, retired directors of other firms, as well as interlocking (concurrent) directors. While these are often considered an important factor of corporate networking in Japan,[29] the retired bureaucrats significantly outnumber the "corporate Old Boys". This comparison underscores the relevance of the overall OB phenomenon.

Table 1 shows a 30% increase in total number of directors in the course of the 1980s, from 2,608 in 1979 to 3,605 in 1991. This increase is referred to as the "inflation of directors" which is ascribed to demographic changes in the Japanese promotional system; that is, a large number of postwar baby-boomers advanced to the position of director in the corporate hierarchy, not all of whom could be dispatched to leading positions in affiliated firms.[30] Because the implicit lifetime employment system rules out dismissal, more managers had to be promoted to the board of directors than in the past.

The total number of "bureaucrat OBs", defined as board members who "descended" either directly from a ministry ("government OBs") or indirectly via a public corporation, tripled between 1977 and 1991. This is partially due to demographics as well: with the increase in civil servants in the 1950 and 1960s, more bureaucrats retire each year. For instance, *Blumenthal* shows that the Personnel Authority permitted a total of 165 officials to assume positions in private firms for the year 1963, and a total of 249 in 1981.[31] However, the increase in number of OBs is steeper than the increase in total directors. While the OBs accounted for 2.13% of all directors in 1979, this percentage increased to 4.9% in 1991. More importantly, not only was there an increase in total numbers of OBs hired (which could be due to the fact that firms that have always employed an OB now hire two or more of them), but there is also a 90% increase in the number of firms that hire OBs, from 35 to 67 of the largest 100 firms. This increase is counterintuitive to the argument that large Japanese firms have gained some independence from the tight controls of the "developmental state". It suggests an increase in external constraints, so that

---

29 *See*, e.g., M. GERLACH, Alliance Capitalism: The Social Organization of Japanese Business (1993); P. SHEARD, Bank Executives on Japanese Corporate Boards (Osaka University Working Paper, 1994); J.R. LINCOLN, M. GERLACH & C. AHMADJIAN, Keiretsu Networks and Corporate Performance in Japan (University of California, Berkeley, Working Paper, 1993); S.N. KAPLAN & B. MINTON, Outside Intervention in Japanese Companies: Its Determinants and Implications for Managers (NBER Working Paper No. 4276 1994).

30 NIHON KEIZAI SHINBUN-SHA (ed.), *Zeminâru. Gendai kigyô nyûmon* [Seminar Introduction to Modern Enterprises] (1991).

31 BLUMENTHAL, *supra* note 19.

more large firms felt they needed direct access to the government by hiring an OB.

The nature of the external constraints that would lead to this increase can be explored by dividing the data set into industry groups. The analysis focuses on seven industries (based on the number of firms in the sample): electronics and electric machinery (in short "electronics", but including everything from stereos to supercomputers), automobiles, steel, construction, commercial banking, investment banking, and insurance. The three latter, banking and insurance, are highly regulated and subject to specific industry laws. On the other hand, electronics and cars are known for their clashes with the industrial policy of the Ministry of International Trade and Industry (*Tsûsan-shô*, hereinafter MITI) since the 1950s (Honda, Sony), and have a reputation for being "stubborn" vis-a-vis the regulators.

Table 2 breaks down the number of firms in the sample in these industries showing the total number of OBs in these industries, and the percentage of firms in the industry that employ at least one OB.[32] This latter category indicates the distribution of OBs across the industry, and it is presented graphically in Figure 1. The industries fall into two categories: those where less than 50% of all firms hire OBs (this includes commercial banking, investment banking, and insurance), and those where more than 75% of all firms hire OBs (electronics, cars, steel, and construction). We can also observe some changes over time in the second group: automobile manufacturers started to hire OBs in the early 1980s, around which time the number of OBs also increased in electronics. The steel industry shows a continuous increase of OBs from 1984 through 1989.

In order to explore the reasons for this division into two groups, the number of OBs in a firm was regressed on a set of firm characteristics such as ownership concentration, the size of the board, *keiretsu* affiliation, the existence of industry laws, and a factor labelled "trade industry" for the year 1991. "Trade industry" refers to industries that are directly affected by cross-border business (export of products, import of raw material or products), and where a firm's profits or market share depends directly on trade volume, as opposed to firms that are primarily domestic. The results of these analyses were insignificant, with one exception: there was a significant positive association between a firm being in a "trade industry" and the number of OBs on the board ($\beta = 0.54$; $p < .01$).

32 The number of firms in the sample varies due to mergers, and because some firms included in the top 100 in 1991 were not listed on the stock exchange or did not exist 10 years ago, so that earlier data are not available. For instance, Mitsubishi Motors was listed only in 1988.

Table 2: Number of OBs by Industry (1979-91)

	Export/Import (Trade) Industries												Domestic Industries								
	Electronics/ Electric machinery			Automobiles			Commercial Steel			Investment Construction			Commercial Banking			Investment Banking			Insurance		
	#	OB	%	#	OB	%	#	OB	%	#	OB	%	#	OB	%	#	OB	%	#	OB	%
1979	15	8	40	3	2	67	4	0	0	10	33	70	20	13	30	4	0	0	5	1	20
1981	15	10	40	3	1	33	4	1	25	10	32	70	20	13	25	4	0	0	5	0	0
1983	15	7	33	3	2	67	4	1	25	10	38	80	20	14	30	4	0	0	5	0	0
1985	15	23	60	3	4	100	4	4	50	10	47	100	20	20	95	4	0	0	5	0	0
1987	15	30	67	3	8	100	4	7	75	10	52	100	20	19	43	4	0	0	5	0	0
1989	15	25	87	4	7	75	4	9	100	10	58	100	19	15	47	4	0	0	5	1	20
1991	15	38	93	4	9	100	4	7	75	10	58	90	19	16	47	4	1	25	5	0	0

Notes: # = number of firms in sample
OB: = total number of OBs hired in this industry
% = per cent of firms in the industry group that hire at least one OB director
Source: NIKKEI, *Kaisha nenkan*, various issues.

One explanation for the strong "trade" correlation is as follows. The "domestic" industries (banking and insurance) are subject to specific industry laws, which tend to align primary lobbying needs around protection, deregulation, and other industry-wide matters. Most of the trade associations are headed by retired government officials. Firms in these industries can lobby their industry-wide interests through the association.[33] In contrast, the "trade industries" are subject to external constraints that do not apply industry-wide, but rather to individual firms. For this reason, lobbying through the trade association is not possible: while the trade association can effectively lobby for interests that are aligned across an industry, it is not a feasible forum if industry interests diverge. In this case, each firm has to go out and lobby on its own. Trade restraints restrict market share of the firms within an industry, so that they compete with each other for allotment quotas. While the types of constraints that apply for the industries in this sample vary, the mechanisms of the constraint, and accordingly the reactions to it, are similar. To illuminate this point, let us briefly look at some trade constraints in the 1980s.

The automobile and electronic industries are major exporters in an environment characterized by trade policy battles with the U.S. and the European Community. One reaction to the increasing Japanese trade surplus was the introduction of bilateral "voluntary export restraints" (VERs) in TV sets (1977, USA), VCRs (1983, EC), semiconductors (1986-1991, USA), automobiles (1980s, USA and EC), and steel (1980s).[34] Between 1977 and 1980, the U.S. restricted the number of TV sets to be exported by Japan. In order to comply with the VER, MITI formed an "export association" for the electronics industry. This association was an export cartel exempt from Japanese antitrust regulation which allowed TV makers to allocate export quotas among themselves (albeit with MITI guidance). Although the U.S. President had requested the VER, the U.S. Attorney General judged that this export cartel was a violation of U.S. antitrust regulation. One of the Japanese

33 When associations' interests converge, they can lobby through the *Keidanren* (Federation of Economic Organizations), which is the largest and most influential business organization, consisting of about 110 industry-wide associations and 800 large corporations. The important role of OBs in the associations is reflected by the fact that five out of the nine postwar presidents of *Keidanren* were former bureaucrats.

34 The rationale for VERs is home industry protection. Europe launched EU-wide voluntary export restraints for Japanese video cassette recorders in 1983 (with a limit of 4.55 million) and on Japanese automobiles in 1988; automobile restraints differ by country. The first VER on cars by the U.S. in 1981 set the limit at 1.68 million vehicles per year. A revision in 1984 lifted the import ceiling to 1.85 million. For VERs by the EU, *see* K. ISHIKAWA, Japan and the Challenge of Europe 1992 (1990).

producers was sued by a U.S. competitor.[35] Thus, Japanese TV manufacturers needed MITI support in the early 1980s.

Given this experience in electronics, MITI had to structure the VERs imposed by the U.S. on automobile exports in the first half of the 1980s in a different way. Rather than forming an export cartel which left the primary quota allocation in the hands of the manufacturers, MITI crafted an "export control scheme". Under this scheme, MITI, employing the mechanisms of administrative guidance, prescribed the maximum number of cars that each manufacturer could export to the U.S. Prior to implementation, MITI presented the scheme to the U.S. Attorney General who issued a statement that it was "believed" that this scheme did not violate U.S. antitrust rules.

Effectively, this export control scheme elevated MITI to a control position over export shares of individual car manufacturers. The basis for allocating quotas is discretionary (MITI decides on the basis of past performance and other non-quantifiable attributes, which seem to include the "tit-for-tat" mechanism of administrative guidance, i.e., compliance with previous and current extra-legal directives). Because the export control scheme did not invoke a U.S. antitrust suit, it served as a precedent for other VERs, such as the semiconductor agreement in 1986.[36]

The VERs force firms to turn to MITI in order to ensure a large share of the limited "export pie". By hiring an OB, the manufacturers can ensure access to information on political developments relating to quotas and they can also ensure that their allotment will not be cut in favor of a competitor who did hire an OB. The fight for pieces of the export pie constitutes intra-industry competition. Trade associations are not a means for lobbying among firms within the same industry; rather, individual firms need to contact the ministry directly in order to assure favorable consideration.

Figure 1 plots the change in number of firms in seven industries that hired OBs between 1979 and 1991. Automobile manufacturers began to hire OBs in 1981, and by 1984 all car makers had hired an OB. In electronics and electric machinery, there was a first push in the early 1980s, when the VERs on TV sets were enforced. The number of firms that hired an OB climbed further in the late 1980s, when the "export control scheme" was implemented for semiconductors. In both industries, the increase of firms with OBs therefore closely maps the developments in trade policies in the 1980s. The increase in the number of firms and the number of OBs hired is consistent with the

---

35 M. MATSUSHITA, International Trade and Competition Law in Japan (1993). This haggling highlights the inconsistency of VER requests with existing U.S. economic policies, and it shows how divided U.S. policy makers are about the issue. For details on the lawsuit, see *Zenith Radio Corp.* v. *Matsushita Electrical Industrial, Ltd.*, 475 US 574, 1986, quoted in MATSUSHITA (Ibid.) 233-234.

36 MATSHUSHITA, *supra* note 35, at 236-237.

conclusion that the motivation for hiring an OB is a response to the competitive constraints within the industry as a result of voluntary export restraints.

The case of the construction industry, which employs the largest number of OBs, adds a further dimension. Most of the OBs in this industry come from the Ministry of Construction (access to public procurement contracts), the Ministry of Agriculture, Fishery and Forestry (access to land), and the Land Agency, or from public corporations related to these industries to which bureaucrats "descended" from the ministries earlier. The Japanese construction industry is characterized by secret bidding procedures (*dangô*) for public work projects, where private firms collude to predetermine both the winner of the auction and the price this winner is to bid.[37] This means that an OB can be invaluable in acquiring prior information on planned public projects and government price ceilings on these projects. A second effect of the closed bidding procedure is that it is impossible for foreign firms to join the auction. Accordingly, *dangô* was included in the trade negotiations with the U.S. in the mid-1980s.[38] The OBs in the construction industries therefore perform two functions: access to price and project information in the bid-rigging process, and lobbying for protection from foreign competition.

The steel industry was subject to special regulation between 1983 and 1988, under the Structurally Depressed Industry Law (*Kôzô fukyô hô*). This law excluded industries designated by MITI as "depressed" from intervention by the Fair Trade Commission (*Kôsei Torihiki Iinkai*) in production cartels, and it enabled MITI to prescribe rationalization measures, input and production quotas (most of the inputs being imported raw materials), and prices.[39] Accordingly, steel makers had an incentive to hire an OB in order to ensure stable market quotas, access to limited imports of raw materials, and lobbying with MITI against competing steel makers. The increase of OBs in the steel industry between 1983 and 1988, and the subsequent decrease, give evidence of a direct relation.

---

37 In this way, the colluding firms ensure that everyone will get a major project over time, and they prevent price-cutting; the designated winner usually shares some of the profits with the collusion partners. *See* J. MCMILLAN, *Dangô*: Japan's Price-Fixing Conspiracies, 3 ECONOMICS AND POLITICS 201 218 (November 1991); S. KAWAMOTO, *Kore ga zenekon dangô da* [This is the General Construction *dangô*] (1994); K. MAEDA, *'Dangô Kokka' wa suibô suru* [The *dangô* State Falls into Decay] (1993), Y. KANEMOTO, *Seifu-chotatsu no keizai-gaku* [Economics of Governmental Supply], *in*: *Kôkyô sekutaa no kôritsuka* [Making the Public Sector Efficient] 89-110 (Y. Kanemoto & H. Miyajima, eds. 1991); R. MAKINO, *Kyôsô nyûsatsu to dangô* [Competitive Bids and *dangô*] (1984).

38 *See* C. JOHNSON, Trade, Revisionism, and the Future of Japanese-American Relations (105-136), and E. KRAUSS & I. COLES, Built-in Impediments: The Political Economy of the U.S.-Japan Construction Dispute (333-358), both *in*: Japan's Economic Structure: Should it Change? (K. Yamamura, ed. 1990).

39 UPHAM, *supra* note 24, at 188-198.

Among the non-trade industries, commercial banks represent a mixed case. About one third of the commercial banks in this sample are either former government financial institutions or used to be closely affiliated with the government in the prewar period (such as Bank of Tokyo, Hokkaido Takushoku Bank, Industrial Bank of Japan). These banks hire OBs for reasons of historical affiliation, and possibly protection. In contrast, the major city banks (such as Mitsubishi, Sumitomo, Fuji, etc.) hire no OBs at all. If former government banks were excluded from the sample, the commercial bank group would look very similar to investment banking. The history of Japanese banking explains the mixed pattern.

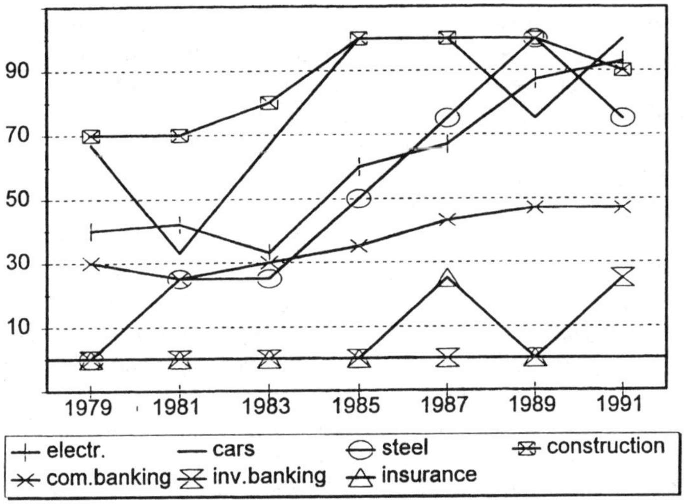

Figure 1: "Old Boys" by Industries, 1979-91 (% of firms in industry that hire OBs)

Finally, the investment banking and insurance industries rarely hire OBs. All firms in these industries represented in the sample hired a total of only two OBs over the twelve-year period. This is counterintuitive, as one might have expected many OBs in these strictly regulated industries. That is, the three industries in the sample that are subject to a specific industry law - banking, investment banking, and insurance - do not show a pattern of hiring OBs, and most firms in these industries do not hire OBs at all. One explanation is that the primary objective of lobbying by these firms are the restrictions exposed by the law. For instance, Article 65 of the Securities and Exchange Law[40] created a

40 *Shôken torihiki-hô*, Law No. 25 of 1948 as amended by Law No. 106 of 1995. For an English translation *see* CAPITAL MARKETS RESEARCH INSTITUTE (ed.), Securities and Exchange Law (1994, suppl. 1995).

firewall between commercial and investment banking until its revision in 1993. In lobbying for this revision, the interests of the securities firms were aligned in their opposition of inroads for the banking industry, and vice versa. In order to lobby this change in financial structure, securities firms can utilize their trade association, as can the banks. There is no need for the individual firm to hire an additional OB for lobbying.[41]

The division of firms into two large groups - those that hire many OBs in systematic patterns, and those that hire none or only a few - suggests that the primary differentiation of firms in terms of their OB structure is between firms involved in intra-industry competition under external constraints controlled by the regulator, and firms involved in industry-wide lobbying with the government agency. A primary strategy behind hiring a retired government official is to ensure direct access to information and to incumbent bureaucrats under intra-industry competition for limited resources (public works, export constraints). The need for such a strategy is even more pronounced if the regulator controls the degree of intra-industry competition. In other words, the ultimate reason for a firm to hire a former government official is to affect relations with the regulator under policy-induced intra-industry competition.

This argument can be tested by one final data analysis. If the "management of regulation" model holds, then there should be a high incidence of the origin of OBs in one industry with the ministry in charge of that industry; i.e., OBs should originate predominantly from the ministries responsible for regulation. Unfortunately, no data base exists that reliably tracks the background of those OBs that "descend" indirectly from public corporations.[42] In focusing on the

41 A further explanation why financial institutions did not hire OBs in the second half of the 1980s may be that financial deregulation created many regulatory loopholes at the time, and firms tried to exploit these to gain competitive advantage in the industry by outsmarting the regulator. At the end of the decade, many banks and securities firms also engaged in fraudulent behavior, as was revealed when the financial scandal erupted in 1991. Under such conditions, an OB on the board of directors could be inconvenient. In contrast to the large firms, small- and medium-sized financial institutions hired many OBs in order to lobby for continued protection under financial deregulation; *see* CALDER *supra* note 4, and van A. RIXTEL, Amakudari in the Private Banking Industry: Empirical Verification of the Equalization Hypothesis, ASSOCIATION OF JAPANESE BUSINESS STUDIES (ed.), Best Papers Proceedings (7th Annual Meetings, 1994).

42 The *Amakudari hakusho* [White Paper on *amakudari*] provides detailed background data on the "public corporations OBs", but it does not list the private firms that these OBs eventually descend into; *see* SEIROREN [*Seifu-kankei hôjin rôdo-kumiai rengô*] [Federation of Labor Unions of Public Corporations] (ed.), *Amakudari hakusho - Seifu kankei ni okeru amakudari kanryô no jittai, 1993 nenpô* [White Paper on *amakudari*: State of the *amakudari* Bureaucrats in Governmental Relations] (1993). Within the data set of this paper, the public corporations from which OBs where hired were in all cases directly related to the ministries in charge of the hiring industries; however, no exact numbers are available.

Table 3: Total Goverment OBs by Ministries and Industries, 1979 - 1991 (Bi-Annual Totals)

Industry	Ministry in Charge	MOF	BOJ	MITI	MPT	MC	MAFF	MFA	Other	Total
Electronics/ Electric Machinery	MITI/MPT	9	4	**39**	**7**	0	0	1	15	75
Automobiles	MITI	0	0	**12**	0	0	0	6	1	19
Steel	MITI	1	2	**17**	0	0	0	0	0	20
Construction	MC	15	1	9	6	**37**	18	2	32*	120
Commercial Banking	MOF/BOJ	**62**	**35**	0	0	0	0	4	2	103
Total		87	42	77	13	37	18	13	50	337

MOF = Ministry of Finance; BOJ = Bank of Japan; MITI = Ministry of International Trade and Industry; MPT = Ministry of Posts and Telecommunications; MC = Ministry of Construction; MAFF = Ministry of Agriculture, Forestry, and Fisheries; MFA = Ministry of Foreign Affairs

* Predominantly from Land Agency

"government OBs" only, Table 3 shows the total number of OBs in the years 1979, 1981, 1983, 1985, 1987, 1989, and 1991, by origin (ministry) and destination (industry). Note that the total is smaller than the actual number of OBs hired due to bi-annual data and the omission of public corporation OBs. The table shows an overall high incidence of ministries in charge and OB origin. Interestingly, OBs hired by the construction industry have the most diversified background, indicating the pervasiveness of the *dangô* process across government sectors.

To investigate the hypothesis that the origin of the OB was related to the destination, a series of chi-square tests were performed.[43] Using the data in Table 3, for each industry a 2x2 breakdown of the data was made as follows: the number of OBs for the focal industry was compared to the sum of OBs in all other industries; and these totals were further broken down by the origin of the OBs (relevant ministry) compared to all other ministries. Figure 2 illustrates this analysis using data from the banking industry.

	MOF / BOJ	other
Banks	97	6
other	32	204

c^2 = 37.3 p<.001

Figure 2: Chi-Square Test for the Banking Industry

Recall that the "management of regulation" hypothesis proposes that firms will be more likely to hire OBs from relevant ministries than government agencies that have little or no regulatory relevance for them. In the banking industry this implies that firms should employ more OBs from MOF and the Bank of Japan (BOJ). Thus, Figure 2 shows that of a total of 129 MOF/BOJ OBs hired in the seven years, 97 were employed in the banking industry. Similarly, of the 103 OBs employed in the banking industry, only 6 did not come from MOF or BOJ. In contrast, of the 236 OBs employed outside the banking industry, 204 came from ministries other than MOF/BOJ. Thus, the chi-squared for this test is $x^2 = 37.3$ ($p < .001$).

43 S. SIEGEL, Non-Parametric Statistics (1956).

Using a similar logic, each industry was examined and chi-square tests computed. In each instance, the relevant ministries were identified *a priori* and the number of OBs from these compared to other OBs across other industries. All results were statistically significant as shown in Table 4. These results offer strong support for the general hypothesis that industries employ OBs from ministries that have regulatory relevance, and they refute the argument that OBs are hired because of individual skill characteristics. This is consistent with a resource dependence perspective suggesting that OBs are a mechanism for dealing with external dependencies arising from regulatory uncertainty.

Table 4: Summary of Chi-Square Test Results

Industry	Ministry	Chi-suare test
Electronics	Ministry of International Trade and Industry, Ministry of Posts and Telecommunications	$x^2 = 110.7, p < .001$
Automobiles	Ministry of International Trade and Industry	$x^2 = 217, p < .001$
Steel	Ministry of International Trade and Industry	$x^2 = 208, p < .001$
Construction	Ministry of Construction	$x^2 = 7.97, p < .01$
Banking	Ministry of Finance/ Bank of Japan	$x^2 = 37.3, p < .001$

The three initial assumptions of the "management of regulation" model were that firms hire more OBs if they are (1) subject to extensive regulation by specific industry laws; (2) subject to extensive administrative guidance, even without an industry law basis; and (3) dependent on the regulator for market share allotments. The first assumption has been refuted by the data. The existence of a specific industry law does not lead to industry-wide systematic hiring of OBs. The reason is that the primary interests of firms in these industries tend to be aligned around major topics, so that they can be lobbied for through the association. The second assumption holds as an extension of the rejection of the first: firms in industries without a specific industry law that are regulated heavily through administrative guidance are likely to have diverse interests and therefore hire more OBs than those that are regulated by specific legislation. The third assumption is the most powerful: the data shows that those industries hire most OBs that are subject to external constraints (such as trade agreements) which are under the control of the ministry in charge of the industry. Statistical results strongly support this hypothesis. Firms hire an OB in this situation to (a) compete for the favor of the regulator against each other, and (b) have direct access in the presence of discretionary regulation. The fact that hiring OBs is strategic, rather than random, is highlighted by the high incidence of industry-relevant OBs hired.

From the perspective of the government, the very same logic applies. First, the government has an overall interest to secure further employment for civil servants who need to retire early for systemic reasons of seniority promotion. Second, firms that are regulated by specific industry with concrete stipulations of what constitutes non-compliance are easier to monitor than firms that are primarily guided through extralegal means. In particular, compliance with political regulation, such as VERs, is difficult to enforce unless there is a direct relation to the firm. It is therefore desirable for the government to place OBs in firms that are predominately regulated on a discretionary basis. Accordingly, the government will try to place its best and brightest retired servants strategically, either in trade associations that monitor behavior and represent interests of firms under specific industry laws, or in individual firms that the government wants to "guide".

D. Conclusions

Contrary to widespread assumptions, the phenomenon of government "Old Boys" in large Japanese firms has increased over the last decade. This is counterintuitive to the notion that large Japanese multinationals are freeing themselves from direct government control. This paper has developed a model that explains this increase.

The "management of regulation" model supports the notion of Japanese "consultative capitalism", in that it shows *why* government and business interact in the process of public and corporate strategy formulation. The model partially refutes the "equalization argument" as data show that industry leaders (the number one firms in an industry) are as likely to hire OBs as are the number two firms; among large firms, equalizing power is therefore not a motivation for hiring an OB.

The model offers three predictions concerning when and why large firms might hire OBs. First, the OB phenomenon is pronounced in Japan due to the high uncertainty of situational regulation through administrative guidance. Second, firms that face external constraints that (a) influence competition within the industry, and (b) that are controlled by the regulators, will hire more OBs than firms in industries where interests are aligned. Interests in industries tend to be more aligned when the industry is subject to a specific law, and in these cases, the interests are represented by the trade association (which is often headed by an OB). Third, the external constraints that impact intra-industry competition are most conspicuous in those industries that derive a large portion of their profits from cross-border transactions (exports of products as in cars).

The model is based on the three different sets of incentives by the three parties involved: (1) The government aims to ensure the implementation of regulation and, as a side effect, keep the former officials employed in the absence of a well-endowed pension system for civil servants. (2) The government official aims to increase his lifetime employment income by assuming a higher-paying position after early retirement. (3) Corporations pursue three simultaneous goals: (a) to ensure access to information in an environment of non-transparent regulation; (b) to ensure intermediation in times of clashes of interests with the government; and (c) to lobby under the framework of encompassing regulation, and thereby manage the dependency on the regulator in an environment of administrative guidance. The rewards to be reaped from complying with administrative guidance may be instrumental for gaining an edge in intra-industry competition.

The difference to similar networks in other countries is that the Japanese bureaucrats are dependent on a de facto government employment agency for their further *amakudari* career. They are also kept involved in ministry activities after retirement; they therefore act under shared loyalties. The dialectic between being loyal to, involved with, and dependent on the government, while being paid by the corporation, translates into three functions that OBs in Japan, but not in other countries, perform: (1) they smooth the information flow between government and business; this is particularly relevant under non-transparent regulation; (2) they impact the formulation of corporate strategies in that they represent the understanding of the regulating ministry in the board discussion; and (3) they impact the formulation of public policies in that they know how to effectively represent the firm's interest in the formulation of administrative guidance. The resulting system can be called a system of "consultative capitalism", where market mechanisms are supplemented by cooperative efforts of government and business to ameliorate potential antagonism between their respective interests.

Three major implications can be drawn from this. First, the specific form of Japanese regulation leads to the OB phenomenon; accordingly, the phenomenon will not disappear as long as administrative guidance prevails. In the 1980s, the export-related industries were subjected to an increase in managed trade. Managed trade in combination with discretionary regulation elevates the ministry in charge into the position of a referee of intra-industry competition, since it is in control of export (or market) share allotments. Therefore, managed trade increases the power of the bureaucrats in these industries; hence, the increase of the number of firms in export industries that hire OBs. While managed trade is not the only reason for the extensive network, a decrease in intra-industry market share prescriptions would most likely lead to a decrease in OBs in the two strongest Japanese export industries, electronics/electric machinery and automobiles.

Second, the government OB network constitutes an institutionalized system for lubricating government-business relationships that must not be overlooked. This system helps overcome some of the inherent antagonism between public and private interests. What is often interpreted as a result of the Japanese "consensus culture" is rather an institutional safeguard to economize on conflict costs and costs of implementation of regulation. Accordingly, in contrast to the U.S., where the adversarial stance of the government versus business has often led to impasses, the system of "consultative capitalism" may translate into efficiency effects in terms of savings in regulatory conflict.

Third, the OB phenomenon highlights the institutional embeddedness of corporate strategies by Japanese multinationals. These firms currently compete internationally under ministerial guidance; in the tit-for-tat mechanism of administrative guidance, this also includes protectionism. Managed trade therefore has the ironic effect that it glues the firms to the regulators through personal relations of the OB network, which also opens the door to favorable treatment by the government of firms in competition with foreign manufacturers. In contrast to the intended effects, managed trade may put foreign competitors at a disadvantage by feeding the tit-for-tat mechanism.

Part Five: Discussion and Concluding Remarks

Chapter Fifteen

Informality, Flexibility, and The Rule of Law: A Report of the Discussion

Dörte Liebrecht

Contents

The following report summarizes the various intense discussions during the conference. It is organized around five main topics rather than structured in a strictly chronological mode. Although some major themes came up more than once and were discussed in different sessions under varying topics, they are represented here in a unified context.[1]

A. Consensus vs. Individual Rights: The Japanese Legal System as a Model to be Exported?

In her opening statement, *Annette Marfording (Sydney)* raised some of the central questions of the conference: Does the visible economic success of Japan suggest that basic features of its legal system - or at least elements of it - should be exported to and could be introduced in Western societies? More specifically, does an exemplary institutional framework exist in Japan which promotes - for the sakc of greater economic efficiency - alternative dispute resolutions? At the same time, have subtle structural barriers to litigation been implemented to discourage people to sue, thereby suppressing individual rights' consciousness? What additional or alternative role do social standards of behavior play with respect to the avoidance of conflicts? And finally, how is the functioning of the Japanese legal system to be evaluated in a comparative perspective?

1 For information about the contributors to the discussion and their respective positions, *see* List of Contributors *supra* p. XIII-XIV.

Regarding the institutional framework of nonjudicial settlements of conflicts, the precise analysis of various concrete examples of administrative dispute resolution in the presentation of *Toshiyuki Kono (Fukuoka)* received broad acknowledgment. However, his question as to whether the parties involved are actually finding a "voluntary" solution and whether the administration can be described as "motionless" in this process provoked a number of comments. A lively discussion elucidated the actual role and power of administrative agencies in this area. Skeptical voices emphasized that the so-called "mediation process" results, in effect, in a suppression of disputes, as those who might have promising legal claims do not bring them to court.

Kono seconded this view and voiced a preference for a replacement of this process through the litigation system. He emphasized the obvious pressure put on the parties by the administration. For example, if a government agency refused without any legally sound reason to accept an application of a developer or a construction company for a building permit, and also refused to transmit it to the higher authorities, the party applying could file suit against the administration. But, quite surprisingly from a Western perspective, this rarely if ever occurs, even though the administrative refusal is blocking the whole project. Two main reasons for this restraint were named in the discussion. The first was seen in the fact that Japanese courts are still very reluctant to make decisions against the state or the administration; secondly, the suing party might face future disadvantages when dealing again with that administration. The construction company in the example might be excluded from future governmental construction projects. For these reasons, refraining from filing suit and resorting instead to some kind of administrative mediation could be very rational economic behavior, in spite of the costs involved in the inevitable compromise.

The general opinion emerged during the discussion that this form of conflict resolution is not truly a "voluntary" one, nor is the administration solely "motionless" when intervening in a dispute in such cases. *Zentaro Kitagawa (Kyoto)* pointed out that these difficulties are enhanced by the fact that the administration in Japan is often acting in ignorance of any legal standards. But, on the other hand, given the legally granted discretional power the administration has in most cases, not every refusal for action should qualify in his view as being illegal per se.

Lorenz Ködderitzsch (Düsseldorf) warned against using the terms "government", "bureaucracy", and "administration" in a too monolithic way. Rather, quite different roles and competencies of the central government - as opposed to those of local government entities - should be distinguished clearly. As a case in point, he mentioned the difficulties in applying the Construction Law cited in

Kono's paper.[2] In that specific case, the local governments had no choice but to apply a building law enacted by the central government although that law does not provide sufficient means on how to solve the foreseeable social problems arising from its application. From *Ködderitzsch*'s point of view, cases like those show that the local governments have virtually no influence on the laws enacted by the central government and only little power to enact ordinances. In setting out standards through the *kaihatsu shidô yôkô* - local guidelines the municipalities use to regulate construction - the lower agencies have tried to make up for the insufficient legal means. However, he saw the administrative system in general as not being without any corrective mechanisms. Thus it is possible for higher agencies to intervene. The press can also have considerable public influence, if it decides to pick up a specific theme. But, of course, these kinds of restraining mechanisms do not grant the individual relief in a particular case. Of a more direct use to the citizen may be the changes brought about by the Administrative Procedure Law[3] enacted in 1994. Although the scope of application is limited to the central government, the local governments are obliged to enact ordinances which work in a similar way on the local level (The impact of the law will be elaborated in greater detail later.[4])

Shifting the perspective from the institutional framework to social behavioral standards, the question arose as to the role these standards play in the avoidance of conflicts. The discussion of several stereotypes formed the starting point for the forum: the picture of Japan as a hierarchical, harmonious society composed of disciplined, immobile, obedient, positively-minded people who allow the political and administrative leaders to direct an immense amount of social energy in a focused way towards the single goal of economic growth. These stereotypes are partly linked to the widespread idea that high social density (a constant living and working environment and strong affiliation to social groups) must be listed as one of the reasons for the dearth of lawsuits and the effectiveness of social mechanisms in solving disputes.

This tentatively drawn picture of "harmony" drew comments and criticism that emphasized the necessity of a careful and differentiating analysis in coping with Japanese social reality. The question was raised as to whether dispute resolutions do occur in Japanese social groups, or whether these groups simply suppress individual rights instead. *Kono* pointed out that differences in the community norms for settling conflicts vary according to social sector. For example, disputes between individuals should be treated differently than those between companies. According to statistics of the *Shihô Kaikaku Kyôgi-kai*

---

2 *Cf. supra* p. 69 *et seq.*

3 *Gyôsei tetsuzuki-hô*, Law No. 88 of 1993. For an English translation *see* 25 LAW IN JAPAN 141-159 (M.A. Levin, trans. 1995).

4 *Cf. infra* p. 387.

(Committee to Reform the Judicial System, consisting of members of the courts, the Ministry of Justice, and the Japanese Bar Association), most Japanese are reluctant to file suit in a dispute of less than U.S.$5,000. In claims exceeding this value, the first consideration - just as in Western countries - is to consult a lawyer or to go to court. *Kono* concluded from this evidence that the typical Japanese phenomenon of "harmony" is only found in low claim cases, although the question of harmony should not be reduced to a mere question of costs.

Guntram Rahn (Munich) criticized that the concept of "harmony", though a basic idea in Japanese society, was too broad a concept to be a criterion or a basis of evaluation for different forms of dispute resolution. He gave two examples of rather different attitudes toward dispute resolution, both of which would fit into the Japanese concept of harmony. The first was the attitude of *naki neiri*, which means to "cry oneself to sleep" because one cannot or does not want to enforce one's interests or rights; personal interests or rights are sacrificed for the ideal of harmony. In the second example, the attitude of *hanashiai* (negotiation), problems are first discussed before litigating or putting emphasis on rights and legal arguments.

The role of reputation in Japanese society was brought up as another social factor promoting alternative dispute resolution. Are people involved in a lawsuit (still) regarded as untrustworthy in present-day Japan, resulting in serious efforts to settle disputes outside the courts to avoid gaining a bad reputation? *Kitagawa* expressed doubt that such kind of community norms exist, or at least that they exert any strong influence on the amount of litigation. In contemporary Japan, he maintained, people no longer take loss of face seriously. In contrast, *Rahn* emphasized the continuing existence of a reputation mechanism. He reported cases in which the Japanese party did not file suit although that would have been rational and was universally expected. Their reasons for refraining were fear of negative publicity that would have resulted from press reports about the litigation.

The question of how to evaluate the Japanese legal system and whether it would be desirable for Western countries to borrow elements of it led to a lively discussion with sometimes strong emotional overtones. Personal experiences of the Western participants with Japan were reflected in the discussion as well as Japanese sensitivities towards a comparative approach which was sometimes perceived as one-sided. A pointed statement was made by *Dan Fenno Henderson (Seattle)*, who characterized Japanese society and its legal order as "almost paramilitary", where "rights don't count and power prevails". In his view, the system works well for the Japanese due to social norms; in American society, however, where value is placed on individual rights that can be voiced and used to achieve a rational solution of disputes rather than their suppression, the Japanese system would never work. *Henderson* defined "law" as essential justiciable law, which creates rights that are secured by judicial procedure "from the bottom up instead of the top down". Top-down law, on the contrary, should be called "order" or "administration" rather than "law". Unless there were a realistic alternative of resorting to litigation - as guaranteed by the Japanese Constitution[5] - and unless clear and measurable criteria for the decision of the administration in a mediation process were defined, he maintained that the process could not be described as a legal one in the classical sense.

Henderson's rather critical evaluation of the Japanese legal system with respect to the rule of law provoked many comments. *Matthias K. Scheer (Hamburg)* proposed measuring Japanese law by its own rather than American legal standards. Furthermore, he maintained that the reality of Japanese law should not be compared with the ideals of American law, but rather with the legal reality in the U.S. European practitioners in the audience elaborated on this point and stated that, based on their personal and professional experiences in both countries, they would rather do business under Japanese rules than under American ones. It was conceded that the scope of enforceable rights for an individual is much lower in Japan than in the U.S., but the mere existence of enforceable rights as such was not seen as a sufficient means to guarantee an adequate protection of the individual. On the contrary, the dangers of individual damages were in this view perceived as possibly higher under_the American legal system. This was accounted for by the fact that American attorneys generally work on contingent fee bases that eliminate most of the financial risks for the plaintiffs; the defendants, on the other hand, have a loss regardless of the outcome of their case as they are usually not entitled to reimbursement for their own attorney costs even if they are winning. Furthermore, the punitive damages system was perceived to be an incalculable risk because of its quite often excessive awards, and the decision-making competence of the American jury system in general was questioned. *Kitagawa* pointed to recent developments in America of even big law firms showing increasing interest in alternative dispute resolution. He suggested taking the Japanese "harmonious settlements of conflicts" as a model.

B. Contracts, Torts, and Value Judgments

The practice of contracts may be another promising angle from which to look at the way a society uses its legal system. *Frank Bennett (London)* opened the discussion on this topic with an examination of the possible purposes of study and empirical research on how private ordering operates in Japan. He set up

5 *Cf.* Article 32 of the Japanese Constitution [*Kenpô*] from November 3, 1946.

three possible goals: first, to learn to cope with the customary system of norms as it exists within the Japanese business community through engagement in practice; second, to establish a prerequisite for future legal reforms within Japan; third, and most far-reaching, to adapt that system or to borrow aspects of it. Concerning the use of contracts in Japanese society, *Bennett* saw a great need for empirical research on contracts and the informal methods of enforcement which distinguishes between the different types of transactions. He raised the question of freedom of contract in the Japanese context: Is the formal legal system of Japan more strictly bound to the principle of freedom of contract, causing an absence of rules of equity which would reduce the impact of a harsh bargain? Or is this principle realized more robustly in the informal Japanese system so that parties can react more flexibly to changing economic situations?

The question of how contractual freedom is manifested in the Japanese courts led to a broad discussion about characteristics of court decisions and the phenomenon of value judgments, perceived as a typical Japanese way of finding compromises in contract litigation and - to an even higher degree - in tort litigation. *Rahn* explained the strong tendency of Japanese courts to decide cases on the basis of a value judgment, using legal arguments or even the written law only as a vehicle to substantiate the verdict already decided. For contract cases, he pointed out that the principle of freedom of contract does not lead the judge to abstain from a value judgment just because the parties agreed upon the contract. *Rahn's* impression was that the Japanese court does not feel bound by contract provisions but tries instead to evaluate the concrete situation. If the judge finds that the provision is not fair (*datô*), he will not hesitate to come to a decision which is in clear contrast to what the parties had agreed upon when concluding the contract. As an example, *Rahn* gave termination clauses in long-term business relationships, where in many cases the court did not allow a termination in accordance with the contract.

Following that line of arguing, *Kitagawa* gave a detailed description of how Japanese judges usually find reasons for their judgments. He pointed out that judges adhere to legal doctrines and study scholarly views so that in many cases a judgment can appear to be based entirely on legal arguments although it is actually a value judgment. Because the reasons behind the judgment lack transparency, the difficulty lies in ascertaining to what extent legal theories have influenced the decision as opposed to values and morals. With reference to contract litigation, *Kitagawa* characterized the interpretation of contracts as a special issue. From an abstract point of view, the subject of a contract should be a matter of fact to be left to the parties' decision, or at least the judge should try to find out their hypothetical intention. But in practice, according to *Kitagawa*, Japanese judges do not make a clear distinction between questions of fact and questions of law, causing them to actually interpret a contract as if they were interpreting legal statutes. This rather exceptional characteristic of Japanese legal practice leads to value judgments which in certain cases may even override an existing agreement on a contract provision.

Yoshiaki Sakurada (Kyoto) cautioned that value judgments typically have a tendency to make the judgments intransparent, causing considerable unforeseeability for the parties about the outcome of a suit. These negative results are further enhanced by a slow legislation process which intentionally leaves many problems to be solved by the courts rather than by the law. *Rahn* pointed out that due to the possibility of very formalistic judgments of Japanese courts, the real challenge for an attorney is to get the judge involved in the case so that he feels the necessity to make a value judgment. If the attorney can reach this goal, the intense desire of the judge to make a fair and just decision can bring the case to a solution that is far beyond any written legal rule. *Rahn* pointed to the present HIV litigation in Japan as an example. In a comparative perspective this litigation is of special interest because of the worldwide occurrence of cases of HIV infection through blood products, providing opportunities to study the resulting reactions of the legal system, society, and government in every individual country. According to *Rahn*, reactions in Germany and Japan have been completely different. German courts have decided these cases mainly on the rules of proof and causation. One plaintiff lost his suit because he could not prove the causal link between his infection and an individual blood product. In Japan, the HIV trials are far from being settled, with suits continuing for more than six years as of the mid-1990s. Although probably the same problems of proof of causation are present as in German trials, *Rahn* saw no chance that the claims would be rejected due to lack of evidence.

Luke Nottage (Wellington) emphasized the importance of distinguishing tort litigation from contract litigation. Regarding contract litigation, he noted that from a comparative perspective, Japanese decisions applying substantive reasoning to set aside for "unfair" contracts are generally rather limited. However, *Nottage* maintained that the role of the administration's interest in certain types of contract transactions - for example, consumer and insurance or saving contracts in the banking industry - should not be forgotten. Together with the influence of the bureaucracy, he also saw some influence by consumer groups in improving of standard contract terms in cooperation with industry. Furthermore, to evaluate the situation in the business context, he said, it is important to look at particular types of transactions. Regarding the termination of distributorship arrangements in Japan, for instance, *Nottage* recognized various types of judicial approaches. In some cases the courts take a very formal approach, whereas in others they reach a more substantive solution, perhaps because of specific characteristics of the case under consideration.

Daniel H. Foote (Seattle) drew attention to the results of research concerning abusive dismissals in labor relations. Over a number of years, Japanese courts have developed a huge body of doctrine for labor relations which essentially dictates that only a just cause of termination will be recognized, regardless of the actual contractual termination clause. This doctrine in labor relationships and parallel cases in landlord-tenant relationships could be interpreted as a matter of balance of power between big business and the individual, with the courts somehow seeking to ameliorate this balance in favor of the individual. Pointing to similar cases in distributor, franchiser-franchisee, and supplier-retailer relationships where courts held termination provisions to be invalid, *Foote* assumed that a broader interpretation might have been correct. According to *Foote*, the judicial process should be regarded as reflecting notions of community and therefore maintaining long-term relationships.

In response to *Rahn*'s statement concerning value judgments, *Foote* asked whether those judgments are as well rendered with regard to the interpretation of more general provisions of, for example, prices or delivery, or whether the elimination of contractual provisions through court decisions is limited to termination clauses as an aspect of maintaining long-term relationships. *Rahn* agreed that the courts will probably focus not only on termination clauses but consider the entire relationship as well; he conceded, though, that he himself had not experienced cases where anything other than termination clauses were eliminated by a value judgment. In relation to *Foote's* statement, *Kitagawa* pointed out the existence of judicial doctrines governing labor cases and special statutes governing landlord-tenant relationships as mandatory rules of decision. In contrast, distributor relationships in Japan do not have mandatory termination rules comparable, e.g., to those in Germany[6]; they are left to private autonomy which is open to the judge's intervention. *Christopher Heath (Munich)* elaborated that a protection of employees is obviously not to be found with respect to the remuneration for inventions made by employees. In these cases, courts normally would not decide in favor of the employee asking for compensation, but would instead leave the level of payment to the discretion of the employer.

Hideki Kanda (Tokyo) pointed out that court decisions in commercial matters which adjust prices the parties have agreed upon are very rare. Instead of direct intervention in contractual price agreements, Japanese courts would rather come to a value judgment in damage litigation for contractual remedy, perhaps reflecting the idea of what the correct price should have been in the first place. Through the legal institution of comparative negligence (*kashitsu sôsai*), judges will usually allow 30% to 70% of the original alleged remedial amount, but rarely 100%. He classified this attitude towards remedy claims as very common

6 *Cf.* § 89 through § 89b Handelsgesetzbuch [Commercial Code] of 1897, RGBl. 219 / BGBl. III 4100-1.

among Japanese courts, although this judicial practice had been widely criticized from a scholarly point of view.

Another international aspect of contract practice was raised by *Bernd J. Götze (Singapore)*, who pointed out that at least in business with foreign parties - in contrast to the 1960s when oral contracts were widely used - usually only written agreements are to be found nowadays. In spite of Japan's civil law legal system, these contracts are drafted more often than not in a typical Anglo-Saxon style. However, in the case of a dispute, the Japanese style of dispute resolution returns, regardless of the style of contract and its settlement provisions. In practice, this mixture of different legal approaches often leads to problems. *Kitagawa* saw the reason for the increasing use of Anglo-Saxon-style contracts in the uniform adoption of contracts made by American attorneys for international business transactions with Japan. The attorneys insist on their familiar style of contracting without trying to figure out the relevant Japanese law. On the other hand, he attributed the typical Japanese style emerging in dispute situations to a lack of personal and organizational interfacing inside the big Japanese corporations. While the legal department is responsible for the drafting of contracts, disputes are handled by the top management, which *Kitagawa* perceived to be still strongly adhering to the traditional Japanese concept of business relationships.

Rahn emphasized the differences between the Japanese and the Western approaches to business relations and the potential resulting misunderstandings. Western companies traditionally thought of their rights in legal terms, so the possibility of a judicial action is primarily judged to be an aspect of the business relationship only. For the Japanese side, in contrast, the legal aspect is a rather new phenomenon which has only existed in its present form for about one hundred years. The main focus in business is personal relationships; questions of legal actions or contractual commitments play a secondary role. To change the terms of a business relationship, Japanese first talk in an informal manner (*hanashiai*), whereas Western parties take legal actions such as termination as a first step, and then try to enter into negotiations. Therefore the strategy of the Western side often - involuntarily - offends the Japanese partner. The different approach can be clearly seen in the so-called "sincere negotiation clause" normally found in Japanese contracts. Such a clause would have no meaning from a German legal point of view, and accordingly such clauses are not to be found in a typical German contract. Rather, the contract itself provides the legal framework to settle any dispute, removing the need for such a clause. However, as *Rahn* pointed out, in the interests of better understanding he normally includes a sincere negotiation clause when formulating contracts between Japanese and European parties.

C. Shareholders and Employees as Stakeholders in the Japanese Enterprise

One aspect of the ongoing international debate on corporate governance is the role of employees as stakeholders in their corporation - a topic intensely discussed with respect to Japanese enterprises. The *uchi no kaisha* syndrome (the firm as a family) with its so-called life-long employment system, promotion of managers more or less entirely through the ranks, low dividend pay-outs to the shareholders, enterprise unions, and other features, seems at first glance to incorporate a special role for employees. However, *Dörte Liebrecht (Hamburg)* raised doubts as to whether the common view of employees as the "owners" of Japanese corporations is indeed correct. In legal terms it is obviously not the case, but in terms of balance of actual power, this statement - referred to, for example, by *Eiji Takahashi (Osaka)* - also appears dubitable. A balance in favor of the employees would mean that the employees have the means to actively influence managerial decisions in their own interests. As expressive legal powers are missing under Japanese law, the question is whether informal ways exist to exercise rights formally reserved for the shareholders as the legal owners of the firm. Various facts combine to cast doubts on the existence of this kind of balance of power within Japanese corporations. First, as *Masaru Hayakawa (Kyoto)* pointed out, the rights of employee shareholders who are beneficiaries of employee stock ownership plans seem to be exercised de facto in the interest of the acting management rather than in the interest of the ordinary employee. Second, the labor management consultation body, *rôshi kyôgi-kai*, which exists in most big enterprises and is praised as an institution for cooperation and participation, is more a place to transmit and discuss managerial directives concerning production methods than a place of participation in management decisions. Third, the problems in achieving rights for employees - as vividly presented in *Foote's* presentation - rather imply that employees have only very limited influence on management decisions.

Kanda agreed that employees are not the owners of Japanese companies. But he stressed that Japanese companies are run *as if* the employees were the owners, i.e., in the *interests* of the employees. Although a legally grounded, German-style codetermination does not exist in Japan, *Kanda* maintained that the fact that all managers in large corporations are former employees leads de facto to total power of decision by this group of stakeholders. A harder question is whether the shareholders are necessarily victimized by this. *Kanda* concluded from the fact that there has been no shareholder revolt in Japan so far that the shareholders - at least in the past - must have somehow been satisfied.

Harald Baum (Hamburg) warned against oversimplifying the question of worker participation. He pointed out that there are great differences between employees in middle-sized and smaller enterprises, which comprise up to 70% of the market, and employees of big companies. Even within these large companies, only 30% of the employees enjoy life-long employment. Only the core employees in big corporations can be considered participants. But, according to *Baum*, those are indeed more closely interconnected with management and the decision-making process than, e.g., employees under the German system of mandatory codetermination. Regarding employee participation, *Foote* warned against two potentially misleading stereotypes: shareholders are neither as insignificant as stakeholders nor, on the other hand, are employees insignificant merely because Japanese unions are enterprise unions and therefore supposedly so tied up with the economic future of the firm that employees do not have an effective voice. *Foote* saw these two views as extremes on both sides of a middle reality. It is true that the shareholders are not considered to be as important as in the United States, and the balance of interests works very differently in Japan. But it would be an exaggeration to state that business exists for the employees only, just because the managers were once employees. Furthermore, *Foote* maintained that the notion of the enterprise union being totally ineffective is vastly overstated. He pointed to the mechanism of the annual spring offensive, *shuntô*, in which unions join together to try to improve working conditions and to raise salaries. He rated the tradition of consultation through the labor management consultation body as being influential, at least in large corporations..

A particularly interesting aspect of the situation of Japanese employees is the struggle to reduce working hours, which was the focus of *Foote*'s presentation. He rejected the statement made by *Scheer* that the reduction of working hours was a reaction to American *gaiatsu* (foreign pressure). In fact, *Foote* claimed that the Japanese Ministry of Labor was engaged in these efforts long before the United States ever mentioned it. Among other features, the debate did have a certain element of *gaiatsu* in the orchestration of the international press as a tool in the campaign of the Japanese anti-*karôshi* (death because of overwork) movement, which gained a great deal of attention as a result of articles in the New York Times and other foreign publications. *Foote* considered a main reason for the reduction of working hours to have been a tight labor market in the late 1980s when businesses had to be competitive in that area to attract young people. Controversy was raised by the question of whether the reduction of working hours will be continued in the future. The lasting recession of the mid-1990s, however, with its surplus of university graduates and others looking for employment, may tend to reduce the need for companies to promise further reduction of working hours to attract young people.

Rahn generally doubted whether the legislation aimed at the reduction of working hours was actually of any substance. He suggested instead that it has the character of *tatemae-honne*, which means that it is supported as a formal principle while its true intentions are different. He supported his doubts by reports of Japanese employees to whom the legislation either did not apply or in whose companies it was not respected. *Foote* agreed with *Rahn* on the *tatemae-honne* character of the legislation and additionally pointed to the fact that a large amount of *sâbisu sangyô* (unpaid overtime work) is done which is not recorded and typically not subject to investigations. Furthermore, there still seems to be evidence that many employees go to work as a matter of principle even when they are entitled to a day off. Reliable statistics which take these facts into account, however, are apparently still nonexistent.

With respect to the position of the shareholders in large Japanese corporations, two main questions attracted special attention. The first point was whether the amount of cross-shareholding *(mochiai)* will be reduced in the future. *Henderson* referred to recent news in the media about *mochiai* shareholders selling their shares, and questioned to what extent the cross-shareholding up to now had been reduced. *Takahashi*, based on his own inquiries, doubted that there had been a strong trend of selling shares and thought it highly unlikely that the system of cross-shareholding would disappear in the foreseeable future. *Ulrike Schaede (San Diego)* agreed with *Takahashi* that no real conclusion could be drawn yet. Furthermore, she cautioned that even the actual amount of cross-shareholding is uncertain. Only on two days during the year, when the corporation updates its books on shareholding, does the corporation know who its shareholders are. Because of that, the so-called "stable shareholders" must merely make sure that they own the shares on these two days; otherwise they can trade the shares. This is done anonymously so that there is no way of knowing at any given point of time what has been traded and what has not. For that reason it is probably safe to assume that of the 70% of the outstanding stock statistically held by banks and other corporations, it may very well be that only some 30% are in fact cross-held.

A second aspect discussed was the impact of the recent reform of the corporation law: the easing of derivative suits. *Baum* pointed out that an abuse of derivative suits, which have been brought in quite a large number during the last two years, could already be observed in Japan. He believed that many of these legal actions have been initiated for their so-called nuisance value, meaning that shareholders are expecting to be paid for withdrawing their suit - a phenomenon not unknown in Germany either. Regarding derivative suits in Japan, *Kono* voiced the apprehension that this might become yet another crucial issue between Japan and the United States in the future. If an American investor holding shares of a Japanese corporation files suit against the company in the United States according to U.S. case law - which is rather generous in assuming U.S. jurisdiction - U.S. courts would have jurisdiction over this case if only one single subsidiary or branch of the Japanese company were located in the United States. As a result, American procedural law would be applied, including the rules of pre-trial discovery, which could compel the Japanese company to make available all information and possibly reveal know-how and trade secrets. Because of the high costs of lawyers and of discovery, the Japanese company might tend to resolve the disputes outside of court, thus potentially leading to an abuse of derivative suits by Japanese as well as American shareholders.

D. Bureaucrats and Old Boys: Influence and Control

An intense and animated discussion was ignited by the report of *Schaede* on the Japanese *Old Boys* (OB) system. It soon broadened into the central question of the role of the bureaucracy in present-day Japan. Who is influencing or controlling whom? Do companies, via former bureaucrats they have hired (OBs - a standard term in Japanese), influence the supervising ministries? Or, on the contrary, do the ministries exercise paralegal control via their ex-officials over the industry?

Scheer saw the balance tipped rather in favor of the industry. The kind of *senmpai-kôhai* (master-apprentice) relationship between the (elder) OBs in the companies and the (younger) bureaucrats who followed them in the office, suggested that companies are actually influencing ministries. *Kono* did not dispute the ministries' practice of using OBs as a tool to exercise control, or at least influence in general, but he doubted that the system was still as efficient nowadays as it had been in the 1970s. He cited various examples of corporations refusing to accept an OB, or not respecting the appointed OB in his new job and openly rejecting his attempts of influencing in line with his former ministry's policy. *Kitagawa* confirmed *Kono's* observation that companies are increasingly rejecting proposed appointments of OBs to their boards of directors, thereby accepting friction with the concerned government agency. He further cautioned that the OB system was not as simple as is often assumed because the interests on the side of the government were often divided by rivalry between different government agencies.

Kanda raised the objection that the OB system is not unique to Japan and can also be found in deregulated industries in other industrialized countries. For example, American SEC officials frequently move into big law firms specializing in securities business, or trade officials in the U.K. shift to private trade associations and their subsidiary networks. *Schaede* conceded that the OB system as such is not an exclusively Japanese phenomenon. But, in her view, the system in other countries functions differently. The comparable group in the U.S. are lobbyists, political appointees in an administration who leave the government if the administration changes after an election. They then join a firm and lobby against the government, but after the next election they may work for the government again. In this way, some lobbyists work for three or four firms that may actually compete with each other. In contrast, Japan has a neatly arranged, institutionalized system, with the *Jinji-in* (the National Personnel Authority) making sure that the OBs represent - or at least do not contradict - government interests.

This point was partially disputed by the objection that in the U.S., most officials who leave the government to go to the private sector are not political appointees but so-called "lifers", who are theoretically appointed for a life-long position. It was therefore suggested that the U.S. OBs as well as the Japanese ones change into the private sector for the same reason: the market for their expertise. Their work for the government allows them to accumulate a considerable amount of technical knowledge that makes them valuable for private firms, whereas the relation to the appropriate regulator is only a side-effect. *Schaede* disagreed, claiming that in Japan the specialization of public employees is more limited than in the U.S. due to the rotation of staff within ministries. Only small firms would try to hire an OB because of his knowledge which they otherwise could not afford to buy. Large firms would have the money to buy the knowledge they want, so there would be no need for them to employ an ex-official for this specific reason.

E.B. Keehn (Los Angeles) suggested that OBs in Japan are not only hired for their connections to the ministries but also for their special knowledge of the handling of the institutional informality that is built into the legislation itself, which he regarded as a unique problem of the Japanese legal and administrative system. He explained that when a piece of legislation is proposed in Japan, every ministry must sign it before it goes to the Cabinet. Because it is almost impossible to get a unanimous decision of 13 different ministries - and there are always some ministries which will not agree - unpublished secret sideletters are drafted to accompany the legislation. These contain promises of one ministry to the other, including how the specific legislation will be used in practice regardless of its wording. The knowledge of these informal promises is what an OB can transfer to the company he is hired by. *Rahn* also suggested that the OB system is a phenomenon of informal communication. Because personal relationships are held in high esteem in Japan, it is possible to get crucial non-public information in an informal way from the ministries via the ex-official, which can prove vital for the business success of the company. This obviously contributes to efficient management, at least for insiders.

A question controversially discussed was whether the Japanese administrative system produces more uncertainty than its Western equivalents, as was suggested in *Schaede*'s presentation. *Kanda* pointed out that, in his perspective, there has actually been more certainty in Japan than in the West, at least until now. As Japan deregulates and internationalizes its industries, however, this process will probably be accompanied by increasing uncertainty. The Japanese way of ex-ante monitoring, as described in greater detail in *Kanda*'s contribution,[7] has essentially been producing more security than the Western model of ex-post monitoring by litigation. He maintained that Western systems also contain many unwritten rules - as an example *Kanda* pointed to the SEC practice in the U.S. - whose scope of application and requirements are also uncertain. Parties are then forced into ex-post litigation to find out whether prior actions were legal or not. *Kanda* criticized this as a very costly and time-consuming procedure. If this kind of uncertainty existed in Japan, the industry concerned would have talks with the competent ministry, followed by traditional administrative guidance either permitting or banning this action. In this way, certainty is reached without the need to resort to a prior filing of an action. The advantage of the U.S. form of monitoring was seen in its stronger transparency, particularly for outsiders. *Kanda* believed that Japan, moving to the American style of financial services, will in the future have more transparency but less certainty in this area. He suggested that the whole system of administrative guidance is likely to change with more ex-post litigation in the future, but was not sure whether this change would be welcomed by the Japanese.

Schaede conceded that any kind of ex-post litigation introduces uncertainty. On the other hand, though, she pointed out that the very characteristics of administrative guidance imply uncertainty. As an example from the financial markets, she mentioned the Ministry of Finance's (MOF) sudden change in August 1995 of the rule concerning the percentage that life insurance companies are allowed to invest abroad. To help the Japanese industry, among other reasons, MOF intended to return to an exchange rate of 100 yen to 1 U.S. dollar. One of its tools was the lifting of the investment restrictions for life insurers. The rule was virtually changed overnight by administrative guidance; simultaneously, MOF informally "encouraged" the industry to actually invest in the dollar. The result was, predictably, a quick move of the exchange rate in the direction desired. Though other countries might follow comparable policies, the striking difference in the case of Japan is that MOF could change the rules overnight through administrative guidance, a procedure which would be impossible, for example, in the U.S. This flexibility, concluded *Schaede*, introduces a strong element of uncertainty.

An especially interesting question in this context is the future impact of the above-mentioned Administrative Procedure Law (hereafter APL), enacted in 1994.[8] In his paper, *Kanda* suggested that the APL is consistent with the ex-ante monitoring model and the informal approach taken by the financial markets bureaucracy because it fosters and encourages an increase of formalism at the

---

7 *Cf. supra* p. 305 *et seq.*
8 *Cf. supra* note 3 and text accompanying note 3.

ex-ante stage. *Nottage* responded by questioning whether the APL may also open up more opportunities for ex-post-monitoring - i.e., suits - thereby encouraging the administrative agencies to start using - or calling for - more substantive guidance in the hope of lessening the risk of ex-post control through the courts. In *Ködderitzsch's* view, the new APL is likely to eliminate at least a part of the former uncertainty through its requirement of national agencies to publish precise review standards by which they will handle future applications. However, he cautioned that the APL does not give hope for dramatic changes. He suggested taking the process of the implementation of the new review standards as an indicator for judging the future relevance of the law. A study conducted one year after the enactment of the APL showed that by and large the agencies concerned had issued review standards, regarded by *Ködderitzsch* as a major achievement. An open question remains, however: Will the citizens actually take advantage of their rights and challenge the administration by insisting on written statements of administrative guidance? As it is still too early to answer this question, the practice of *gyôsei shidô* remains undecided. Although the APL was promoted by large businesses that were frustrated by a regulation which put large sectors of the economy in very uncompetitive surroundings, these same groups seem to have shown little interest so far in utilizing their rights to get written statements of *gyôsei shidô* in their dealings with ministries. At the level of the central government, therefore, the APL obviously has not yet been effective. However, *Ködderitzsch* reported a visible change at the level of medium and small businesses confronted by regional branches of central ministries contravening national regulations. According to reports in the media, businesses here have taken advantage of the new rules.

Although the APL was generally designed as a mechanism for Japanese companies - not as a product of *gaiatsu* as is sometimes voiced abroad - it may very well prove to be helpful to foreign companies entering or already doing business in the Japanese market, the eternal outsiders in the game of getting things done the informal way. This leads to the more general question which frequently surfaced throughout the discussions, the subject of the following final section.

E. Suitability for the Global Economy?

From an international perspective it appears to be quite a sensitive issue as to whether the Japanese legal system fulfills the modern requirements of an increasingly integrated global economy, or whether it is shaped instead in a peculiar, non-compatible way that - purposefully or by chance - constitutes a kind of non-tariff trade barrier. This question must be distinguished clearly from the opening discussion of whether aspects of the system should be borrowed by Western nations. Quite apart from its desirability or undesirability, the fact is that, in contrast to the famous "Japanese style of management" - to use a common but rather simplifying phrase - Japan's characteristic legal features have yet to be exported worldwide. At least until the present, therefore, the standard has been set by the majority of North American and European players in the global market - for better or worse. Whether that will be the case in the future, too, remains to be seen; it is far from being certain. As *Keehn* pointed out, in speaking of global markets one must increasingly consider the East Asian market, where the Japanese model of trade and Japanese networks are predominant - again, for better or worse.

Henderson once again set the focus by expressing doubts that the Japanese method of regulation, which according to his above-mentioned definition must be regarded as an administrative rather than a legal system, could be characterized as that of a "team player in the global market". The subtly organized system is particularly intransparent to foreigners. He feared that Japan still had to be called a "quasi-state trader". In spite of having to some extent an internal free-market system, managed trade continues to prevail in international business. Consequently, all efforts of the U.S. in the past to open the Japanese market have been more or less futile, and all (formal) liberalization on the Japanese side has yet to produce substantial results. In *Henderson*'s view, the only alternative for the U.S. will be to manage its own trade to cope with Japan. He called this a tactical victory for the Japanese side, but a victory that would bring nobody much gain in the long run.

This critical and pointedly formulated statement raised foreseeable opposition and was contested by various contributions. *Kitagawa* countered vehemently that in his opinion the U.S. was trying to force its own ideas upon other countries. He interpreted *Henderson's* argument as implying that Japan should change everything in accordance with American ideas - a concept to which he was strongly opposed. *Rahn* pointed out that, in his view, the criteria for the evaluation of a legal system and of society norms of another democratic country could only be the legal principles of that system itself. He would be hesitant to criticize the Japanese system from a foreign - for example, German - point of view. *Keehn* stated that a model for managed trade with Japan already exists in the European Union, which, in spite of negative aspects such as high costs, technological deficiencies, and lack of competitiveness, somehow still seems to work overall. He added that the U.S. is actually benefiting from the kind of trade Europe has with Japan, for example from exclusive dealerships that exist as anticompetitive measures against the Japanese.

Peter Rodatz (Tokyo) raised the question of whether the existence of Japanese enterprise groups, the *keiretsu*, which dominate large sectors of the Japanese trade and industry, should be regarded as a non-tariff trade barrier. He characterized the vertically structured *keiretsu* rather than the horizontal ones as a hindrance for foreign companies trying to enter the Japanese market. Within the vertical *keiretsu,* he further differentiated between the distribution and the production types. Past experience had shown that whereas it might be possible for foreigners to do profitable business with or via the existing distribution channels, larger problems existed with respect to the production *keiretsu.* These are composed of a tight network between a core company and various layers of subcontractors. The subcontractors, in a more or less exclusive relationship, sell their products mainly to the core company, which on the other hand uses only "its" subcontractors who design custom-tailored products according to its instructions. There may be good economic reasons for this relationship, according to *Rodatz*, but for foreign firms trying to enter the Japanese market it will continue to cause serious difficulties. As it would be more or less impossible to change the *keiretsu* structure by law, no easy solution exists which could be reached in negotiations on the government level.

Takahashi objected that one should first compare a production *keiretsu* like *Toyota* with its Western equivalent, in this case a company like *General Motors,* before drawing conclusions on market access. The amount of cars produced by both is about the same. The production system of GM is structured inside the firm and therefore especially inaccessible for outsiders. As the core company of the Toyota *keiretsu* is much smaller than General Motors, *Takahashi* maintained that it consequently relies much more on subcontractors, which could be termed a kind of outside production system. However, in *Takahashi's* view, the degree of accessibility is rather less in the case of GM, making it unfair to single out a company like Toyota for criticism. *Götze* suggested that the real problem was not only the structure of *keiretsu,* but to a greater extent their large number. Whereas the United States has only five to six unpenetrable companies or networks, in Japan there are about 60 to 80. The result is that significant parts of the Japanese market are dominated by them in one way or the other.

Baum stated that the existence of legal and/or structural barriers are strongly indicated by the unbalanced relation of foreign direct investments in Japan to the investments of Japanese enterprises abroad, which is in a relation of 1 to 14 in favor of the Japanese side (cumulated foreign direct investments from 1952 to 1992). In comparison, the corresponding proportion in Germany, for example, is more or less balanced. He pointed out that, in the first decades after World War II, this imbalance had direct legal reasons in the form of outright restrictions on foreign direct investments in Japan (as was also the case in other countries). This gave way to more subtle administrative hindrances in the 1970s and 1980s (in contrast to most other OECD countries with the possible exception of France), which in turn were slowly removed to allow structural impediments alone to take over the "task" of hindering foreign engagements in a unique way. According to *Baum*, to a significant degree - though not exclusively - because of the cross-shareholding structure mentioned earlier, it is still almost impossible for foreign companies to acquire domestic Japanese corporations as a way of entering the market, notwithstanding some recent exceptions. Start-ups as a greenfield venture are equally difficult due to various other reasons such as rigidities of the labor market. In *Baum's* opinion, the instruments supplied by Japan's legal system seem at the very least to be fairly ineffective tools for coping with these difficulties, although it obviously supported their formation.

As a summary of the discussion, it seems fair to state that regarding the question of whether the legal system in itself functions as non-tariff trade barrier, there was a consensus that informality of norms and intransparency of administrative processes are detrimental to the economic activities of outsiders, be they Japanese or foreign. However, a quite different - and rather provocative - evaluation was finally voiced with respect to the actual condition of the Japanese economy. Assuming that the Japanese legal system is indeed protecting the Japanese market and therefore functioning as a trade barrier, does it help the country or - as the question was posed - does it harm the Japanese more than the foreigner? 65% of Japanese industry was described as not being competitive worldwide because of a lack of foreign investment and competition. These facts have allegedly been confirmed repeatedly by *Keidanren*, *Nikkeiren,* and even the Ministry of International Trade and Industry during the structural recession of the 1990s. As a result of these barriers, Japanese consumers must often pay double the prices charged in Germany or the U.S. for consumer goods, and Japanese employees must work significantly more, for example, than their European colleagues. From this perspective, it was considered doubtful whether the legal system with its restrictions on individual rights had had any significant positive influence on the economic success of the individual Japanese.

Concluding remarks

Peter Rodatz

The conference papers published in this book and the discussions at the conference itself have covered a very wide field, making it difficult - if not impossible - to summarize the proceedings. I therefore would like to limit myself to some impressions:

1. I believe we have agreed on the definition of law. Professor *Henderson* suggested - and here I simplify - that law is a set of rules which can be enforced in court.

This is important because we repeatedly heard that disputes are settled outside the framework of the law courts. Settlement in this context can, for instance, mean "voluntary" agreement by the parties concerned based on guidance by the authorities. Guidance can mean the threat - express or implied - to remain inactive (the *motionless* mediator as mentioned by Professor *Kono*).

It is not clear to me what such de-facto refusals of access to dispute settlement really mean - the disputing parties in any case seem not to be overly aggrieved. Law does not appear to be always an essential part of the relationships between people.

2. While no black and white description is possible, the partial but not complete absence of law does not mean that Japan is less flexible, less tolerant, or less effective. On the contrary, a member of the audience, based on his experience in both countries, even prefers the Japanese to the American legal environment, which to many seems to be the mother of all law (or at least all lawyers). Mr. *Nottage*, by the way, called our attention to differences among common law countries and the apparent closeness of systems which in theory should be wide apart.

3. If I understand Professor *Henderson*'s theses correctly, law is replaced to a considerable extent by social governance. Social density (a term used by both Professor Henderson and Professor *Haley*) enhances this system. Professor *Haley* remarked in his paper that decision making within a community - the village replaced by the company - provides a framework for resolutions which are closer to the expectations of the parties (and therefore better controllable).

This phenomenon is connected to an apparent unwillingness to be subjected to institutions which are outside the control of the parties (this includes individual and private and bureaucratic organizations) as judgments here are unforeseeable and therefore undesirable. Professor *Kono* also reported that the bureaucrats tend to avoid independent committees outside the control of the mainstream bureaucracy.

4. A consistant thread through nearly all papers is the relationship between law and bureaucracy or, more appropriately worded, between law and the multitude of bureaucracies resulting from the fragmentation of the Japanese government into several sub-governments. I refer here also to Professor *Foote*, who indicated that the Ministry of Labor (seemingly a part of the government) is actually different from the government as a whole, at least as far as the subject of his paper on working hour reduction is concerned.

In the opening speech, Dr. *Baum* mentioned the questionable role of the state. Professor *Henderson* remarked at the beginning of his paper on the strong position of the bureaucrat who seems to shape the law. Professor *Kitagawa* pointed out the large role of administrative standards on contracts. And Professor *Foote* gave an impressive description of the workings of the all-important *shinji-kai*, illustrated by the influence of the bureaucrats on one aspect of labor relations.

Nevertheless, Professor *Kanda* warned against overemphasizing the power of the bureaucrats of the Ministry of Finance, and presumably those of other bureaucratic entities as well. With his remark on "no rule means prohibition" however, he indicated that, in this case, the public has to remain motionless in the absence of bureaucratic regulations. Bureaucrats are powerful even if they do nothing.

The opinion that law is interpreted by bureaucrats and not by courts, was supported by Dr. *Keehn*. Mr. *Heath* conceded that in his field the courts play some role, but reminded us that the protection of Japanese interests and not the neutral interpretation of international treaties still governs much of Japan's intellectual property right legislation and practice - a relict from bygone times, it seems, but of utmost interest in view of the importance of new technologies. Finally, Professor *Schaede* advised us of the evils of *amakudari* and the OB system.

Two papers - as far as I remember - did not include major references to bureaucrats: those of Professor *Takahashi* on *keiretsu* and of Professor *Hayakawa* on shareholder rights. To me, at least, this is an indication that in the field of the organization of business bureaucratic influence is not strong.

5. What does this all mean? Dr. *Rahn* warned against oversimplification (of which I am in danger now in these remarks) by applying mono-causal theories. He reminded us that Japan is a pluralistic society - I would say: an extremely complex society - to a much higher degree than the West. In the discussion, he also reminded us that the concept of harmony is a very broad one, ranging from real harmony to mere absence of conflict to suppression of disputes, and thus maybe we should follow Professor *Henderson* and omit mention of harmony as one of the determining forces in Japan's law.

The lower rate of litigation as shown by Professor *Wollschläger* in his remarkable statistical investigations has many reasons and roots: social density, the stronger position of the bureaucrats in comparison with that of the courts, the lack of a long-standing tradition of law and rights and the unwillingness to be subjected to entities completely outside one's own control, to mention but a few. We were told that in spite of the many inadequacies - Dr. *Baum* mentioned the present mess of Japan's financial system - the Japanese system works reasonably well.

Can we learn from Japan? In my opinion, this is a very wrong question. The search for "goodies" in the Japanese system, to be taken over or adopted by the non-Japanese, will limit our ability to understand the Japanese system as it is and the Japanese as partners or competitors or just because they exist. If learning means understanding regardless of our ability or willingness to adopt, then we can and should learn. I hope that this conference has contributed to such a continuing learning process.

Is Japanese law and its application a barrier to foreign investment and activities in Japan? And if so, should the Japanese change their system to achieve compatibility with the systems of those foreigners who want to have greater access to commerce and business in Japan? The second question, in my opinion, is a comment on the relevance of the first. Japanese applied law - or the "shallow bite" of it - determines important aspects of relationships among the Japanese. In view of the overall success of the system outside pressure will not cause major changes. And maybe it should not, in spite of the admirable Professor *Henderson*'s call in the final discussion to strengthen the role of law in Japan. In my opinion, Japanese law is a barrier only as long as we wish to impose our systems, however well they work in our own countries. In Japan we should adapt to the Japanese system, and train our business people accordingly to look far less to lawyers for remedies.

6. At the end I wish to repeat thanks to Dr. *Brenn* and his staff who very ably organized the conference in such a way that we hardly noticed their organizational skills; in this case, no complaints is high praise indeed.

Two more persons must be mentioned: *Graf Brockdorff*, who impresses me every time we meet, gave the go-ahead to the conference in a one-hour meeting some time ago in between attempts to light his pipe and listen to our proposals (of course there was some *nemawashi*). I believe this conference was of mutual benefit, and perhaps this is all the thanks which *Graf Brockdorff* needs.

Lastly I wish to mention one nother person, and I mention him at the end so that one may better appreciate what he has achieved. He brought together scholars from four continents who are great admirers - some less, some more - of Japan, and, in spite of some critical remarks, he is also one of them. Of course, I am writing about Dr. *Baum* to whom hearty thanks for arranging the conference and editing this book should go.

Index